The

OXFORD
Children's *Pocket*
Encyclopedia

D0882318

The OXFORD Children's *Pocket* Encyclopedia

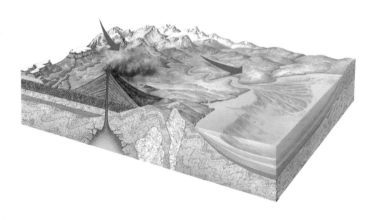

OXFORD
UNIVERSITY PRESS

OXFORD
UNIVERSITY PRESS

Great Clarendon Street, Oxford OX2 6DP

Oxford University Press is a department of the
University of Oxford. It furthers the University's
objective of excellence in research, scholarship, and
education by publishing worldwide in

Oxford New York

Athens Auckland Bangkok Bogotá Buenos Aires
Calcutta Cape Town Chennai Dar es Salaam Delhi
Florence Hong Kong Istanbul Karachi Kuala Lumpur
Madrid Melbourne Mexico City Mumbai Nairobi Paris
São Paulo Singapore Taipei Tokyo Toronto Warsaw
with associated companies in Berlin Ibadan

Oxford is a registered trade mark of Oxford University
Press in the UK and in certain other countries

Copyright © Oxford University Press 2000

Database right Oxford University Press (maker)

First published 2000

British Library Cataloguing in Publication Data available

ISBN 0-19-910570-7

1 3 5 7 9 10 8 6 4 2

Typeset by Oxford Designers and Illustrators
Printed in Spain

Contributors

Editor: Ben Dupré

Coordinating editors: Joanna Harris, Andrew Solway

Assistant editors: Nina Morgan, Susan Mushin,
Louise Spilsbury

Indexer: Ann Barrett

Design: Jo Cameron, Oxford Designers and Illustrators,
Mara Singer, John Walker

Art editing: Jo Samways, Hilary Wright

Photo research: Charlotte Lippmann

Consultants: Dr R. E. Allen, Bridget Ardley, Neil Ardley,
Norman Barrett, Professor Warwick Bray, Karen Brittin,
John R. Brown, Ian Chilvers, Dr Stuart Clarke, Dr Stuart
Corbridge, Ian Crofton, Tony Drake, Dr Frank Eckardt, Foster
and Partners (Architects), Gal Gerson, Naranjami Gupta,
Professor David Harris, Esmond Harris, Peter Holden,
Rosemary Kelly, Dr Adrian Lister, Brian Loughrey, Dr George
McGavin, Vivien McKay, Massey Ferguson, Dr Stuart Milligan,
Colin Mills, Dr Jacqueline Mitton, Professor Kenneth
O. Morgan, Peggy Morgan, Ruth Nason, Iain Nicolson, Dr Chris
Norris, David Parkinson, Professor J. H. Paterson, Joyce Pope,
Stephen Pople, Judy Ridgway, Alisdair Rogers, Stewart Ross,
Angela Ryalls, Elspeth Scott, Michael Scott, Spemco
Engineering Ltd, Professor Charles Taylor, Peter Teed, Eric
Tupper, Patrick Wiegand, Elizabeth Williamson, Gillian Wolfe,
Professor Ted Wragg, Dr Robert Youngson

Authors: Dr R. E. Allen, Bridget Ardley, Neil Ardley, Jill Bailey,
Nicola Barber, Norman Barrett, John and Susan Becklake,
Dr Michael J. Benton, Ian Chilvers, Mike Corbishley, Judith
Court, Ian Crofton, Tony Drake, John L. Foster, David Glover,
Susan Goodman, Neil Grant, Joanna Harris, Sonia Hinton,
Peter Holden, Dr Terry Jennings, Rosemary Kelly, Kenneth and
Valerie McLeish, Haydn Middleton, Dr Nick Middleton,
Dr Jacqueline Mitton, Nina Morgan, Peggy Morgan, Iain
Nicolson, John O'Connor, Dr Stuart Owen-Jones, Chris Oxlade,
David Parkinson, Joyce Pope, Stephen Pople, Philip Pullman,
Judy Ridgway, R. J. Ritchie, Dr Alisdair Rogers, Stewart Ross,
Theodore Rowland-Entwistle, Michael Scott, Nigel Smith,
Andrew Solway, Louise Spilsbury, Jonathan Stock, Gian
Svennevig, Peter Teed, Teresa Thornhill, Dr Philip Whitfield,
Patrick Wiegand, Elizabeth Williamson, Jill A. Wright

Contents

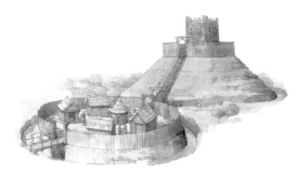

Finding your way around

The Oxford Children's Pocket Encyclopedia has many useful features to help you find the information you need quickly and easily. This guide will help you to get the most out of your book.

Articles are arranged alphabetically, so that it is easy to find the topic you are looking for.

Fact boxes set out dates, records and amazing facts clearly, while **feature boxes** cover a particular aspect of the topic in depth.

Attractive **maps** illustrate geographical and historical articles.

The **opening paragraph** gives a lively and friendly introduction to the topic.

The **main text** gives a detailed account of the topic.

Clear **headings** tell you what each section is about.

Key terms are picked out in bold.

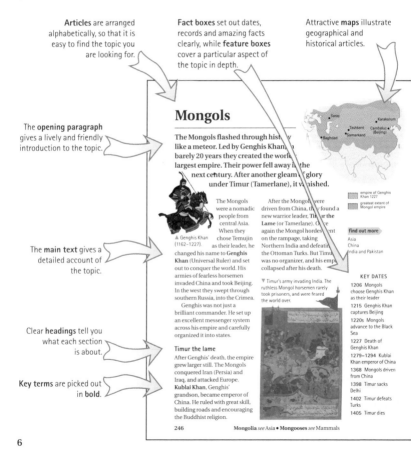

Mongols

The Mongols flashed through history like a meteor. Led by Genghis Khan, in barely 20 years they created the world's largest empire. Their power fell away in the next century. After another gleam of glory under Timur (Tamerlane), it vanished.

The Mongols were a nomadic people from central Asia. When they chose Temujin as their leader, he changed his name to **Genghis Khan** (Universal Ruler) and set out to conquer the world. His armies of fearless horsemen invaded China and took Beijing. In the west they swept through southern Russia, into the Crimea. Genghis was not just a brilliant commander. He set up an excellent messenger system across his empire and carefully organized it into states.

▲ Genghis Khan (1162–1227).

Timur the lame

After Genghis' death, the empire grew larger still. The Mongols conquered Iran (Persia) and Iraq, and attacked Europe. **Kublai Khan**, Genghis' grandson, became emperor of China. He ruled with great skill, building roads and encouraging the Buddhist religion.

After the Mongols were driven from China, they found a new warrior leader, **Timur the Lame** (or Tamerlane). Once again the Mongol hordes went on the rampage, taking Northern India and defeating the Ottoman Turks. But Timur was no organizer, and his empire collapsed after his death.

▼ Timur's army invading India. The ruthless Mongol horsemen rarely took prisoners, and were feared the world over.

find out more
Asia
China
India and Pakistan

KEY DATES

1206 Mongols choose Genghis Khan as their leader
1215 Genghis Khan captures Beijing
1220s Mongols advance to the Black Sea
1227 Death of Genghis Khan
1279–1294 Kublai Khan emperor of China
1368 Mongols driven from China
1398 Timur sacks Delhi
1402 Timur defeats Turks
1405 Timur dies

246   **Mongolia** *see* Asia • **Mongooses** *see* Mammals

The **articles** in the encyclopedia are arranged in alphabetical order from Africa to Zoos. When you want to find out about a particular topic, the first step is to see whether there is an article on it in the A–Z sequence. If there is no article, there are two things you can do.

First of all, look at the **footers** at the bottom of the page. These may include the topic you want, and tell you where you can find out about it. If there is no footer, the next thing to do is to look the topic up in the alphabetical **General index** at the back of the book. This will tell you which page or pages to look at to find out what you want to know. Also, if you want to find out about a famous person, you can look them up quickly in the **Index of people** on page 431.

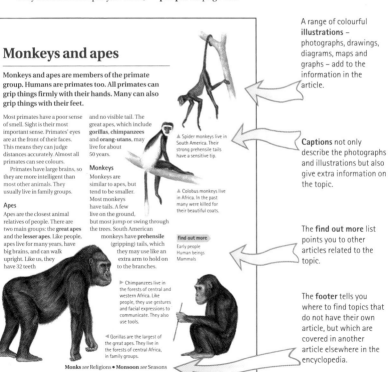

A range of colourful **illustrations** – photographs, drawings, diagrams, maps and graphs – add to the information in the article.

Monkeys and apes

Monkeys and apes are members of the primate group. Humans are primates too. All primates can grip things firmly with their hands. Many can also grip things with their feet.

Most primates have a poor sense of smell. Sight is their most important sense. Primates' eyes are at the front of their faces. This means they can judge distances accurately. Almost all primates can see colours.

Primates have large brains, so they are more intelligent than most other animals. They usually live in family groups.

Apes

Apes are the closest animal relatives of people. There are two main groups: the **great apes** and the **lesser apes**. Like people, apes live for many years, have big brains, and can walk upright. Like us, they have 32 teeth

and no visible tail. The great apes, which include **gorillas**, **chimpanzees** and **orang-utans**, may live for about 50 years.

Monkeys

Monkeys are similar to apes, but tend to be smaller. Most monkeys have tails. A few live on the ground, but most jump or swing through the trees. South American monkeys have **prehensile** (gripping) tails, which they may use like an extra arm to hold on to the branches.

▲ Spider monkeys live in South America. Their strong prehensile tails have a sensitive tip.

▲ Colobus monkeys live in Africa. In the past many were killed for their beautiful coats.

find out more
Early people
Human beings
Mammals

▶ Chimpanzees live in the forests of central and western Africa. Like people, they use gestures and facial expressions to communicate. They also use tools.

◀ Gorillas are the largest of the great apes. They live in the forests of central Africa, in family groups.

Captions not only describe the photographs and illustrations but also give extra information on the topic.

The **find out more** list points you to other articles related to the topic.

The **footer** tells you where to find topics that do not have their own article, but which are covered in another article elsewhere in the encyclopedia.

South Africa
(see page 348)

Ethiopia

Congo, Democratic
Republic of

Algeria

Sudan

Tanzania

Kenya

Mozambique

Ghana

Uganda

Africa

Africa is the world's second largest continent. There are 53 different countries, each with many different languages and peoples. Two-thirds of the countries are very poor. The forests, swamps and grasslands of Africa have a huge variety of wildlife.

Nearly all of Africa is hot. At the heart of the continent is **tropical rainforest**, where it is wet all year round. Away from the forest stretches the savannah: tall grassland dotted with trees. The savannah has two seasons, a wet season and a dry one. The Sahara, Namib and Kalahari deserts are huge areas of sand and bare rock. Very little grows there, and it is dry all year round.

Africa has four of the world's biggest rivers: the Nile, the Congo, the Niger and the Zambezi. It also has some of the world's largest freshwater lakes.

Nigeria

Population: 97,220,000

Area: 973,768 sq km

Nigeria is named after the Niger, Africa's third largest river. It has more people than any other African country. High plains cover most of northern and central Nigeria, with high mountains in the east. Along the southern coast are sandy beaches, swamps and mangrove forests. Two-thirds of Nigerians live in farming villages, but Nigeria makes most of its money from oil.

▶ A giraffe drinking at a waterhole in Tanzania. Africa has more large mammals than any other continent. Many of them live in the national parks, and millions of tourists come each year to see them.

8

Africa

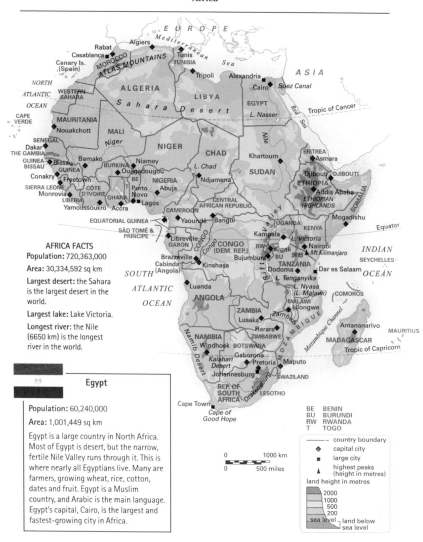

AFRICA FACTS

Population: 720,363,000

Area: 30,334,592 sq km

Largest desert: the Sahara is the largest desert in the world.

Largest lake: Lake Victoria.

Longest river: the Nile (6650 km) is the longest river in the world.

Egypt

Population: 60,240,000

Area: 1,001,449 sq km

Egypt is a large country in North Africa. Most of Egypt is desert, but the narrow, fertile Nile Valley runs through it. This is where nearly all Egyptians live. Many are farmers, growing wheat, rice, cotton, dates and fruit. Egypt is a Muslim country, and Arabic is the main language. Egypt's capital, Cairo, is the largest and fastest-growing city in Africa.

BE	BENIN
BU	BURUNDI
RW	RWANDA
T	TOGO

	country boundary
◆	capital city
■	large city
▲	highest peaks (height in metres)

land height in metres

2000
1000
500
200
sea level | land below sea level

0 — 1000 km
0 — 500 miles

Lakes Tanganyika and Malawi (Nyasa) lie in a great fault (split) in the Earth's surface called the Rift Valley.

African animals

Farming, building and forest clearance have greatly reduced the wild areas in Africa, but there is still a rich variety of wildlife. The **savannah** is home to lions and other big cats, zebras, antelopes, giraffes, elephants and ostriches. Crocodiles, hippos and many birds are found in African **wetlands**, while monkeys, chimpanzees and gorillas live in the rainforests. Many African countries have huge **national parks**, where the animals and plants are protected.

People and places

Most of the people in Africa live in just a few areas, such as the coast of West Africa, the Nile Valley and the area around Lake Victoria. In between are huge areas of desert or forest where there are very few people.

Africa has few large cities and factories. Mining is important in some places: South Africa, Congo and Botswana produce diamonds, while copper is mined in Zambia and Congo.

Most Africans live in small villages. Many are farmers, keeping a few cattle, sheep or goats, or growing food crops such as cassava, maize or sweet potatoes. Larger farms produce coffee, tea, peanuts (groundnuts), bananas,

▲ The Victoria Falls, on the Zambezi River, is one of the largest waterfalls in the world. It was given its English name by the explorer David Livingstone. Its African name means 'smoke that thunders'.

▲ These village children in Zambia are preparing flour to make bread. Most Africans can grow only enough food to feed themselves: they have no extra to sell or exchange.

pineapples and other crops to sell abroad.

African history

Scientists believe that the first human beings lived in Africa. Very little is known of Africa in prehistoric times, but from about the year 4000 BC powerful empires grew up beside the River Nile. The most famous of these was ancient Egypt.

From the 5th century AD, new empires in West Africa used camels to carry gold, salt and

slaves across the Sahara. Cities on the east coast sent ivory, gold, copper and gum by sea to Arabia, India and China. The gold came from the powerful inland state of Zimbabwe.

In the 16th to 18th centuries the trade in slaves grew enormously as Europeans took millions of Africans to be sold abroad. In the 19th century European nations took control of most of Africa. They created countries with artificial borders, separating groups of people who spoke the same language.

Since 1956, the states of Africa have one by one achieved their independence. But lack of rain in some countries has led to food shortages, hunger and disease. In other countries wars have caused much poverty and hardship.

find out more

Dance
Empire, Age of
Grasslands
Music
Slaves
South Africa

▼ The ruins of Great Zimbabwe, in modern Zimbabwe. In the 14th century it was a great religious centre and trading city. Gold mined nearby was sold to traders from Arabia.

Air

Air is a gas that is all around us. We cannot see, smell or taste it, but we can feel it moving when the wind blows.

Air is not just one gas: it is a mixture of gases. It also contains many other things besides gas: dust, water vapour, pollen, seeds, microscopic creatures, and pollution from cars and factories.

neon, helium, krypton, xenon

other gases 1%

oxygen 21%

carbon dioxide

argon

nitrogen 78%

▲ The gases found in air. The main gases are nitrogen and oxygen, plus small amounts of carbon dioxide. There are also tiny amounts of other gases.

Layers of air

Air is wrapped around the Earth in a layer several kilometres thick. This blanket of air is called the **atmosphere**.

The atmosphere has several different layers, which merge

▼ The different layers of the atmosphere.

The **exosphere** is where the Earth's atmosphere really becomes part of space. Temperatures in this layer can be as high as 1000 °C.

satellite

Radio signals from Earth bounce off the **ionosphere** before returning to Earth hundreds of kilometres from where they started.

Space Shuttle

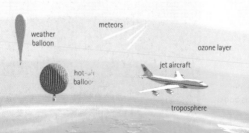

weather balloon

meteors

ozone layer

jet aircraft

hot-air balloon

Long-distance aircraft fly in the lower part of the **stratosphere**, where the thin air offers less resistance. They are sometimes helped by high-speed 'jet-stream' winds.

troposphere

clouds

Auroras

High up in the atmosphere, between 80 and 600 km above the ground, huge patches of glowing coloured lights sometimes appear in the night sky. Scientists call these displays **auroras**. The pattern of lights can look like searchlights, twisting flames, shooting streamers or shimmering curtains.

into one another. We live in the lowest layer (the **troposphere**).

In the **stratosphere**, the air is much thinner. It contains a gas called ozone (a type of oxygen), which soaks up harmful ultraviolet rays from the Sun.

The **ionosphere** is above the stratosphere. Here there are layers of particles called ions, which carry electrical charges. The ionosphere is very important for bouncing radio signals around the world.

Heavy air

Air is not weightless – a bucketful weighs about the same as two pages of this book. The weight of air in the atmosphere is always pressing down on us. This pressing force is called **atmospheric pressure**. It is like having a 1-kilogram weight pressing on every square centimetre of our bodies. This pressure does not squash us because we have air inside our bodies as well as outside.

Air to live

Without air our planet would be a waterless desert with no living creatures. Green plants use the carbon dioxide in air, together with sunlight and water, to make their food. As they do so, they produce oxygen. Humans and other animals breathe air to get this oxygen. Animals need oxygen to get energy from the food they eat.

find out more

Plants
Pollution
Radio
Solids, liquids and gases
Weather

▼ Scuba divers carry their own air supply in metal tanks filled with compressed air, which are strapped onto their backs.

jumbo jet

MIG-29 Fulcrum fighter plane

Cessna propeller-driven plane

Bell 222 police and rescue helicopter

Schweizer stunt glider

flexi-wing microlight aircraft

hot-air balloon

advertising airship

Aircraft

All kinds of flying machine are called aircraft – aeroplanes and helicopters, gliders, balloons and airships. Some are heavier than air, and need wings to fly. Others float through the air, just as boats float in water.

The first aircraft to carry people was a balloon. It flew over 200 years ago. The very first aeroplane, with wings and an engine, was not built until 1903. It was made of wood, canvas and wire. Aeroplanes today are made of light, very strong materials. Designers have developed wings that slip through the air, and engines that are quieter and use less fuel.

Aeroplanes and helicopters

Aeroplanes come in many shapes and sizes, but all of them have **wings**. The shape of these wings is important. Straight wings work best for carrying heavy loads at low speeds, but swept-back wings are better for fast flying. Helicopters have several long, thin wings, called **blades**. Instead of being fixed, these blades spin around to lift the helicopter into the air.

Aeroplanes also need an **engine** to move them along. Tiny microlights have a motorcycle engine. This turns a propeller that pushes the plane through the air. Most bigger aircraft have powerful jet engines. These can push an airliner along at over 850 kilometres per hour (km/h), or a fighter plane at over 3000 km/h – more than twice the speed of sound.

Most aeroplanes have movable **flaps** on the wings and on the tailplane and fin at the back. The pilot uses these to control the plane. A helicopter is controlled in a different way. By tilting the helicopter blades, the pilot can make the helicopter take off and land, hover, or move in any direction.

No engine!

Gliders do not have engines: they use the force of the wind to keep them up in the air. The glider is very light, and the wings are long, to create as much lift as possible. Gliders are towed up into the air by an aeroplane, or by a car or powered winch. Once in the air, the pilot releases the towline and is free to soar.

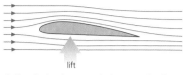

▲ Aircraft wings have an arched cross-section. The shape is called an *airfoil*. Air moving around this airfoil creates lift. As the aircraft builds up speed, the air rushing past the wings produces enough lift to raise it into the sky.

A glider can gain height in a thermal, a current of warm air that rises from the ground on a sunny day. The pilot circles the glider in the thermal, and the rising air carries it upwards.

Balloons and airships

To float, a balloon or airship has to be lighter than the surrounding air. So it has a large bag, called the envelope, filled with a light gas or hot air. Airships have engines and can travel in any direction, but balloons travel where the wind blows them.

AIRCRAFT FIRSTS

1783 First hot-air balloon flew in France.

1852 Henri Giffard made first airship flight.

1853 George Cayley built first glider to carry a person into the air.

1903 The Wright brothers' biplane *Flyer* made first powered flight. It flew for just 12 seconds.

1919 Alcock and Brown made first non-stop flight across Atlantic.

1927 Charles Lindbergh made first non-stop solo flight across Atlantic.

1930 Amy Johnson first woman to fly from UK to Australia.

1939 Heinkel He-178 first jet aircraft to fly.

1952 De Havilland Comet first jet airliner in service.

1970 Boeing 747 first wide-bodied jet.

1976 Concorde first supersonic (faster-than-sound) airliner in service.

1995 Steve Fossett made first solo balloon crossing of Pacific.

1999 Brian Jones and Bertrand Piccard make first round-the-world balloon flight.

▼ This Boeing 747 airliner can carry over 300 passengers. Large airliners have an autopilot – a computer that can navigate and fly the plane for most of its journey.

Airships and gas balloons are usually filled with **helium gas**, which is very light. **Hot-air balloons** use gas burners to heat the air inside them. Hot air is lighter than cool air, so the balloon rises.

Hot-air balloons are used for pleasure or for sport. The balloons race each other to see which can go farthest in a day. Gas balloons are used for weather forecasting or for scientific experiments. Airships are used for taking aerial photographs and television pictures because they can fly very slowly or stay exactly in one position.

▼ A cutaway view of Hong Kong airport. The terminal building is over 1 km long, the largest enclosed public space ever made. An airport has two basic jobs: ensuring that aircraft take off and land safely, and getting passengers on and off the aircraft. Planes are directed, both on the ground and in the air, by air-traffic controllers in the control tower. Landing lights and radar landing systems make it possible for planes to fly at night and in bad weather.

find out more
Engines and motors
Weapons

control tower

runway

docking bays
departure hall

raillink

carpark

Algae

Algae do not have leaves, stems, roots or flowers, but in important ways they are like plants. Algae are found in wet places everywhere, from rivers and ponds to the damp sides of trees. They also make up most of the plant life in the oceans.

Algae are not true plants, but they can use sunlight to make their food in the same way that plants do. There are many different kinds of algae, and they live in many different ways.

sacs containing sex cells

frond

air sacs help some seaweeds to stand upright in the water

holdfast, to attach seaweed to rocks

◀ The structure of a typical seaweed.

Floating life

Many kinds of algae are microscopically tiny. They are found in lakes and rivers, and most importantly in the sea. Tiny single-celled floating algae known as **phytoplankton** are the basic food for many of the animals that live in the sea. The seaweeds that cling to rocks on the seashore or get washed up on the beach are also algae.

Seaweed is a food for many sea animals. In Japan and China it is a popular food for people, too. Seaweed is also used in many parts of the world to fertilize crops.

Mixed–up algae

Some types of algae live together with a fungus (another group of living things) to form another sort of 'plant' called a **lichen**. Lichens form growths that look like coloured crusty patches on rocks, walls and roofs.

▲ This picture shows several types of phytoplankton, magnified many times. The ones with the spiky shapes are called diatoms.

Pollution patrol
Some algae can give us clues about pollution levels. For example, a bright-green, powdery alga called *Pleurococcus* grows in very polluted air.

find out more
Life on Earth
Mushrooms and
toadstools
Seashore

Alligators *see* Reptiles • **Alloys** *see* Metals • **Alphabets** *see* Languages

American Revolution

The American Revolution began when Britain's American colonies rebelled against King George III. The colonists defeated the British and set up a new country: the United States of America (USA).

In the 1760s the British began taxing their 13 North American **colonies**. The Americans said this was wrong because they were not represented in the British parliament. 'No taxation without representation!' was their cry.

The British removed all taxes – except on tea. The Americans were still not content, and fighting broke out in Massachusetts.

War and independence

The fighting flared into a full-scale war. The Americans, guided by Thomas **Jefferson**, wrote a **Declaration of Independence** saying they now

▶ The territories of eastern North America at the time of the Revolution, and the sites of the major battles.

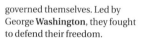

The Thirteen Colonies
✕ major battle with date
— boundary of the United States in 1783

governed themselves. Led by George **Washington**, they fought to defend their freedom.

France, Spain and the Dutch joined in on the American side. After General Cornwallis surrendered at Yorktown, Virginia, the British knew they could not win.

Peace was made at Paris and the **USA** became an independent country. Leading Americans then wrote a new **constitution**. It set out how the USA would be governed and gave its citizens human rights.

KEY DATES

1773 Boston Tea Party

1775 Fighting begins

1776 Declaration of Independence

1778 France declares war on Britain

1781 British army surrenders at Yorktown

1783 Peace of Paris ends the war

1787 Constitution drawn up

1789 George Washington elected first president of USA

◀ On 16 December 1773 a group of Boston citizens disguised as Mohawks boarded British tea ships and threw tea into Boston harbour – in protest at the tea tax. The 'Boston Tea Party' brought the Americans and British closer to war.

find out more

Britain, History of
Empire, Age of
North America
United States of America

Amoebas *see* Life on Earth • **Amphibians** *see* Frogs, etc.

Ancient world

Over 5500 years ago (3500 BC), the first civilization grew up around the rivers Tigris and Euphrates. Over the next 3500 years more civilizations appeared. The best known were in Mesopotamia (now Iraq), Egypt, Greece and Italy (Rome), but there were many others.

The first humans moved around, hunting and gathering food that grew wild. When **farming** began about 10,000 BC, people settled in villages. Some were farmers, others were craft workers, priests and organizers. This was the beginning of **civilization**.

In about 3500 BC, the **Sumerians** of Mesopotamia set up the earliest civilization. They built **cities** and huge towers, called ziggurats. They also invented a kind of writing. Sumerian merchants traded by land and by sea. But the most famous **traders** of the ancient world came from **Phoenicia** (modern-day Syria and Lebanon). The Phoenicians traded across the Mediterranean from the cities of Tyre and Sidon.

About 2000 BC, the **Babylonian** people took control of Mesopotamia. Their king, **Hammurabi**, was one of the first rulers to write down his laws. The warlike **Hittites** set up yet another civilization to the north, in what is now Turkey.

▲ The great ziggurat, known as the **Hanging Gardens of Babylon**. It was probably built by King Nebuchadnezzar of Babylon about 500 BC. It was one of the Seven Wonders of the World.

▼ The Sumerians returning from war after a victory. These scenes were carved in 2500 BC on a box known as the Standard of Ur.

Some of the 7000 life-size clay soldiers that were buried in the tomb of the Chinese emperor Qin Shi Huangdi about 200 BC.

find out more
Archaeology
Egyptians, Ancient
Greeks, Ancient
Law
Romans

Emperors, merchants and artists

Several kings of the ancient world ruled huge **empires**. The **Assyrian** empire (900–650 BC) stretched from Egypt to the Persian Gulf. The **Persian** empire of King Darius I (from 521 BC) was the biggest the world had ever seen.

Other civilizations were smaller, but just as important. The **Minoans** and **Mycenaeans**, who lived on the island of Crete from about 2000 BC, were stylish craftspeople. In the 8th century BC, **Carthage** in North Africa grew rich from trade. At about the same time, the **Etruscans** of Italy were using styles of art and building later copied by the Romans.

China, India and America

People were building and trading in other parts of the world, too. One of the grandest civilizations started in about 2500 BC beside the River Indus, (modern-day Pakistan). It built several fine cities. One of the largest, Mohenjodaro, had broad streets and houses with bathrooms.

The first Chinese civilization grew up in about 1500 BC, around the Huang He (Yellow River). Its citizens, the **Shang**, used a type of picture writing.

Around 1200 BC, the **Olmecs** built a civilization in Mexico, and the **Chavins** set up another in Peru. They put up huge buildings, but did not discover the wheel or know how to make metal tools.

TIMELINE

BC

about **10,000**
Farming begins, in Asia

about **7500**
City of Jericho built

about **3500**
Sumerians invent writing

about **2600**
Egyptian pyramids built

about **2500** Indus civilization begins

about **2000** Minoan civilization begins

about **1790**
Hammurabi becomes king of Babylon

about **1500** Shang civilization begins; Phoenicians trading in Mediterranean

about **1200** Olmec and Chavin civilizations beginning

about **900–650**
Assyrians at their most powerful

814 Phoenicians set up city of Carthage

about **800** Etruscan civilization beginning

about **753** City of Rome built

521 Darius I king of Persia

▼ Some ancient civilizations and cities.

Sumerians (about 3500 to 2000 BC)

Egyptians (about 3100 to 30 BC)

Indus Valley civilization (about 2500 to 1600 BC)

Mediterranean Sea

Tigris

Euphrates

MESOPOTAMIA

Babylon

Jericho

Memphis

Ur

Nile

Red Sea

EGYPT

ARABIA

Persian Gulf

PERSIA

Harappa

Mohenjodaro

Indus

INDUS VALLEY

INDIA

Arabian Sea

Anglo-Saxons

The Anglo-Saxons were a group of peoples from northern Europe who settled in Britain in the 5th century AD. They eventually united to form a single nation – Angleland, or England.

The Anglo-Saxons began to settle in Britain after the Romans left in 410 AD. They pushed the Celtic Britons back into Cornwall and Wales, and established seven separate kingdoms: Essex, Wessex, Sussex, Mercia, East Anglia, Northumbria and Kent. There were many wars between the different kingdoms.

The Anglo-Saxon way of life

The Anglo-Saxons were farmers, craftspeople and traders. Most lived on farms and in villages. They kept sheep, cattle and pigs, and hunted deer, fish and wild birds. Women wore long gowns fastened at the shoulders with brooches. Men wore short tunics over leggings, and cloaks for warmth. The Anglo-Saxons were skilled at metalwork, and produced much fine jewellery.

Viking invaders

In the 9th century Britain was invaded by the Vikings from Denmark. The Vikings defeated all the Anglo-Saxon kings except Alfred, King of Wessex. The country was divided into two. The Vikings ruled the north and east, while King Alfred ruled the south and west. In time, Alfred's successors reconquered the lands to the north and east, and established the kingdom of England. Saxon and Viking kings ruled England until the Norman invasion in 1066.

▲ This warrior's helmet was found in the remains of an Anglo-Saxon ship at Sutton Hoo, in England. Sutton Hoo may have been the grave of Raedwald, king of East Anglia and High King of Britain, who died in 624 or 625.

• In 597 the Pope sent Augustine, a monk in Rome, to convert the people of Britain to Christianity.

• The English spoken today comes from the language Anglo-Saxons spoke 1500 years ago.

find out more

Britain, History of
Celts
Normans
Vikings

◀ All the buildings in an Anglo-Saxon village were made of wood, thatch and wattle (woven twigs and dry mud). Peasant families usually lived in a single room, with an earth floor and a fire in the middle for cooking and heating.

Animals

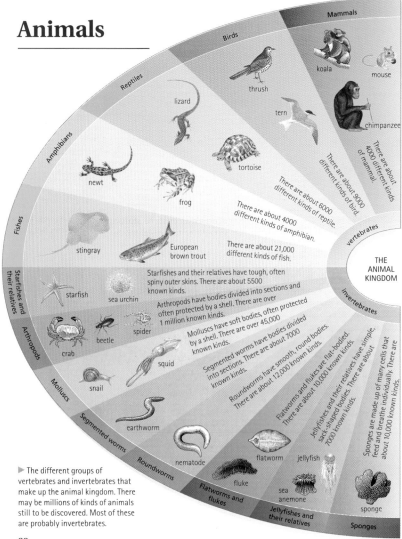

Mammals
koala
mouse
chimpanzee

There are about 4000 different kinds of mammal.

Birds
thrush
tern

There are about 9000 different kinds of bird.

Reptiles
lizard
tortoise

There are about 6000 different kinds of reptile.

Amphibians
newt
frog

There are about 4000 different kinds of amphibian.

Fishes
stingray
European brown trout

There are about 21,000 different kinds of fish.

vertebrates

THE ANIMAL KINGDOM

invertebrates

Starfishes and their relatives
starfish
sea urchin

Starfishes and their relatives have tough, often spiny outer skins. There are about 5500 known kinds.

Arthropods
crab
beetle
spider
snail
squid

Arthropods have bodies divided into sections and often protected by a shell. There are over 1 million known kinds.

Molluscs

Molluscs have soft bodies, often protected by a shell. There are over 45,000 known kinds.

Segmented worms
earthworm

Segmented worms have bodies divided into sections. There are about 7000 known kinds.

Roundworms
nematode

Roundworms have smooth, round bodies. There are about 12,000 known kinds.

Flatworms and flukes
flatworm
fluke

Flatworms and flukes are flat-bodied. There are about 10,000 known kinds.

Jellyfishes and their relatives
jellyfish
sea anemone

Jellyfishes and their relatives have simple, sack-shaped bodies. There are about 7000 known kinds.

Sponges
sponge

Sponges are made up of many cells that feed and breathe individually. There are about 10,000 known kinds.

▶ The different groups of vertebrates and invertebrates that make up the animal kingdom. There may be millions of kinds of animals still to be discovered. Most of these are probably invertebrates.

22

There are millions of different kinds of animals. Some are very large. Others are so tiny you can only see them through a microscope.

Animals can be divided into many groups. An important group includes animals with backbones, which are called **vertebrates**. Animals without backbones are called **invertebrates**.

Almost all the bigger, more complicated animals are vertebrates. Fishes, amphibians, reptiles, birds and mammals are all vertebrates. Ninety-nine per cent of all animals are invertebrates. These include insects, jellyfishes and worms. Invertebrates do not have bones, but many are supported by some kind of hard shell inside or outside their bodies.

Warm- or cold-blooded

Some vertebrates, like birds and mammals, are **warm-blooded**. This means they can stay active when their surroundings are cold. But they must eat a lot of food to keep their bodies warm.

Most animals, including reptiles, amphibians, fishes and all the invertebrates, are **cold-blooded**. They have to warm up in the sun before they can move around quickly. But they don't need to eat so much food.

What do animals eat?

All animals eat things that were once alive. Some, like horses and bees, are **herbivores**. They only eat plants. Others, like tigers and sharks, are **carnivores**. They catch and eat other animals. Still others, like people, are **omnivores**. They eat both plants and animals. **Scavengers**, such as vultures, eat dead and rotting plants and animals.

Reproduction

All animals reproduce themselves. In many animals males and females must mate in order to produce young. In a few, such as water fleas, females can produce young without mating. Some, like sea anemones, split off pieces of their own bodies to produce young.

find out more ▷

Birds
Evolution
Fishes
Frogs and other
  amphibians
Insects
Life on Earth
Kangaroos and other
  marsupials
Mammals
Migration
Reptiles

• All animals have some things in common. All eat food to survive, and all are able to move about.

Animal records

The *largest* animal is the blue whale, which can be about 30 m long and weigh over 100 tonnes.

The *tallest* animal is the giraffe. Giraffes can grow up to 5.3 m tall.

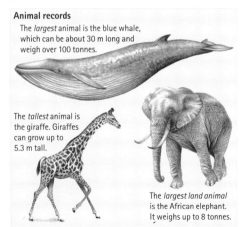

The *largest land animal* is the African elephant. It weighs up to 8 tonnes.

Antarctica

Antarctica is the Earth's coldest continent. It is covered by a vast sheet of ice, built up over millions of years. On land there is very little wildlife, and until recently there were no people. Today, a few scientists live and work on Antarctica.

The Antarctic ice-sheet is over 3 kilometres thick in places. Parts of the ice-sheet spread beyond the land on to the sea. Huge pieces break off from the edges to become **icebergs**.

Antarctic life

The Antarctic interior is almost empty of life. Simple plants and one or two kinds of insect are all that can live there. But the ocean is full of life. There are seaweeds, corals, starfish and sponges. And millions of tiny creatures called **krill** provide food for fishes, sea birds, seals, penguins and whales.

Exploration

Seal hunters were probably the first people to reach Antarctica, in about 1820. In 1895 Belgian explorers spent a winter on the ice, and in 1901 Captain Robert Scott led an unsuccessful British expedition to the South Pole.

The Norwegian Roald Amundsen was the first explorer to reach the Pole, in December 1911. An expedition led by Captain Scott reached the Pole soon after Amundsen, but tragically Scott and his companions all died on the journey back.

• Geologists studying Antarctic rocks have discovered that until about 150 million years ago, Antarctica had a warm climate.

◀ The tallest peaks in the Antarctic are over 4000 m high. But the ice sheet is so thick that in places three-quarters of this height is under the ice.

find out more

Arctic
Climate
Continents
Ice

Archaeology

The world is full of things left behind by people who lived long ago. Archaeologists study these things to find out how people lived at different times and in different parts of the world.

Historians find out about the past mainly from written records, but archaeologists look at **objects**. These objects include buildings, pottery and jewellery, and plant, animal and human remains such as bones or corpses (dead bodies). Some archaeologists even study ancient rubbish tips and toilets to find out what people ate.

The remains of some **ancient civilizations** are so big they are easy to see, like the great Inca city of Machu Picchu in Peru. But many smaller sites are difficult to find. **Aerial photographs** can help to reveal ancient remains. And sometimes a small, accidental **find**, such as a coin, can lead to an exciting new discovery.

▶ An archaeologist at work at an Aztec burial site in a cave near the Pyramid of the Sun in Teotihuacán, Mexico.

Archaeological digs

When archaeologists **dig** a site, they remove the soil carefully with trowels and brushes. They record the position of every object before removing it. Archaeologists can tell a lot about an object from where it is found and from other objects that are found with it.

▼ An aerial view of the ancient city of Jericho, in Palestine. Jericho is one of the oldest cities in the world – people first settled here 10,000 years ago. In the last 100 years archaeologists have begun to dig into the piled-up remains of thousands of years of human occupation.

FAMOUS FINDS

1871 Heinrich Schliemann finds the site of **Troy**, the city beseiged by the Greeks in the ancient Greek poem, the *Iliad*. It was destroyed in 1200 BC.

1922 Howard Carter discovers the tomb of the ancient Egyptian boy king, **Tutankhamun**, who died in 1323 BC.

1974 People digging a well in Xi'an in China stumble upon the burial site of the **Chinese emperor Zheng**, who died in 210 BC.

Architecture

Architecture is the business of designing and creating buildings. The Roman architect Vitruvius said that a well-designed building should be useful, stable (well built) and beautiful. This is still true for buildings today.

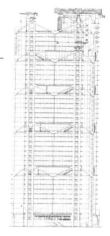

For centuries European architecture was based on the ideas of the ancient Greeks and Romans. Other cultures have their own architectural rules and traditions. However, in the 20th century Western styles spread to many countries.

The work of an architect

Architects have to work with many different people in designing a building. They talk to the client (the person who is paying for the building) about the size and purpose of the building. They talk to the surveyors about the building site, and to the builders about details of construction.

Architects express their ideas in drawings: first rough sketches, then plans, and finally a detailed model, picture or computer simulation.

Classical architecture

The architecture of ancient Greece and Rome is known as 'classical architecture'. Greek buildings were built simply, using upright posts (**columns**) and horizontal beams (**architraves**). Roman buildings were often bigger and more complicated than those of the

▲ Before building work starts, an architect does drawings to show what a new building will look like. These two drawings are an elevation (a view of one face of the building) and a plan (a 'footprint' of the building) of a famous building in Hong Kong: the Hong Kong–Shanghai Bank.

▼ This temple was built by the ancient Greeks over 2000 years ago. It shows the column and beam style of building very well.

find out more

Bridges
Buildings

▶ The Taj Mahal at Agra, one of the most beautiful buildings in the world. It was built in the 17th century by the Mughal emperor Shah Jahan.

Greeks. This was partly because they made use of **arches**, which could span wider spaces than horizontal beams. The Romans also often used **domes** to cover square or circular spaces, and **vaults** (arched roofs) over long, narrow spaces.

Roman architecture formed the basis of much European architecture for many centuries. Arches and domes were also an important part of Islamic architecture.

Gothic and Renaissance

In the 12th century a new style of architecture, called Gothic, arose. It used pointed arches, which are stronger than rounded ones. Instead of having massively heavy stonework, Gothic buildings have a more skeleton-like system of construction, and therefore look more elegant and airy.

The Gothic style dominated most European architecture

▲ Bourges cathedral in France. Large Gothic churches often use flying buttresses – external supports that are connected to the wall by an arch.

Church buildings

The earliest western churches were copied from the halls (basilicas) where the Romans held law courts. The names for the parts of a basilica, including the nave, the transept, and the aisle, are used for parts of a church.

Churches in western Europe are often built in the shape of a cross. Many have huge windows filled with stained glass. Eastern (Orthodox) churches were built with many arches and domes. They are called 'Byzantine' after Byzantium (now Istanbul), the capital of the Eastern Roman Empire.

SOME FAMOUS ARCHITECTS

Andrea Palladio (1508–1580). Italian who reinterpreted classical Roman architecture.

Antonio Gaudí (1852–1926). Spanish architect with a distinctive style.

Frank Lloyd Wright (1867–1959). American known for 'organic architecture', which reflects the natural surroundings.

Le Corbusier (1887–1965). Swiss-born architect, one of most innovative of the 20th century.

from about 1200 to about 1500. It was then replaced by a revival of Classical features. This revival was part of the Renaissance (meaning 'rebirth') period, in which the glories of the ancient world were rediscovered.

Modern styles

Classical architecture was given many variations over the next few centuries. In the 19th century some architects began experimenting with entirely new styles and techniques, using industrial materials such as iron and steel.

This revolution in architecture continued after World War I. Many European architects began to experiment with simple-looking buildings made from materials like reinforced concrete and large sheets of glass. The most famous of these architects was the Swiss-born Le Corbusier.

The German architects Walter Gropius and Mies van der Rohe

took the new ideas to the USA in the 1930s. There they developed the type of glass-walled, steel-framed office blocks that have since been built in cities all over the world.

By the 1960s some architects began to think that this style was too plain and unfriendly. They started to mix new styles with ideas copied from older buildings in a more decorated 'post-modern' style. They also created buildings that were designed to express the different cultures in the world.

▲ More and more architects are designing buildings that use natural materials, fit in with their environment, and need less energy for heating. This house on the east coast of the USA is built mostly from wood. It has very thick insulation, which keeps the house warm in cold weather, and cool in hot weather.

◀ The Sydney Opera House in Australia was designed by the Danish architect Jørn Utzen. Its bold design made the building an international landmark. Many problems had to be overcome before the Opera House was completed in 1973.

Arctic

The Arctic is the area inside the Arctic Circle around the North Pole. It is a huge frozen ocean, surrounded by islands and by the northern coasts of Asia and North America. Cold water flows out from the Arctic into the Atlantic and Pacific Oceans, carrying icebergs with it.

The Arctic is cold all year round. In winter the sun never comes above the horizon, and the sea is completely frozen over. In summer, temperatures creep above freezing, the edge of the Arctic Ocean melts, and for weeks the sun never sets. The Arctic Ocean is rich in plankton and fish. These are food for millions of sea birds, which nest in the Arctic in summer, and for seals, whales and other sea creatures.

The land areas around the Arctic Ocean are generally flat and treeless. In winter, the soil is frozen and covered with snow. In summer, the snow melts and the top layer of soil thaws out. Plants grow and flower, providing food for animals such as reindeer (caribou) and musk oxen. Meat-eaters like the Arctic wolf and polar bear survive by hunting.

The Arctic region is one of the most sparsely populated areas in the world. The **Inuit** (Eskimo) have survived here for hundreds of years. More recently, the discovery of oil, natural gas and other minerals has brought people from further south to work in the Arctic.

------	country boundary
	ice cap
	sea covered by ice all year
	sea covered by ice for part of the year

First to the Pole?
In 1909 two Americans, Robert Peary and Frederick Cook, both claimed to have been the first to reach the North Pole. However, neither could provide real proof. Various studies since have suggested that Peary may have come at least within a few kilometres of the Pole.

◀ When summer arrives, huge herds of reindeer (caribou) come to the Arctic to benefit from the rich feeding here. The caribou are followed by packs of hungry wolves.

find out more
Antarctic
Climate
Ice

Argentina *see* South America • **Armies** *see* Weapons • **Arthur** (king) *see* Knights

ARCTIC OCEAN

EUROPE

RUSSIA

Arctic Circle

**RUSSIA
(RUSSIAN FEDERATION)**

Sea of
Okhotsk

Sakhalin

URAL MOUNTAINS

Don Volga

Ob

Yenisey

S i b e r i a

Kolyma

Amur

Lake
Baykal

ALTAI MOUNTAINS

MONGOLIA

Gobi Desert

Sea of
Japan

Black Sea

TURKEY

GE
AZ
AR

Caspian
Sea

KAZAKHSTAN

Aral
Sea

S   t   e   p   p   e

Irtysh

LE
IS
SYRIA
JO
IRAQ

Tigris

SAUDI
ARABIA

KUWAIT

BAHRAIN

QATAR

The Gulf

UAE

YEMEN
REPUBLIC

OMAN

Red Sea

AFRICA

IRAN

TU

UZBEKISTAN

KIRGYZSTAN

TAJIKISTAN

AFGHANISTAN

HINDU KUSH

K2
▲8611

Jammu and
Kashmir

CHINA

NK

SK

JAPAN

Huang He
(Yellow)

East
China
Sea

TAIWAN

Tropic of Cancer

PACIFI

OCEAN

PHILIPPINES

PAKISTAN

Indus

TIBETAN
PLATEAU

HIMALAYAS

Mt Everest
▲8848

NEPAL

BH

Chang Jiang
(Yangtze)

Arabian
Sea

Ganges

INDIA

DECCAN

BANGLADESH

BURMA
(MYANMAR)

LAOS

THAILAND

VIETNAM

CAMBODIA

South
China
Sea

WESTERN GHATS

Bay of
Bengal

MALDIVES

SRI LANKA

INDIAN OCEAN

Mekong

BR

MALAYSIA

Borneo

SINGAPORE

INDONESIA

Sumatra

Java Sea

New
Guin

Eq

OCEANI

OCEANI

0   1000 km
0   500 miles

country boundary
ice cap
▲ highest peaks
(height in metres)
land height in metres

5000
2000
1000
500
200
sea level land below
sea level

AR   ARMENIA
AZ   AZERBAIJAN
BH   BHUTAN
BR   BRUNEI DARUSSALAM
GE   GEORGIA
IS   ISRAEL
JO   JORDAN
LE   LEBANON
NK   NORTH KOREA
SK   SOUTH KOREA
TU   TURKMENISTAN
UAE UNITED ARAB EMIRATES

Asia

Asia is the largest continent in the world, and it has the most people. Asia covers one-third of the Earth's land surface, and about two-thirds of the world's population live there.

Central Asia is very hot in summer, but extremely cold in winter. In winter cold, dry winds blow out from the centre of the continent. In summer wet winds blow in from the sea, bringing heavy **monsoon** rains to the south. However, the barrier of the Himalayas stops the wet winds from reaching central Asia, western China and Mongolia, which stay dry.

ASIA FACTS

Population: 3,608,799,000

Area: 44,387,000 sq km

Highest mountain: Mount Everest, 8848 m, is the highest mountain in the world

Longest river: Chang Jiang (Yangtze), 6300 km

Largest lake: Caspian Sea, 371,000 sq km, the largest lake in the world

Deepest lake: Lake Baykal, 1714 m, is the deepest lake in the world

Landscapes

Asia is so large that it has nearly every kind of landscape. Flat frozen plains cover much of the far north, while further south a band of coniferous forest called the **taiga** stretches right across the continent. The **steppes** of western Asia are grasslands, with rich, black soils that are excellent for farming. Much of central Asia, from the Red Sea to Mongolia, is desert. The greatest area is the bare, rocky Gobi Desert.

The **Himalayas** separate central Asia from the tropical lands of southern and South-east Asia. They form the largest mountain system in the world. The rivers that drain the Himalayas, such as the Ganges, the Indus and the Brahmaputra, carry silt and mud to the flood plains to the south, forming rich, fertile soils.

• Asia has some of the world's poorest countries, and some of its richest. The average life expectancy in Laos, for example, is about 50 years, whereas people in Japan usually live to be nearer 80. The death rate for babies is higher in Cambodia than in any other country in the world.

find out more

China
Continents
Grasslands
India and Pakistan
Japan
Middle East
Mongols
Mountains
Ottoman empire
Russia
South-east Asia

China
(see page 77)

India
(see page 196)

Indonesia
(see page 346)

Russia
(see page 320)

Bangladesh
(see page 196)

Japan
(see page 210)

People

Most Asians live in the southern part of the continent, in India, Bangladesh, the eastern half of China, Japan, Indonesia and Sri Lanka. The most crowded areas are on the coasts and along the flood plains of rivers in China, India and Bangladesh. There are also vast areas where few people live.

The majority of Asians live in the country and make their living from some kind of farming. Rice is the main crop in most of India, China and South-east Asia; wheat is the main crop in Russia and Kazakhstan; and the plains of central Asia are grazed by herds of cattle, goats or yaks. However, in southern and South-east Asia, more and more people are moving to cities. Seoul, Bangkok, Jakarta and several Chinese cities now have more than 5 million people. Many of these cities have tremendous problems because of overcrowding.

▲ Rice is the most important crop in large parts of southern and eastern Asia. The seeds are sown in special seed beds, then transferred to a flooded field, or paddy. This Vietnamese woman is taking some seedlings to a paddy for planting.

◀ There are many kinds of farming and industry in the Himalayas. Farmers grow rice and sugar cane, and keep sheep, goats and yaks. About one-third of the Himalayas is forest, used mainly for paper and firewood. The mountains also contain valuable minerals, iron and coal.

Pakistan
(see page 196)

Vietnam
(see page 346)

Turkey
(see page 241)

Philippines
(see page 346)

Thailand
(see page 346)

Iran
(see page 241)

Asthma *see* Medicine • **Astronauts** *see* Space exploration

Astronomy

When you look up into the night sky, what are the lights that you see? A few are planets, many are stars, and some are huge galaxies, each one full of billions more stars. Astronomy is the study of the planets, stars and galaxies that make up our Universe.

Astronomers try to explain the things you can see in the night sky. They also try to work out things like the age of the stars and their distance from Earth.

Seeing further

People have always been interested in the stars and planets. Early astronomers had only their eyes to watch the sky, but when **telescopes** were invented in 1608, astronomers were able to see the stars and planets more clearly. One of the first people to study the sky using a telescope was the Italian scientist **Galileo Galilei**.

Today astronomers use many types of telescope to collect information about the Universe. Some telescopes collect the faint light from distant objects. Others measure other types of radiation given off by stars and galaxies, such as **X-rays**. Most telescopes are on Earth, but some, like the Hubble Space Telescope, orbit in space. Today's astronomers also get information from **space probes**, which travel far out into space.

▲ New stars are forming in the glowing gas of the Orion Nebula, shown here. This picture was taken by the Hubble Space Telescope.

find out more

Galaxies
Lenses and mirrors
Solar System
Stars
Sun
Universe

◄ Astronomical observatories, like this one at Kitt Peak in Australia, have many different telescopes, each making different sorts of measurement. Most observatories are built on the tops of mountains, far from city lights, to give a clear view of the sky.

Atoms and molecules

Atoms are the building blocks that make up everything. But they are very, very tiny. If you lined up 4 billion atoms side by side they might just cover the full stop at the end of this sentence.

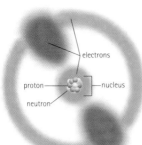

electrons

proton

neutron

nucleus

Elements are basic substances made up of atoms. Elements cannot be broken down to make other substances. An atom is the smallest bit of an element that you can have.

Making up molecules

Although there are only about 100 elements, there are millions and millions of different substances. This is because the atoms in the elements can join together to make new substances called **compounds**.

Molecules are made up of several atoms joined together. A molecule is the smallest bit of a compound that you can have.

Some molecules, like the oxygen we breathe in air, have only two atoms. A molecule of water is made up of just three atoms.

Other molecules are much bigger. Some of the molecules that make up our bodies have millions of atoms.

Inside atoms

Atoms themselves are made up of smaller particles called **electrons**, **neutrons** and **protons**. The neutrons and protons form a clump in the middle of the atom. This is called the **nucleus**. The electrons whizz around the

▲ A cloud of electrons whizzes around the cluster of neutrons and protons that make up the nucleus of an atom.

The molecules of oxygen we breathe are made up of two atoms of oxygen.

The water molecules we drink have two atoms of hydrogen and one atom of oxygen.

Methane gas can be burnt as a fuel. A molecule of methane has four atoms of hydrogen and one atom of carbon.

hydrogen atom

oxygen atom

carbon atom

◄ Three simple molecules.

▲ Nuclear weapons make use of the energy released by splitting atoms to cause huge explosions. When an atomic bomb explodes it releases as much energy as thousands of tonnes of dynamite.

nucleus. They are much lighter and smaller.

Releasing power

There are massive amounts of energy locked in an atomic nucleus. Scientists have found that they can split certain types of nucleus and release some of this energy. This is called nuclear **fission**. Fission has been used in nuclear weapons to cause huge explosions. It is also used more peacefully in atomic power stations, to make electricity.

KEY DATES

about 400 BC Greek philosopher Democritus suggests that everything is made of tiny particles called atoms

1803–1805 British chemist John Dalton discovers elements

1897 British physicist J. J. Thomson discovers electrons

1911 British physicist Ernest Rutherford discovers that most of an atom is made up of empty space

1919 Ernest Rutherford discovers the proton

1932 British physicist James Chadwick discovers the neutron

1938 German chemist Otto Hahn and Austrian physicist Lise Meitner discover nuclear fission

Empty atoms!
Most of the space inside an atom is empty. If there was an atom as large as a football stadium, its nucleus would be about the size of a pea.

find out more

Elements
Solids, liquids and gases
Power stations
Radiation

small nucleus

neutrons

gamma radiation

small nucleus

neutron

fission

uranium-235 nucleus

▶ Nuclear fission. If a neutron with a certain energy hits a uranium nucleus it makes the nucleus unstable, causing it to split. Splitting the nucleus releases lots of energy.

Australia

Australia is one of the largest and flattest countries on Earth. It is also a land of great natural beauty. Many of the plants and animals that live in Australia are found wild nowhere else on Earth.

AUSTRALIA FACTS

Capital: Canberra

Population:
18,400,000

Area:
7,692,300 sq km

Language: English

Religion: Christian

Currency:
1 Australian dollar =
100 cents

Wealth per person:
$18,720

The hot, dry area in the middle of the country is known as the '**outback**'. A large part of it is desert. Only animals and plants that can survive with little water live in the outback. Most people live on the coast to the east of the Great Dividing Range, where it is cooler and wetter.

Animals and plants

Some of Australia's most famous animals – kangaroos, koalas, possums, wallabies and wombats – belong to a special group of mammals called **marsupials**. Marsupial young live in a furry pouch on their mothers' stomachs.

• Australia is the main country in the continent of Oceania, which also includes New Zealand, Papua New Guinea and many Pacific islands.

find out more

Continents
Exploration, Age of
Oceans and seas

--- state boundary
— main roads
— main railways
◆ capital city
■ large cities
·-·-· seasonal rivers, lakes
sand desert
▲ high peaks
(height in metres)
land height in metres

1000
500
200
sea level land below
sea level

Austria *see* Europe • **Avalanches** *see* Mountains

▶ A group of Aboriginal children. Today many Aborigines live in the big cities or towns. They prefer to be known as Kooris. Some of their sacred sites are being returned to them.

Echidnas (spiny anteaters) and duck-billed platypuses belong to another tiny group of mammals called **monotremes**. They are the only mammals that lay eggs. **Eucalyptus** trees are the most famous Australian trees.

People and work

Although most people live in towns and cities on the east coast, some live in country towns or on farms. Farmers produce mostly beef, mutton and wool from sheep, and wheat. There are huge cattle and sheep ranches, called 'stations', in the outback.

Another important industry is mining. Australia is the world's largest exporter of coal and opals (a precious gem). Australia's other main industries include timber production, fishing and tourism.

Australia's history

The first inhabitants of Australia were the **Aborigines**. They probably arrived at least 45,000 years ago, and spread over the country in large family groups called tribes.

In the 1640s the Dutch explorer Abel **Tasman** became the first European to sail round Australia. Then in 1770 the British explorer James **Cook** claimed Australia for Britain. The first European settlers were criminals and soldiers sent from Britain. In the 19th century settlers fought with the Aborigines and took over their lands.

In 1901 Australia became a self-governing country. In the last 50 years people from all over the world have moved there. Today, Australia is an exciting country of many cultures and languages.

▼ One-fifth of all Australians live in **Sydney**, the largest city in Australia. Sydney is famous for its great harbour and the Opera House (centre).

Aztecs

For almost 200 years the Aztecs ruled an area that is now part of Mexico. Although the Aztecs were great builders and fine craftworkers, their civilization was also extremely bloodthirsty.

▲ The Aztec empire at its height.

The Aztecs came to central Mexico about 650 years ago. They built a huge city, called **Tenochtitlán**, in the middle of a lake. Here lived the emperor, his courtiers and the chief priests. Aztec life was carefully organized, but the Aztecs did not have writing or money; and they did not make metal tools.

Worshippers of the Sun

The Aztecs worshipped a **Sun god**. They believed he needed fresh blood to make him rise each day. So the priests sacrificed animals and birds to the god. They also sacrificed living people – often prisoners they had captured in war.

Conquest by Cortés

The Aztec civilization was ended by the Spanish conqueror Hernán **Cortés**. Cortes landed in Central America in 1519. The Aztecs had never seen a European before. Some believed he was a god.

Cortés made friends with the Aztecs' enemies and captured the emperor **Montezuma**. This led to fierce fighting. The Spanish, with their horses, guns and metal weapons, triumphed and destroyed Tenochtitlán.

Have a heart!
The Aztecs cut the hearts out of their human sacrifice victims when they were still alive. On very special religious occasions as many as 20,000 people were killed in a day!

find out more
Empire, Age of
North America

▼ The temple area of Tenochtitlán was dominated by a huge pyramid, on top of which stood twin temples to the gods.

Babies *see* Children *and* Sex and reproduction • **Bach, J. S.** *see* Classical music

Bacteria and viruses

Bacteria and viruses are very simple living creatures. They are found everywhere on Earth. Many live inside plants and animals.

Bacteria are some of the oldest and simplest living things on Earth. In the classification of living things, bacteria are placed in their own kingdom, the Monerans.

Bacteria are also among the most common organisms. They reproduce very quickly, by dividing into two.

Like plants, some bacteria make their own food using the energy of the Sun. But most live by breaking down dead plants and animals. Many live inside other living things.

Some bacteria are useful. Bacteria that break down dead organisms return important nutrients to the soil, and bacteria in our stomachs help us digest food. But some bacteria are dangerous and cause serious diseases.

Viruses

Viruses are so tiny that they can only be seen under a very powerful microscope. They are thought to be the smallest living things, but they cannot reproduce on their own. Viruses can only reproduce themselves by infecting, or getting inside, the cells of another organism.

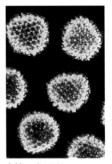

▲ More than 200 different types of virus can cause colds. This picture shows one of them – adenovirus.

> **Quick work!**
> If it had unlimited supplies of space and food, a single bacterium could produce 4000 million million million others in just one day.

> **Deadly diseases**
> Some diseases caused by bacteria and viruses are killers. Tuberculosis, pneumonia, cholera and typhoid are all caused by bacteria. Aids, polio, rabies and some forms of cancer are just a few of the serious diseases caused by viruses.

find out more

Algae
Cells
Diseases
Life on Earth

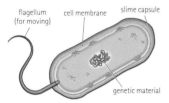

flagellum (for moving)
cell membrane
slime capsule
genetic material

▲ A typical bacterium.

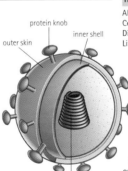

protein knob
inner shell
outer skin
genetic material

◀ This diagram shows the human immuno-deficiency virus (HIV) that causes the disease Aids. When the virus reproduces itself it destroys the white blood cells that help our bodies fight off disease.

Bears

Bears are huge creatures. Some, like polar bears, live in the frozen Arctic. Others, like brown bears, live in forests.

Like people, bears are mammals. They are related to flesh-eating animals such as dogs and cats.

Although bears can stand upright, they usually walk on all fours. They have an excellent sense of smell, but cannot see or hear very well.

Eating and sleeping

Bears eat both animals and plants. **Polar bears** feed mainly on fish and seals. Other kinds of bear eat small animals, fruit, nuts and honey. The **giant panda** lives mainly on bamboo.

In the autumn bears eat a lot of food to build up layers of fat.

▶ The giant panda is one of the most striking-looking animals in the world. Pandas are extremely rare – they live only in three remote mountain areas of China. There may be only 500 left in the wild.

This helps them survive the winter. Most bears sleep through the winter in a den. But they do not hibernate (go into a deep winter sleep). They can usually wake up quickly.

Baby bears

Most bear cubs are born in winter. At first they are no bigger than guinea pigs, and they stay with their mother until they are at least a year old. A family of cubs may stay together for up to three years.

Bear facts
There are eight different kinds of bear. The largest is the Alaskan Kodiak bear, which is the largest meat-eater that lives on land. It can weigh up to half a tonne.

find out more
Animals

▼ This brown bear is fishing with her cubs. There used to be lots of brown bears in Europe and North America. Today they live mainly in Alaska, Canada and remote parts of Asia.

Beavers *see* Mice and other rodents

Bees and wasps

Bees and wasps are closely related. They are some of our most familiar insects.

There are about 25,000 different kinds of bee and over 50,000 different kinds of wasp. Many bees and wasps live alone, but some, such as **honeybees** and **bumble-bees**, live in big family groups in a hive or nest.

Life in the **hive** is very organized. There is just one **queen bee** who lays eggs. The eggs are fertilized by a few male bees, called **drones**. All of the other bees are **worker bees**. One of their jobs is to look after the grubs that hatch from the queen's eggs.

Gathering food

The worker bees also collect the sugary liquid nectar from flowers. They use this to feed the grubs, and also to make **honey**. The bees feed on the honey during the winter.

When they visit flowers, they fill 'pollen baskets' on their hind legs with **pollen**. As they travel from flower to flower, they brush some of this pollen onto other flowers they visit and so pollinate (fertilize) them.

▲ A social wasp feeding. There are many different kinds of wasp. Social wasps are usually striped black and yellow, and sting. They live in large family groups like bees. But digger wasps and potter wasps are solitary hunters, and gall wasps are parasites that feed on plants.

◀▼ Worker bees at work.

Worker bees follow the queen when she lays eggs.

They use wax that they make in their bodies to build a comb inside the hive.

A worker bee collects nectar and pollen.

Dancing bees
When a worker bee finds a good supply of pollen, it goes back to the hive and does a special 'dance'. This dance tells the other bees where the food is.

find out more
Animals
Insects

Bicycles

Bicycles are used for transport all over the world. In poorer countries, where most people cannot afford cars or trucks, bicycles are used for carrying heavy loads and as taxis. In richer countries, they are used mostly for short trips and for pleasure.

The **first bicycles** were wooden, with iron tyres and no brakes or pedals. The first pedal bicycle was built in 1839, and in 1888 air-filled tyres were invented. By the early 1900s, bicycles looked much like they do today. Lightweight bicycles, BMX bikes and mountain bikes were introduced in the 1970s.

Bicycle parts

Most bicycles have a strong but light **frame** made from hollow metal tubes. The air-filled **tyres** ride smoothly over small bumps. There is a **brake** on each wheel. A pull on the brake levers slows the bicycle down by pressing rubber brake blocks against the wheel rim.

▲ Mountain-bike racing.

▲ Hobby horse (velocipede), 1817.

▲ Penny farthing, 1860s.

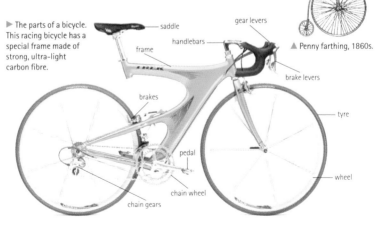

▶ The parts of a bicycle. This racing bicycle has a special frame made of strong, ultra-light carbon fibre.

saddle
gear levers
handlebars
frame
brake levers
brakes
tyre
pedal
wheel
chain wheel
chain gears

Bicycle racing
There are many kinds of bicycle
racing, from road and track
racing to BMX and mountain
biking. The most famous road
race is the Tour de France, which
covers thousands of kilometres
and lasts three weeks.

Bicycles work by **muscle
power**. Pressing on the pedals
turns the chain wheel, which
pulls on the chain. The chain
turns the back wheel, and drives
the bike along. Many bicycles
have **gears** to make riding easier.

Bicycle design

Different kinds of bicycle are
designed with different jobs in
mind. A **mountain bike** is
designed for riding over rough
ground. It has a very strong
frame and wheels, chunky tyres
for good grip, and lots of low
gears for steep hills. A **track-
racing bike** is designed for
speed, with thin tyres, high gears
and a very light frame. A **touring
bike** is designed to be fast but
comfortable on long journeys.

Motorcycles

A motorcycle is like a bicycle
with an engine. It has a steel
frame, like a bicycle, and the
engine, fuel tank, saddle and
other parts are all bolted to this.
The front and rear wheels have
dampers (shock absorbers) to
stop the bike bouncing up and
down too much. The
engine is connected to a
gearbox. It usually turns
a chain, which turns the
back wheel.

▲ This bicycle is being
used to transport
bananas in India.

● In 1885 the German
Gottleib Daimler made
the first motorcycle with
a petrol engine.

find out more

Engines and motors
Transport

▶ Motorcycle
engines range in
capacity from less
than 50 cc (cubic
centimetres) to over
1200 cc. The engines
of larger machines
like this one have a
water cooling system
instead of being
cooled by air.

Birds

Birds are the only animals with feathers. Any animal that grows feathers is a bird. All birds have wings, and most, although not all, can fly.

Birds are warm-blooded animals, and do not have teeth. The earliest known bird is the *Archaeopteryx*, which lived about 147 million years ago, and was about the size of a magpie. It had teeth and was like a small dinosaur in many ways. Some scientists think that birds evolved from dinosaurs.

Today there are around 8700 different kinds of bird. They come in all shapes and sizes. An ostrich can grow taller than a person. A bee hummingbird can fit into the palm of your hand.

Birds all over

Birds live in all parts of the world and in all kinds of habitat. Many live in gardens, cities and parks. Others live in rainforests, deserts, forests or oceans, and in the icy wastes of the Arctic and Antarctic.

Many birds **migrate** – they move to a different part of the world for part of the year. Some birds fly thousands of kilometres to spend the winter in warmer places where there is plenty of food.

▲ This red kite is a hunting bird. As it soars high in the sky, it uses its keen eyesight to spot its prey.

RECORD-BREAKING BIRDS

Biggest bird: Ostrich, 2.5 m tall and weighs 150 kg

Smallest bird: Bee hummingbird, 6 cm long

Largest wingspan: Wandering albatross, up to 4 m

High flyers!

Some birds fly as high as jumbo jets. In 1973 a vulture collided with a plane over West Africa. The bird was flying at 11,277 m.

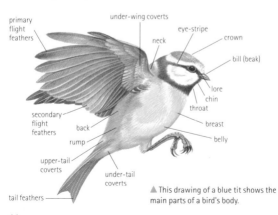

primary flight feathers

under-wing coverts

neck

eye-stripe

crown

bill (beak)

lore

chin

throat

breast

belly

secondary flight feathers

back

rump

upper-tail coverts

under-tail coverts

tail feathers

▲ This drawing of a blue tit shows the main parts of a bird's body.

Feathers

Feathers cover most of a bird's body. They are made by the birds' skin, like our skin makes hair or fingernails. Adult birds shed their old feathers and grow new ones in a process called **moulting**.

Feathers keep birds warm and dry. They can also provide **camouflage** – their colours blend in with their surroundings and make them difficult to see. Female birds are often camouflaged, because they need to stay hidden while sitting on their eggs. On the other hand, male birds often have brightly coloured feathers. This helps them attract mates.

Taking flight

Most important of all, feathers help a bird to fly. They are light and strong, and the shape of the wing feathers helps to create an upward lift. This lift keeps a flying bird in the air. Feathers also streamline the bird's body, which makes it fly better.

A bird's bones are also designed for flight. The bones are very light, and some are hollow. This makes it easier for them to fly.

Not all birds fly in the same way. Starlings fly in a straight line, moving their wings all the time. Hummingbirds can hover, beating their wings up to 100 times a second. Vultures glide through the air, hardly moving their wings at all.

▲ The Arctic tern migrates longer distances than any other animal. It can travel up to 35,000 km in one year.

—— main migration route
····· alternative migration routes

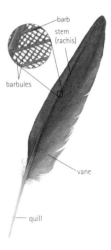

barb
stem (rachis)
barbules
vane
quill

▶ A typical feather includes the stem (rachis), the base of the stem (quill) and the vane. The vane is made up of separate branches called barbs. These are linked to each other by small hooks called barbules.

▼ A little owl in flight. Birds use powerful muscles attached to a strong breastbone to flap their wings.

◀ Cuckoos lay their eggs in other birds' nests, and leave the foster mother to take care of the young cuckoo. When the baby cuckoo hatches, it pushes the other eggs out of the nest.

Eggs

All birds lay eggs on land, usually in a **nest**. The young hatch and grow up in the nest.

A bird's egg has a hard outer shell for protection. Inside there is a watery substance, the egg white, which protects the growing chick. In the centre is the yolk. This is made up of fat and proteins to feed the chick as it develops.

The parents sit on the eggs to keep them warm. When the chick is fully developed, it hatches by breaking out of the egg.

Songs and calls

Most birds use songs and calls to communicate. Many birds have a language with calling sounds that have distinct meanings. These sounds are innate – they do not have to be learned. The songs, however, have to be learned and it is usually only the male birds who really sing.

Danger signals are short and loud. Other calls may be used to keep a flock together. Courting birds use special calls to attract mates.

▲ Ducks (left), geese (centre) and swans (right) are all wildfowl. They usually live near water, and have webbed feet, short legs and oily feathers.

find out more

Animals
Camouflage
Conservation
Dinosaurs
Life on Earth
Migration

▼ Songbirds make up the largest group of birds. Most land birds are songbirds.

waxwing (Europe and North America)

black-headed weaver and nest (Africa)

scarlet tanager (North America)

song thrush (Europe)

Gouldian finch (Australia)

Food

Some birds eat only plants. Others eat only fresh meat. And still others eat a mixture. The shapes of birds' **beaks** and feet often give us a clue as to what they eat. Sparrows and finches, for example, have short, strong beaks for cracking seeds.

Ducks, **geese** and **swans** live near water. They have webbed feet to help them paddle through the water, and use their flattened beaks for plucking plant food from water or mud.

Most **wading birds** have long legs so they can wade into the water, and strong beaks which they poke into the mud to find worms or shellfish.

▼ Wading birds find food in many different ways. Curlews (1) probe in the mud. Pratincoles (2) sometimes feed off insects in the air. Turnstones (3) search under stones. Phalaropes (4) feed from the surface water, and avocets (5) scoop food from water.

Birds of prey like eagles, falcons and hawks live by hunting and killing other animals for food. They have powerful feet with talons (claws), and hooked beaks for tearing meat.

Most **sea birds** live by catching fish. Many can glide for hours without flapping their wings. Some have spear-shaped beaks, ideal for catching or snapping up fish.

Birds don't have teeth, so they can't chew their food. Instead they swallow their food whole and crush it using the muscles in a special grinding organ called a **gizzard**.

Protecting birds

Young birds have a hard time finding food and shelter and avoiding their enemies. Most die in their first year. But generally enough survive to produce the next generation. By hunting birds and destroying the places where they live, people can upset this balance. For example, whenever marshes are drained or forests are cleared, the habitats of many birds are destroyed.

▲ Albatrosses are great ocean travellers. They are spectacular gliders and only come on land to breed.

▲ Gulls are a very adaptable group of sea birds. Some kinds even live inland.

▶ Cormorants are among about 300 different kinds of bird that get their food mainly from the sea. With their powerful webbed feet and long bodies cormorants are champion divers.

Birth *see* Sex and reproduction

Black Death

The Black Death is the popular name of a killer disease also called the plague. It first appeared about 700 years ago, spreading death and terror across Asia and Europe. Millions died.

The official name for the Black Death is 'bubonic plague'. Nasty dark lumps swell up under a victim's arms and in their groin. They get a raging fever and usually die within a few days.

The march of death

The plague spread from northern India to China and west to Constantinople (Istanbul). From there it passed into Europe. It reached England in 1348 and Moscow three years later. Where it struck, the plague wiped out between one third and one half of the population.

God forgive us!

The plague terrified medieval people because it was mysterious as well as murderous. Some said it was God's punishment for wicked behaviour. They thought infected air carried the disease. In fact, it was carried by fleas that lived on rats.

Not all the effects of the plague were bad. After it had died down, there were far fewer labourers to work in the fields and workshops. Those who were left got higher wages and better conditions.

▲ Unknown to people at the time, the Black Death was spread by fleas that lived on rats. In the often filthy living conditions of the Middle Ages, the disease spread quickly.

Nasty medicine!
All sorts of strange cures for the plague were tried. People ate dung and ashes, cut off the black lumps, and even placed a living toad on a victim's chest!

find out more
Diseases
Middle Ages

◀ Burying plague victims. During a really bad outbreak, the bodies were all buried together in a mass grave, or just piled in a heap and covered with earth.

Bones and muscles

Your bones are the hard parts of your body. They form your skeleton – the frame around which your body is built. All these bones have muscles attached to them. Together your muscles and bones make it possible for you to move.

You have more than 200 bones in your body, and more than 650 muscles. All **vertebrates** (animals with backbones) have bones inside their bodies that give them shape. And all animals have muscles of some sort. Without muscles they would not be able to move about.

Bones

Bones contain living cells and can regrow if they break. They are made of a mixture of protein and minerals, and they are very strong. At the centre of many bones is a soft

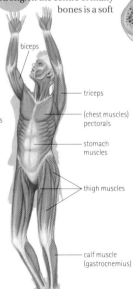

this end fits into hip bone

hard outer bone

bone marrow

soft living bone

this end forms part of knee joint

▲ A human thigh bone. The thigh bone is the longest bone in the human body.

find out more

Heart and blood
Human beings

skull
jawbone
collar bone
breastbone
upper arm (humerus)
ribs
lower arm ⎡ ulna
⎣ radius
spine
pelvic bones
thigh bone (femur)
knee cap (patella)
lower leg ⎡ tibia
⎣ fibula

biceps
triceps
(chest muscles) pectorals
stomach muscles
thigh muscles
calf muscle (gastrocnemius)

◄ The human skeleton and muscular system.

49

tissue called **bone marrow**. Blood vessels in the marrow supply the bone with food and oxygen. New blood cells are also made in the marrow. The ears and the tip of the nose are made out of **cartilage** – a smooth gristly substance that is much softer than bone.

Joints

Joints are the bending and sliding places where bones meet. The bones at joints are covered in cartilage, and oiled by joint fluid. This allows them to move over each other easily. Different types of joint allow different movements. **Hinge joints**, such as the elbow and the knee, move in two directions only. **Ball-and-socket joints**, such as the shoulder and hip, can move in many directions.

Muscles

There are three types of muscle in your body. The first type is attached to your bones and you use it to move your body. This sort of muscle only works when you want it to, so it is called a **voluntary muscle**. When you move, it pulls against your

▲ This crab has just shed its cuticle (shell). Cuticles are hard and do not allow the crab to grow.

skeleton, bending it at joints such as the elbow and the knee.

The second type of muscle can contract (shorten) without you thinking about it, so it is called an **involuntary muscle**. The muscle around the gut is an involuntary muscle.

The third type of muscle – the **cardiac muscle** – is found in the heart. It pumps blood around the body and can work for years without getting tired.

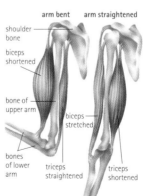

arm bent   arm straightened

shoulder bone

biceps shortened

bone of upper arm

biceps stretched

bones of lower arm

triceps straightened   triceps shortened

◀ There are at least two muscles at each joint. In the upper arm the biceps and triceps muscles work together to bend and straighten the arm. To bend the arm, the biceps contracts (shortens), and this stretches the triceps. To straighten the arm, the triceps contracts, and this stretches the biceps.

Brain and nerves

The brain is the body's control centre. Nerves carry messages to and from the brain and the rest of the body. Together, the brain and the nerves make up the nervous system.

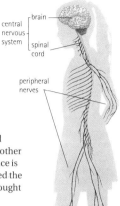

▲ Nerves reach out from your spinal cord into every part of your body.

Most animals have a nervous system. In people and other animals with backbones (vertebrates), it is made up of the brain, the **spinal cord** and a network of **peripheral nerves** throughout the body. Nerves carry electrical messages, called **nerve impulses**. For example, some nerves carry information about your surroundings from your eyes and other sense organs to your brain. Your brain uses this information to decide how your body will behave. Other nerves carry information and instructions from the brain to all parts of your body. Different parts of your brain carry out different jobs.

Humans have larger and more complex brains than other animals. The main difference is in the part of the brain called the **cerebrum**, the centre of thought and memory.

Reflexes
Your body does some things without you thinking about them. For example, if you touch something hot, you pull away your hand automatically. This kind of action is called a **reflex**. Reflexes happen because some nerve signals can trigger an automatic response in the spinal cord, without the brain being involved.

Well connected!
Human brains have about 100 *trillion* nerve connections. There are about 100 billion neurons (nerve cells) in the brain, each one of which is connected to about 1000 others.

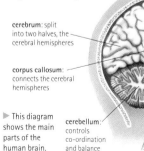

cerebrum: split into two halves, the cerebral hemispheres

corpus callosum: connects the cerebral hemispheres

thalamus: the brain's 'telephone exchange', sending nerve signals to different parts of the brain

hypothalamus: the site of emotions

cerebellum: controls co-ordination and balance

spinal cord

▶ This diagram shows the main parts of the human brain.

find out more
Cells
Human beings
Senses

Breathing

You breathe all the time – if you stopped breathing you would die. When you breathe in, you take air into your lungs. When you breathe out, you push air out of your lungs.

Human beings, like all animals, need a substance called **oxygen** to live. Air contains oxygen. When we breathe in, oxygen passes from our **lungs** into our **blood**. At the same time, another gas called **carbon dioxide**, which the body does not want, passes out of the blood into the lungs. So when we breathe out we get rid of carbon dioxide.

Why oxygen?

The oxygen we breathe reacts with food in our body to release energy, in a process called **respiration**. All animals and plants respire, but only certain animals breathe. Breathing is just one way of getting oxygen. Fishes, for example, use their gills to extract oxygen from water.

How respiration works

The blood carries oxygen to every cell in the body, where respiration takes place. Inside the cells, oxygen reacts with sugars and fats in food to release **energy**, plus some water and the waste gas carbon dioxide. The blood then carries the carbon dioxide back to the lungs, where it is breathed out.

● The oxygen in the air is produced by plants through a process called photosynthesis. They use energy from the Sun to turn carbon dioxide and water into sugar and oxygen.

find out more
Energy
Heart and blood
Human beings
Plants
Solids, liquids and gases

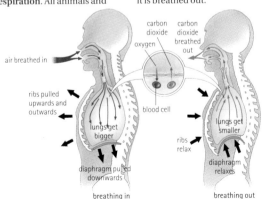

carbon dioxide
oxygen
carbon dioxide breathed out

air breathed in

ribs pulled upwards and outwards

blood cell

lungs get bigger

lungs get smaller

ribs relax

diaphragm pulled downwards

diaphragm relaxes

breathing in

breathing out

◄ Breathing in and breathing out.

Bridges

Bridges are structures built to get people or vehicles across rivers or valleys, or over a road or railway.

The earliest bridges were probably **beam bridges**, in which a wooden beam or stone slabs rested on supports or on the banks of a stream. Other early bridges used vines or ropes slung across a river to make a simple suspension bridge.

Arches in stone and steel

A curved arch can span a wider space than a simple beam. The Romans built many such arched bridges. At the end of the 18th century, the first iron bridges were built. These could span much larger distances than wooden or stone arches. By the 1880s steel was being used instead of iron.

BRIDGE RECORDS

Longest bridge:
Pontchartrain Causeway, Louisiana, USA (over 38 km long)

Longest suspension bridge:
Akashi–Kaikyo Bridge, Japan (main span 1991 m long)

Longest stone arch:
Wuchaohe Bridge, Fenghuang, China (spans 120 m)

find out more
Architecture
Construction
Trains

▲ In cable-stayed bridges, the cables that support the deck are attached directly to towers, rather than to a suspension cable. This bridge over the River Seine in Normandy, France, is the longest cable-stayed bridge in the world. The main span is 856 m.

Modern bridges

There are many types of modern bridge. Modern beam bridges have hollow beams made of steel or concrete instead of stone or wood; arch bridges are made of concrete or steel. **Cantilever bridges** are balanced about a support in the middle of the beam, rather than at the ends.

Suspension bridges and **cable-stayed bridges** are best for very large spans. In suspension bridges the deck of the bridge is suspended from steel cables, which hang between towers.

▼ With all bridges, the problem is to design structures that will not sag or crack under the weight they have to carry. Different bridge designs solve this problem in different ways.

early beam bridge

arch bridge

cantilever bridge

suspension bridge

Britain see United Kingdom

History of
Britain

For centuries Britain was a divided and fairly unimportant island. Then, after England, Scotland and Wales united, it enjoyed about 250 years of great power. Although this faded, today English is the world's leading language and many countries have a British-style parliament.

▲ Stone circles were built in Europe from about 3000 BC to about 1200 BC as ceremonial or religious monuments. Archaeologists think that Stonehenge in England was also used to observe the Sun and Moon.

Britain's prehistoric inhabitants worked with stone tools, then bronze and finally iron. The mysterious standing stones at **Stonehenge** are among the monuments from these times. The **Celts**, the last prehistoric people to come to Britain, arrived about 500 BC.

Invasions

From the 1st century AD, Britain was invaded many times. The **Romans** conquered England but struggled to overcome Wales and Scotland. Christianity first came to Britain in Roman times. After the Romans came tribes of **Anglo-Saxons**, whose language is the basis of modern English.

The **Vikings** took over much of north and west Scotland and eastern England. For a time Viking kings ruled all England. But in 1066 came the **Norman conquest**. The Normans were keen builders, and many of their castles and cathedrals are still standing.

▶ Robert the Bruce (1306–1329), Scotland's hero-king who drove the English from his country.

KEY DATES

AD
43 Romans invade Britain

5th century Anglo-Saxon invasions

597 St Augustine arrives to convert English to Christianity

793 First Viking raid on England

about 843 Kenneth McAlpin king of all Scotland

973 Edgar king of all England

1066 Norman conquest

1284 Edward I conquers Wales

1338–1453 Hundred Years' War

1348–1351 Black Death

1381 Peasants' Revolt

1455–1485 Wars of the Roses

1535 Henry VIII becomes head of Church of England

1540s Scotland becomes Protestant

1559 Elizabeth I sets up Protestant Church of England

1603 Scottish and English crowns united by James VI of Scotland (also James I of England)

1638 Scots rebel against Charles I

The age of kings

During the **Middle Ages** everyone had to attend church. Britain was run by kings and churchmen. The two did not always get on.

Kings frequently went to war. England's Edward I conquered Wales. But daring leaders such as Robert the Bruce beat off English attacks on Scotland. There were civil wars, too, such as the **Wars of the Roses** between the families of York and Lancaster.

Medieval Britain was closely linked to Europe. All European Christians belonged to the Roman Catholic Church. Henry II's lands stretched from Newcastle to the Pyrenees. Other English kings fought the **Hundred Years' War** for the French crown.

► Elizabeth I, who ruled from 1558 to 1603.

1642–1648 English civil wars

1649 Charles I executed. England a republic (to 1660)

1688–1689 Glorious Revolution. Mary II and William III share power with parliament

1707 Act of Union unites England and Scotland

1721 Robert Walpole first prime minister

1780s Industrial Revolution begins

1783 American colonies win independence

1830 First mainline railway between Liverpool and Manchester

1832 Great Reform Bill increases number of male voters

1851 Great Exhibition of British arts and sciences

1914–1918 First World War

1918 Women over 30 gain vote

1926 General Strike

1939–1945 Second World War

1946 National Health Service set up

1947 India gains independence

1974 Britain joins European Union

1999 Scottish parliament and Welsh assembly set up

Britain's revolution

By 1500 the population of Britain was growing rapidly. Scotland and England were also getting richer. When they became **Protestant**, kings and nobles got much of the Church's land and wealth. Henry VIII was England's grandest king yet, and his daughter, Elizabeth I, was a wise and careful queen. Scotland's Stuart rulers, including Mary Queen of Scots, were less successful.

In the 17th century **civil wars** rocked England and Scotland. They were fought for religious reasons, and to decide whether king or parliament should rule. Under Oliver Cromwell, England had no king at all. Finally, in the **Glorious Revolution**, parliament came out on top.

▼ The execution of Charles I (1649) by parliament, a major turning point in British history. Afterwards no one governed for long without a parliament.

◀ London in the 'swinging sixties', when British pop music and fashions were copied all over the world.

find out more ▶

American Revolution
Anglo-Saxons
Black Death
Celts
Empire, Age of
Industrial Revolution
Middle Ages
Normans
Reformation
Romans
Slaves
United Kingdom
Vikings
World War I
World War II

Industry and empire

Britain was the first country to make goods in power-driven factories. These were carried by road, canal, ship and railway across the globe. Britain's villages swelled to towns, and its towns grew into cities. By the mid-19th century it was the wealthiest nation on Earth.

Meanwhile, Britain had gathered many overseas lands into an enormous **empire**. The Americans broke away in the 18th century, but India and parts of Africa were added.

Democratic Britain

By the 20th century German and American industry had caught up with Britain. The country also suffered greatly in the **First** and **Second World Wars**. Afterwards, it was no longer a great power and its empire broke up.

The country was changing fast. All men and women got the right to vote. Racism was outlawed. People became richer, and the country joined the **European Union**. In this new, multi-cultural country sport, design and the arts flourished.

▼ Chartist protesters take their petition to Parliament in 1842. The Chartists collected huge petitions (charters) calling for ordinary men to be given the vote.

Buddhists

Buddhists are people who follow the teachings of Siddharta Gautama, an Indian prince who lived 2500 years ago. He became known as the Buddha, and today he has followers all over the world.

Siddharta wanted to find an explanation for the sickness and death he saw all around, so he began to **meditate**. When you meditate you concentrate on things that are really important. Buddhists believe that Buddha meditated until he finally came to see the truth about the way things are. He became 'enlightened'.

Teachings

Buddha spent the rest of his life teaching others what he had discovered. He taught four **noble truths**:

1 Life can never be perfect because there will always be suffering.

2 Suffering is caused by our greed or selfishness.

3 Suffering can only end when you no longer want anything for yourself.

4 The way to reach enlightenment, and a feeling of inner peace called *nirvana*, is to follow the **eightfold path**.

The eightfold path

Right understanding – seeing the world as it really is

Right thoughts – those of kindness

Right speech – speaking simply and truthfully

Right actions – not harming living things, not stealing

Right living – earning a living in a fair and honest way

Right effort – doing what you can do well

Right awareness – of the world around you

Right concentration – meditating and concentrating on what you do

▲ Buddhists have statues of the Buddha in temples and in their homes. They place offerings such as flowers and candles in front of the statues.

• Buddhists believe in karma, the idea that good and evil deeds get a just reward either in this life or, through rebirth, in other lives.

◀ Most boys and men in Thailand spend at least part of their lives as monks. Monks and nuns spend their time meditating, studying and teaching. Other Buddhists give monks and nuns food, clothing and a place to live.

find out more

India and Pakistan
Religions
South-east Asia

Buildings

Buildings are used for many different purposes. They are made out of all sorts of materials, and come in all shapes and sizes.

The choice of materials for a building depends on many things. These include the size and shape of the building and what it will be used for. It is also important to consider the climate in the area, and the types of material available there.

Local traditions

Buildings can be built from materials brought in from far away, but in many places local materials are used. This helps to give different places their own special character.

In countries that have large forests, such as Canada and the Scandinavian countries, many buildings are made of wood. In other places, buildings are built of stone dug from the ground. Other traditional materials include clay, straw and reeds.

Traditional materials are used by local people to make buildings that are cheaper and especially well suited to the local

◄ The idea of building blocks of flats to save space is a very old one. Flats called tenements, which were built about 400 years ago, still stand in Edinburgh, Scotland. They are built from local stone.

▲ In some places, like the coastal areas of Benin in Africa, huts are built on stilts to raise them above the water level. The huts are made of bamboo from nearby bamboo forests.

conditions. The Inuit, who live in the Arctic regions, use snow blocks to build the igloos that they live in during hunting trips. The snow blocks cost nothing, but make a windproof shelter. Near the Congo River in Africa, cool and airy houses are made from woven bamboo mats. In Saudi Arabia, the desert earth

▲ The nomadic (wandering) people of central Asia live in large, round tents called *gers*. The *ger* has a light wooden frame, covered with felt and canvas. Inside, the walls are covered with brightly coloured rugs.

◀ Houses similar in style to this mud brick house in Yemen, in the Arabian desert, are found throughout the Middle East and North Africa.

is pressed together to make mud-brick houses with thick walls that keep out the heat.

Modern materials

Many modern buildings are built from materials such as concrete, steel, bricks and glass. These materials are useful because they are strong, and they are easy and quick to build with. Buildings made from these materials often have a similar 'international' style, and look the same all over the world.

In towns and cities houses and offices are often built in rows. Where land is scarce or expensive, tall blocks of offices or flats are built. In South-east Asia, these blocks may be more than 50 storeys high. Some very tall buildings, called **skyscrapers**, are over 100 storeys high.

find out more
Architecture
Construction
Iron and steel
Wood

Back to nature
Some new buildings are built using natural materials in new ways. These buildings are designed to fit in with their environment, and to use less energy for heating and cooling.

▼ People have been building tall buildings for thousands of years. As engineers have learned more about how structures work, it has become possible to build them ever taller.

CN Tower, Canada, 1976: 553 m

Petronas Twin Towers, Malaysia, 1996: 452 m

Empire State Building, USA, 1931: 381 m (with mast 449 m)

Eiffel Tower, France, 1889: 300 m

Lincoln Cathedral, UK, AD 1307: 160 m

Great Pyramid of Khufu, Egypt, about 2580 BC: 147 m

Pharos lighthouse, Egypt, about 280 BC: 135 m

Butterflies and moths

Butterflies and moths are found almost everywhere in the world. Most butterflies have brightly coloured wings and fly during the day. Moths are usually active at night and their wings are dull in colour.

There are around 20,000 different kinds of butterfly and about 120,000 different kinds of moth in the world.

Most butterflies and moths live for less than a year. Before they die, they mate. The females usually lay their eggs on leaves. When the caterpillars hatch, the leaves provide their first meal.

▶ Silkworms are the caterpillars of a kind of moth. They build their cocoons out of very fine thread – silk. For thousands of years people have used silk to make a luxurious and expensive textile.

Butterflies and moths cannot chew their food. Instead they use their long, tube-like tongues to suck up the sugary nectar from flowers.

In some parts of the world butterflies and moths are dying out because the places they live and the plants they feed on are being destroyed.

From caterpillar to adult

Butterflies and moths **metamorphose** (change form) in the course of their lives. First they hatch out of their eggs as **larvae**, or **caterpillars**, and begin feeding. When they are big enough, they change into **pupae** (chrysalis) and build a cocoon around themselves. Inside the cocoon the pupa changes into an adult butterfly or moth.

Long-distance flight!
Comma butterflies can fly from the Sahara Desert to northern Europe, a distance of 3000 km, in just 14 days.

find out more

Insects
Migration
Textiles

▼ Butterfly metamorphosis.

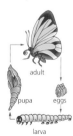

▼ This monarch butterfly is coming out of its cocoon to spread its wings for the first time.

Byzantine empire

In AD 330 Constantine the Great, the first Christian emperor of Rome, made the city of Byzantium (now Istanbul in Turkey) the capital of the Roman empire. He changed the city's name to Constantinople.

The Roman empire later split into two. The western empire was destroyed, but **Constantinople** remained the capital of the eastern part. This became known as the Byzantine empire.

The Byzantine empire reached its height in the 6th century, under **Justinian I**. Justinian conquered Egypt and parts of Italy, Spain and North Africa. Constantinople became one of the largest and richest cities in the world. Architects built grand churches, richly decorated with paintings and mosaics. But within 100 years the empire was under attack.

First Muslim Arabs conquered much of Spain and North Africa. When the Turks occupied Asia Minor (Turkey) and Palestine in 1071, the emperor asked the Christian kings of western Europe for help. This led to the wars known as the **Crusades**, in which European Christians fought against the Muslims of the Middle East.

In 1204 the crusaders attacked and destroyed Constantinople. The emperor recaptured it, but the Byzantine empire now had little territory left. The city itself held on until 1453, when it was captured by the **Ottoman Turks**.

▲ The walls of the cathedral of **Saint Sophia** in Istanbul are covered in glowing mosaics. This one shows Empress Zoe, who ruled the Byzantine empire from 1028 until 1050.

find out more

Architecture
Christians
Middle Ages
Ottoman empire
Romans

▼ Saint Sophia was the greatest of all the Byzantine churches. It was built during the reign of Justinian. During the Ottoman period it became a mosque. It is now a museum.

Camouflage

Camouflage helps animals to hide themselves. When an animal is camouflaged, its colours and markings help it blend into the background.

Many wild animals rely on camouflage as a source of protection, to hide from their enemies. But hunting animals use camouflage to help them creep up unseen on their prey.

Spots, stripes and changing colours

There are many types of camouflage. An animal's colours or markings may match its background – some moths, for example, blend with the bark of certain trees. Another kind of camouflage is **disruptive coloration**. Animals such as tigers and leopards have spots or stripes on their skin or fur. This makes them blend into the background when there is a mixture of sun and shadows.

Some animals can **change colour** to match their surroundings. Chameleons, for instance, change colour to match their background within minutes. Some animals that live in snowy areas change their colour with the seasons. In summer, an Arctic fox's fur is brown, which makes it hard to see against bare ground. But in winter the fox's fur turns white, making it almost invisible against the snow.

▲ Some insects take camouflage to extremes. This leaf insect lives in the rainforests of Costa Rica. Its camouflage is so perfect that it is very hard to tell apart from a real leaf.

> *Copycat camouflage!*
> Some animals protect themselves from enemies by copying the colours and patterns of animals that sting or taste unpleasant. Harmless hoverflies, for example, are striped like stinging wasps.

▼ This blue shark relies on **countershading** for camouflage. The shark's back is darker than its underside. Seen from below, the lighter underside blends with the lighter water above it. But from above, the shark's darker back blends with the darker water below. Countershading also makes animals look flatter when seen from the side, which makes them harder to see.

find out more
Animals
Cats
Skin and hair

Canada

Canada is the second biggest country in the world, but much of it is almost empty of people. Northern Canada is a vast land of snow and ice. To the west rise the Rocky Mountains, and wide grasslands (prairies) stretch across the centre.

• Canada became an independent country in 1867. For the history of Canada before independence, see the article on North America.

Snow covers much of Canada from November to April. There are ice caps in the far north, and large parts of the country are forested. Wheat is grown on the central **prairies**.

▲ Clearing snowy roads in Ottawa.

People

Many Canadians are descended from French and British settlers who first arrived in the 16th century. Most French-speaking Canadians live in Québec. Many would like Québec to become an independent country.

There are also about 500,000 **Native Americans** in Canada. They include the Inuit, who live in the north; the Haida of the

west coast; and the Cree, who invented the toboggan.

Resources

Canada is rich in natural resources. It exports grains, timber and minerals such as zinc and gold. There are huge deposits of oil, natural gas and coal. Canada's factories make many kinds of product.

CANADA FACTS

Capital: Ottawa

Population: 30,200,000

Area: 9,971,500 sq km

Languages: English, French

Religion: Christian

Currency: 1 Canadian dollar = 100 cents

Wealth per person: $19,380

find out more

Empire, Age of
Exploration, Age of
North America
United States of America

▶ Peyto Lake in Banff National Park, in Canada's Rocky Mountains. Banff became Canada's first national park in 1885.

Cancer see Diseases • **Carbohydrates** see Food • **Carbon** see Elements   63

Caribbean

The Caribbean is the name given to a group of sunny tropical islands scattered across the Caribbean Sea, between North and South America.

There are more than 20 countries in the Caribbean, and hundreds of smaller islands. Cuba, the largest island, is over 1100 kilometres long and has 10 million people. Some islands are built up from **coral reefs**, and hardly rise above the sea. Others have steep-sided mountains covered with thick **rainforest**.

Caribbean life

The Caribbean has a warm, tropical climate. Rainfall is heavy, but there is plenty of sunshine too. Most rain falls from June to November. During the rainy season there are sometimes tremendous **hurricanes**.

Many Caribbean people make their living from farming, growing **sugar cane**, bananas, coffee, spices and other tropical crops. Bauxite (the material from which aluminium is made) is mined

• As well as all the islands around the sea, the Caribbean includes some coastlands in Central and South America, and the countries of Guyana, Suriname and French Guiana (see map under South America).

----- country boundary
—— main roads
◆ capital city
land height in metres

| 2000 |
| 1000 |
| 500 |
| 200 |
| sea level |

USA

ATLANTIC OCEAN

Gulf of Mexico

Nassau

Str. of Florida

Havana

THE BAHAMAS

Turks & Caicos Is. (UK)

Yucatan Channel

MEXICO

CUBA

Cayman Is. (UK)

JAMAICA

Kingston

HAITI

Port-au-Prince

DOMINICAN REPUBLIC

Santo Domingo

San Juan

Virgin Is. (USA/UK)

Anguilla (UK)

ANTIGUA & BARBUDA

Puerto Rico (USA)

ST KITTS & NEVIS

DOMINICA

Guadeloupe (Fr.)

Martinique (Fr.)

ST LUCIA

BARBADOS

BELIZE

HONDURAS

Caribbean Sea

ST VINCENT & THE GRENADINES

GRENADA

NICARAGUA

TRINIDAD & TOBAGO

COSTA RICA

Panama Canal

PANAMA

VENEZUELA

PACIFIC OCEAN

COLOMBIA

0   500 km

0   300 miles

on a few islands, and there is some oil and gas. The long sandy beaches and warm tropical seas make the Caribbean islands popular with tourists.

Early history

Five hundred years ago the Caribbean islands were home to two groups of Native Americans, the **Arawaks** in the west and the **Caribs** in the east.

In 1492 Christopher **Columbus** sailed to the Caribbean from Spain, and other Europeans soon followed. Within 50 years the Spanish had conquered the Caribbean. Later French, Dutch and English sailors captured some islands from the Spanish. Many Caribs and Arawaks were killed in the fighting, and others died from European diseases.

Slavery and independence

The European settlers brought West Africans to the Caribbean to work as **slaves** on sugar and

▲ Bananas are an important crop on Grenada, St Vincent, St Lucia and Dominica. The workers at this plantation are washing and sorting banana bunches.

tobacco plantations. Slavery in the Caribbean lasted for about 200 years, until 1886. Once the slaves had been set free, the Europeans did little to see that they had land or jobs. Many slaves were desperately poor.

In the 1920s and 1930s Caribbean countries began to press for **independence**. Cuba gained independence in 1898, Jamaica in 1962 and Suriname in 1975. Today some islands are still under French control, while others have strong links with the USA, the Netherlands or Britain.

▲ Toussaint l'Ouverture was a slave on the island of St Domingue. In 1791 he became the leader of a slave army that fought against French rule. Toussaint was imprisoned and died, but his army defeated the French. In 1804 they named their new country Haiti.

◀ In 1959 Fidel Castro led a communist revolution against the dictator Fulgencio Batista. He became leader of Cuba, and has remained in power ever since.

find out more

Africa
Exploration, Age of
Slaves
South America

65

Cars

There are more than 500 million cars in the world today. They come in a variety of shapes and sizes. Most have four wheels, though there are some three-wheelers, and at least one has 26!

There are many different types of car: small saloons for city driving; powerful Formula 1 cars with top speeds of over 300 km/h; and rugged four-wheel drive cars designed for rough terrain.

Parts of a car

The **engine** is the heart of the car. It runs on petrol or diesel fuel and provides power to drive the wheels. The **transmission** takes power from the engine, through the gearbox, to the wheels. The **gears** allow the car to be driven at different speeds with the engine working efficiently. The **suspension** joins each wheel to the body. It uses springs to give a smooth ride.

To control the car, the driver has a **steering wheel**, an **accelerator** pedal to go faster, and **brakes** to slow down. An **electrical system** uses a battery and an alternator (a type of generator) to power the starter motor, spark plugs and lights.

Designed for safety

Modern cars are designed with safety in mind. The passenger compartment is very strong, while the front and rear parts of the car's body are designed to crumple. which lessens the impact of an accident. Other safety features include seat belts, special locks that stop the doors from bursting open, and safety glass, which has no sharp edges.

▲ Many motor cars are now made using robots. This robot arm has been programmed to perform welding on a car production line.

Amazing cars

Fastest car: Thrust SSC, which in October 1997 set a world land speed record of 1228 km/h – faster than the speed of sound

Longest car: a specially built US car, 30 m long, with 26 wheels and a swimming pool in the back

Most popular car: the Volkswagen Beetle: over 20 million sold worldwide

◀ Rally cars are based on regular road cars, but adapted for racing. The races are run on ordinary roads, and last several days. The drivers set out at regular intervals, and are timed over the course.

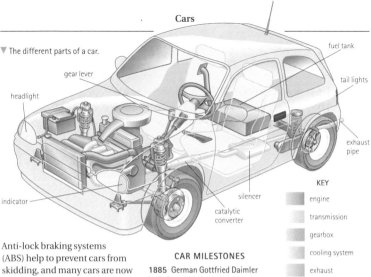

▼ The different parts of a car.

fuel tank

tail lights

gear lever

headlight

exhaust pipe

indicator

silencer

catalytic converter

KEY

engine

transmission

gearbox

cooling system

exhaust

steering

brakes

electrical system

suspension

Anti-lock braking systems (ABS) help to prevent cars from skidding, and many cars are now fitted with airbags that inflate in an accident and cushion the people inside the car.

Dirty cars

Car engines produce exhaust fumes that pollute the air around us. One of the gases, carbon dioxide, traps heat from the Sun and contributes to global warming. Petrol engines also produce other pollutants that can cause smog in city areas. **Catalytic converters** can get rid of some of these harmful fumes, but they cannot remove carbon dioxide gases.

CAR MILESTONES

1885 German Gottfried Daimler built first vehicle powered by a petrol engine: a wooden motorcycle

1886 Karl Benz built first true motor car, a three-wheeler

1890s Daimler and Benz manufacture four-wheeled cars

1907 Henry Ford, in USA, begins making the Model T, the first mass-produced car

1920s Wide choice of cheap cars available. Closed-in saloon cars become popular

1960s onwards More and more electronic equipment used in cars

1980s First air bags fitted to cars

1990s Some car manufacturers build hybrid cars, which are electric-powered at low speeds

find out more ▸

Design
Engines and motors
Pollution
Transport

▶ Thrust SSC, the fastest car in the world. It was powered by two Rolls-Royce jet engines, the type used in Phantom aircraft.

Cartoons and animation

A cartoon can be a single picture, a comic strip or a film that has been made using a technique called animation.

Cartoons that are just a single picture appear in newspapers and magazines. They usually make a joke, or a political point.

Comic strips also appear in newspapers and magazines. They use a few pictures (**frames**) to tell a funny story. Some comic strips run for many years. One of the most popular is 'Peanuts', featuring Charlie Brown and Snoopy the dog.

Comics are magazines that are full of stories told in cartoon strips. Some of the most popular comics feature superheros, such as Superman or Spiderman.

Animation

When people make **animated films** they use a series of pictures similar to the frames of a cartoon strip. The pictures may be drawings, or they may be photographs of **puppets**. Each frame in the series is slightly different from the one that went before. To show an animated film, the film-maker runs the pictures together very quickly, one after the other. This creates the effect of movement.

It takes 24 drawings to make one second of animated film. This means that you need about 14,400 pictures to make a 10-minute film.

▲ Live puppet shows are a kind of animation. Puppeteers move (animate) puppets with their fingers, or by pulling strings or pushing rods attached to the puppets. This Thai puppeteer is performing a show using finely carved shadow puppets attached to rods.

▼ 'Peanuts' by Charles Schulz first appeared in 1950. Since then it has appeared in more than 2000 newspapers in 68 countries, in 26 different languages.

◄ Model animation can be used to create special effects within live-action films, like the model gorilla in *King Kong* (1933). Today entire films are made this way. Nick Park has made some very successful films featuring his popular characters, Wallace and Gromit. Here he is adjusting the model of Gromit for the next shot.

Cel animation

The first animated films were made in the early 1900s. They were cartoons. These films took a lot of time to make because the backgrounds had to be redrawn for each frame, as well as the moving figures.

Cartoon-making was transformed by the invention of **cels** in the 1920s. Cels are transparent sheets on which the artist draws the sequence of pictures needed for a particular movement. The cels are then laid over the background and photographed.

Almost all cartoons used the cel method until **computer animation** was introduced in the 1990s. *Toy Story* (1995) was the first animated film made entirely of computer images.

Walt Disney

Walt Disney is the most famous cartoonist of all. In the 1920s he created characters such as Mickey Mouse and Donald Duck, who starred in short cartoons and were hugely popular. He then took the brave decision to produce a full-length animated film. Critics thought that people would be bored by an 80-minute cartoon, but *Snow White and the Seven Dwarfs* (1937) was a box-office hit. The Disney company is still making worldwide hits, such as *The Lion King* (1994) and *Mulan* (1997).

find out more

Films
United States of America

▼ This series of eight pictures, showing a clown taking a bow, would work as a flip cartoon. If you put these pictures one after another into a tiny notebook, and flipped through them with your thumb, the clown would appear to move.

Castles

Castles are strong buildings that were specially designed to protect the people who lived in them from attack.

The earliest castles date from the 10th century. They were **motte and bailey castles**, which had a simple wooden tower (the keep) built on a high mound (the motte), with a fenced area (the bailey) at the foot of the mound. Motte-and-bailey castles were built all over western Europe. From these strongholds, kings and their barons could control the surrounding lands.

Walls of stone

Castles grew stronger as builders found ways to make them safer from attack. The early wooden walls were rebuilt in stone. Builders made the outer walls much thicker, usually with a second wall inside. Along the top was a walkway, protected by a wall called a **battlement**. The **drawbridge** at the main gateway could be raised at the first sign of an attack.

In the 15th century, powerful cannons were developed that could break through the thickest castle walls. Castles became less important as strongholds, but many magnificent castles were still built to show off the power and riches of the owner.

Siege!
Enemy attempts to capture castles were called sieges. Defenders in the castle fired arrows through narrow slits in the walls or through the gaps in the battlements. If the attackers came closer, the defenders could drop heavy objects on them or pour hot oil through holes under the battlements.

find out more

Crusades
Knights
Middle Ages
Normans
Weapons

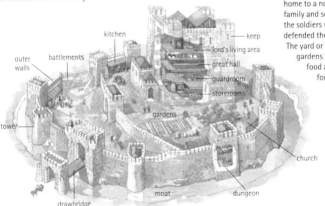

▼ A cut-away view of a medieval castle. It was home to a nobleman, his family and servants, and the soldiers who defended the castle. The yard or bailey had gardens for growing food and stables for keeping animals.

kitchen
keep
lord's living area
great hall
guardroom
storerooms
outer walls
battlements
gardens
tower
church
moat
dungeon
drawbridge

Cats

The pet cats that people keep in their homes are just one of the many types of cat in the world. The cat family also includes wild cats such as lions, tigers, leopards and cheetahs.

All cats are hunters and feed mainly on meat. Their strong legs and padded feet help them move quickly and silently as they sneak up on their prey. They can move very fast over short distances. Cats have extremely sharp eyesight and keen hearing. Their long whiskers help them to sense their surroundings.

There are 37 different kinds of wild cat. The lion, tiger, jaguar, leopard and snow leopard are known as the 'big' cats. And lynxes and ocelots are two kinds of smaller wild cat.

Many types of wild cat – for instance tigers, cheetahs and jaguars – are in danger of dying out in the wild. This is mainly because the places where they live are being destroyed. Laws have been introduced to try to protect them, but many are still killed by hunters, for their fur or to protect farm animals.

▲ An adult male lion can eat up to 40 kg of meat in a single meal, but afterwards he probably won't eat again for several days.

TOP CATS

Largest: Tiger, head-and-body length up to 2.5 m.

Fastest: Cheetahs can reach speeds of 100 km/h. They are the fastest land animals.

• Cats were first tamed by the ancient Egyptians, more than 3500 years ago. Today there are about 500 million domestic cats in the world.

▲ **Jaguars** live mainly in the forests of South America. They hunt at night, and sometimes feed on fish and even crocodiles.

▼ **Tigers** are big cats that live in the forests of India, Sumatra and Siberia. They hunt mainly at night and are excellent swimmers and climbers.

find out more
Animals
Mammals

Cattle *see* Farm animals • **Cave paintings** *see* Early people

Caves

A cave is a natural hole in a hillside or cliff, or under the ground. The most spectacular caves are found in areas where the rock is mostly limestone.

Limestone is rock that is dissolved by rainwater. Water seeping through cracks and joints in the limestone gradually washes it away, widening the cracks and joints into tunnels and holes. Rivers may soak into the limestone and form large caves.

Over thousands of years, impressive **stalactites** and **stalagmites** form in many

▲ Stalactites in the Carlsbad Caverns, New Mexico, USA. Stalactites form very slowly. Every time water drips from a cave roof, a tiny deposit of calcium carbonate is left behind. These deposits gradually grow to form stalactites. Deposits can also pile up on the cave floor to form stalagmites.

limestone caves. Stalactites are like icicles of rock hanging down from the ceiling of a cave. Stalagmites are thin pillars of rock rising up from the floor. They can join together to form a column of rock stretching from ceiling to floor.

In rocks such as basalt (cooled lava from volcanoes), caves can form when the surface lava cools and hardens, but the liquid lava beneath flows away, leaving a space. **Sea caves** are formed by waves pounding against a cliff, enlarging natural cracks and weaknesses. In desert areas, caves are formed when wind blows sand at a rock face, gradually wearing it away.

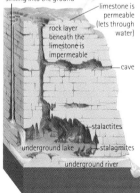

swallow hole, formed by water sinking into the ground

limestone is permeable (lets through water)

rock layer beneath the limestone is impermeable

cave

stalactites

underground lake — stalagmites

underground river

◀ An underground cave system.

CAVE FACTS

Deepest cave: Réseau du Foillis, French Alps (1455 m deep)

Biggest cave system: Mammoth Cave system, Kentucky, USA (over 530 km)

Longest (unsupported) stalactite: Gruta do Janelã, Brazil (10 m long)

Tallest stalagmite: in Krásnohorská cave, Slovakia (32 m tall)

find out more
Erosion
Rocks and minerals

Cells

Cells are the building blocks of life. All living things are made up of cells. Most cells are so tiny that you can only see them with a powerful microscope.

Some very simple plants and animals are made up of just one cell, but most living things are made up of many millions of cells. An adult person has over 50 million million cells in their body.

Groups of similar cells that work together are called **tissues**. Nerve tissues and muscle tissues are two examples. The **organs** in your body, such as your heart, are made up of different kinds of tissue that work together.

Inside a cell

The cell **membrane** is a thin 'skin' that surrounds the cell. It holds the cell together and controls which substances come into or go out of the cell.

The cell's **nucleus** contains the body's **genes**. The genes control what features a plant or animal will have. Genes contain a chemical called **DNA**, which sets out how the cell will develop.

The **cytoplasm** surrounds the nucleus. It contains food and other substances.

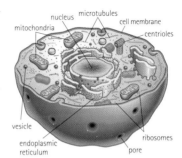

▲ An animal cell. Animal cells are surrounded by a thin cell membrane. In the cytoplasm are tiny structures called organelles, for instance mitochondria and endoplasmic reticulum, which have their own particular tasks.

• The oldest forms of life are microscopic, single-celled organisms, such as bacteria and algae. They appeared on Earth 3500 million years ago.

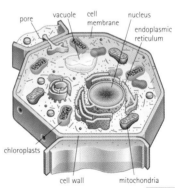

▲ A plant cell. Plant cells have a thick cellulose wall outside the cell membrane. They have special organelles called chloroplasts. These contain the green pigment, chlorophyll, that plants use to trap the energy from sunlight.

find out more
Animals
Bacteria and viruses
Genetics
Life on Earth
Plants

Celts

The Celts are an ancient tribal people who settled in much of Europe 2500 years ago. Many Europeans are descended from the Celts, and a few people still speak Celtic languages.

The Celts probably came originally from central Europe. They were farmers, traders and warriors. They were also skilled craftspeople and metalworkers.

In the fifth century BC Celtic tribes settled in France, Spain, Italy and the British Isles. They then moved on into the Balkans and Turkey. But after 200 BC they lost ground – to the Germans in the north, the Dacians in the east and the Romans in the south.

▲ This Celtic silver cauldron was probably made in south-eastern Europe. The Celts were superb artists. Their metalwork and stone carvings show that they were skilled at creating elaborate patterns and illustrating scenes from mythology in a lively way.

The Celtic way of life

The Celts lived on farms and in small villages. They grew crops and kept cows, horses, pigs and sheep. They also hunted wild boar. Their clothes were colourful and elaborately embroidered, and they wore bronze or gold jewellery.

Celtic people worshipped many gods, including the Sun and Moon. Their priests (**Druids**) made both animal and human sacrifices to these gods. Druids could be male or female and they acted as chiefs and judges as well as priests.

The Celts were terrifying warriors. They combed their hair to make it stand on end, tattooed their bodies, and rushed shouting into battle.

▼ The Celts built hillforts to defend themselves against enemy tribes. This is the entrance to the hillfort of Crickley Hill, England. Attackers would break through the outer gate only to be trapped before the inner gate.

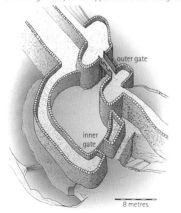

outer gate

inner gate

8 metres

• The warrior-chief **King Arthur** is the hero of many Celtic myths and legends. The stories say he ruled all Britain and conquered most of western Europe. His 12 most trusted warriors were known as the Knights of the Round Table.

find out more

Anglo-Saxons
Britain, History of
Knights
Romans

Chemistry

If you want to know what something is made of – ask a chemist! Chemistry is the science that looks at substances. Chemists study how substances are made and how they change.

Chemical changes, or **reactions**, are going on around us all the time. For example, they help us cook food – when you boil an egg, it is a chemical reaction that makes the egg go hard. Batteries make electricity using chemical reactions. And plastics, medicines, fertilizers and many other products are made using chemical reactions.

Mixing, making and breaking

An **element** is a basic substance made of just one kind of **atom**. In chemical reactions, atoms of different elements join together to form compounds.

Compounds contain two or more different elements. In a compound the atoms are joined together through **chemical bonds**. These bonds can only be broken by another chemical reaction.

Mixtures are different from compounds. You do not need a chemical reaction to make a mixture or to separate out the different parts of a mixture.

▼ Chemists help to make many of the things we use every day, such as paints, plastics, glass, soap and medicines. Chemists also use tests to find out what a substance is made from.

▲ In crystals, the atoms are arranged in a regular pattern. These are salt crystals.

find out more

Atoms and molecules
Elements

Acids and alkalis

Acids and alkalis are chemical opposites. Paper, explosives and fertilizers are made with acids. Alkalis are used to make glass and soap.

Weak acids, like lemon juice and vinegar, taste sour. Weak alkalis feel soapy. But strong acids and alkalis can burn into skin, wood, cloth and other materials.

If you mix the right amount of an acid and an alkali, you can make a substance that is **neutral**, and does not burn.

Children

Baby boom!
252 babies are born every minute. And over a third of all the people in the world are under 18.

Children are young human beings. Childhood is the period of your life when you do all of your growing and most of your learning.

▶ Children learn different skills at different ages.

At four months babies smile, hold toys and try to reach things.

At about a year children can stand, or even walk, and say a few words.

At 3 years children can dress themselves, catch a ball, and join in conversations.

At around 6 children learn to read and write.

At 12 children can carry out investigations by themselves.

In the first few months of life, a child is a **baby**. It soon grows into a **toddler** and then a little girl or little boy. A few years later, the child begins to develop physically into a young adult.

All children are dependent on adults to care for, educate and protect them. In many countries, children legally become **adults** when they are 18. They then get rights that they did not have as a child, for instance the right to vote.

▶ These Indian children work carrying heavy stones to help build a dam.

School and work

In rich countries, children go to school until their late teens. In poor countries, not all children get the chance to go to school. Some children have to work to help their families. Girls are sometimes given less education than boys are, and may be expected to marry at 14 or 15.

find out more

Families
Growth and development
Human beings
Schools and universities

Children's rights
The United Nations Convention on the Rights of the Child says that every child has the right to education, health care and freedom from abuse. It also says that children have a right to have their wishes considered in all matters affecting them.

China

China has the world's largest population: over 1.2 billion people live there. For over 4000 years it was ruled by a series of emperors, but since 1949 it has been led by the Chinese Communist Party.

Western China is a land of high plains, deserts, grasslands and mountains. Two rivers, the Huang He (Yellow River) and the Chang Jiang (Yangtze), flow east from here. The Huang He carries fine silt that enriches the eastern farmlands.

Bamboo forests cover much of central China. They are home to the giant **panda** and other rare animals. Southern China is hot and humid.

CHINA FACTS

Capital: Beijing
Population: 1,210,000,000
Area: 9,597,000 sq km
Language: Mandarin, Catonese and others
Religion: Atheist, Confucian, Taoist, Buddhist
Currency: 1 yuan = 100 jiao
Wealth per person: $620

country boundary
disputed boundary
main roads
main railways
capital city
large cities
sand desert
marsh
high peaks (height in metres)
land height in metres

5000
2000
1000
500
200
sea level

KAZAKHSTAN

KIRGYZSTAN
TAJIK-ISTAN
Tien Shan
154
K2 8611
Takla Makan Desert
Jammu and Kashmir
Kunlun Shan
Ürümqi
Nan Shan
Qaidam Basin
Tibetan Plateau
INDUS
NEPAL
Lhasa
Mt Everest 8848
BHUTAN
INDIA
BURMA (MYANMAR)

MONGOLIA
Gobi Desert
Huang He (Yellow)
Great Wall
Lanzhou
Lancang Jiang (Mekong)
Nu Jiang (Salween)
Chengdu
Red
Chongqing Basin
Kunming

RUSSIA (RUSSIAN FED.)
Amur (Heilong Jiang)
Harbin
Changchun
Shenyang Fushun
Anshan
NORTH KOREA
Beijing (Peking)
Tianjin Dalian
Taiyuan Jinan Zibo
Huang He
Xi'an
Zhengzhou Xuzhou
Nanjing
Chang Jiang (Yangtze)
Wuhan
Shanghai
Wenzhou
Guangzhou (Canton)
Macao Hong Kong
TAIWAN
Yellow Sea
SOUTH KOREA
Qingdao
South China Sea
Hainan
VIETNAM
LAOS

0   800 km
0   500 miles

77

For 30 years Mao Zedong was the most powerful figure in China. The children around this picture of him are holding copies of the 'little red book' that set out Mao's thoughts on communism.

Chinese life

Most of China's enormous population lives in the lowlands of eastern and south-eastern China. Ninety per cent of the population belong to a people called the **Han**.

Many Chinese live in the countryside and work the land. In the north they grow mostly wheat and potatoes. In the south, the climate is good enough to grow three crops of **rice** a year. Villages often have small factories and workshops, which have been set up to stop people moving to the cities.

In the past 20 years, China's cities have grown rapidly. Chinese factories make half the world's **toys**. They also produce steel, textiles, shoes, ships and cars. These new industries have made many city people rich, although the countryside remains quite poor.

Early history

Chinese civilization is one of the oldest in the world. From at least 2000 BC until the 20th century, China was ruled by dynasties (families) of **emperors**.

The early dynasties united China as a single country, introduced irrigated rice-

Hong Kong

Hong Kong was a British colony from 1842 until 1997. Its position on the main trade routes between the Pacific and Indian Oceans and its natural harbour made it a thriving trading and financial centre. In 1997 China took control of the colony again. The Chinese government hopes that this will give a further boost to the country's economy.

The Great Wall of China is 3460 km long. It was first built between 221 and 210 BC, then rebuilt in the 15th and 16th centuries. It is the only man-made object that can be seen from space.

growing, and built the Great Wall to keep out 'barbarians' from the north. Buddhism came to China during this period, and the arts and writing flourished.

Conquerors and traders

In the 13th century China was conquered by the **Mongols**, who swept over the Great Wall and set up the Yuan dynasty. The Mongols were defeated in 1368 by the Chinese Ming dynasty. The Ming emperors built the Forbidden City, where China's emperors continued to live until 1911.

Portuguese explorers reached China by boat in 1517, and began European trade with the powerful Chinese empire. But by the 19th century, China's power had weakened. Europeans trading with China found excuses to seize Chinese ports. Some Chinese began to worry that their country might be conquered by the Europeans.

End of empire

In 1911, followers of **Sun Yixian** (Sun Yat-sen), overthrew the emperor, Pu Yi, and declared China a republic. But their democratic government quickly collapsed, and after a period of unrest General **Jiang Jieshi** (Chiang Kai-shek) came to power. His most serious rivals were the communists, under their popular leader **Mao Zedong**.

Marco Polo
In 1271 the 17-year-old Marco Polo set out from Venice with his father and uncle. They were travelling to the magnificent court of Kublai Khan, the Chinese emperor. Marco worked for the emperor for 17 years, travelling all over China. When he returned, he wrote a remarkable account of his travels.

▲ A road junction in the Chinese city of Kunming. Bicycles are a much more important form of transport in China than cars, buses or lorries.

After World War II, in 1945, civil war broke out between Jiang Jieshi and the communists. Mao emerged victorious in 1949, and set up the communist People's Republic of China.

Under communism education, health and the rights of women improved a lot, but private businesses were not permitted. After Mao's death in 1979, the new leaders began to allow some private enterprise. Industries have since done well and the economy has grown, but opposition to the government is still not allowed.

Inventive Chinese
The compass, the ship's rudder, the horse collar, paper, steel, gunpowder and movable-type printing are among the many inventions that originally came from China.

find out more
Ancient world
Asia
Buddhists
Mongols
Religions

Christians

Christians are people who follow the teachings and example of Jesus, who they believe was the Son of God. Jesus and his first followers lived in the land of Israel over 2000 years ago. Now there are millions of Christians all over the world.

▲ Christians in the Orthodox Church use pictures called icons, like this one of Jesus, in their worship.

Jesus taught that God cares for people like a loving father and that by trusting in God they would find happiness on Earth and, after death, in heaven. To live as God wishes, they should love and worship God, and care for all people, particularly the poor and unhappy.

▼ A man called Saul had been persecuting Christians, but one day he had a vision of Jesus, which changed him completely. Renamed Paul, he became one of the most important Christian teachers.

Jesus

Jesus was born a Jew in Bethlehem in Judea in about 4 BC. At about the age of 30 he began to teach, and to heal the sick. People came to believe that he was **Christ**, which means 'God's chosen one'. His followers came to be known as Christians.

The Jewish religious authorities did not like Jesus, and the Roman rulers of Judea were worried by the power he had. Jesus was eventually put to death by **crucifixion**. This meant being nailed to a cross and left to die. But Christians believe that, three days later, Jesus rose from the dead (came alive again). They call this the **Resurrection** and celebrate it on **Easter Sunday**.

Christians believe that the risen Jesus appeared to several of his followers and told them to spread his teachings. Then he returned to God in heaven.

Christians today

Some Christians try to study the Bible and pray every day. On Sunday, the Christian day of rest, many go to **church** or **chapel** to worship with other believers. Others may almost never go to church, but they still try to live in a Christian way.

Christian groups

All Christians around the world belong to the Christian Church, but within this single body there are several different branches. The three main branches are the **Orthodox Church**, the **Roman Catholic Church** and the **Protestant Church**. And within these large groupings there are many smaller ones. These Churches differ from each other in exactly what they believe and how they worship.

▼ Baptism (often called christening) is a special service in which people are given their Christian names and become members of the Christian Church. Christians are usually baptized in holy water in the font of a church or in a river or the sea, like this woman in the Caribbean.

▶ The Christmas festival celebrates the birth of Jesus. Most Christians celebrate Christmas Day on 25 December. The festival ends on 6 January, when three kings are said to have visited the baby Jesus. In Germany children dress up as kings on this day.

The Bible
The Bible is the Christian holy book. It consists of the Old Testament and the New Testament. The Old Testament is almost the same as the Jewish Bible and contains myths, legends, history, hymns and laws for living as God wishes. The New Testament includes the four Gospels of Matthew, Mark, Luke and John. They tell of the life and teachings of Jesus. 'Gospel' means 'good news'.

find out more
Architecture
Reformation
Religions

• The **apostles** were the people who went out to teach people about Christianity. The first apostles were Jesus's disciples (followers). Another apostle was St Paul.

• A **saint** is a Christian who has lived a particularly good life. Saints who have died for their beliefs are called martyrs.

Classical music

Most people have heard the names of Bach, Mozart and Beethoven. They are composers (writers) of classical music. When we talk about classical music, we usually mean the kind of music that is performed by orchestras or smaller groups, in religious services or to accompany opera or ballet.

The best-known classical music is European (or Western). But there are strong traditions of classical music in many parts of the world, for example in India and Japan.

Western classical music

Until the 16th century most music in the West was religious, although some poetry was set to music. During the **Baroque period**, from 1600 to about 1750, both religious and non-religious music became more elaborate, and opera was born.

Claudio **Monteverdi** was an important early Baroque composer who wrote many operas. But the most famous composer of the Baroque period is Johann Sebastian **Bach**. Bach wrote both court music, such as concertos, and Church music. The late-Baroque composer George Frideric **Handel** wrote beautiful operas and oratorios.

The Classical period

'Classical music' can also mean music from the Classical period of Western music, from about

▲ By the time he was 5, Mozart could play and compose pieces of music himself. He travelled in Europe with his father and his sister Anna, giving performances, which were very popular.

▼ A concert party in Venice in the early 1700s. The harpsichordist in the centre directs the other players – oboes, horns and strings.

1750 to 1820. Franz Joseph **Haydn** wrote many symphonies and tried out new kinds of music for chamber orchestras. Others followed his lead.

Wolfgang Amadeus **Mozart** composed at great speed and produced a huge number of works including symphonies, piano concertos, string quartets, sonatas and operas.

Ludwig van **Beethoven** wrote powerful and dramatic music that seems to speak to its listeners of his feelings and thoughts.

Modern classical music

Nineteenth-century music is called **Romantic** music. Composers such as Franz **Schubert**, Frederick **Chopin**, Giuseppe **Verdi** and Johannes **Brahms** expressed their feelings and thoughts in poems set to music and operas full of emotion and drama.

In the early years of the 20th century some composers reacted against the Romantic style. They wrote music that was very different to what had gone before. Igor **Stravinsky's** music made use of strange harmonies and exciting rhythms.

Types of classical music

Symphonies are played by orchestras. Many different instruments are needed to perform a symphony. In a **concerto** one musician, or a small group, plays with an orchestra accompanying them. **Solo music** is for one instrument only. Long pieces of music for one instrument, or for one instrument and a piano, are called **sonatas**.

Chamber music is played by a small group of instruments. **Songs** are for one or more singers, often with piano or other instruments. **Choral music** is for much larger groups of singers – choirs. **Operas** are stories told through music and acting. **Oratorios** are like operas, but without acting, scenery or costumes.

▲ Beethoven began to lose his hearing when he was 28. In spite of this he went on to write some of his finest music – much of which he never heard.

find out more

Music
Musical instruments
Orchestras and bands
Pop and rock music

◀ The ballets Igor Stravinsky wrote for the Ballets Russes between 1910 and 1913 made him the most talked-about composer in Europe. This is a scene from *The Firebird*.

Climate

The climate of a place is the pattern of its weather over many years. Places near the Equator have hotter weather than places nearer the North and South Poles. But mountains, oceans and winds affect climate, too.

Weather and climate are not the same thing. The weather may be hotter on one particular day in New York than it is in Bombay. But averaged over many years, the climate in Bombay is hotter than in New York.

What affects climate?

How far a place is from the Equator has the most effect on its climate. This is because the further a place is from the Equator, the less heat it receives from the Sun. At the North and South Poles, which are far from

▲ Winds move around the world in a series of wind belts. Hot air rising at the Equator is replaced by cooler air from the north and south. This creates a belt of winds called the trade winds in the tropics. To the north and south of the tropics are two other wind belts, the westerlies.

the Equator, the **polar** climate is cold, with short summers and long dark winters. Areas near the Equator get more sunlight than anywhere else. They have a **tropical** climate, which is warm all year, often with a dry season and wet season.

▼ This map shows the climate in different regions of the world.

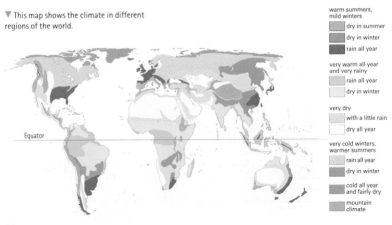

warm summers, mild winters
- dry in summer
- dry in winter
- rain all year

very warm all year and very rainy
- rain all year
- dry in winter

very dry
- with a little rain
- dry all year

very cold winters, warmer summers
- rain all year
- dry in winter

- cold all year and fairly dry
- mountain climate

Between the polar regions and the tropics are the **temperate regions**. Here the Sun is low in the sky in winter, and high in summer, resulting in long, warm summer days and shorter, colder winter ones.

Other things that affect climate

The height of a place above sea level affects its climate – the higher you go, the cooler it becomes. So mountainous areas usually have cooler climates than nearby lowlands. Some of the highest mountains, for example Mount Kilimanjaro in tropical Africa, have snow all year round.

Oceans can affect climate, too. Water warms up and cools down much more slowly than land. So in winter the sea is often warmer than the land, and in summer it is often cooler. Because of this, places near the sea have milder winters and

Global warming
The climate of the whole Earth is slowly changing. There are many natural reasons for climate change, but scientists believe that some recent changes are due to human activity. Burning fuels such as coal and oil releases large amounts of gases such as carbon dioxide into the air. These gases act like a blanket around the Earth, causing global warming – a rise in the world's temperatures.

cooler summers than places that are far inland.

In any particular area of the world, the wind blows most often from one direction – it is the **prevailing wind** for that area. Prevailing winds can have a large effect on the climate. In the Sahara desert, the prevailing winds are hot and very dry, so there is very little rainfall. But winds that blow from the sea, such as the monsoon winds in South-east Asia, are very moist and bring lots of rain.

▲ This icy landscape in the north of Alaska has a polar climate.

• A temperature of −89.2 °C was recorded at Vostok research station, Antarctica, in 1983. This is the lowest temperature ever recorded on Earth.

find out more

Deserts
Mountains
Seasons
Weather

Clothes

People wear clothes to keep warm, and to cover and decorate their bodies. The kinds of clothes they wear depend on whether they are male or female, where they live, and what sort of lives they lead.

Climate has a huge influence on dress. In hot climates, thin, light-coloured clothes are popular because they are cooler. In colder regions, clothes are made out of thicker materials, and people often wear several layers.

Clothes around the world

In many parts of the world, especially in developing countries, people wear styles of dress that are particular to that region or country. This is partly because certain materials are produced locally, for example cotton in South-east Asia. It is also because traditional styles and patterns have developed, which are handed down from one generation to the next.

In Western, developed parts of the world, however, people in different countries often wear the same styles of clothing. Most people buy **ready-to-wear** clothes that are mass-produced in factories and sold around the world. Some Western styles, such as Denim jeans and T-shirts, are becoming popular in developing countries too.

Clothes for work and play

People who do certain jobs have to wear special clothes for their work. Police officers, nurses and people who work in super-markets, for example, wear **uniforms** so that members of the public can recognize them. In other jobs, workers need to

▲ Firefighters wear special fire-resistant clothing to protect them from getting burnt. The fluorescent (glowing) stripes on their clothes help them to see each other through thick smoke.

▼ Some styles of clothing around the world.

Berber, Morocco   Inuit, Canada   India   Masai, Kenya   Japan   Cameroon   Native American, Bolivia

▲ Today **fashion** is big business. Designers show their clothes at international fashion shows. Styles that catch on are then adapted and sold around the world. Fashions are sometimes set by ordinary people too, especially by groups of young people.

complete freedom of movement. American footballers wear helmets and special padding to guard against injury.

Making clothes

When clothes are produced for the mass market, they are usually made in factories. Much of the work is done by machine, although skilled workers are needed for certain jobs, such as sewing. A designer decides what a piece of clothing will look like and produces a pattern. The separate pieces of the pattern are laid flat on the material and cut out. Sewers then sew the different parts of the garment together.

wear special **protective clothing** because their work is dangerous. They may work with poisonous chemicals, or in places where there is a high risk of an accident, such as mines or building sites.

Sports players wear clothes specially designed for their sport. Runners wear leotards or shorts and vests to allow

find out more

Textiles

Jewellery

People have worn jewellery to decorate their bodies since prehistoric times. Jewellery can be made from all sorts of materials, but is often made out of precious metals and stones. Such jewellery may be worn not just for decoration but also to show how wealthy or important a person is. In Rajasthan in India women traditionally wear a lot of jewellery, partly as a mark of their status.

Coasts

A coast is a place where the land meets the sea. The world has about 312,000 kilometres of coastline, but the pattern of these coastlines is always changing. The sea wears away some coasts, while others are built up by mud and sand.

Some coasts are constantly being **worn away** (eroded) by the sea. Waves pounding against the shore break off pieces of rock and carve out caves. When the sea cuts deep into the rock at sea-level, the ground above may fall away too, leaving a cliff (a sheer wall of rock).

Other areas of coast are gradually being **built up**. Pieces of rock broken off at one part of the coast are worn down into smaller and smaller pieces.

These are then swept along the coast by the sea currents. Eventually the pieces are washed up on the shore as **beaches**.

Coastlines are also built up by the billions of tonnes of sand and silt that are carried to the oceans by rivers. This material is washed in by the breaking waves and gradually builds up on the shore.

▲ The cliffs of Moher in County Clare, on the west coast of Ireland, rise to a height of 230 metres.

Bird life

Many kinds of sea bird nest on sea cliffs, where their eggs are safe from egg-eating hunters like rats and foxes. Razorbills, kittiwakes and gannets nest on the sheer cliff face. Guillemots nest on ledges, resting their eggs on their feet. Puffins nest in burrows on the grassy cliff-top.

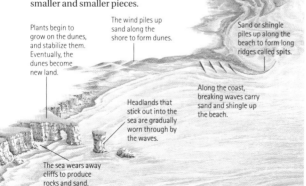

Plants begin to grow on the dunes, and stabilize them. Eventually, the dunes become new land.

The wind piles up sand along the shore to form dunes.

Sand or shingle piles up along the beach to form long ridges called spits.

Headlands that stick out into the sea are gradually worn through by the waves.

Along the coast, breaking waves carry sand and shingle up the beach.

The sea wears away cliffs to produce rocks and sand.

◄ How the coastline is shaped by the sea.

find out more

Climate
Erosion
Oceans and seas
Rivers
Seashore

Communications

Speaking, writing and signalling with your hands are all types of communication. So are talking on the telephone, sending faxes, watching television or listening to the radio. Modern devices help us to communicate more easily and quickly than ever before.

Animals use sounds and gestures to communicate, and for thousands of years people have communicated through speech. But for long-distance communication, the information being sent usually has to be turned into a series of **signals** – like a code that carries the information.

Sending signals

In telephones and faxes the signals are usually short bursts of electricity that travel along wires. Other times the signals are pulses of light that speed down very thin fibres of glass called **optical fibres**.

When the signals reach their destination, they are changed, or **decoded**, to reveal the original information.

Mobile phones send voice messages using a kind of radio wave called **microwaves**. Other **radio waves** are used to **broadcast** radio and television programmes. Radio waves are a type of **electromagnetic wave**. They do not have to travel through wires or optical fibres. Instead, they can travel through the air, or even through space. Radio waves and microwaves are picked up and re-transmitted by communications satellites orbiting the Earth. Using such satellites, information can be sent all around the world.

Communication history

About 5000 years ago people started writing. Before printing was invented in 1450, most books and writings were copied out by hand. Printing made it possible to spread ideas and information more easily.

When the telegraph was invented in 1837, information

▲ Pulses of light are coming out of the end of these optical fibres. The fibres are made of glass. They are so thin that the fibres can bend. But they can carry a lot of information. Just one optical fibre cable can carry more than 40,000 phone calls at once.

find out more
Internet
Newspapers
Printing
Radiation
Radio
Satellites
Telephones
Television

◄ Egyptian hieroglyphs were among the earliest forms of writing. The names of pharoahs were written in oval frames called cartouches. This is Queen Cleopatra's cartouche.

could travel even more quickly. The telegraph sent coded messages along electric wires as a series of long and short bleeps.

In 1876 Alexander Graham Bell invented the telephone. It allowed people to speak to each other over long distances. Later, in 1895, Guglielmo Marconi discovered how to send messages using radio waves instead of wires.

▼ Communications networks. (a) A telephone network uses electrical signals, optical signals and microwaves to carry information from place to place. (b) A television station can broadcast its programmes either through cables, via a radio transmitter, or by satellite.

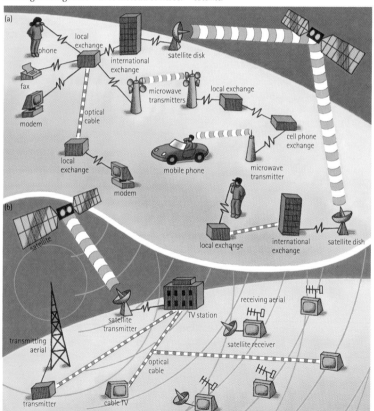

Communism

At its simplest, communism means a group of people sharing equally everything they have. In the 20th century it became a way of running a country. Although it helped some poor people, it was not a great success.

▲ A poster of the Russian communist Vladimir Lenin (1870–1924), designed to make him look like a hero.

The German thinker Karl **Marx** dreamed up modern communism. It was unfair, he said, that a few rich people owned the **capital** (money), property and businesses, while the poor did most of the work.

Marx urged the workers to take over their country and make it communist. Everyone would own everything, and there would be no rich or poor.

Communism in action

Communists did take over in two huge countries, **Russia** and **China**. But things didn't work out as planned. The countries' leaders behaved like old-fashioned kings. People were not allowed to say or write what they wanted. The government controlled their lives.

Also, because no one could make much money, they had no reason to work hard. Russia and China lagged behind other countries. Finally, at the end of the 20th century, Russia gave up communism, while China watered it down.

▼ The Red Guards of the Chinese communist leader **Mao Zedong** (1893–1976). Mao used the young Guards to help him stay in power.

KEY DATES

1848 Karl Marx and Friedrich Engels publish *Communist Manifesto*

1917 Russian Revolution, led by Lenin, sets up communism in Russia

1928 Stalin takes over as leader of Russia (now the USSR)

1945 Communists begin to take over eastern Europe

1949 Communists take over China

1989–1991 Communism collapses in eastern Europe and the USSR breaks up

find out more

China
Governments
Russia

Computers

Computers are electronic machines that can be programmed to do a huge number of tasks. Today, they are familiar parts of our daily lives.

Computers work by processing data. Data is any type of information, ranging from numbers and words to pictures and sounds. A computer follows sets of instructions, called **programs**, which are stored in its memory. A single computer can run many different types of program. This means that the same computer can be a word processor, a games machine or a powerful calculator.

Hardware and software

A computer system is made up of two parts, the hardware and the software.

The software includes the programs that the computer uses to do jobs. The hardware includes the actual computer (the processing unit), and parts such as the

▲ Today's personal computers use one microprocessor and carry out around 300 million instructions per second (MIPS). But supercomputers, like this CM-5, which is as tall as a wardrobe, use many microprocessors working at the same time. It can operate at speeds of over 10,000 MIPS.

keyboard, the mouse and the printer (**peripherals**). The keyboard and the mouse are called **input devices**, because they are used to get data into the computer. **Output devices**, such as the monitor and the printer, are used to get data out of the computer.

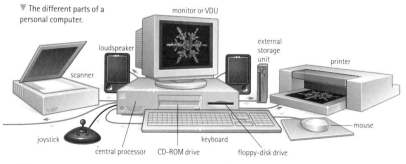

▼ The different parts of a personal computer.

monitor or VDU

loudspeaker

external storage unit

printer

scanner

mouse

joystick

central processor

CD-ROM drive

keyboard

floppy-disk drive

Computer chips

At the heart of every computer is a tiny microchip, called a **microprocessor**. It is a small slice of silicon imprinted with an extremely complicated electronic circuit. The microprocessor does all the calculations and carries out the instructions it gets from the computer's programs.

Computers use another kind of chip, called a memory chip, for storing programs and data. There are two types. **RAM** (random-access memory) chips are used for short-term memory. Data stored on RAM chips is lost when the computer is turned off. **ROM** (read-only memory) chips are used for storing programs, which the computer uses again and again. Data on ROM chips is saved when the computer is turned off.

Uses of computers

Before the 1980s, computers were thought of mainly as tools for scientists and engineers. But once **personal computers** (PCs) were developed, the world of computers was opened up to millions of people.

Information technology (IT) includes all the many uses of computers in science, business and our everyday lives. One of the most common uses of computers is to control machines such as washing machines, microwave ovens and

▲ ENIAC (the Electronic Numerical Integrator and Calculator) was one of the first electronic computers. The only way to change its 'program' was to change its wiring. That is what the technicians here are doing.

video recorders. These kinds of machine have 'dedicated' microchips, programmed to do just one job.

Today, people use computers for a wide range of jobs. In factories, computers are used to control large machines such as lathes and drills. They are also used to control robot arms, which can carry out tasks such as welding and assembling parts. In business, computers are used for sending and receiving messages, for word-processing, for storing information such as names and addresses, and to keep accounts.

Binary numbers

Computers do all their calculations and carry out all their instructions using binary numbers. These are numbers made up only of 0s and 1s. The computer works this way because it can store the numbers as 'ons' and 'offs' in an electronic circuit.

1–10 in binary numbers:

1	1
2	10
3	11
4	100
5	101
6	110
7	111
8	1000
9	1001
10	1010

At home, people use computers to play games, listen to music, surf the Internet or to look at pictures, videos or films. They also use computers to send faxes and emails to friends and relations.

Artificial brains?

Most computers can only do what they are 'told' by a program. But one type of computer, called a **neural network**, works like an artificial brain. It can 'learn' how to tackle new tasks by itself.

Scientists use neural networks to help them understand how real brains work. In one experiment, researchers in the United States are working to develop a very advanced neural network, which is linked to a robot kitten. By studying how the robot kitten's

'brain' learns as it develops, they hope to find out more about how our own brains process information.

▲ This pilot is training in a flight simulator. These devices use five computers to re-create the movements, sounds and views of a real flight.

▼ Even very young children now have access to computers, through the many computerized toys that are available.

Bits and bytes

Computer memory is measured in bytes. One bit of memory can store either a 0 or a 1. One byte of memory is 8 bits. A byte is enough memory to store one letter of the alphabet. A kilobyte (kB) is 1024 bytes; a megabyte (MB) 1,048,576 bytes.

find out more

Communications
Electronics
Internet

Concertos *see* Classical music • **Concrete** *see* Construction • **Conifers** *see* Trees

Conservation

With humans wanting more and more space for houses, factories and farms, there is less and less space for other living things. Conservation is action to stop animals and plants from dying out, and to protect the wild places where they live.

▲ One of the most important conservation organizations is the World Wide Fund for Nature (WWF). Their symbol is a giant panda.

In the past, some animals and plants became **extinct** (died out) because they could not cope with natural changes around them. However, humans have greatly speeded up the rate at which living things are becoming extinct.

Animals in danger

As well as the many species that have died out completely, at least 1000 different kinds of bird and mammal are now extremely rare, as well as countless kinds of insect and plant. None of these living things will survive unless we protect their **habitats** – the wild places where they live.

Many of the rarest animals live in the tropical rainforest. But every minute, people cut or burn down an area of rainforest the size of 20 football pitches, destroying the homes of all the animals that live there. In the sea, coral reefs are also being damaged by pollution and by human visitors.

Rare bird

The rarest animal in the world is probably the Spix's macaw. A single male bird was found in a wood in Brazil in 1990. About 30 other Spix's macaws live in zoos, and a few females have now been released back into the wild, in the hope that they will breed with the male to save the species.

▼ In the last 350 years, 95 different birds and 40 different kinds of mammal have become extinct, through humans hunting them for food, or through the loss of their natural habitat. They include the dodo from Mauritius in the Indian Ocean, the Tasmanian wolf, the flightless moa from New Zealand, and the quagga from Africa.

moa

quagga

dodo

Tasmanian wolf

95

The variety of life

In 1985 an American scientist invented a new word: **biodiversity**. The biodiversity of the Earth is the total variety of all its living things. It is part of the natural 'wealth' of our planet. The sheer variety of living things helps to keep the environment in good working order. Biodiversity is therefore an important measure of the health of the planet.

Positive action

Since about 1970, people who are worried about what humans are doing to the Earth have formed groups to try to protect the environment. Together, these groups are known as the **green movement**.

Charities such as the World Wide Fund for Nature and Friends of the Earth raise money for protecting endangered

animals and their habitats. They also campaign to stop the cutting down of irreplaceable forests and to reduce pollution. Governments have passed laws to stop animals being killed, and they have set up nature reserves and national parks to keep their best pieces of countryside safe. Perhaps the most important change is that people have begun to recognize the value of wild plants and animals.

▲ No more than 400 mountain gorillas survive in the mountain forests of central Africa, yet some are still shot by poachers. A recent war in the countries where they live has reduced numbers still further.

find out more

Ecology
Forests
Pollution
Zoos

◄ Some conservationists try to stop damage to the environment in a very direct way. These members of the charity Greenpeace are trying to stop a fishing trawler from putting out its nets. The nets of this kind of trawler can damage the sea-bed.

Construction

Construction is the process of building things. Engineers and builders construct all kinds of structures – roads, dams, bridges, tunnels, and all sorts of buildings.

The materials and methods used to construct something depend on the job it has to do. Modern materials such as steel and concrete are very versatile, and can be used in most kinds of construction.

Building buildings

There are two main ways of constructing buildings. In the first, solid **load-bearing walls**

▼ How a brick house is built. Strong, firm **foundations (1)** prevent the house from sinking or tilting. Concrete **lintels (2)** span the openings of doorways and windows. The **wall cavity (3)** helps to keep the house warm in winter and cool in summer. Inner walls are often made of **plasterboard (4)**. The roof is made using a timber **framework (5)**, covered with waterproof **felt (6)**. **Battens (7)** (thin strips of timber) are laid on top of the felt, and tiles or **slates (8)** are nailed to the battens. **Insulating material (9)** stops heat escaping through the roof.

▲ In many hot countries bricks are made from clay that is baked hard in the sun.

Scaffolding

While a building or other structure is being constructed, workers use a temporary framework, called scaffolding, to reach all parts of the structure safely. Scaffolding is also used as a temporary support during building. Arches built from bricks or stone, for example, need supporting until the central keystone has been added.

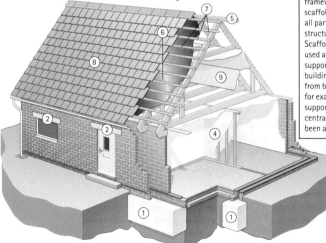

support the weight of the floors and roof of the building. In the second, a **frame** of timber, steel or concrete supports the weight of the floors and roof, and is covered with other materials. The covering materials can be lightweight, because they do not have to support heavy loads.

The strong framework of large modern buildings is often made from **reinforced concrete** – concrete strengthened with steel rods or bars.

Large buildings generally need deep foundations to stop them from sinking, slipping sideways or being blown over in a gale. The foundations may be supported by long steel or concrete posts, called **piles**, hammered deep into the ground.

Dams and tunnels

Dams are barriers built across rivers, streams or estuaries. Embankment dams are wide banks of earth or rock, built so that the base is much wider than the top. Masonry dams are usually made from reinforced concrete.

Shallow tunnels, or underground passages, can be constructed by digging a deep ditch then covering it over to form a tunnel. In deeper tunnels, cutting machines can be used to gouge out soft rock and soil. Harder rock is blown out using explosives. Supports made out of steel or concrete are built into the tunnel to keep it from collapsing.

▼ The Channel Tunnel is really three tunnels in one. It has two main train tunnels with a third service tunnel between them. Cross-tunnels link all the tunnels together.

▲ A tall crane is used to move things around this building under construction in Thailand. Cranes are used in many types of construction. They make use of wires, ropes and pulleys to lift heavy weights and move heavy objects.

find out more

Architecture
Buildings
Bridges

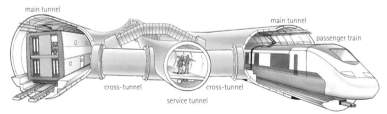

main tunnel

main tunnel

passenger train

cross-tunnel

cross-tunnel

service tunnel

Continents

Almost a third of the Earth's surface is covered by land. This land is divided up into seven continents. Millions of years ago, all the continents were joined in one giant landmass. Gradually this broke up into the continents we know today.

The seven continents are Africa, Antarctica, Asia (the largest), Europe (the smallest), North America, Oceania and South America. Oceania is made up of Australia, New Zealand and the many Pacific islands.

Continental plates

The rocky surface of the Earth (the **crust**) is less than 50 kilometres thick in most places. Below it, the rock is so hot that it is liquid. The crust 'floats' on the liquid rocks beneath. It is broken up into several large pieces, called **continental plates**.

Moving together and apart

Because the continental plates are floating, they move very slowly. Some of the plates move apart, while others bump into each other.

Beneath the oceans, the plates are moving apart. As the plates separate, hot, liquid rock (magma) from below rises to plug the gap. On land, where plates collide the edges buckle, and mountain ranges form. Earthquakes also occur at these boundaries.

250 million years ago

175 million years ago

▲▼ These three maps show how the giant continent Pangaea split first into two parts and then into today's continents. The third map also shows the rocky plates that make up the Earth's crust. These plates move about 2.5 cm each year.

plate boundaries
—— moving apart
- - - moving together
—— passive

Crabs
and other crustaceans

Crustaceans are a large group of animals that include crabs, lobsters, barnacles and woodlice. The name 'crustacean' means 'crusty one' – because all crustaceans are covered in a hard armour or shell.

Some of the most ancient fossils ever found are of crustaceans that lived over 500 million years ago. Today there are about 150,000 different kinds of crustacean. They range from huge lobsters, which can weigh up to 20 kilograms, to tiny copepods just a fraction of a millimetre long.

Most crustaceans spend their lives in water. A few, such as woodlice, live on land. Many small crustaceans are **filter feeders**. They use the fine 'hairs' on their legs to sweep food towards their mouths. Other crustaceans use their legs to catch food.

Life cycles

Most sea-dwelling crustaceans produce large numbers of tiny floating **larvae** (young). The larvae are swept along by ocean currents, where many are eaten by other animals. When they become adults, they settle in one area. As they grow, crustaceans shed (cast off) and regrow their shells many times.

▼ ▶ Some different kinds of crustacean. (These drawings are not to scale.)

Crabs, like this edible crab, are heavily armoured. Most live in the sea.

Lobsters have very big claws or pincers on their first pair of legs. One of these claws is used specially for crushing prey.

Daphnia are water fleas. The females can produce young without mating.

Acorn barnacles are filter feeders. Their hairy feet comb the water for food.

Woodlice are the most successful land-living crustaceans.

Krill

Huge numbers of krill float in the cold waters of the Arctic and Antarctic seas. These small shrimp-like crustaceans are the basic food for many types of bird and seal, and for baleen whales.

find out more

Animals
Bones and muscles
Oceans and seas
Seashore
Whales and dolphins

Crusades

The people of medieval Europe were fiercely Christian and very warlike. They fought many long wars against people of other faiths. Between 1096 and 1291 they waged eight wars, known as the crusades, against the Muslims of the Middle East.

▲ All aboard! Workmen loading supplies onto a ship for the journey to the Holy Land.

In 1095 the pope asked Christian soldiers to drive the Muslims from the **Holy Land** (the Bible lands, including Jerusalem). Thousands answered his call, including kings, knights and many ordinary people.

Crusaders believed the Holy Land should be in Christian hands. They also thought a crusade would be a good chance to win fame and get rich quick.

Success and failure

The first crusade captured Jerusalem and set up a Christian king there. When the Muslims recaptured the city, more crusades were called for. The famous English king **Richard the Lionheart** joined the third crusade against the respected Muslim leader **Saladin**. The crusaders took part of the Holy Land, but not Jerusalem.

Other crusades were even less successful. One, made up of just children, was a tragic disaster. The fourth crusade captured the Christian city of Constantinople (modern Istanbul), nowhere near the Holy Land! When the crusades ended, all of the Holy Land was in Muslim hands.

KEY DATES

1096–1099
First crusade

1099 Crusaders capture Jerusalem

1189–1192
Third crusade

1202–1204
Fourth crusade

1212
Children's crusade

1270–1272 Eighth (and last) crusade

1291 Muslims capture last crusader fortress in Holy Land

find out more

Byzantine empire
Knights
Middle Ages

◀ The routes of the first four crusades.

ENGLAND
FRANCE · Ratisbon
Vezelay
Lyon · Venice
Marseille
ITALY
SPAIN · Rome
Lisbon · Black Sea · Constantinople
GREECE
Mediterranean Sea
Antioch
Acre
EGYPT · PALESTINE

— first crusade
— second crusade
— third crusade
— fourth crusade

▨ western Christendom
▨ eastern Christendom
▨ Muslim lands

Dance

When people dance they move their bodies, usually in time to music. They may dance for many reasons – to celebrate something, as part of a performance, or for pleasure. Dancing is popular all over the world and takes lots of different forms.

◀ Odissi is a flowing, graceful style of dance that began in Kerala, in southern India. It was originally danced in Hindu temples. Female temple dancers used dance to worship and praise the gods, and to tell stories about them.

Dance is often performed in front of an audience, usually by professional dancers. Ballet, modern dance and classical Indian dance are examples of **performance dancing**. Such dances often tell a story. The dancers have to know all the moves, and must be both strong and supple.

Another very important kind of dancing is **social dancing**. This is dancing that people do for fun – and anyone can do it. Jive, ballroom and line dancing are types of social dancing. Dancers usually have to learn special steps and movements, but they are much easier to learn than classical dance movements.

Indian dance

The oldest known dances come from India. Dancers were performing in Hindu temples

▼ In the 20th century, professional dancers broke away from the rigid style of classical ballet. They began to dance much more freely, and used movement to express emotions or states of mind. This dance piece by the choreographer Mark Morris is set to an 18th-century opera, but it uses modern styles of movement.

Ballet is a form of performance dance that first developed in Europe, and is now popular around the world. Ballet involves many energetic and difficult moves, but it must always appear smooth and graceful. The dancers seem to float above the ground. Here, the famous dance partners Rudolf Nureyev and Margot Fonteyn dance a *pas de deux* (a dance for two people).

nearly 2000 years ago. Today there are many different styles.

In most Indian dance styles the legs are bent and there are few jumps. Dancers often wear bells on their ankles and stamp out complex rhythms. The dancer's body, arms, hands and face are very mobile. The moves, gestures and expressions form a kind of language, and have particular meanings. Dance styles throughout South-east Asia have been strongly influenced by Indian dance.

African dance

When Africans were taken to the Americas as slaves, they took their dances with them. Many new styles developed from the combination of African and American styles. Tap dancing, for instance, is a mixture of clog dancing, Irish step dancing and African dance.

In Africa people often dance to celebrate weddings, harvests – in fact, any kind of event. African dancers usually move with the legs bent and the weight low. They often stamp out rhythms with their feet. The back bends and stretches, while the hips circle and sway.

Folk dancing

Today most folk dances are performed for entertainment. But in the past the dances had more serious purposes. Sometimes people danced to bring good luck, or a good harvest. Many dances were part of religious ceremonies.

Each area has folk dances of its own. In Britain, morris dancing is probably the best-known type of folk dance. In South-east Asia, people dressed-up as dragons or lions danced to frighten away evil spirits. People in dry areas, such as the Aborigines in Australia, performed rain-dances to bring rain.

▲ This sequence shows a dance exercise by Merce Cunningham. The exercise is performed smoothly to develop a strong, supple spine.

find out more

Drama
Music

▼ Women dancing in Angola, Africa. In traditional African women's dances, the movements are graceful and fluid, in contrast to the men's dancing which is forceful and fluid.

Deserts

A desert is a large area of extremely dry land. To survive in the desert, people and wildlife have to adapt to the difficult conditions.

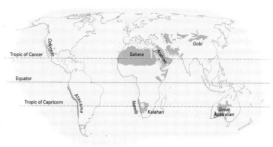

A 'true' desert receives less than 250 millimetres of rain in an average year. But rainfall in the desert can vary a great deal from year to year – a desert may have heavy rains in one year, followed by several years without any rain at all.

Sand, rock and gravel

Most deserts are vast expanses of sand, gravel or rocks. In places, wind piles the sand up to form **dunes**. These sand dunes are constantly moving as sand is blown up one side of the dune and then rolls down the other side.

In a few places in the desert, water lies at or near the surface. These places are called **oases**. The soil here may be quite fertile, and trees and crops can all flourish.

Desert peoples

Many traditional desert inhabitants are **nomads**. They live in tents or build temporary homes, and move from place to

place in search of grazing for their animals. In the Sahara and the deserts of Arabia, the Bedouin graze herds of camels, sheep and goats. The Bushmen of the Kalahari and the Aborigines in Australia are **hunter–gatherers**. They gather desert plants and hunt the animals.

▼ Sand dunes in Africa's Namib Desert. Large animals such as this gemsbok often have to move to other areas during long periods of drought.

▲ The world's main deserts. Most are near the tropics: these are the **hot deserts**. The deserts of central Asia are hot in summer and freezing in winter. There are also polar deserts in Antarctica and Greenland.

find out more

Climate
Erosion
Plants

Today, new settlements have grown up in the deserts, where valuable minerals such as oil have been found under the ground. Water for these settlements comes from deep wells, or is brought in by pipelines or lorries.

Desert wildlife

Desert plants and animals have found ways to survive in hot conditions with little or no water. Many animals avoid the heat by sleeping during the day and coming out to find food at night.

Desert plants survive the dry conditions by storing water in their stems, leaves or roots. Some have a thick waxy coating that reduces the amount of water lost.

Spreading deserts

In some parts of the world, particularly around the Sahara, the desert areas are getting bigger. This is because the cattle are eating all the new grass, trees are being cut down for fuel, and there is not enough rain. New methods of farming are being tried out to reclaim some of these desert areas.

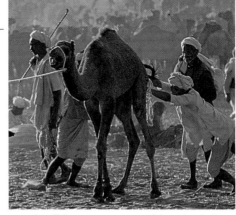

▲ A camel market in northern India. Camels can live for several weeks in the desert without a drink. Their bodies can produce water from fat stored in their humps.

DESERT RECORDS

Largest hot desert:
Sahara Desert, 8.4 million sq km

Highest temperature:
58 °C, Libya 1922

Highest sand dunes:
430 m high, in eastern Algeria

A dry spell
The Atacama Desert in Chile is the driest place in the world. When it rained there in 1971, it was the first rain in 400 years.

◄ A desert landscape. Parts of the desert are sandy, but other areas are bare rock. Canyons, mesas and buttes are formed by the erosion of rocks by wind and sand. An aquifer is a layer of water-bearing rock. Where the aquifer comes to the surface, an oasis forms.

canyon
mesa
butte
bare rock surface
oasis
sandy desert
oasis
aquifer

Design

When people make something, they usually want it to do a certain job – for instance they make a chair to sit in. They may also want it to look a certain way – perhaps they want their chair to be very simple. We call the process of deciding how a new object should be made – and how it should look – **design.**

The people whose job it is to come up with ways of making new objects are called **designers**. Designers work in all sorts of fields. Industrial designers create new versions of familiar objects, such as kettles or cars. Fashion designers design new clothes. Graphic designers design books, advertisements and computer icons. Landscape designers design gardens, parks, or even towns.

Many designers try out a design by making a **model**. If the model doesn't work – or if it doesn't look right – they change it, or start again. They may try out lots of different ideas before they come up with something that works.

◀ The original Coca-Cola bottle was designed in 1916 by Alex Samuelson. Most Coke is now sold in cans or plastic bottles, but the company still uses the original bottle in advertisements because it is so popular and creates a particular image.

▲ Most big companies and organizations have a 'logo'. Logos are examples of graphic design. If the design is a good one, people will remember it.

find out more
Architecture
Building
Clothes

▲ Many designers use computer modelling to help them produce new designs. With a computer model it is possible to see an image from different angles, and to change it. It is even possible to simulate (imitate) real conditions, for instance the effect of speed and wind on a car, before going ahead with a full-sized model.

Digestion

Like all living things, you need food to live and grow. And like every other animal, you get your food by eating. But before your body can use the food, you have to break it down into tiny bits. Some of these are useful to the body, others are waste. This process is called digestion.

Many animals, including humans, birds and fishes, digest their food in a long tube called the **gut**, which stretches from the mouth to the anus. Other, simpler animals, such as jellyfishes, digest their food in a kind of bag in the middle of their body. This bag only has a single opening – to the mouth.

How you digest your food

When humans eat, they bite off a chunk of food with their teeth. The teeth chew it up, and then the tongue pushes it to the back of the mouth, where it is swallowed.

The tube that leads from the mouth to the stomach is called the **gullet**. The gullet pushes the food down into the stomach.

▶ The human digestive system.

gullet

liver: stores extra food

pancreas: makes digestive enzymes

small intestine

stomach

large intestine

appendix: used by some mammals to digest plants, but not used by humans

rectum

The stomach mixes it with acid and special juices called **enzymes**. These juices break it down into its different parts. From the stomach the food moves on into the **small intestine**. The useful parts of the food pass through the intestine wall into the blood. The blood carries the digested food to all parts of the body.

The food that is left is waste. This goes into the **large intestine** and leaves the body through the **rectum**.

find out more

Food
Heart and blood
Human beings
Teeth

rumen

◀ Bison, like all cattle, are **ruminants**. Ruminants have complicated stomachs. When they swallow food it goes first to the rumen. From there it is returned to the mouth as cud, for a second chewing, called rumination.

Dinosaurs

Dinosaurs were prehistoric reptiles that roamed the Earth for 160 million years. They died out 65 million years ago – more than 60 million years before the first human-like creatures lived.

About 200 years ago, people began to find the fossils of huge bones. At first they thought the bones might belong to giants, or even dragons. But gradually they realized that they were the bones of huge lizard-like animals. They called these animals dinosaurs – which means 'terrible lizards'.

Since then scientists have discovered hundreds of different kinds of dinosaur. Many of them were very big – the biggest animals that have ever lived on land. Others were small – some as tiny as chickens.

The first dinosaurs

The earliest dinosaurs lived over 220 million years ago – in the warm swamps and lush forests of the Triassic period. They were quite small and ran on their hind legs.

The main advantage that the dinosaurs had over the reptiles from which they evolved was the position of their legs. Dinosaurs' legs were 'under' their bodies (like human legs), instead of sticking out to the sides. This meant that they could reach

▼ *Triceratops* (left), was a plant-eater that walked on all fours. It had a bony neck shield for protection. Other plant-eaters had horns, or plates of bony armour like this *Scolosaurus* (right).

▲ Some dinosaurs, such as *Stenonychosaurus* (above), walked on their hind legs, rather like chickens.

DINOSAUR RECORDS

Longest dinosaur
Diplodocus 27 m

Tallest dinosaur
Brachiosaurus 12 m

Smallest dinosaur
Compsognathus
75–91 cm; 3 kg

Heaviest dinosaur
Ultrasaurus 120 tonnes

find out more

Continents
Evolution
Fossils
Life on Earth
Reptiles

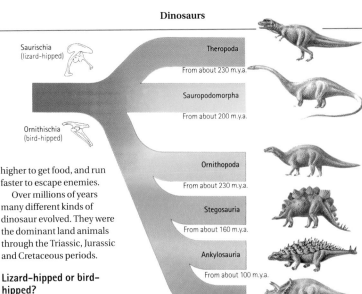

Saurischia
(lizard-hipped)

Ornithischia
(bird-hipped)

Theropoda

From about 230 m.y.a.

Sauropodomorpha

From about 200 m.y.a.

Ornithopoda

From about 230 m.y.a.

Stegosauria

From about 160 m.y.a.

Ankylosauria

From about 100 m.y.a.

Ceratopsia

From about 140 m.y.a

▲ The two main groups of dinosaurs can be divided further into six sub-groups, as shown above. (m.y.a. = millions of years ago.)

higher to get food, and run faster to escape enemies.

Over millions of years many different kinds of dinosaur evolved. They were the dominant land animals through the Triassic, Jurassic and Cretaceous periods.

Lizard-hipped or bird-hipped?

Scientists divide dinosaurs into two main groups, based on the shape of their hip bones. One group is called the Saurischia, which means 'lizard-hipped', because their hip bones are arranged like those of lizards. The other group is called Ornithischia, which means 'bird-hipped', because the hip bones of birds are arranged like this.

The lizard-hipped dinosaurs had their teeth in the front of their mouth. They could bite and tear, but they could not really chew their food. All the meat-eaters were lizard-hipped. The bird-hipped dinosaurs had teeth at the back of their mouth. They could grind up tough plant

food. All the bird-hipped dinosaurs fed on plants.

Warm-blooded or cold-blooded?

Scientists do not know whether dinosaurs were warm-blooded or cold-blooded. A cold-blooded animal needs heat from the Sun to become active. Warm-blooded animals can be active all the time.

Because the Earth's climate was warmer, it would have been easier for cold-blooded dinosaurs to keep active. The bigger dinosaurs could stay warm through the night because

Dinosaurs in your garden!
Did all the dinosaurs really die out? Perhaps they didn't. Some scientists think that birds are probably the direct descendants of the dinosaurs.

it would take a long time for their bodies to cool down. Smaller dinosaurs may have been warm-blooded.

The end of the dinosaurs

At the end of the Cretaceous period, 65 million years ago, the dinosaurs suddenly disappeared. What happened?

One suggestion is that the climate changed abruptly. The dinosaurs could not adapt to the new conditions and just died out. Another theory is that the Earth was hit by a giant **meteorite**. The impact sent up a huge cloud of dust, which blacked out the Sun. The Earth became much colder. Only those animals that could withstand the cold survived.

Discovering dinosaurs

Everything that we know about dinosaurs we have learned from

fossils. Scientists study a dinosaur's fossilized bones to work out the shape of its body. They can also use fossils to learn how dinosaurs lived.

Sometimes lots of dinosaur bones are found together, so perhaps certain dinosaurs lived in herds. Fossils of leaves, insects or shells tell us about the climate and the plants that lived at the time. Dinosaur teeth tell us whether the animal ate meat or plant food. Dinosaur eggs that have been found suggest that some kinds of dinosaur did not look after their young, although a few did.

But there are many things that we do not yet know about dinosaurs. What colour were they? Were they noisy? How long did they live? Scientists are still searching for the answers to these questions.

◀ Fossilized dinosaur footprints like this one help scientists find out how big dinosaurs were and how fast they moved.

▼ *Tyrannosaurus* was one of the biggest meat-eaters that has ever lived, and was probably one of the last dinosaurs to evolve. It was as tall as a two-storey building.

Disabilities

A disability means that part of your body does not work properly. There are two kinds of disability – physical and mental. People with a disability often have special needs.

Some kinds of disability stop you hearing or seeing properly. These are called **sensory disabilities** because they affect your senses. Blindness and deafness are sensory disabilities. Some people have **learning disabilities**. This means that they cannot learn as easily as other people. Down's syndrome is a learning disability.

Why are people disabled?

We do not always know why people are disabled. Sometimes they inherit a disability from their parents. Occasionally problems during birth cause a baby to become brain damaged. Other disabilities are caused by disease or by accidents.

Living with disability

In richer countries there may be special teachers or schools for disabled children. Today many new buildings are built so that people in wheelchairs can use them. And cars and buses can also be designed to cater for disabled users.

Many people who have disabilities take an active part in sport. There are also workshops that teach people with disabilities skills they can use to earn a living.

▲ This 4-year-old girl has Down's syndrome, a mental disability. About one in 650 babies is born with the syndrome. Many of them grow up to lead fulfilling lives.

find out more
Health and fitness

▼ Many deaf people communicate using sign language. This woman is using sign language to say 'Hello! I am pleased to meet you.'

| Hello! | I | (am) | pleased | to meet | you |

Diseases

Some diseases, such as the common cold, may make us feel a bit miserable but they do no lasting damage. Others, such as diabetes, are serious but can be kept under control by the use of drugs. But some diseases, such as cancer or Aids, can kill.

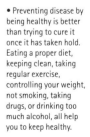

People may be born with a disease, or they may get one as a result of injury, from an infection, or from some other cause. The causes of many diseases are still unknown. Scientists are researching ways of preventing and curing disease all the time.

Infectious diseases

Many diseases are infectious. This means that the germs that cause them pass from one person to another, either carried in the air or through some sort of physical contact. These germs include bacteria, viruses and fungi.

Diseases caused by **bacteria** include food poisoning, whooping cough and tuberculosis (TB). Bacteria can be killed by antiseptics or antibiotics. People can also be protected against certain types of bacteria by

▲ This girl has diabetes, a fairly common disease which means her body does not produce the chemical insulin naturally. The body needs insulin to break down sugar in the blood. Diabetics inject themselves daily with insulin.

◀ Louis Pasteur (1822–1895) was a French scientist who discovered that bacteria cause diseases. He developed vaccines for several diseases in animals, including anthrax, a disease that kills cattle and sheep.

• Preventing disease by being healthy is better than trying to cure it once it has taken hold. Eating a proper diet, keeping clean, taking regular exercise, controlling your weight, not smoking, taking drugs, or drinking too much alcohol, all help you to keep healthy.

receiving vaccines. This protection is called **immunization**.

Viruses cause several diseases in humans, including Aids, rabies, measles, chicken pox, influenza (flu) and the common cold. Viruses also cause diseases in other animals and plants. Antibiotics will not cure viral infections, but there are some anti-viral drugs.

Fungi cause athlete's foot, ringworm and other infections in humans. They also cause foot rot in cattle and many plant diseases. Fungal infections can be treated with special powders and creams.

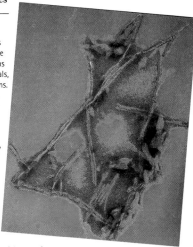

▶ Prions are protein particles that attack nerve cells in the brains of various animals, including humans. Scientists think that they cause BSE (mad cow disease). This picture is magnified many times.

Epidemics

When a large number of people get the same disease at the same time in the same place, it is called an epidemic. Epidemics of diseases such as measles and flu are caused by germs that are spread by coughing and sneezing or by touching someone who has the disease. Epidemics of diseases such as cholera and typhoid are often caused by people eating dirty food and drinking dirty water.

> **find out more**
> Bacteria and viruses
> Cells
> Drugs
> Medicine

Cancer

Most people know someone who has been affected by the disease called cancer. There are many different types of cancer. Cancers develop when cells in the body increase rapidly and form a swelling called a tumour. Sometimes cells break off the tumour, spreading the cancer to a different place in the body. Many cancers can be cured, especially if they are found early enough, but in many countries, especially in richer parts of the world, cancer is one of the main causes of death.

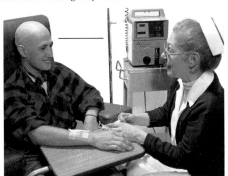

▲ This cancer patient is undergoing chemotherapy, a drug treatment.

Allergies

You have an allergy when your body reacts against what should be a harmless substance as if it were a germ. Some people are allergic to certain foods, others to dust or animal fur. Allergies may make you sneeze, your eyes and nose run, or your body itch.

▶ Asthma is a disease that causes difficulty in breathing. It can be brought on by an allergic reaction to pollen and dust. This magnified picture of a windpipe shows the pollen (pink) and dust (blue) particles that the person has breathed in.

• Today heart disease is one of the biggest causes of death in Western, developed countries. People may get heart disease if they eat a lot of fatty foods and do not take enough exercise.

• Smoking is known to be a major cause of disease. For example, smokers are at least twice as likely to die of heart disease as non-smokers, and 90% of lung cancers are caused by smoking.

Inherited and developmental diseases

Inherited diseases are passed by parents to their children. Haemophilia, a disease in which the blood is slow to clot, is one example. Special treatment can help people with inherited diseases, though often they cannot be completely cured.

Sometimes a baby is born with part of its body not working properly. For example, the heart may have a hole between the right and left sides, causing the blood to flow incorrectly. This is a developmental disease. Such conditions can often be cured by surgery.

Mental illness

Mental diseases, also called mental illness, are problems of the mind. They often cause people to behave in an unusual manner, and some sufferers may see and hear things that are not there. They may also hurt themselves or other people.

Some people become very unhappy and are said to be suffering from **depression**. This may be caused by overwork, stress or the death of someone close. Doctors called **psychiatrists** treat people with mental illness.

▼ The Austrian doctor Sigmund Freud had a huge influence on psychology in the 20th century. He introduced the idea that the unconscious mind influences people's thoughts and behaviour.

Dogs

TOP DOGS

Tallest: Irish wolfhound, shoulder height about 1.1 m

Heaviest: St Bernard, weight about 100 kg

Smallest: Chihuahua: weight less than 1 kg

Fastest over long distances: Saluki

Fastest over short distances: Greyhound

Good hunting!
African hunting dogs are among the most successful hunters of all mammals. They catch their prey in up to 70% of their hunts.

find out more

Animals
Farm animals
Mammals

There are more than 100 different kinds (breeds) of domestic dog. All are descended from just one ancestor, the grey wolf. But there are many relatives of domestic dogs that live in the wild – including wolves, foxes and jackals.

All dogs are hunters. Most can run very fast and have excellent senses of sight, hearing and smell. They use smell to communicate with each other. They are very intelligent animals. People first domesticated (tamed) dogs about 10,000 years ago.

Wild dogs

There are about 35 different types of wild dog, including two kinds of wolf, 21 kinds of fox and

▲ Wolves were once widespread. Now they are only found in some parts of North America and Asia and are very rare indeed in Europe.

four kinds of jackal. Other wild dogs include African hunting dogs, bush dogs, dingos, dholes, coyotes and racoon dogs.

Wolves live and hunt together in family groups called **packs**. They hunt mainly deer. **Jackals** usually live in pairs, in the warm and dry areas of Africa, Asia and south-east Europe. **Foxes** tend to hunt alone, but they often live in pairs or small groups. The red fox has even taken to living in towns.

▼ People have bred dogs for all sorts of jobs, so the variety among breeds is enormous. But all domestic dogs can breed with each other to produce cross-breeds (mongrels).

Afghan hound

bulldog

Airedale

bouvier

chihuahua

cocker spaniel

cairn terrier

chow chow

Drama

A drama is a story that is performed, often in the form of a play. The people who perform are called actors. All over the world, and in almost all cultures, people enjoy watching and acting in drama.

Many people go to the **theatre** to see **plays** being performed live. People also go to the cinema to watch films, which are a form of drama. And millions of people watch 'soaps', situation comedies and other dramas on television. Drama can thrill us or frighten us – it can make us laugh or even cry.

The beginnings of drama

Prehistoric people may well have acted out dramas – but because they were never written down, we know nothing about them. As civilization and writing developed, people began to write plays down. This meant that they could be performed over and over again.

▼ Three types of stage are used in modern theatres. The most common type is the **proscenium stage**, in which the stage is framed by an arch, and the audience seated in front. In **theatre-in-the-round** the stage is in the middle of the audience. The **platform stage** has seats on three sides. The theatre below has a proscenium stage.

1 The **proscenium arch** is like a picture frame through which the audience watches the performance.
2 **Lights** help to create the atmosphere of a scene, or highlight particular actors.
3 The **curtain** can be opened at the beginning of the play to reveal the scene.
4 The **safety curtain** is a fireproof screen that can be lowered in case of fire.
5 **Trapdoors** are useful if actors need to make a surprise entrance or exit.

6 **Scenery** and **props** make a performance more realistic.
7 The performers get dressed and put their make-up on in **dressing rooms** before going on stage.
8 The **costumes** are made and stored in the **wardrobe room**.
9 The **wings** are where the performers wait just before they make their entrance.
10 The **lighting director** operates the lights from the lighting control room.
11 Scenery and props to be used for different plays are stored.

The Greeks

About 2500 years ago, the Greeks developed a very powerful kind of drama. Their plays told of the lives of men and women and usually had unhappy endings. They were called **tragedies**. The three greatest writers of Greek tragedies were Sophocles, Euripides and Aeschylus. The Greeks also wrote **comedies**: plays that make people laugh, and which end happily.

Medieval and Elizabethan drama

In Europe in the Middle Ages, most drama told stories from the Bible. These plays were known as **mystery plays**, and were performed by ordinary people. But in England in the 16th century, people began to use drama to tell all kinds of stories. Theatres were built where people could go to see professional actors perform new plays. The playwright William **Shakespeare** was writing at this time.

Modern drama

In the 19th century **melodramas** became very popular. These are plays with fast-moving plots, and obvious heroes and villains. In the 20th century some writers wrote plays that were more about ideas than action. **Television** and the **cinema** provided dramas that were watched by millions of people around the world.

Eastern theatre

Drama has a long history in South-east Asia, especially in Japan and China. **No** is an ancient Japanese form of theatre that uses music, dancing, and elaborate costumes and masks. It is based on religious ritual. **Kabuki** is a more recent and popular form, which mixes music, dance and mime.

Beijing opera is a Chinese theatre form that features acrobatics, operatic singing, and dancing.

▲ This mask from Japanese **No** theatre represents a demon. It was made in about 1280.

• In mime, actors do not speak or make any noise at all. They show their feelings through movement and facial expression. They can make the audience believe in things that are not physically there, such as walls and tables. Elaborate forms of mime are used in an Indian classical dance form called 'Kathakali', in which male actors dance to epic stories about ancient India.

William Shakespeare

William Shakespeare (1564–1616) is considered by many people to be the greatest playwright of all time. Thirty-seven of his plays have survived and all of them are still performed today. Among his most famous plays are the tragedies: *Hamlet*, *Macbeth*, *Othello* and *King Lear*. He also wrote popular comedies, such as *A Midsummer Night's Dream* and *Twelfth Night*. The company Shakespeare worked with was based at the Globe Theatre in London (right). A reconstruction of the theatre, on the same site as the original, was completed in 1997.

find out more
Dance
Films
Poetry
Television
Writers

Drugs

Drugs are chemicals that affect our minds or our bodies. Drugs can help to make sick people better. But sometimes people take drugs just because they like the way the drugs make them feel.

In the past, all drugs were made from plants or animals. For example, the painkiller **opium** was made from a type of poppy. Scientists studied many of these early drugs to learn how they work and how to produce them using chemicals. Now many drugs are made from chemicals.

There are several main types of drug used in medicine. **Analgesics**, such as aspirin, are used to fight pain. **Antibiotics** like **penicillin** kill bacteria that cause serious infections. **Tranquillizers** help to calm people down, while **sedatives** help people to sleep.

Dangerous addictions

Sometimes people feel they cannot manage without a particular drug – they become **addicted**. The alcohol in alcoholic drinks is a kind of drug. So is the nicotine in tobacco. Even drinking too much coffee can become addictive. There are also other, much stronger addictive drugs, such as heroin or cocaine. Often people need help to overcome their addiction.

▲ These drugs are used by doctors to help sick people get better. The drugs shown here are used for many diseases, including gout, malaria and tuberculosis.

● As well as curing people, drugs can have unpleasant or dangerous side-effects. This is why many drugs can only be prescribed by a doctor.

Smoking
The nicotine in tobacco is addictive. This is why millions of people continue to smoke cigarettes, in spite of the fact that cigarettes damage their health.

◀ It is illegal to sell addictive and dangerous drugs like heroin and cocaine. These drugs officers have just uncovered a large amount of cocaine that is being smuggled through the Panama Canal.

find out more
Bacteria and viruses
Diseases
Medicine

Early people

The first human-like creatures lived in Africa about 5 million years ago. Modern humans appeared about 100,000 years ago, and gradually spread around the world.

▲ This ancient painting of a buffalo is one of many paintings of animals and hunters on the walls of the Lascaux caves in the Dordogne, France. They were painted between 15,000 and 14,000 BC.

millions of years ago

Homo sapiens made carvings, delicate stone tools, and wonderful cave paintings.

modern humans

Neanderthal people wore clothes and used flint knives.

Homo erectus ('upright man') had a bigger brain than *Homo habilis*, was able to make better tools, and made fires.

Homo habilis ('handy man') was about 1.6 m tall, had a larger brain than *Australopithecus* and probably used tools.

other australopithecines

The best example of *Australopithecus afarensis* is known as Lucy. Lucy was 1.5 m tall and had a small brain. She could walk upright.

Australopithecus ramidus (*Australopithecus* means 'southern ape')

▲ ▶ How modern humans evolved. Many human-like species such as *Homo habilis* and Neanderthals are not direct ancestors of modern humans.

Our ancestors separated from the ancestors of the great apes over 5 million years ago.

The long period before people kept written records is known as 'prehistory'. Archaeologists have to work out how people lived in these times from the little physical evidence that survives.

Hunters and gatherers

Through most of prehistory, people everywhere got their **food** from wild plants and animals. They hunted, fished and gathered fruits, roots and other plant foods. They moved seasonally from camp to camp and became expert observers of plant and animal life.

Early people made **tools**, mostly of stone and wood, and lived in small family groups. They also expressed themselves artistically in rock and **cave paintings,** and by carving and making models of animals and people.

▶ This timeline shows the development of prehistoric peoples around the world, from the time when the first human-like creatures evolved, about 5 million years ago, until 700 BC.

5,000,000– 2,000,000 BC	2,000,000– 250,000 BC	250,000– 120,000 BC	80,000– 30,000 BC	50,000– 25,000 BC	25,000– 10,000 BC	10,000– 8000 B
Early tree-dwelling hominids evolve in Africa	Upright humans *Homo erectus* evolve, and spread to Asia and Europe.	Modern humans *Homo sapiens* evolve in Africa and spread north.	Neanderthals live in Europe and the Middle East.	Modern humans (*Homo sapiens sapiens*), spread through Europe into Asia and Australia and the Americas. A wide variety of tools made in a variety of materials.	Early round houses, cave-painting and carving in Europe and western Asia.	Climate changes as ice age ends.

Farmers

About 10,000 years ago, at the end of the last ice age, some hunter-gatherers began to cultivate plants and keep animals. This change took place earliest in the **Middle East**, where some people were already living all year round in small **settlements**.

The first farmers grew **cereals** such as barley and wheat, and other grain crops. They also raised goats and sheep, and later pigs and cattle. These **animals** provided regular supplies of meat and other useful products. As agriculture developed,

settlements got larger and people began to specialize in different **crafts** such as pottery, weaving and metal-working.

In other parts of the world people also began to cultivate plants they had previously gathered, such as rice in China and maize in Mexico. Agriculture gradually spread and, as it did so, more plants and animals were 'domesticated'. By 3000 BC farming had replaced gathering and hunting as the dominant way of life in Europe. And in the Middle East the first **civilizations** were developing.

▼ A camp in France about 12,000 years ago. The people who lived here would have spent their time hunting reindeer for food and skins, gathering plant food and cooking.

Ears *see* Human beings *and* Senses

8000–7000 BC	7000–6000 BC	5000–4000 BC	4000–3000 BC	3000–2000 BC	2000–1000 BC	1000–700 BC
Beginning of farming in western Asia. Village settlements in Syria, Palestine, Cyprus. Beans and wild cereals (wheat and barley) cultivated.	Goats, sheep, pigs and cattle domesticated in western Asia. Linens, textiles and pottery first made. Copper used. Rice cultivated in China.	Domestication of ass, horse and camel in western Asia. Cotton grown in Peru.	Sumerian civilization. First writing. Metalwork in copper, tin, bronze, lead, silver, gold. Maize cultivated in Mexico. Llama domesticated in Peru. Agriculture established across Europe. Stone temples and tombs in Europe.	Pharaohs in Egypt. Chariot invented in Mesopotamia. Indus civilization with cotton textiles.	Bronze technology throughout Europe. Stonehenge completed.	Olmec culture in Mexico. Celts spread into Central Europe and Britain. Iron technology in Europe.

Early technology

In many parts of the world early people used flint and other types of stone to make **tools** and **weapons**. As they became more skilful, they developed specialized tools, such as stone axes for butchering large animals, flint blades for skinning them, and stone and bone barbs for spears and arrows. They also made **baskets** for collecting plant foods. The first farmers needed new tools, such as stone axes for felling trees, and grindstones for processing grains. Most prehistoric peoples also learned how to make **pottery** and how to spin and weave.

Discovering metals

Early people discovered how to use metals to make tools at different times in different parts of the world. **Copper** was first used before 6000 BC in western Asia. Craftspeople discovered that if they mixed copper and tin, they got a harder metal: **bronze**.

The first people to use **iron** lived in Anatolia (part of Turkey) in about 2000 BC. They made the iron by 'smelting': melting iron ore and charcoal together. They then beat it into shape to make knives and other tools and weapons. People began using iron in China in the 6th century BC, in Britain in about 700 BC, and in West Africa before 500 BC.

find out more

Africa
Ancient world
Archaeology
Aztecs
Celts
China
Evolution
Human beings
Incas
Life on Earth

◄ In 1991 two hikers in the Austrian Alps found the body of a man who had died about 5300 years ago. With the body they found the remains of clothes, boots, a quiver, arrows, an axe, a small flint dagger, a simple haversack, a sewing kit and lots of trapping equipment.

Earth

The Earth is one of the nine planets that travel around the Sun in our Solar System. The Earth is a rocky ball whose surface is two thirds water and one third land.

The Earth is the planet that we live on. It is surrounded by layers of air that contain oxygen. So far as we know, it is the only planet with living things on it.

Always on the move

Like all the planets, the Earth is constantly moving. It spins around its axis like a top. (The Earth's axis is an imaginary line that passes through the Earth from the North Pole to the South Pole.) The Earth also travels in a path, called an orbit, around the Sun.

▲ From space the Earth is like a blue ball with brown and green patches. The blue areas are the oceans; the brown and green areas are the land. There are white ice caps at the North and South Poles, and parts of the surface are covered with swirling white clouds.

It takes one day for the Earth to make one complete spin around its axis. It takes one year for the Earth to make one complete orbit around the Sun.

Born of gas and dust

The Earth began as a swirling cloud of gas and dust. Around 4.5 billion years ago some of this material clumped together in the centre of this cloud to form the Sun. At the same time, smaller lumps of gas and dust were clumping together away from the centre to form the planets. One of these planets was the Earth.

◀ Satellites in space can take photographs and make measurements of the Earth's surface. This is called remote sensing. Remote sensing helps scientists predict the weather. It can also give information about how the surface of the Earth is changing. This photo shows northern Africa and part of the Red Sea. The darker line across the middle is the River Nile.

At first the surface of the Earth was very hot, but gradually it cooled down. After hundreds of millions of years it cooled enough to form a solid crust.

Inside the Earth

The Earth is made up of three main layers. The outer layer is called the **crust**. The middle layer is called the **mantle**. At the centre of the Earth is the **core**.

The crust

The crust includes the oceans and the land areas where we live. It is made up of a layer of hard rock, broken up into 13 huge pieces, called plates. The plates move around over the Earth's surface. Under the oceans the crust is only around 5–6 kilometres thick. Under the land it can be up to 35 kilometres thick.

The mantle

The mantle is around 2900 kilometres thick. Heat from inside the Earth causes some of the rocks in the mantle to melt. This molten rock comes to the surface when a volcano erupts.

The core

The Earth's core is made of two layers. The outer layer is about 2000 kilometres thick. It is made of liquid metals. The inner core is a ball of solid metal. The temperature in the core is around 5000 °C.

▼ A cutaway view showing the inside of the Earth. Scientists find out what it is like by studying how waves from earthquakes travel through the different layers.

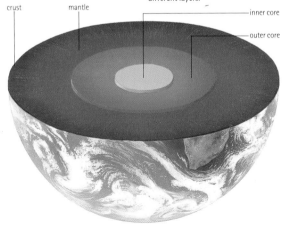

crust   mantle

inner core

outer core

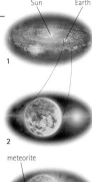

▲ How the Earth and Moon formed. **1** The Sun and planets, including the Earth, developed from a huge spinning cloud of gas. **2** When it was first formed, the Earth was a ball of molten rock. **3** Before the Earth cooled, it was hit by a giant meteorite, and a huge piece split off. **4** The piece broken off by the meteorite became the Moon.

find out more

Continents
Oceans and seas
Rocks and minerals
Seasons
Solar System

Ecology

Ecology is the science which studies how plants and animals live together, and their connections with the world around them.

There are many complicated links between plants and animals and their surroundings (their **environment**). It is the job of an ecologist to try to understand how these connections work.

Food chains and webs

One way that living things are connected is through **food chains**. Green plants use the Sun's energy to make their own food. Animals then eat the plants, or they eat other animals. In a garden, for example, caterpillars may eat a cabbage plant. Some of the energy stored in the cabbage is passed to the caterpillars. If a thrush then eats a caterpillar, some of the caterpillar's energy passes to the thrush. Cabbage, caterpillar and thrush are all links in a food chain. In real life, food chains are connected in many ways, forming complicated **food webs**.

The studies of ecologists show that a lot of energy is lost with each link in a food chain. At each step along the chain there are fewer animals.

thrush eats berries

seeds in droppings

new tree

mountain ash

▲ Thrushes eat the berries of trees like the mountain ash. The seeds come out in the bird's droppings, and new trees grow. The thrush needs the tree's berries for food, while the mountain ash needs the thrush to spread its seeds.

The arrows in the food chain always point from food to feeder.

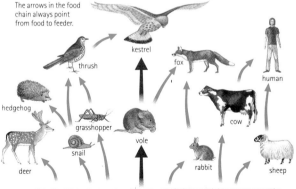

kestrel
thrush
fox
human
hedgehog
grasshopper
cow
snail
vole
deer
rabbit
sheep

◀ A food web. In many meadows, voles eat grass. Kestrels often hunt and kill the voles. The grass, voles and kestrels make a simple food chain. But other kinds of animal – cattle, sheep, deer, rabbits, snails and grasshoppers – also feed on grass. In turn, there are many animals – such as humans – that feed on these grass-eaters.

Living spaces

Plants and animals are linked not just through food, but also through their environment. So cacti and rattlesnakes, for example, are adapted (designed by nature) to live in the desert environment (their **habitat**). To survive in the desert, they must have ways of saving water, keeping cool, coping with the shifting sands and avoiding their enemies.

The lives of all the plants and animals in any habitat are interconnected. The living system that ties them all together is known as an **ecosystem**.

Lessons for life

One of the lessons of ecology for humans is that if we disturb the balance of an ecosystem, the result is often damaging to us. The story of the Californian sea otter illustrates this.

Early in the 20th century, so many sea otters were hunted that they almost died out. Sea otters feed on animals such as

sea urchins, and once the sea otters had gone, sea urchin numbers exploded. The sea urchins ate all the large seaweeds (giant kelps), and underwater 'forests' of kelp became bare, rocky areas. With the kelp forests gone, many fishes, which had bred in the kelp, died out. As a result, the Californian fishing industry closed down, and hundreds of people lost their jobs – all because the killing of sea otters had disturbed the balance of nature.

◄ Moorland, like this in Lancashire, UK, is often the result of human activity. Many moors and heaths were formed when people cleared woodland trees for hunting or to graze sheep or cattle. Without grazing, the land would soon return to woodland.

find out more

Conservation
Energy
Food
Forests
Grasslands
Oceans and seas
Plants
Wetlands

• Deserts, rainforests and coral reefs are examples of ecosystems. Even a small pond can be an ecosystem in itself. If a ship sinks at sea, a whole ecosystem of fishes and other sea creatures will soon be formed around the wreck.

◄ The disappearance of the Californian sea otter, as a result of hunting, had unexpected effects that led to many fishermen and factory workers losing their jobs.

Ancient
Egyptians

The Egyptians created one of the most amazing civilizations of the ancient world. It lasted almost 3000 years (from about 3200 BC to 340 BC). Its power and influence stretched over a huge area of Africa and the Middle East. And we are still dazzled by its art and buildings, especially the famous pyramids.

The Egyptians depended on the **River Nile**. It was their main highway, a place to bathe, and provided fish to eat. More important, its waters allowed crops to grow in the desert land. Most ordinary Egyptians farmed land near the river. They dug channels to bring water to their fields. The Nile was such a key part of their lives they believed it was a god, called Hapy. When the river flooded or got low, it meant Hapy was annoyed.

Kings and gods

Egypt was ruled by a royal family, or dynasty. Members of the family married close relatives, even their brothers and sisters. The king, later called the **pharaoh**, was head of the family. He was also a godlike high priest, chief judge and commander of the army. He had enormous power.

Religion was a vital part of the Egyptians' everyday lives. They had over 750 gods. There were Sun gods and crop gods, gods of love and war, gods in human form and animal form, and several gods that were half-human, half-animal. Sobek, the crocodile god, even had his own pool at Crocodilopolis.

▲ The golden mask of Tutankhamun (about 1370–1352 BC), whose tomb was found in 1922. It contained amazing treasures. There were weapons, chariots, a solid gold coffin, and this gold mask of the handsome teenage pharaoh.

Mummies and monuments

The gods ruled the upper world, where people lived. They were also in charge of the

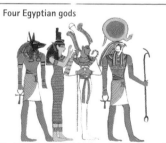

Four Egyptian gods

The falcon-headed Ra (right) was the chief Sun god.

Anubis (left) was the jackal-headed god of tombs.

Osiris and Isis (centre), brother and sister, were once king and queen of all humans. Osiris was killed and went to rule the underworld. Each year Isis' tears of unhappiness flooded the Nile.

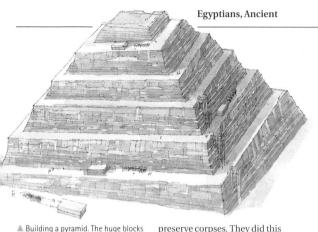

▲ Building a pyramid. The huge blocks of stone arrived by boat. Slaves, working in gangs of about 20, hauled them into position.

underworld, where the dead went. In the underworld people lived the sort of lives they had lived on Earth. A king, for example, went on being a king.

Because they might need their bodies in the underworld, the Egyptians learned how to preserve corpses. They did this by taking out the bits that might rot and drying out the rest. A preserved body is called a '**mummy**'. A person was buried with objects, or pictures of objects, they might need.

Important Egyptians, especially the pharaohs, were buried in magnificent tombs. Some were cut out of solid rock. Other royal tombs were hidden inside enormous stone **pyramids**. It took thousands of slaves, working for years, to build a large pyramid.

▲ A tenth life for an Egyptian cat. This mummified cat was found wrapped in the same shape as a human mummy.

The bearded lady!
All the pharaohs were men except one, a princess named Hatshepsut. She came to power in about 1478 BC and ruled Egypt for 20 years. To show everyone that a female pharaoh was just the same as a male one, she wore a pharaoh's false beard!

◀ The noble Nebamun hunts birds with his throwing stick. This ancient Egyptian tomb painting gives a lot of information about the birds, fishes, boats and clothes of Ancient Egypt.

find out more

Africa
Ancient world
Archaeology
Romans

Electricity

Electricity is a very useful form of energy. You can turn it on at the flick of a switch, and switch it off again when you don't need it.

Electricity can travel along wires from a power station or battery to wherever it is needed. It can power trains, lights, heaters and many kinds of machine.

Electricity and atoms

Electricity is due to **electrons**, one of the tiny particles that make up atoms. Each electron has a very small electric charge. Everything is made of atoms, so there is electricity in everything. But you do not see its effects unless the electrons move from their atoms.

Rubbing can make electrons move. When two different materials rub together, electrons move from one material to the other. An electric charge, called **static electricity**, builds up.

Lightning is caused by static electricity, and so are the crackling sparks you get when you pull a woolly jumper over your head.

When electrons flow along a wire, this is what we call **current electricity**. This is the kind of electricity we get from batteries or from the mains.

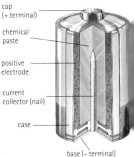

▲ A battery has a positive electrode and a negative electrode, with a chemical (the electrolyte) between them. Electrons flow out of the battery via the negative terminal. In this battery, the negative electrode is mixed with the electrolyte to form a chemical paste.

▼ Electricity travels along wires called power lines from the power station to the places where it is needed. Tall metal pylons hold up the power lines. A transformer steps up (increases) the voltage of the electricity before it leaves the power station. This helps to reduce the amount of energy lost in the wires. Step-down transformers reduce the voltage again so that the electricity can be used in offices and homes.

Generating electricity

Mains electricity is made in power stations by machines called **generators**. These machines turn a coil of wire in a magnetic field, which produces electricity.

Batteries are a useful source of portable electric power. They rely on a chemical reaction to produce electricity. Some kinds of battery, such as the large lead-acid batteries used in cars, can be recharged by connecting them to mains electricity.

Electricity on the move

Batteries and generators push electrons along wires to make the current flow. The amount of current that flows is measured in amperes or amps. Volts are a measure of how hard a battery or generator pushes out electrons. The more volts, the harder the electrons are being pushed.

Some materials let current flow through them. They are called **conductors**. Copper,

Danger!
The electricity that flows out of a mains socket is very dangerous and could kill you.

◀ Electromagnets, like this one at work in a scrap yard, have an iron core which only becomes magnetized when an electric current passes through a coil of wire wrapped around the core.

aluminium and carbon are all conductors. Copper is usually used to make wires. Materials such as rubber and most plastics do not let current flow through them. They are called **insulators**.

In order for electricity to flow, the conductors must form a continuous path, or **circuit**. If the circuit is broken, electricity stops flowing.

Close connection
Michael Faraday, an English scientist, showed how magnets could be used to make electricity. Other scientists had shown that a wire with electricity flowing through it behaved like a magnet. In 1831, Faraday showed that electricity could be made by moving a magnet in and out of a hollow coil of wire. This is basically how generators in power stations make electricity today.

positive (+) terminal

negative (–) terminal

current (flow of electrons)

filament

wire

light bulb

switch

◀ In this electric circuit, the battery pushes a stream of electrons from the negative terminal through the wires to the positive terminal. As the current flows through the filament in the bulb, it makes it hot, and it glows brightly. You can turn the bulb off by using the **switch**. This breaks the circuit by cutting off the electricity.

find out more
Atoms and molecules
Electronics
Energy
Engines and motors
Power stations

Electronics

Electronics is a way of controlling small electric currents to make them do something useful. Televisions, radios, computers and CD players are just a few of the many devices that rely on electronics.

In an electronic device, changing electric currents, called **signals**, are used to carry information. The signals can produce sounds from loudspeakers or pictures on a TV. They can be used to send messages across the world, or to control the flight of an airliner.

Circuits

The different basic parts (the components) of an electronic device are joined together to form an **electronic circuit**.

Different circuits do different jobs. For example, an **amplifier** is a kind of circuit used to make weak electric signals stronger. Computers have another kind of circuit, called an **adder**, which can add two signals together.

The circuits of a modern electronic device are formed on a tiny slice of silicon called a **microchip** or chip. Each chip can contain thousands of electronic components.

Chips are cheap to make and very reliable. They help to make electronic devices smaller, cheaper and more efficient.

▲ Although microchips may be only 1 or 2 millimetres square, they contain thousands of electronic components.

ELECTRONIC COMPONENTS

Electronic circuits are built from a few basic components.

Transistors amplify electric current and are able to switch it on and off.

Diodes only let current pass through in one direction.

Light-emitting diodes (LEDs) give out light when a current passes through.

Resistors restrict the amount of current flowing in a circuit.

Capacitors can store an electric charge.

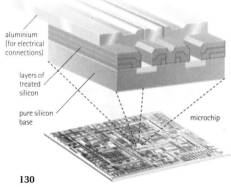

aluminium (for electrical connections)

layers of treated silicon

pure silicon base

microchip

◀ The different components of a microchip, such as transistors, resistors and diodes, are made up of layers of silicon that have been treated in slightly different ways.

find out more
Computers
Electricity

Elements

The Earth, the Universe and everything in it is made up of elements. An element is a basic substance made of just one kind of atom. It cannot be split up into different materials.

Most of the materials we notice around us are **compounds**. Compounds are substances made up of two or more elements. Water is an example of a compound. It is made up of atoms of hydrogen and oxygen.

There are around 90 different elements in nature. In addition, scientists have made more than eleven 'new' elements. These elements do not occur in nature because they are too unstable. Some of them break down after less than a second.

Every one is different

Every element has its own characteristics. They freeze and melt at different temperatures. At normal temperatures, some are **solids**. Others are **liquids**. Still others are **gases**. Some elements, such as carbon and oxygen, react easily with other substances. Other elements, such as helium, do not.

The way an element reacts with other substances depends on the structure of its atoms, especially the way its electrons are arranged.

▲ Drops of the element mercury. Mercury is a metal, but unlike other metals it is a liquid at room temperature. It is extremely poisonous to humans and other animals.

• Atoms are made up of smaller particles called *protons*, *neutrons* and *electrons*. The protons and neutrons are clumped together in a central *nucleus*. The electrons whizz around the nucleus.

◄ The element oxygen is one of the gases in air. Oxygen is necessary to make things burn. Welders burn a mixture of oxygen and other gases in their torches. The torch flame is so hot that it can melt steel. Oxygen is also essential for life. We cannot live unless we have oxygen to breathe.

Periodic patterns

To make it easy to see how the different elements react with each other, the Russian chemist Dimitri Mendeleev arranged all the chemical elements in a pattern. This is called the **periodic table.**

In the periodic table, the elements are arranged according to how many protons they have in their nucleus. The table starts with the lightest element, hydrogen (H), which has only one proton, and ends with Lawrencium (Lr), which has 103.

The elements are arranged in columns, called **groups**: each group has elements with similar properties. The elements in each group are similar because their electrons are arranged in a

similar way. This means they tend to react with other elements in the same way.

The periodic table helps chemists to understand the properties of the different elements, and to guess how they will react with other substances.

Code names

Scientists use letters called **chemical symbols** as a code to name the different elements. Some of the chemical symbols are easy to understand. For example, the chemical symbol for oxygen is 'O'. But others are more difficult to recognize. The chemical symbol for gold, for example, is Au, from the Latin word for gold, *aurum*. The 'code name' or chemical formula for water is H_2O.

find out more

Atoms and molecules
Chemistry
Metals
Solids, liquids and gases

• Diamonds, graphite (the 'lead' in your pencil) and soot all look very different. But they are all made of the same element – carbon. In each of these materials the carbon atoms are arranged differently. This gives them different properties.

▼ The periodic table. The elements are divided into several broad types. Most important are the metals and the non-metals.

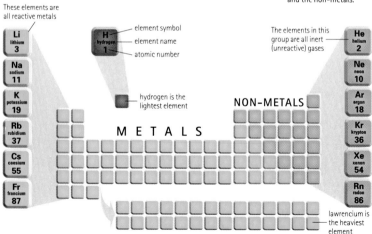

These elements are all reactive metals

Li lithium 3		
Na sodium 11		
K potassium 19		
Rb rubidium 37		
Cs caesium 55		
Fr francium 87		

H hydrogen 1 — element symbol, element name, atomic number

hydrogen is the lightest element

M E T A L S

NON-METALS

The elements in this group are all inert (unreactive) gases

He helium 2
Ne neon 10
Ar argon 18
Kr krypton 36
Xe xenon 54
Rn radon 86

lawrencium is the heaviest element

Elephants

Elephants are the biggest land-living animals. In the past there were many kinds of elephant in most parts of the world. Now there are just two, African elephants and Asian elephants.

African elephants are the bigger of the two. They can be up to 7.5 metres long and weigh up to 7500 kilograms. They live south of the Sahara Desert. African elephants are rarely tamed.

Asian elephants are often trained to move heavy objects for people. Although they are smaller than African elephants, they are still very large. They can

▼ Asian elephants are sometimes trained to take part in processions.

be up to 6.4 metres long and weigh up to 5000 kilograms.

Both kinds of elephant live in **herds**. These herds are led by older females. Each herd stays together for many years.

Big eaters

Elephants eat huge amounts of food – around 150 kilograms of grass, leaves, twigs and fruit each day. They chew this food using grinding teeth in the back of their mouths. Elephants have only four teeth for chewing. Their other two teeth are very big and are called **tusks**.

Elephant alert

Elephants are in danger because people are taking over the land where they live. Many elephants are killed for their ivory tusks.

▲ This young African elephant is using its **trunk** to pull up grass to eat. An elephant's trunk is formed from its upper lip and nose. Elephants use their trunks for breathing, smelling, touching and picking things up.

find out more

Animals
Life on Earth
Mammals

Age of
Empire

About 500 years ago, European countries began conquering lands overseas. These lands became colonies – they were governed by European countries. A country that has a lot of colonies is said to have an empire. By the 19th century many European countries had huge empires. But in the 20th century, these empires broke up.

Spain and Portugal were the first European nations to conquer empires – in South and Central America. The Europeans came looking for wealth, and treated the local people very badly. They shipped hundreds of tonnes of gold and silver back to Europe.

Settlers from Europe migrated to the colonies. They brought in **slaves** from Africa to do the hard work. In the 17th century the same thing happened in North America, where the British, French and Dutch set up

▲ Stolen gold. The Spanish gold mine at Cerro Rico in South America, in the 18th century. The wealth from such mines, worked by unpaid slaves, made Spain the envy of Europe.

colonies. By 1760 Britain was the main power in the region.

▼ This map shows the main European empires.

empires about 1750 in the Americas and about 1900 in the rest of the world

- Belgian
- British
- Danish
- Dutch
- French
- German
- Italian
- Portuguese
- Russian
- Spanish

NORTH AMERICA
EUROPE
ASIA
AFRICA
SOUTH AMERICA
AUSTRALIA

134

Independence for the Americas

Over time the American colonies developed their own way of life. Not surprisingly, the colonies disliked being under European control. In 1775–1783 the North American colonies fought for independence and won. They became the United States of America (USA). Canada and the Caribbean remained in the British empire. In the early 19th century Spain and Portugal's colonies also rebelled, and countries such as Brazil, Mexico and Argentina were formed.

Age of empire

Meanwhile, Europe was collecting colonies elsewhere. Britain claimed Australia and New Zealand, India and Malaya. The French took Indo-China (Cambodia and Vietnam). Russia pushed south into Asia.

Africa suffered most. The Europeans carved up most of the continent. Britain's territory stretched almost from Cairo to Cape Town. Even Germany, a new world power, joined in. The conquerors were very proud of their empires. Sometimes they took lands simply to stop other countries getting them.

▶ Fighting for their homeland. South African Zulu warriors defeated the British at Isandhwlana in 1879. In the end, the Zulus were defeated and almost all their land passed into the hands of the white conquerors.

End of empire

Europeans hoped the colonies would bring great wealth. Some did. British businessmen made fortunes from the mines of South Africa, for example. But colonies were also costly. They required governors and soldiers to control them, and needed huge sums for building roads and railways.

By 1945 Europe's empires were falling apart. Some colonies, such as Australia and Canada, already governed themselves, and other colonial people were crying out for **independence**. Gradually, starting with India in 1947, all Europe's remaining colonies became independent. The change often involved bloodshed. But by 1997, when Britain handed Hong Kong back to China, the age of empire was over.

▲ An Indian soldier in the French colonial army, 1761. Until the middle of the 18th century Britain and France fought bitterly to control India. Britain won and India became the 'jewel in the crown' of the British empire.

find out more

American Revolution
Britain, History of
Exploration, Age of
India and Pakistan
North America
South America
Spain

Energy

Energy is the ability to do work. Without energy nothing would live, move or change. Our bodies and everything we do depends on energy. The Sun is the source of nearly all energy on Earth.

Energy exists in different forms. Heat, light, electricity and chemical energy are all forms of energy. Things that are moving, such as cars and winds have **kinetic energy**. Springs or other stretched or compressed (squashed) materials have **potential energy**. When hot materials cool down they give off heat, or **thermal energy**.

Changing energy

Energy can change from one form to another. For example, when you kick a ball, your muscles change chemical energy from your food into kinetic energy.

Although energy can be changed into different forms, it cannot be made or destroyed. People talk about 'using energy', but in fact energy never gets used up. It just gets passed on in another form. Often the energy ends up as heat.

Energy from fuels

People living in industrialized countries use huge amounts of energy to run their homes, vehicles and factories. More than 80 per cent of this energy

▲ Some types of plastic can be recycled to conserve energy. The plastic waste shown here has been shredded at a recycling plant.

• Energy is measured in units called joules (J). A **joule** is a measure of how much **work** can be done. Power, measured in watts (W), tells us how many joules are being used each second.

▼ The solar-powered car *Sunraycer* has rows of solar cells on the back and sides, which make electricity from sunlight. The electricity charges up the batteries that power the car's motors.

find out more

Conservation
Electricity
Oil
Pollution
Power stations
Sun

comes from burning fuels such as petrol (which comes from oil), coal, and natural gas (**fossil fuels**). Once fossil fuels have been used up, they cannot be replaced.

We use other fuels, too. Fuels made from plant and animal matter, such as wood, are renewable. We can grow more of these. We can also get energy from sources such as the wind, moving water, the Sun and nuclear power. Even so, it is hard to meet all our energy needs.

Conserving energy

One important way to make sure we always have enough energy is to use less energy in the first place. This is known as **energy conservation**. There are many things that you can do to save, or conserve, energy. For example, you can use your bicycle rather than going by car. You can make sure your house is well insulated, so that it doesn't need so much heating to keep it warm. Recycling waste products also saves energy, and saves raw materials too.

Shine on!

The Sun runs on nuclear energy. In the Sun, lots of energy is released when atoms of hydrogen join together, or fuse, to form an atom of helium. Thanks to this fusion reaction the Sun has enough energy stored to keep it shining for another 5000 million years.

◄ How the Sun provides the Earth's energy.

Energy radiated from the Sun.

Green plants use energy from the Sun to produce their own food from water and carbon dioxide.

Animals, including humans, get energy from food. This food may be plants, or animals that feed on plants.

Coal, oil and natural gas are formed from the buried remains of plants and animals that lived millions of years ago.

We burn fossil fuels to get energy for engines, to make electricity and for heating.

137

Engines and motors

Engines are a type of machine. They burn fuel to make heat, then turn the heat into motion. Engines produce the power to drive vehicles and other machines.

The first successful engines were steam engines. Today, internal-combustion and jet engines are more common. Electric motors are also used to power machines, but they are not 'real' engines because they do not produce motion from heat.

Steam engines

In a steam engine the heat from a burning fuel, such as coal, heats water to make steam. The steam pushes on a piston to produce movement – for example, by turning a wheel.

A more modern type of steam engine is a **steam turbine**. In this, steam pushes against a **turbine** – a large fan with many blades – and makes it spin around very fast. Large steam turbines are used in power stations to produce electricity.

▲ Electric cars do not cause pollution while they are running because they do not create exhaust gases. This electric car has a top speed of 100 km per hour and can travel up to 150 km before its batteries run out.

▼ How a petrol engine works. The heavy flywheel helps to keep the crankshaft and piston moving after the power stroke. Most petrol engines have four or more cylinders. The cylinders fire one after another so that power is supplied smoothly to the wheels.

Power stroke
A spark from a spark plug explodes the mixture of petrol and air in the cylinder. The expanding hot gases push the piston down.

Exhaust stroke
The piston moves in again, pushed by the heavy flywheel. As it moves in, the piston pushes the burnt gases out of the cylinder.

Induction stroke
The inlet valve opens as the piston moves down once more. A mixture of petrol and air is sucked into the cylinder.

Compression stroke
Both valves close as the piston moves in, compressing the petrol/air mixture. The cylinder is ready for the next power stroke.

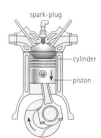

spark-plug

cylinder

piston

outlet valve

crankshaft

flywheel

inlet valve

petrol/air mixture

Internal-combustion engines

The petrol and diesel engines used to power cars, motorcycles, trucks and buses are internal-combustion engines. In an internal-combustion engine the fuel is mixed with air and exploded inside a closed **cylinder**. The force of the explosion pushes out a **piston**. The movement of the piston pushes round a **crankshaft**, which in turn drives the wheels of the vehicle.

Jet engines

Jet engines are very powerful. The biggest ones produce as much power as 500 large car engines. Jet engines need less looking after than internal-combustion engines.

In a basic jet engine, air is sucked in at the front, then compressed and forced into a **combustion chamber**. Fuel is added, and the fuel and air burn. This produces very hot gases, which shoot out of the back, driving the aircraft forward. The gases also turn a turbine, which powers the compressor sucking in air at the front.

find out more

Aircraft
Cars
Power stations
Space exploration
Trains

Rocket engines

Rocket engines burn fuel to produce a jet of gases. The gases shoot backwards through a **nozzle** at the back of the rocket, pushing the rocket forwards.

In all engines, oxygen is needed to make the fuel burn. In most types of engine the oxygen comes from air. But rocket engines have to carry their own oxygen supply with them. This means that they can work in space, where there is no air.

> **James Watt, the father of steam**
> James Watt was born in 1736 in Greenock, Scotland. As a child he became interested in steam power. When he was 28 he began to study existing steam engines, and improving them. By 1775 Watt had produced a more efficient and useful steam engine. Watts' engine was soon taken up for use in many different industries.

● The first jet engine was designed in 1937 by the British engineer Frank Whittle.

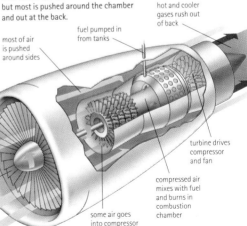

▼ Cutaway of a turbofan jet engine. Most airlines use turbofan engines rather than the basic turbojet, because they are quieter and use less fuel. Turbofans have huge fans at the front to collect air. Some of this air is mixed with fuel in the combustion chamber, but most is pushed around the chamber and out at the back.

hot and cooler gases rush out of back

fuel pumped in from tanks

most of air is pushed around sides

turbine drives compressor and fan

compressed air mixes with fuel and burns in combustion chamber

fan sucks in air

some air goes into compressor

Erosion

All around us, the rocky surface of the Earth is being slowly worn away by water, ice, wind and sun. Tiny pieces of rock are then carried away. This process is called erosion.

The breaking-down of rocks by snow and frost, sun and rain is called **weathering**. Rainwater is a weak acid; it can dissolve or soften some rocks. Trickles of rainwater running over the surface wear the rocks away.

Constant heating and cooling can also break down rocks. Water gets into tiny cracks in the rocks, and when it freezes, it expands, and the cracks widen. Plant roots and burrowing animals can speed up weathering.

New land from old

The rock pieces that have been broken up by weathering are moved away by water and wind. These pieces eventually settle somewhere else. This is called **deposition**. Material carried away by a river, for example, may find its way to the sea. There, over many years, it may form new rock on the sea-bed, or be washed up on the shore to form beaches, and eventually new land.

▲ Erosion by the wind has created these unusual sandstone rock shapes in the Arches National Park, Utah, USA.

Storm force
Erosion is usually a slow process. But during storms, water and wind are much more powerful. They carry bigger fragments of rock and erode the land more quickly. A river in flood can erode more land in a few hours than it would normally do in years.

▼ The pounding action of sea waves has formed a cave in the face of this cliff.

▼ The jagged shape of these rocks is due to ice erosion. Piles of rock fragments (scree) build up around the base.

scree

find out more

Coasts
Ice
Mountains
Rivers
Rocks and minerals

Ethnic groups *see* Human beings • **Etruscans** *see* Ancient world

Europe

Europe is the smallest continent, yet it is the most crowded. It has about one-eighth of all the world's people.

Europe has a huge variety of landscapes for such a small continent. The Mediterranean region has warm, wet winters and hot, dry summers. It is a popular place for holidays.

Northern Europe lies in the cold Arctic region. There are wild mountainous areas in Scandinavia, the Alps and the Balkans. The North European plain stretches from Brittany to Russia. It is mainly flat and provides rich farmland. Long rivers such as the Danube, Rhine and Volga have been important trade routes for centuries.

▼ Kiev, the capital of Ukraine, is built on the banks of the River Dneiper.

EUROPE'S HISTORY

395	Division of Roman Empire into eastern and western parts
about 700	Muslim Moors conquer Spain
1095	First crusade of Christian soldiers to Jerusalem
1347–1351	Millions die in Black Death
1400s	Renaissance of art and science starts in Italy
1492	Columbus sails to the Americas
1517–1648	Religious conflict between Roman Catholics and Protestants
1700s	Industrial Revolution
1789	French Revolution
1890s	Europe's empires rule 80% of the world
1914–1918	First World War
1939–1945	Second World War

find out more

Black Death
Byzantine empire
Empire, Age of
Exploration, Age of
France
French Revolution
Germany
Greeks, ancient
Industrial Revolution
Ireland, Republic of
Italy
Middle Ages
Reformation
Renaissance
Romans
Russia
Spain
United Kingdom
World War I
World War II

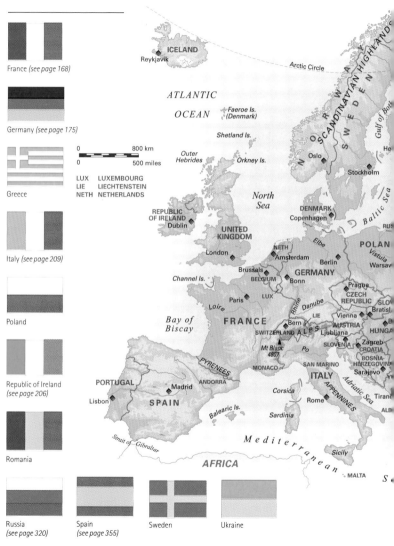

France *(see page 168)*

Germany *(see page 175)*

Greece

Italy *(see page 209)*

Poland

Republic of Ireland
(see page 206)

Romania

Russia
(see page 320)

Spain
(see page 355)

Sweden

Ukraine

0   800 km
0   500 miles

LUX   LUXEMBOURG
LIE   LIECHTENSTEIN
NETH NETHERLANDS

ICELAND
Reykjavik

Arctic Circle

ATLANTIC
OCEAN

Faeroe Is.
(Denmark)

Shetland Is.

Outer
Hebrides

Orkney Is.

Oslo

Stockholm

NORWAY

SWEDEN

SCANDINAVIAN HIGHLANDS

Gulf of Both

He

North
Sea

DENMARK
Copenhagen

Baltic Sea

REPUBLIC
OF IRELAND
Dublin

UNITED
KINGDOM

London

NETH
Amsterdam

Brussels
BELGIUM

Elbe

Berlin

GERMANY
Bonn

POLAND

Vistula

Warsaw

RU

Channel Is.

Paris

LUX

Loire

Rhine

Danube

Prague

CZECH
REPUBLIC

SLO

Bratisl

Bay of
Biscay

FRANCE

LIE

SWITZERLAND

Bern

ALPS

Vienna

AUSTRIA

HUNGA

Mt Blanc
4807

Po

Ljubljana

SLOVENIA

Zagreb

CROATIA

B

MONACO

SAN MARINO

BOSNIA-
HERZEGOVIN

Sarajevo

Y

PYRENEES

PORTUGAL

Madrid

ANDORRA

ITALY

APPENNINES

Adriatic Sea

Tirane

Lisbon

SPAIN

Corsica

Rome

ALB

Balearic Is.

Strait of Gibraltar

Sardinia

Mediterranean

AFRICA

Sicily

MALTA

S

142

European Union

In 1957 six countries – Belgium, France, West Germany, Italy, Luxembourg and the Netherlands – signed the Treaty of Rome to form the European Economic Community. By 1995 the Community had grown into a European Union of 15 countries. These countries have agreed to make it easier to trade across national boundaries. They help one another to develop and try to create common laws. In 1999 11 members participated in the launch of a common currency, the euro.

• There is no clear boundary between Europe and Asia. But the Ural Mountains in Russia are a convenient place to draw a line on the map.

Barents Sea

White Sea

North Dvina

URAL MOUNTAINS

RUSSIA

(RUSSIAN FEDERATION)

Lake Ladoga

Moscow

Volga

ASIA

Minsk

ELARUS

Kiev

Dnieper

Caspian Sea

UKRAINE

MOLDOVA

Chişinău

Mt Elbrus 5642

CAUCASUS

GEORGIA

Tbilisi

ATHIANS

IA

arest

Black Sea

Danube

BULGARIA

Sofia

NIA

ASIA

Aegean Sea

Nicosia

CYPRUS

Crete

	country boundary
◆	capital city
ᔕᔕᔕ	ice cap
▲	highest peaks (height in metres)

land height in metres

2000
1000
500
200
sea level — land below sea level

United Kingdom
(see page 381)

Yugoslavia

143

Evolution

Evolution is the process by which new kinds of living things come into being. It happens through lots of very small changes over a long period of time.

Fossils found in ancient rocks show us that over millions of years many new kinds of living things have appeared. At the same time some kinds of living things have become **extinct**, which means they have died out.

Natural selection

In the 19th century, the biologists Charles **Darwin** and Alfred Russel Wallace presented the theory of natural selection, or **survival of the fittest**, to show how evolution takes place.

This theory says that those animals or plants that are best suited to the conditions they are living in are the most likely to survive and to produce young. In turn their young inherit the special characteristics that helped to make their parents fit, and go on to pass them on to their own young.

After a few generations, the **species** gradually changes to include more characteristics of the 'fit' members. This gradual change can eventually lead to the development of a new species.

Darwin's theory angered many people because they thought it went against the idea that God created all living things. Although some people still believe this, most now think that Darwin's theory is right.

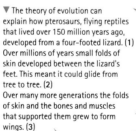

▲ Charles Darwin published his theories in his book *The Origin of Species*.

find out more

Animals
Dinosaurs
Fossils
Genetics
Life on Earth

▼ The theory of evolution can explain how pterosaurs, flying reptiles that lived over 150 million years ago, developed from a four-footed lizard. (1) Over millions of years small folds of skin developed between the lizard's feet. This meant it could glide from tree to tree. (2) Over many more generations the folds of skin and the bones and muscles that supported them grew to form wings. (3)

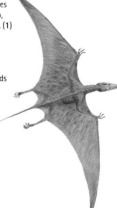

Age of Exploration

Until about 500 years ago, people living in different parts of the world knew very little, if anything, about each other. Map-makers understood the Earth's geography only vaguely. During the Age of Exploration, Europeans travelled right around the world. They got to know its different lands and peoples for the first time.

▲ Christopher Columbus (1451–1506).

Europe and Asia had traded since ancient times. But goods were passed from merchant to merchant, and no one made the whole journey. **Marco Polo**, who travelled from Italy to China and back in the 13th century, was an exception. Not long afterwards the Arab explorer **Ibn Batuta** journeyed from Egypt through much of the Middle East and on to eastern India. And in the 15th century, the remarkable Chinese explorer **Cheng Ho** sailed to Persia, Arabia and down the coast of Africa.

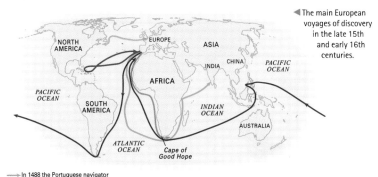

◄ The main European voyages of discovery in the late 15th and early 16th centuries.

→ In 1488 the Portuguese navigator Bartolomeu Dias sailed round the southern tip of Africa.

→ In 1492 Christopher Columbus sailed to the West Indies. He thought they were part of Asia. He made three more voyages but still did not believe he had found a new continent.

→ In 1497 John Cabot, an Italian navigator working for the king of England, reached North America.

→ From 1497 to 1499 Vasco da Gama sailed all the way to India.

→ In 1519 Ferdinand Magellan, a Portuguese navigator working for the king of Spain, set off to find a western route to Asia. He was killed in the Philippines, but Elcano took over and returned to Spain in 1522 with one ship – the first to sail right round the world.

Eyes *see* Senses • **Factories** *see* Industry

India and beyond

At the same time, the Portuguese tried to find a sea route round Africa to India. In 1488 **Bartholomeu Dias** reached the Cape of Good Hope. Ten years later **Vasco da Gama** continued across the ocean to India. Before long, Portuguese sailors had pressed on to China and Japan. But it was another 100 years before a Dutch sailor, **Abel Tasman**, sailed to New Zealand and Australia.

America

Although the **Vikings** reached North America 1000 years ago, their voyages were forgotten. Then, in 1492, **Christopher Columbus** sailed across the Atlantic looking for a way to China. Instead, he reached the West Indies. The newly discovered continent was

named after Amerigo Vespucci, who explored South America.

French, Dutch and British explorers tried to sail round North America. They failed because this **North-west Passage** is frozen solid. Sailors seeking the North-east Passage, round Asia, were also unsuccessful. Despite its failures, a great deal was learned during the Age of Exploration. By 1650, the world was far less strange and frightening than it had been 200 years earlier.

Later exploration

The Age of Exploration produced a rough outline of the continents. The details were filled in over the next 250 years. **James Cook** mapped the Pacific Ocean. Lewis and Clarke crossed the American continent. Mungo Park, David Livingstone, Henry Stanley and others explored Africa's mysterious interior. Finally, in the 20th century, explorers reached the North and South Poles.

▲ The British naval captain James Cook (1728-1779). Cook explored the Pacific Ocean. On one of his voyages he claimed New Zealand and Australia for Britain.

find out more

Empire, Age of
Pirates

▼ The fleet of the Dutch navigator William Barents. Barents was one of the first explorers to try and find the North-west Passage round North America. He made three unsuccessful voyages, and died at sea while returning from the third in 1597.

Families

A family is a group of people who belong together. They are usually related by birth and marriage, but not always. Your immediate family is your parents, brothers and sisters. Your wider family includes your grandparents, aunts, uncles and cousins.

In some parts of the world **extended families** live together. An extended family can include grandparents, parents, children, aunts, uncles and cousins.

Some people live in **nuclear families**. This means one or two parents and a child or children. The parents may be married to each other, but they may not be. If there is only a mother or a father, the family is known as a **one-parent** family.

Sometimes parents separate or get divorced. If one of the parents takes a new partner or remarries, the new person becomes a **step-parent** to the children. If the step-parent has children of their own, the children of the new family are called **step-brothers** and **step-sisters**.

Fostering and adoption

If a child's parents are unable to look after him or her properly, the child may go to live with a **foster family**. This may be just for a short time or it may be till the child grows up. **Adoption** is when a child goes to live with a new family permanently, and takes the surname of that family.

▲ These pictures show a grandmother, mother and daughter of the same birth family. You can see that they look like each other.

find out more

Children
Genetics

▼ A family tree shows you how different members of a family are related to each other. It is divided into different 'generations' – in each generation people are about the same age.

Famine *see* Food

Farm animals

Farm animals are domestic animals. This means that they are tame and that they breed happily in captivity. Some farm animals, such as pigs and chickens, are reared for food only. Others are used to help with the work around the farm. Pets are also domestic animals.

All domestic animals were originally bred – over hundreds of years – from wild animals. People first began to breed animals about 9000 years ago, in western Asia. The first animals to be tamed were goats, sheep, pigs and cattle. Over the next few thousand years, horses, donkeys, dogs, camels and, in South America, llamas followed.

Cattle

Cattle are large plant-eating animals. They include cows, oxen, buffaloes and bison. Most farm cattle are descended from the aurochs, which once roamed wild across Europe.

There are about 200 different breeds of cattle on farms today. Most cattle are raised for milk, meat and leather. But some are also used for pulling ploughs and heavy loads. And cattle droppings are a useful source of fertilizer, and even fuel.

Sheep and goats

Sheep and goats are related to cattle. They are now very rare in the wild, but many different kinds are used in farming. Sheep and goats are sturdy animals, and excellent climbers.

▲ In parts of the world that are very dry, people have to move their herds from place to place to find fresh grass. These people are known as nomadic pastoralists. This woman belongs to the nomadic Masai people of East Africa. The Masai depend almost entirely on meat, milk and blood from their cattle.

• Pets are tame animals that we keep just for company. Cats and dogs, fishes, guinea pigs and hamsters are common pets. All pets need to be looked after properly, for instance given proper food and exercise, and kept clean.

◀ Cattle bred on farms, such as the Friesian (top), look quite different from wild cattle, such as the gaur of South-east Asia (bottom).

Clean as a pig?
In spite of their reputation for being dirty, pigs are really quite clean animals. They do sometimes wallow in mud, but that is probably to keep their skin cool.

People started to keep sheep for their thick coat of fine wool (fleece). But they are also raised for meat. Sheep can graze on grasslands that are too steep and dry for other animals. Dogs may help to round them up, and to protect them from wild animals such as wolves and eagles.

Goats are usually kept in herds. They are useful for their milk, meat and skins. The coats of angora and Kashmir (cashmere) goats are used to make wool.

Pigs

▲ The European wild boar is the ancestor of the farm pig.

Pigs have short legs, heavy bodies and a snout for a nose. They feed on grasses and small plants, and often use their long snouts to dig up roots. People keep them for their skin and meat. Pigs are often fed on farm scraps, such as meat, corn and grain.

▶ Some people think that the conditions in which farm animals are often kept are cruel. Some animals, such as these pregnant sows, spend most of the year inside, unable to move around. This form of intensive farming was banned in the European Union in 1998.

▲ The mouflon from southern Europe and south-west Asia is the smallest of the wild sheep. It was domesticated about 9000 years ago, and is the ancestor of domestic sheep.

Chickens

Chickens are found on farms in many regions of the world. They are kept for meat and eggs. In western Europe and North America large numbers of chickens are sometimes kept indoors in row upon row of small cages, called batteries. This is a form of **intensive farming**, in which farmers organize their animals to get the maximum food from them.

find out more

Animals
Cats
Dogs
Early people
Elephants
Farming
Food
Grasslands
Horses

▲ Many different kinds of bird have been domesticated. This picture shows a turkey (1), a Chinese goose (2), a rooster (3), an Indian runner duck (4), a hen (5) and a Rouen duck (6).

Farming

Farming is the process of growing crops and raising animals to provide food and other products that people use, for example cotton and leather. People first began to farm about 10,000 years ago and most of the people who have ever lived have been farmers. Even today, more people work in farming than in any other industry.

Almost all humans rely on farming to produce the food they eat. Types of farming vary widely around the world. Different crops grow well in different climates and types of landscape.

Growing crops

The most commonly grown crops are **cereals** – a type of grass. Cereal seeds are very rich in carbohydrates, which are filling and give the body energy. Cereals such as rice, wheat and maize are the main food source for most people around the world. Cereals can be made into many different kinds of food.

Wheat is mainly eaten as bread, but it can also be made into pasta. The USA, Argentina, Australia and the Ukraine are the world's biggest wheat producers. Farming in these countries is mostly intensive.

In **intensive farming** the heavy use of machines, **fertilizers**, **pesticides** and **herbicides** means farmers can produce much more grain from the same piece of land than they would do using simpler methods.

▲ Rice is grown in water. Over half the people in the world eat rice as their staple (main) food.

• Recently scientists have begun to develop **genetically modified** (GM) crops. This means that the genetic make-up of these crops has been changed, for example so that they resist certain herbicides. Many people are opposed to GM crops. They think that these crops might have a harmful effect on the environment.

◀ Farmers in Kenya ploughing with oxen. Farmers everywhere plough the land to bury weeds and break up the earth ready for planting seeds. In developed countries ploughing is done by tractor.

Mixed farming

Mixed farming involves both growing crops and rearing **livestock** (animals). The main areas of mixed farming are parts of the USA and Europe. These farmers grow wheat for people to eat, and **fodder crops** (crops to feed animals), for example maize, oats and hay.

Mediterranean farming

Mediterranean farming is found in areas where winters are mild and wet and summers are long and dry. Crops grow in winter as well as in summer. Winter crops include wheat and barley, and summer crops include peaches, citrus fruits, tomatoes, grapes and olives.

Shifting cultivation

Shifting cultivation is a common type of farming in many tropical countries. In shifting cultivation, farmers grow crops in one place for only as long as the soil allows the crops to grow well. After a year or so they move on, and leave the land to return to its natural state. Common crops are maize, rice, manioc, yams and millet.

Organic farming

There are problems with some modern farming methods. Fertilizers and pesticides can cause pollution and harm plants and animals. Traces of chemicals may be left in our food.

Some farmers farm without chemicals (organically). They fertilize their land with compost and manure, and they use other plants to control insect pests.

▲ Sprinkler systems create vast circular areas of irrigated farmland in Colorado, USA. Without such irrigation much of this land would be too dry to support crops.

find out more

Early people
Farm animals
Food
Grasslands

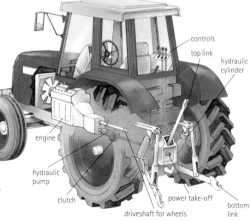

▶ A cutaway of a tractor, showing how power from the engine is used to drive a separate power take-off (orange) and hydraulic system (green). The power take-off can be used to power any attachment on the back of the tractor. The hydraulic system lifts or lowers the attachment.

controls
top link
hydraulic cylinder
engine
hydraulic pump
clutch
power take-off
bottom link
driveshaft for wheels

Films

Films, or movies, are moving pictures that tell a story. The first films were made only about a hundred years ago, but today films are a popular source of entertainment and an important art form. Some film actors and actresses have become stars, their names and faces known all over the world.

The first films to be made were very short. But soon people began to produce longer films as entertainment, called **feature films.** Cinemas opened around the world and many countries developed their own film industries. **Hollywood** in California, USA, quickly became and has remained the most important film-making centre in the world.

▲ Charlie **Chaplin** (1889–1977) was the most famous comedian of silent films. He often played a little tramp, who was bullied but who managed to win through in the end. Here he is in *The Gold Rush* (1925), one of his most popular films.

• The age of cinema began in 1895, when the **Lumière** brothers held the first public film screening in a Paris café.

• India has the world's biggest film industry. It makes about 900 films every year. The USA makes about 250. The Indian film industry is based in Mumbai (Bombay), and is known as 'Bollywood'.

1 director
2 actors
3 **camera crew:** includes the camera operator, the clapper loader, the focus puller and the grips, who move the camera during shots
4 **cinematographer:** controls the lighting, camera movement and framing of shots
5 sound team
6 lighting team
7 **continuity assistant:** checks that the details in each scene are correct
8 actors are carefully dressed and made-up
9 **editor:** puts together the shots that form the final film
10 **sound mixer:** mixes the dialogue, the background sound and the music (soundtrack) into a single track

◀ Making a film.

The 'golden age' of cinema

Early films had no sound, although musicians often provided a live accompaniment. The first major sound film was *The Jazz Singer* in 1927. This was the beginning of a 'golden age' of Hollywood films, which lasted until the 1950s.

By the 1930s millions of people were going to the cinema, often several times a week. Huge film studios turned out more and more new films. People often went to see films because their favourite stars were playing the leading roles.

Certain kinds of film proved especially successful and popular. These included comedies, romances, westerns, horror movies, and science fiction and action movies.

It was the age of 'classic' films such as *Gone With The Wind* (1939), *The Wizard of Oz* (1939), *Citizen Kane* (1941) and *Casablanca* (1942). Popular stars included Humphrey Bogart, Clark Gable, Cary Grant, Greta Garbo and Ingrid Bergman.

▶ *Gone With the Wind* (1939), starring Vivien Leigh and Clark Gable, won 10 Oscars and topped the box-office charts for 25 years.

Films in the age of television

The arrival of television in the 1950s meant that fewer people went to the cinema. Film-makers had to invent new ways of attracting audiences. With the arrival of the **wide screen**, film-makers started to make more spectacular films, such as *Ben Hur* (1959), with extravagant sets, and often a cast of thousands. In the 1970s directors introduced spectacular **special effects**. Films such as *Jaws* (1975) and *Star Wars* (1976) attracted a new, younger audience into cinemas.

Cinema audiences did begin to rise again in the 1990s. Blockbusters such as *Jurassic Park* (1993) drew audiences with action-packed storylines and ever more thrilling special effects.

Today most people watch films on **video** rather than at the cinema. And soon digital video on CD-ROM will make it possible for viewers to join in with the action!

◀ *Titanic* (1997), starring Leonardo DiCaprio and Kate Winslet, is the most expensive film ever made. With its huge cast and amazing special effects, it cost over £200 million to make. It has also taken more money than any other film at the box office.

find out more

Cartoons and animation
Drama
Photography

Fishes

Fishes are cold-blooded animals with backbones and fins. They all live in water and breathe using gills. They can be found in the sea and also in ponds, lakes and rivers.

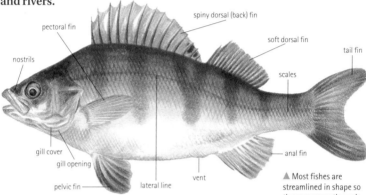

- spiny dorsal (back) fin
- pectoral fin
- soft dorsal fin
- nostrils
- tail fin
- scales
- gill cover
- gill opening
- anal fin
- pelvic fin
- lateral line
- vent

▲ Most fishes are streamlined in shape so they can move through the water easily.

When they swim, most fishes use powerful zigzag muscles to move their bodies from side to side. They use their fins mainly for balancing and slowing down.

Most fishes also have a **swim bladder** inside them. This gas-filled bag keeps them from sinking in the water even when they are still. They breathe by passing water over their **gills**. Oxygen dissolved in the water passes through the gills into the fish's blood.

Female fishes generally lay huge numbers of eggs. When they hatch, the young usually have to look after themselves.

Fish senses

Like people, fishes can see, hear, touch, smell and taste. Many fishes can see colours. Most have eyes on the sides of their heads to give them all-around vision.

Many fishes make noises to communicate with each other. Fishes' ears are inside their skulls. Their ears also help fishes to balance.

Fishes use organs called **lateral lines** to sense the nearness of enemies or prey. These are a series of nerve endings just below the skin which are sensitive to changes in water pressure. Some fishes

FISHY FACTS

Largest fish: whale sharks can be up to 18 m long and weigh over 40 tonnes

Smallest fish: Pygmy gobies are about 11 mm long, and weigh 4–5 mg

Fastest fish: cosmopolitan sailfish can swim at a speed of 109 km/h

also have 'whiskers', called **barbels,** around their mouths. They use these to explore the sea- or river-bed.

Most fishes have a good sense of smell. They use smell to find their prey. Fishes' sense of taste is related to their sense of smell. Some fishes have lots of taste buds in and around their mouths.

Fish food

Fishes living in rivers and ponds eat all sorts of food. These can include water plants, snails, worms, insects and their larvae, and even other fishes.

In the open sea, where there are no rooted plants, most fishes are **carnivores.** This means they eat other animals such as shrimp, squids and other fishes.

Others feed on very tiny animals, called plankton. They

catch these by taking in mouthfuls of water and pushing it out over combs attached to their gills. The plankton get caught in the combs.

Sharks, skates and rays

Sharks, skates and rays form a special group of fishes. Their skeletons are made of cartilage rather than of bone. Cartilage is the bendy material found in your nose and ears. Some sharks feed by filtering sea water for plankton, but others are powerful hunters. Rays and skates are flat-bodied fishes that live close to the sea-bed.

▲ A lion fish hunting cardinal fishes. Cardinal fishes, like many kinds of fish, live in groups called schools. Fishes in a school behave as a single unit. When they are threatened, they swim close together and twist and turn like a single fish.

▼ These are just a few of the 21,000 different kinds of fish in the world.

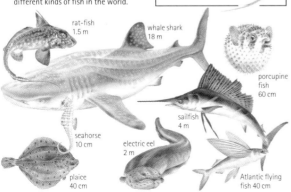

rat-fish
1.5 m

whale shark
18 m

porcupine fish
60 cm

sailfish
4 m

seahorse
10 cm

electric eel
2 m

plaice
40 cm

Atlantic flying fish 40 cm

find out more

Animals
Oceans and seas
Rivers

Fishing

Fishing – or angling – is the most popular sport of all in some countries, including the UK and the USA. But most people who fish catch fish for food – either to feed themselves or to sell for profit.

Millions of people around the world are employed catching, processing and selling fish.

Industrial fishing

Industrial fishing includes inshore fishing and deep-sea fishing. **Inshore fishing** boats stay near the coast and catch fish using rods and lines or small nets. They sail and return the same day.

But most of the world's fish catch comes from the deep oceans. Large **deep-sea fishing** ships can stay at sea for months.

In some oceans fishing fleets have caught too many fish. Stocks are very low, and not enough fish are left to breed.

Sports fishing

There are three main kinds of sports fishing. **Coarse fishing** is the most popular. You use a simple rod, a reel and line, hooks, weights, floats and **bait** (food to lure the fish). **Sea angling** is similar to coarse fishing, except that you catch fish from the sea.

Game fishing, or fly-fishing, involves catching edible fish, such as salmon or trout. The angler's hooks are often dressed (disguised) as artificial flies to attract the fish.

▶ Purse-seining, trawling and drift-netting are the three main types of industrial fishing. In purse-seining, the boat first encircles a shoal with the net (**1, 2**) and then closes the bottom of the net to trap the fish (**3**).

▲ In fly fishing, the fisher propels the line forward to land gently on the water. Tinsel, wool, fur and feathers can be used to dress the flies.

• In fish 'farms', lakes, rivers and parts of the coast are stocked with fish which are kept in cages or released to be caught and eaten.

find out more

Conservation
Fishes
Oceans and seas
Sports and games

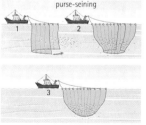

purse-seining

trawling

drift netting

Flowers and fruits

We have all seen flowers in parks and gardens, and eaten fruits such as apples and bananas. But flowers are not just there to look pretty, and fruits do not just grow so that we can eat them.

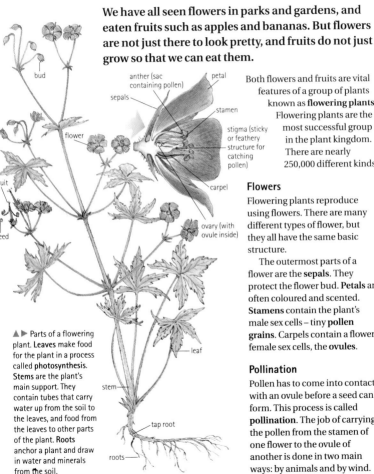

bud

anther (sac containing pollen)

petal

sepals

stamen

flower

stigma (sticky or feathery structure for catching pollen)

carpel

fruit

seed

ovary (with ovule inside)

leaf

stem

tap root

roots

▲ ▶ Parts of a flowering plant. **Leaves** make food for the plant in a process called **photosynthesis**. **Stems** are the plant's main support. They contain tubes that carry water up from the soil to the leaves, and food from the leaves to other parts of the plant. **Roots** anchor a plant and draw in water and minerals from the soil.

Both flowers and fruits are vital features of a group of plants known as **flowering plants**. Flowering plants are the most successful group in the plant kingdom. There are nearly 250,000 different kinds.

Flowers

Flowering plants reproduce using flowers. There are many different types of flower, but they all have the same basic structure.

The outermost parts of a flower are the **sepals**. They protect the flower bud. **Petals** are often coloured and scented. **Stamens** contain the plant's male sex cells – tiny **pollen grains**. Carpels contain a flower's female sex cells, the **ovules**.

Pollination

Pollen has to come into contact with an ovule before a seed can form. This process is called **pollination**. The job of carrying the pollen from the stamen of one flower to the ovule of another is done in two main ways: by animals and by wind.

Flowers and fruits

◀ Wild flowers in the Namaqaland Hills, Cape Province, South Africa. This small region probably has more variety of flower species than anywhere else in the world.

Insects are the most common **animal pollinators**, especially bees and butterflies. They come in search of nectar, a sweet, sugary liquid in flowers. While the insect is visiting the flower, pollen grains stick to its body, and so the insect carries the pollen to the next flower it visits. **Wind-pollinated flowers** have small, light pollen that blows in the wind.

Once a pollen grain has reached another flower of the same kind, it grows down into the carpel and joins up with the ovule inside. Here the two cells combine. This is **fertilization**. The fertilized ovule develops into a **seed**, and the ovary swells to form a fruit.

Fruits

The fruit encloses and protects the seeds as they grow, and helps to spread them when they are ripe. Different kinds of fruit spread their seeds in different ways. Fruits we eat, like apples and bananas, are called 'soft fruits'. Other fruits form dry or papery containers round the seeds. These are 'dry fruits'.

Animals spread the seeds of some fruits. They eat the flesh of soft fruits, and drop the seeds. Fruits that are sticky or have tiny hooks ('burs') hitch rides on an animal's fur or feathers.

Many plants use the wind to spread their seeds. To help this, sycamore, maple and ash all have winged fruits, while the fruits of dandelions and thistles have parachutes of hairs.

Smallest and tallest

The smallest type of flowering plant is the least duckweed, a tiny water plant scarcely 1 mm across. The tallest flowering plants are trees, which can grow to 100 m.

▲ A honeybee on a swamp rose. As the bee searches for nectar, pollen gets stuck to its body. It then carries this pollen to the next flower it visits.

• Grasses are the most successful flowering plants. They survive because they grow quickly and produce many seeds.

▼ Some types of fruit.

Pea pods are dry fruits. They split to release their seeds.

Oranges are a soft fruit.

Winged fruits like this field maple spread by flying.

Strawberries are 'false fruits'. The fleshy part is actually a swollen stem.

find out more
Insects
Plants
Trees

Food

Everything the body does needs energy. Energy keeps your body warm, your heart beating and your lungs working. Food supplies your body with energy. Food also gives your body the materials it needs to grow and to stay healthy.

The substances the body gets from the food you eat are called **nutrients**. There are five types of nutrient: carbohydrates, fats, proteins, vitamins and minerals.

Types of food

Carbohydrates are our main source of energy. They are found in sugary foods such as honey, and in starchy foods such as bread, potatoes and rice. **Fats** are even more energy-rich. Fatty foods include butter and cream, and plant oils such as olive oil and sunflower oil.

You need **proteins** to help your body replace damaged and worn-out parts. Everyone needs plenty of protein because bodies are rebuilding themselves all the time. Meat, fish, milk, eggs, nuts and beans are high in protein.

Vitamins and **minerals** are nutrients that are essential for staying healthy, although you only need to eat small amounts of them. Vitamins take part in many important chemical changes in the body, while you need minerals such as iron and calcium for healthy blood, bones and teeth.

▼ This diagram shows the kinds of foods that make up a healthy diet. It is shaped like a pyramid because you should eat a lot of the foods at the bottom of the pyramid and just a little of the foods at the top.

▲ Bread is a basic (staple) food in many parts of the world. The ingredients of bread are flour and water, and it can be either unleavened (flat) – like pitta bread and tortillas – or leavened (risen). Leavened bread is made with yeast. This bread is from the world-famous Poilâne bakery in Paris, France.

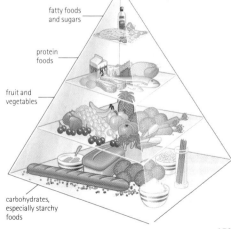

fatty foods and sugars

protein foods

fruit and vegetables

carbohydrates, especially starchy foods

Diets

The range of foods that you eat most of the time is called your diet. A healthy diet is one that provides the right nutrients in the right amounts. A **balanced diet** includes plenty of cereals – such as rice, bread and pasta – and fruit and vegetables. A diet that is mostly made up of fatty and sweet foods – such as chips, crisps and soft drinks – is unbalanced. People who eat this way are more likely to be unhealthy and overweight. If you are very overweight, you are obese. Obesity can lead to heart disease, high blood pressure, diabetes and certain cancers.

People's diets vary from country to country. The people who live around the Mediterranean Sea eat a lot of starchy food such as pasta, plenty of fruit and vegetables, olive oil and a little fish. The people of Japan and China eat a lot of vegetables and cereals, especially rice. These diets are often healthier than those in northern Europe and North America.

▲ This Japanese meal includes rice, raw vegetables and seafood in batter, which will be dipped into the sauces to add flavour.

Cooking

Almost all food can be eaten without any cooking at all. Most people eat raw fruit, and raw vegetables in salads, and the Japanese particularly like raw fish. However, some foods are much softer and easier

• Fruit and vegetables, wholemeal bread and pasta, brown rice, peas and beans all contain lots of fibre. Fibre is not a nutrient but it is important because it helps the body to get rid of waste products.

▼ Some different cooking methods.

boiling

steaming

frying

baking

grilling

microwaving

to chew if they have been cooked, and they may be easier to digest, too. Cooking can also destroy harmful bacteria that might cause food poisoning.

Cooking methods include **boiling** or **steaming**, **frying**, **grilling**, and **baking** or **roasting**. The leaves and flowers of some plants, such as parsley and ginger (**herbs** and **spices**), are added to food during cooking to give it more flavour.

Food processing

Food may just be washed, trimmed and packed before being sold, or it may be processed to turn it into ready-made dishes such as cakes and casseroles.

Foods are also processed so that they stay fresh and do not spoil. This can be done in many ways. **Drying** can preserve foods, as can **pickling** (soaking the food in vinegar). Certain chemicals known as **preservatives** can also help to keep food fresh for longer. **Canning** and **bottling** use heat treatment to kill bacteria. The food is then packed without any air and can be kept for years. Food can also be chilled or **frozen** to preserve it.

▶ When a large number of people are starving, we say there is a famine. This young boy has arrived at a famine relief centre in Somalia.

Feeding the world

More than half the world's population suffers from **malnutrition** – they do not get the nutrients they need. Most of these people live in poorer countries and do not get enough to eat. But some people in Western countries suffer from malnutrition because they eat too much of the wrong kinds of food.

About one tenth of the people of the world suffer from **hunger**. Many of these are children and young people. Every year about 15 million children die of starvation and related causes.

• Additives are natural or artificial substances that are added to food in small amounts. Some are used to keep the food fresh and make it last longer. Others are used to improve the flavour or appearance of the food.

• Water is as important to the body as any food. You can live without food for a week or more, but water is necessary every day. Most people need about 2 litres of water a day.

find out more

Digestion
Farming
Health and fitness
Human beings

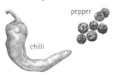

◀ Some popular spices.

nutmeg

ginger

pepper

chilli

cloves

mace

Food chains and webs *see* Ecology

Football

You can find people playing football (soccer) everywhere, from streets and beaches to giant football stadiums. It is the most popular game in the world.

There are several kinds of football, but soccer (association football) is the most popular. Other popular types of football are American football and rugby. These games use an oval ball rather than a round one, and players are allowed to handle the ball.

goal line
halfway line
goal area
centre circle
penalty spot
touch line
penalty area

▲ A soccer pitch.

Soccer

A professional football match is played between two teams of 11 players. The aim is to score goals by kicking or heading the ball into the opponents' goal. Players move up the field by passing or running with the ball (called dribbling). Players may use any part of their body, except hands and arms, to play the ball. Only the goalkeepers are allowed to handle the ball, and then only when they are in their own penalty area.

▶ American football is the national winter sport of the USA. The climax of the season is the Super Bowl, when the two top teams of the National Football League meet.

find out more

Sports and games
See also Sports facts, page 428

▼Germany (in white) face Bulgaria in the 1994 soccer World Cup. The tournament was eventually won by Brazil, world champions for a record fourth time.

Football competitions
World Cup The most important international competition in football. It takes place every four years.
League championship The club champions of each country are decided in this way. Teams get points for a win or a draw. The team with the most points at the end of the season wins the championship.
Knockout competitions Many countries have national knockout competitions. The oldest is the English FA (Football Association) Cup.

Forces

Forces are pushes or pulls. A force can make a still object move. It can make a moving object travel faster or more slowly, or change its direction. Together two or more forces can make something stretch, squash, bend, twist, turn or change its shape.

There are five types of force: gravity, electricity, magnetism and two kinds of nuclear force. But scientists have found that some forces, such as electricity and magnetism, are closely related.

Basic forces

Gravity is a force of attraction. It tries to pull things together. The heavier two objects are, and the closer they are, the stronger the gravitational pull between them. Gravity is the force that holds everything on the Earth.

Electricity and **magnetism** are closely related forces. You can see the effects of an electric force if you pull a comb though your hair and then hold it close to some tiny pieces of paper. You can feel a magnetic force if you hold a magnet close to a piece of iron or steel.

Nuclear forces are the forces that hold the nuclei of atoms together. There is a lot of energy locked up in an atom's nucleus. Nuclear power stations release some of this energy to produce electricity.

Other forces

Friction is a force that tries to stop one material sliding over another. Friction

▲ This climber is clinging to a nearly vertical rock face. Only the force of friction between her fingers and toes and the rock face keeps her from falling.

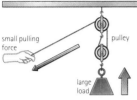

small pulling force

pulley

large load

▲ Machines like pulleys take advantage of forces to make work easier. Pulleys work by changing a small force into a large one. They also change the direction of the force so that you can pull downwards, rather than up. This makes lifting much easier.

find out more
Energy
Physics
Scientific Revolution
Space exploration

Getting moving

You need to apply a force to get an object moving. If it is already moving, a force can make the object move faster or slower, or change its direction. The greater the force, the greater the change in movement. **Acceleration** and **deceleration** are measures of how quickly an object's speed increases or decreases.

Once an object is moving, it has **momentum**. It will keep moving until another force causes it to slow down or stop.

• Scientists measure forces in newtons (N). Pressure tells you how concentrated a force is. Pressure is measured in newtons per square metre (N/m^2).

between your shoes and the floor stops you from slipping over. Air resistance is friction between the air and a moving object. Cars and planes need to minimize air resistance, but parachutists rely on it to get them safely to Earth.

If you stretch a rubber band, you can feel the force of **tension**. When you squash something, you are exerting a force of **compression**.

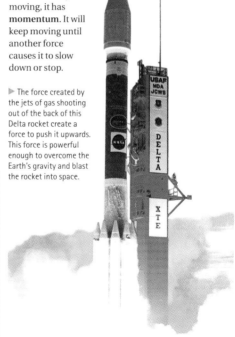

▶ The force created by the jets of gas shooting out of the back of this Delta rocket create a force to push it upwards. This force is powerful enough to overcome the Earth's gravity and blast the rocket into space.

Newton's laws of motion

Isaac Newton was born in England in 1642. He grew up to be one of the most important scientists of all time. He developed three rules, or laws, of motion, as follows:

1 If an object is not being pushed or pulled by a force, it will either stay still or move in a straight line at a constant speed.

2 When a force acts on an object, it will start to move, speed up, slow down, or change direction.

3 If you push or pull an object, it will push or pull back an equal amount.

Forests

Forests are areas of land covered with trees. About a fifth of the Earth's land is forested. There are many kinds of forest, from hot tropical rainforests to northern conifer forests.

Forests create their own special environment. At ground level it is generally shady and still, because the trees give shelter from the sun and wind. The trees also prevent heat being lost into the sky at night, so forests are warmer at night. This makes the forest a sheltered place for wildlife.

Types of forest

Forests can grow in many different climates and soils.

Rainforests thrive where it is hot and wet all year round. Many different kinds of tree grow there: a small region may contain over 100 different kinds. There are huge numbers of other plants. Some even grow on the trunks and branches of trees and fallen logs.

▶ A section through the rainforest. The larger trees form an almost continuous canopy over the roof of the forest. A few very tall trees, called emergents, grow through the canopy into the sunlight above. Below the canopy smaller trees and young saplings form the understorey. Below them, the forest floor is covered by a layer of shrubs and plants. Each layer of the forest has its own community of animals.

▶ Autumn in a deciduous forest in Utah, USA. The colours are produced as the normal green pigment of the leaves is broken down as the leaves die. By shedding their leaves for the winter or during the dry season, deciduous trees are able to save energy and reduce the amount of water they need.

1 harpy eagle
2 macaw
3 spider monkey
4 cock of the rock
5 tree boa
6 sloth
7 ocelot
8 poison frog
9 capybara
10 coral snake

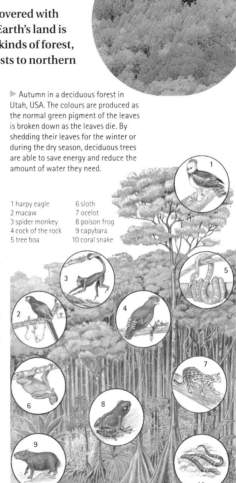

Forests

Deciduous forests are found where it is cool in winter and warm in summer. There are far fewer tree species here than in the rainforest. Many of the trees are deciduous, which means that they shed their leaves in winter, or in the dry season.

Coniferous forests grow in colder climates than any other kind of forest. The main trees are conifers (cone-bearing trees) such as pines. Most are evergreen. Their shape and their tough, needle-like leaves help them shed snow and cope with ice.

The importance of forests

Forests have important functions. Like all green plants, trees absorb carbon dioxide from the air and release oxygen. So forests are major suppliers of the oxygen that all animals need.

A forest acts like a giant sponge, absorbing rainfall and

▲ Cutting down forest in Washington, USA.

only gradually releasing it into rivers. Forest cover also prevents the soil being eroded (worn away).

Forests provide shelter and food for many animals. Leaves, flowers, fruits, seeds and nuts are food for insects, birds and small mammals, such as squirrels and mice, which in turn are food for larger birds and mammals. Forests also provide people with an enormous range of important products, from firewood and building wood to paper, food, varnishes, dyes and medicines.

Vanishing forests
Every year the world's people use 3 billion cubic metres of wood. In Britain and much of north-west Europe, most of the trees have been cut down, and tropical rainforests are also disappearing fast.

Many rainforests grow on very poor soils. Most of the goodness of the land is locked up in the plants. When a rainforest is cut down and burned, the remaining soil is easily washed away in the tropical rains. The area may even turn to desert.

find out more
Conservation
Plants
Trees
Wood

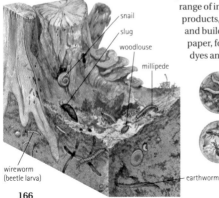

snail
slug
woodlouse
millipede
wireworm (beetle larva)
earthworm

pot worms
ants

◀ The moist forest soil has its own community of worms, centipedes, beetles, ants, and the eggs and larvae (young) of many insects. Hollow trees, crevices under roots and bark, and the moist soil provide sites for nests and burrows.

Fossils

Fossils are the remains of animals and plants that died millions of years ago. By studying fossils we can find out a great deal about the history of life on Earth.

find out more

Dinosaurs
Evolution
Life on Earth
Rocks and minerals

A mammoth meal!
Very occasionally, scientists have discovered whole mammoths that have been deep-frozen for thousands of years in the frozen soil of Siberia. Their flesh is often very well preserved. There are even stories that say that mammoth meat was served at a banquet in 1901, and that the tsar himself tasted it.

▼ These fossils are ammonites. Ammonites were common in the seas between 400 and 64 million years ago.

The most common fossils are the **shells** and **bones** of animals that lived in the sea. This is because most of the rocks that contain fossils were formed in the sea. Also the hard parts of sea creatures do not rot away.

Rare fossils

Other parts of animals and plants can be preserved too. The rarest and most exciting fossils are those that preserve the soft parts of animals. These include insects trapped in **amber**, a resin that oozes from certain trees and then dries hard. Sometimes fossils of baby dinosaurs have been found inside their eggs.

The footprints or burrows of ancient animals can also be preserved. These are called **trace fossils**. It is even possible to find fossilized animal droppings.

Anyone can find fossils. The best place to look is on a beach, where the waves keep uncovering new fossils.

1 When an animal dies it sinks to the sea-bed. Scavenging animals and bacteria remove its flesh. The hard parts – the shell or bones – are left.

2 Sediments, small particles of sand and mud, pile on top of the remains and bury them. Minerals in the sea water replace the hard parts.

3 Gradually the water is squeezed out and the rock becomes hard and compact.

4 Millions of years later the rocks are lifted up and become dry land. Rain, wind or the sea wear them away and uncover the fossils.

France

France is the largest country in western Europe. It is very beautiful and varied, with many different landscapes and ways of life.

FRANCE FACTS

Capital: Paris

Population:
58,800,000

Area: 551,000 sq km

Language: French

Religion: Christian

Currency: 1 French
franc = 100 centimes

Wealth per person:
$24,990

find out more

Europe
French Revolution
Middle Ages
Normans
Romans
World War I
World War II

In the middle of France there is a high plateau (plain) called the Massif Central. France's longest river, the Loire, rises here. To the east are forests, and to the north-west is moorland. High mountains border Italy and Spain.

The climate is varied too. In the north it is mild and damp, while southern France enjoys a Mediterranean climate.

Food and farming

French farmers produce a great variety of foods. They grow wheat, maize (corn) and sunflowers, which provide food for animals and oil for cooking. In the north-west they breed dairy cows, whose milk is used to make famous French cheeses such as Brie and Camembert.

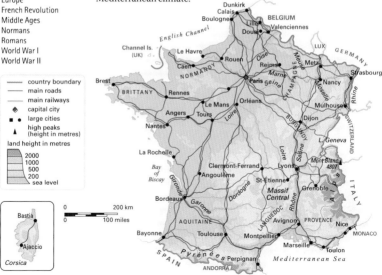

country boundary
main roads
main railways
capital city
large cities
high peaks
(height in metres)
land height in metres

2000
1000
500
200
sea level

0   200 km
0   100 miles

▶ Beaujolais vineyards in the Rhône valley. Each year millions of bottles of French wine are sold all around the world.

France sells its **wines** throughout the world. The biggest vineyards are in the south. The south also produces many other fruits and vegetables.

Industry

Most of France's electricity comes from nuclear power and hydroelectricity. Car manufacturing is an important industry in France, and so is **tourism**. More tourists visit France than any other country.

France's history

France was once divided into small kingdoms ruled by tribes of **Celts**. The **Romans**, who called the region Gaul, conquered it in the 1st century BC. The name 'France' comes from the tribe of **Franks** who took over Gaul in the 5th century AD. The most powerful early French king was **Charlemagne**, who was made emperor in 800. Although the empire broke up after his death, France was now an important European kingdom.

By the end of the 15th century France was also a very rich country. But over the next few centuries its kings spent much of their time and money on wars, and left the people poor and tired.

Revolution and modern times

In 1789 there was a revolution. The people overthrew the king and the old government and set up a parliament to rule the country fairly. When other European nations invaded France, the French drove them back. Under **Napoleon Bonaparte** they conquered most of western Europe.

In the 19th century French industries grew and people became richer. Then, in the first half of the 20th century, France was devastated by two world wars and the Great Depression. But by the millennium France was once again a wealthy, powerful and respected nation and a major force in Europe.

◀ This glass pyramid stands in front of the Louvre, the most famous museum in **Paris**, France's capital city. The Louvre, which was once a palace, was first opened to the public in 1793.

169

French Revolution

During the French Revolution the people of France rose up against their rulers. They changed the way the country was run, executed the king and spread their ideas of freedom and fairness across Europe and beyond.

For centuries France had been governed by a king and a handful of nobles. This small group led easy, privileged lives. Most French people, including wealthy merchant families, had no say in the government.

Liberty, equality, fraternity

In 1789, fed up with the feeble king **Louis XVI**, the people rebelled in the name of **liberty**, **equality** and **fraternity** (brotherhood). They set up a parliament and began to make France a fairer, more democratic country. But they also began executing people as 'enemies of the Revolution'. Eventually thousands of people were killed in a **Reign of Terror**.

War and empire

After the Terror, more moderate leaders, known as the **Directory** took over. By this time France was at war. At first many Europeans had welcomed the Revolution. But when the executions began, other nations invaded France to stop the Revolution spreading.

France hung on, however. And later its most successful general, **Napoleon Bonaparte**, became emperor and master of much of western Europe.

▲ The Revolution begins. The people of Paris attack the Bastille, a large government prison, on 14 July 1789. This date is now France's National Day.

find out more
France
Europe

KEY DATES

1789 Revolution breaks out; storming of the Bastille

1791 King Louis XVI under arrest

1792 France at war with Austria and Prussia

1793 Louis XVI beheaded; Terror begins

1795–1799 Directory governs France

1804 Napoleon makes himself emperor

◀ Maximilien **Robespierre**, the harsh leader of the Terror, was sent to the guillotine himself in 1794. But his tough rule had helped the Revolution survive.

Friction see Forces

Frogs and other amphibians

Amphibians are animals that can live on land as well as in water. Frogs, toads, newts, salamanders and blindworms are all amphibians.

Amphibians are found in all parts of the world except Antarctica. They all have moist, soft skins. They breathe partly through their skin.

Many amphibians hide during the day and move about at night. In this way they protect themselves from predators (animals that eat them). Some have **poison glands** in their skin.

Amphibians are 'cold-blooded' animals. This means that their body temperature depends on the warmth of the air or water around them. When it is warm they are active. When it is cold, they become very slow.

▼ Frogs, like most amphibians, **metamorphose** – change shape. A baby frog (tadpole) breathes with gills. As it grows, its legs and lungs develop, and it can live on land.

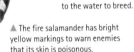

▲ The fire salamander has bright yellow markings to warn enemies that its skin is poisonous.

▶ The marbled newt lives mostly on land, but returns to the water to breed.

Kinds of amphibian

There are three main kinds of amphibian. **Frogs** and **toads** are the most common kind of amphibian. They have long, powerful hind legs, which they use for jumping and swimming. **Newts** and **salamanders** look like soft-skinned lizards. They are often brightly coloured. **Blindworms** live only in the tropics. They have no legs and burrow through the ground.

find out more
Life on Earth

• Amphibians were the first animals with backbones to live on land. Their ancestors began to emerge from the water about 400 million years ago.

• There are over 3500 different kinds of frogs and toads, over 300 different kinds of newts and salamanders and 167 different kinds of blindworm.

egg (spawn).

gills

one day old

one month old

two months old

adult

Galaxies

Galaxies are giant collections of stars. They are so huge that it can take starlight a hundred thousand years to travel from one side to the other. Our Sun is part of a galaxy called the Milky Way.

There are more than 10,000 million galaxies. All started off as huge clouds of gas soon after the birth of the Universe.

Different shapes

The American astronomer Edwin Hubble studied galaxies and classified them into three main types according to their shape.

Spiral galaxies contain both young and old stars. They are disc-shaped with spiral arms. Our galaxy, the **Milky Way**, is a spiral galaxy. It measures about 100,000 light years across and contains more than 200,000 million stars. The Sun is located on one of the spiral arms of the Milky Way. You can see parts of the Milky Way in the sky on clear nights.

Elliptical galaxies look like flattened balls of stars. They are the most common type of galaxy in the Universe. The largest ones are the biggest known galaxies. Elliptical galaxies contain old stars at the end of their lives.

Irregular galaxies have no particular shape. They are the rarest kind of galaxy.

▲ This is M87, an elliptical galaxy 50 million light years away from Earth. It is called an active galaxy because it gives out enormous amounts of energy. Active galaxies are thought to have black holes at their centre. (A black hole is an invisible object with gravity so strong that not even light can escape from it.)

● One light year is equal to 9.5 million million km, the distance light travels in a year.

◀ Spiral Galaxy NGC 1232. Our own galaxy, the Milky Way, is a spiral galaxy. From space it would look like this one.

find out more

Astronomy
Stars
Universe

Genetics

Within any particular type of animal or plant, there will be small differences between individuals. Some of these differences are due to heredity, the inheritance of characteristics from our parents. Genetics is the study of how heredity happens.

▲ Identical twins look very alike because they have identical genetic material. They both grow from a single egg that splits after it has been fertilized.

Some characteristics are not inherited, but are due to the effects of environment and learning. Eye colour is an inherited characteristic. Reading and writing are examples of things that we learn.

Chromosomes and genes

Inherited characteristics are passed on through structures called **chromosomes**, which are found inside the tiny cells that make up living things. Different animals and plants have different numbers of chromosomes – humans, for example, have 46. They are arranged in pairs. On each chromosome there are many small units called **genes**. Each gene carries information about a particular characteristic of the plant or animal.

Passing on genes

A new animal or plant is made by the joining together of two special cells, called **sex cells** – one from each parent. Sex cells are different from all other cells in that they contain only half the normal number of chromosomes – one of each chromosome pair. When two sex cells join, the resulting cell (which becomes the new animal or plant) has the normal number of chromosomes – half from the mother and half from the father.

Making proteins

Genes produce the different characteristics of an animal or plant by controlling the making of proteins. Proteins are the most important substances in

▼ Genes are made from a chemical called **DNA**. Each gene is one section of an enormously long DNA molecule. DNA is like a long ladder twisted into a spiral.

living things. **Structural proteins** make up the bulk of such body tissues as muscles and ligaments. **Enzymes** are proteins that control the chemical reactions in the body. Each gene controls the making of one or a small number of proteins.

Dominant genes

The characteristics we inherit are passed on through pairs of genes. But of the two genes we inherit for any characteristic, one is usually **dominant** over the other. This means that living things carry within their chromosomes many 'hidden' genes. These weaker genes do not show as characteristics when they are masked by a dominant gene, but only if an animal or plant has two weaker genes for a particular characteristic.

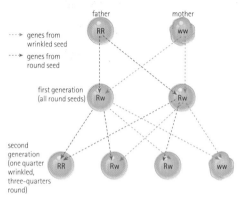

▲ Pea plants have a gene that controls whether their seeds (the peas we eat) are round or wrinkly. The gene for the round seed (R) is dominant over the gene for a wrinkled seed (w). The diagram shows what happens when a plant with two R genes is bred with a plant having two w genes.

find out more
Bacteria and viruses
Cells
Sex and reproduction

Genetic engineering

Scientists can genetically 'engineer' living cells. For example, the chromosomes of microbes (creatures such as bacteria and yeasts) can be modified to produce medicines.

Genetic engineering has important uses, but many people are worried by it. They do not like the idea of eating foods that have been genetically modified, or that one day babies may be 'designed' to have specially chosen characteristics.

▶ Dolly the sheep, born in 1997, was the first large animal to be cloned from an adult. A clone is a living thing that is an exact genetic copy of its parent.

Germany

Germany is a large country in the middle of Europe. It is one of the richest countries in the world, and an important member of the European Union. Germany is famous for its high-quality industrial products, such as electrical equipment, chemicals and cars.

Northern Germany is a land of low hills and flat, fertile plains. To the south are the Black Forest and the snow-capped mountains of the Alps. The climate is mild, which allows German farmers to grow wheat, maize, potatoes and grapes.

People

Most Germans speak German as their first language. However, there are also many people from Turkey and other countries, who came to Germany during the

▼ The Rhine in western Germany is Europe's busiest waterway. Germany's network of rivers and canals is used to transport people and goods across the country and to other parts of Europe.

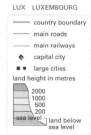

LUX   LUXEMBOURG

————— country boundary
————— main roads
————— main railways
◆ capital city
■ ● large cities
land height in metres

2000
1000
500
200
sea level ⌐ land below
sea level

1960s, when German factories were short of local workers. The majority of Germans work in factories, or in service industries such as banks or hotels.

Germany's history

Until the 19th century, Germany was a jumble of independent states. Then in 1871 the king of Prussia became emperor of Germany, and united most of these states under his rule. Under Otto von Bismarck, the the first chancellor (prime minister), Germany soon became a world power.

Rivalry between Germany and other European nations led in 1914 to World War I. Germany lost the war, and many people blamed the Kaiser (emperor). The emperor was overthrown, and the country became a republic.

In 1933, the Nazi dictator Adolf **Hitler** took power. He led the country into World War II, and under his orders 6 million people, mostly Jews, were killed in concentration camps. Once

Adolf Hitler

Adolf Hitler was the leader of Germany's National Socialist (Nazi) party. He believed that all Germany's problems were caused by Jews and communists. Hitler became president of Germany in 1934, and then supreme leader, or Führer. He invaded neighbouring countries, which began World War II. During the war the Nazis rounded up and killed millions of Jews, in what became known as the 'Holocaust'.

again Germany lost the war, and their opponents divided the country in two parts – East and West. **East Germany** was a communist dictatorship, while **West Germany** was a rich capitalist democracy.

In 1989 the communist government in East Germany collapsed, and the following year the two parts of Germany were reunited. Since then there have been some tensions between the poorer east and the wealthy west. However, Germany remains a powerful and important country.

GERMANY FACTS

Capital: Berlin

Population: 82,300,000

Area: 357,868 sq km

Language: German

Religion: Christian

Currency: 1 mark = 100 pfennigs

Wealth per person: $27,510

◄ The Berlin Wall was put up by the East Germans in 1961. It cut the East German part of Berlin off from the West German part. When the communist government fell in 1989, the wall was torn down by thousands of people, to mark the end of a divided Germany.

find out more

Europe
Governments
Middle Ages
Racism
World War I
World War II

Governments

Large groups of people usually have some sort of government to lead and organize them. Governments collect money (taxes), make laws and see that the laws are kept. Democratic governments do what their citizens want. Other types of government may ignore the people's wishes entirely.

What a government does affects everyone. Government decisions can affect the school you go to for instance, or how much money you have to spend, or how clean the world around you is.

▲ Two democratically elected leaders: US presidents George Bush (left) and Bill Clinton. Americans elect the president separately from the assembly (Congress), but the two have to work closely together.

Monarchs, presidents and dictators

In the past, most governments were run by a single person. This could be an emperor or empress, or a monarch (king or queen). **Monarchy** was the most common type of government. Monarchs had great power – some even believed God had chosen them to rule. When they died, a member of their family took over. A few countries, such as the United Kingdom, still have monarchs, but in most cases these monarchs no longer rule.

Countries without a monarch are known as **republics**. The USA became a republic in 1783. The government of a republic is usually led by a president. Many presidents are chosen (elected) by the people.

Leaders who take over and run the government by force are called **dictators**. Dictatorships are often cruel and unfair because they follow the wishes of the dictator and his party, not the people. The dictator Adolf **Hitler** ruled Germany very ruthlessly from 1933 to 1945.

◀ The Italian politician Benito Mussolini. Head of the fascist party, he became prime minister of Italy in 1922. He then scrapped the country's democratic system and ruled as a dictator until 1943.

177

Democracy

US president Abraham **Lincoln** said democracy was government 'of the people, by the people, and for the people'. The idea started in Ancient Greece. Many countries are democracies. Democratic governments do what their people want. Their countries tend to be peaceful and prosperous.

Democratic governments are made up of politicians who belong to a **political party**. A party is a group with similar ideas about government. Adult citizens vote for politicians in an **election**. The party with the most votes or the most elected politicians sets up the government.

Communist governments also say they are democratic. But voters don't normally have a choice because there is only one party, the communist party. This means that communist governments are often more like dictatorships than democracies.

Governing a country

A democratic government is made up of politicians elected from different parts of the country. These politicians meet in an assembly (a **parliament** or **congress**). The assembly controls law-making, taxes and spending, and the armed forces. Some members of the assembly oppose the government. It is their job to see that the government acts wisely and tells the truth.

▲ Friends help a 75-year-old disabled South African to vote. He is taking part in the country's first democratic elections, in April 1994.

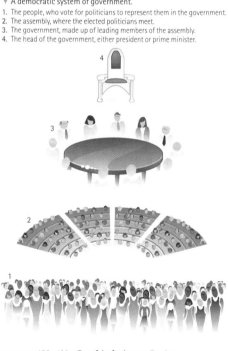

▼ A democratic system of government.
1. The people, who vote for politicians to represent them in the government.
2. The assembly, where the elected politicians meet.
3. The government, made up of leading members of the assembly.
4. The head of the government, either president or prime minister.

A **president** or **prime minister** leads the government, which is split up into departments. Each department looks after an area of our lives, such as health, education, transport or defence. Full-time administrators, or **civil servants**, carry out the politicians' wishes.

Local government

Local government looks after a part of a country, such as a city or state. It is responsible for everyday matters like repairing roads and collecting rubbish. In some countries (Australia, for example) states have their own assemblies and make their own laws. The boss (mayor) of a big city like New York, USA can be very powerful.

International government

National governments run single countries. There are also international governments. They may help run a group of countries, as in the case of the **European Union**. The **United Nations** tries to persuade national governments to co-operate on matters that affect all of them.

▼ Athens, in ancient Greece, was the first city to have a democratic government. A citizens' assembly met regularly to discuss and vote on matters of state, and an elected body called the *boule* ran everyday business. This picture shows the buildings where the *boule* met.

• The world's first woman prime minister was Sirimavo Bandaranaike, who was elected in Sri Lanka in 1960. Other famous women prime ministers include Britain's Margaret Thatcher, India's Indira Gandhi and Pakistan's Benazir Bhutto.

> **find out more**
> Europe
> Law
> Schools and universities
> United Nations

Graphs

A graph is a way of showing numerical information as a picture. Instead of giving a long list of numbers, a graph might show the information as a curved line, a set of coloured bars, or as slices of a pie.

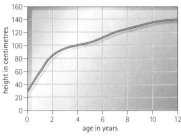

▲ This line graph shows how a girl grows taller as she gets older. The lines with the numbers on are called axes. The bottom axis gives the child's age in years. The side axis gives her height in centimetres. At a glance you can see that the girl grew most quickly during her first two years.

Graphs make it easy to compare sets of numbers. They also show up any patterns in the numbers.

Lines, bars and pies

Line graphs are useful for showing how things change. They can show the temperature of a sick patient changes, or how a child gets taller as she gets older.

Bar charts are useful for comparing different numbers, such as the temperature at different holiday resorts in a particular month, or how many vehicles of different types drive past your school in a day. The taller a bar, the bigger the number it stands for.

A **pie chart** looks like a pie cut into slices. It can be used, for instance, to show the results of a survey of a group of children's favourite colours. The whole pie represents all the children. The size of each slice shows the fraction of the group that chose a particular colour.

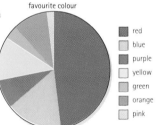

favourite colour

- red
- blue
- purple
- yellow
- green
- orange
- pink

▲ This pie chart shows the results of a survey of the favourite colours of a group of children. Almost half the children chose red as their favourite colour.

find out more

Numbers
Shapes

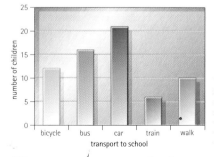

◀ This bar chart shows how a group of children travel to school. More than twice as many come to school by car as walk to school.

Grasshoppers *see* Insects

Grasslands

Grasslands cover more than one-fifth of the Earth's land surface. There are many different types, from the desolate steppes of central Asia to the rich farmlands of North America.

Grass is an important food for many animals, and human foods such as wheat and rice are types of grass.

Animals

All sorts of animals live on the world's grasslands. Most either eat grass themselves (grazing animals), or kill grazing animals

for food. Australia's grasslands are home to kangaroos, emus, kookaburras, and flocks of budgerigars and parrots. On the savannahs of East Africa there are giraffes, elephants, rhinos, gazelles, zebras and big cats. Smaller animals such as prairie dogs and rattlesnakes live on the North American prairies.

People and grasslands

Humans have changed grasslands in many parts of the world. Over the past 300 years, hunting has reduced the numbers of bison ('buffaloes') on the North American prairies from 60 million to fewer than a thousand. During the 20th century, grasslands in North America and eastern Europe were ploughed up and turned into rich farmland. In other areas, such as the pampas of Argentina, grasslands are used to graze beef cattle.

▲ In North America large areas of the prairie are now used to grow cereals such as wheat, maize or, in this case, barley. All these cereals are themselves types of grass.

GRASSLANDS OF THE WORLD

Grasslands have different names in different parts of the world.

East Africa	*savannah*
southern Africa	*veld*
North America	*prairie*
South America	*pampas, chacos*
central Europe and Asia	*steppes*
western Europe	*meadows, downlands*

◀ Elephants cool off at a watering hole on the East African savannah, while wildebeest and zebra graze. Grazing in mixed herds enables animals to help warn each other of danger.

find out more
Farming
Plants

Ancient
Greeks

The Greeks created Europe's first major civilization. Although it ended over 2000 years ago, its arts, architecture, government, language, maths and science still play a part in the modern world.

▲ The open-air Greek theatre at Epidaurus. Drama was very important to the Greeks, and their theatres were superbly designed so the audience could hear every word.

In about 2000 BC, the **Minoans** created a civilization on the isle of Crete. Later, the **Mycenaean** civilization grew up on mainland Greece. But about 1100 BC both of these were destroyed by invaders and earthquakes.

A land of city states

Later Greece divided into **city states**. Each was made up of a city and the land around it. They governed themselves and made their own laws. Only when danger threatened did they join together.

The most important city states were **Athens** and **Sparta**. Athens was a rich city of merchants, thinkers and artists. The Spartans were warriors, dedicated to winning battles. Both states, like the rest of Greece, used **slaves** to do manual labour. And everywhere women were much less powerful than men. They were not citizens and had no say in government.

All citizens had a duty to keep fit and healthy. Physical exercise and public baths were extremely popular. So too were sports meetings. The best known was the **Olympic Games**, held every four years in honour of Zeus, the king of the gods.

The 'golden age' of Athens

Greek civilization was at its finest in Athens in the mid-5th century BC. During this 'golden age', Athenian ships traded across the eastern

◀ The Acropolis (fortress) of Athens as it may have looked in the 5th century BC.

1 Holy place of Zeus
2 Parthenon, the temple of Athene, the city's special goddess
3 Theatre of the god Dionysus
4 Temple of Athene and the god Poseidon
5 Statue of Athene
6 Holy place of the goddess Artemis
7 Gateway

KEY DATES

BC

about 2000 Minoan civilization begins in Crete

about 1600 Mycenaean civilization begins

about 1210 Greeks capture Troy

1100 – about 800 'Dark Age' of Greek civilization

about 900 City of Sparta founded

about 750 Greeks setting up colonies overseas

776 First mention of Olympic Games

508 Athens becomes more democratic

490 Greeks defeat Persians at Battle of Marathon

461 Pericles becomes leader of Athens

about 447 Parthenon built at Athens

431–404 Athens and Sparta at war

336–323 Reign of Alexander the Great

146 Greece under Roman rule

towered over the wealthy city. There were no kings or tyrants. Instead, the citizens chose their own government (called **democracy** or 'people rule').

Alexander the Great

Wars between Athens and Sparta ended the glory of Ancient Greece. In the next century, however, Greek power rose again under Alexander the Great, King of Macedonia. Alexander conquered a huge empire and spread Greek ideas across Asia to northern India. His empire broke up after his death. By the 2nd century BC Greece was under Roman rule.

▲ Alexander the Great, perhaps the finest general the world has ever seen. He set up many new cities and named them 'Alexandria', after himself. He even named a city (Bucephala) after his favourite horse, Bucephalus.

Mediterranean. Her poets wrote wonderful plays and her craftspeople made beautiful decorated pottery. The grand buildings of the **Acropolis**

▲ Poseidon, the Greek god of rivers, lakes and seas. The Greeks believed in many gods and goddesses. These gods were half-human, and often interfered in people's lives. To keep them happy, the Greeks made sacrifices, and held ceremonies.

◀ The myth of the Minotaur tells of the bull-headed monster that lived in the middle of a maze. The picture on this Greek pot shows the hero Theseus killing the Minotaur.

find out more

Ancient world
Drama
Europe

● The Greeks loved a good story, and many of the world's finest myths and legends come from Ancient Greece. They include the stories of Hercules, the Minotaur, Jason and the Argonauts, and the wooden horse of Troy.

Growth and development

All living things grow and change. And all need food to enable them to grow. Most complicated living things go through a number of stages between birth and death – this is their development.

To get bigger, living things make more **cells**. New cells form when existing cells divide in two. Plants and animals use the **food** they take in to make new cells.

Human development

Many plants and animals have periods when they grow and change quickly. Human beings grow fastest when they are **babies**. After infancy their rate of growth slows down – until they reach puberty.

Puberty usually begins when you are in your early teens. It is the time when your body develops to make it possible for you to have babies. Boys and girls go through a period of rapid growth. At the end of puberty – between the ages of 16 and 20 – you stop growing taller.

Growing old

As people get older their bodies continue to change. Their muscles and skeleton become weaker. Women can no longer have babies. When people get very old, their bodies get worn out and they **die**.

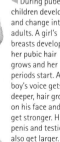

▲ Plants, like this sunflower, grow from **seeds**. When a seed germinates, or starts to develop, roots grow (1), then a shoot pushes its way to the surface (2). Soon the first full-sized leaves appear (3). More leaves appear and the plant grows taller. Finally a flower bud appears, and the flower opens up (4). New seeds develop from this flower.

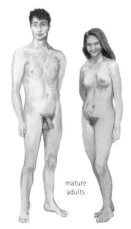

mature adults

children before puberty

◀ During puberty children develop and change into adults. A girl's breasts develop, her pubic hair grows and her periods start. A boy's voice gets deeper, hair grows on his face and he get stronger. His penis and testicles also get larger.

find out more

Animals
Cells
Children
Human beings
Plants
Sex and reproduction

Health and fitness

Good health and fitness depend both on how you live and on where you live.

To stay healthy and fit you need to look after your own body – to eat well and exercise regularly. But the environment you live in also affects your health.

How you live

To stay healthy it is important to eat a balanced **diet**, including lots of fresh food. Eating too much fatty or sweet food will damage your health.

Smoking and drinking too much **alcohol** are also likely to cause disease.

It is also important to keep clean. **Washing** regularly helps to get rid of bacteria that spread diseases.

Keeping fit helps people to live full and healthy lives. The way to keep fit is to do lots of **exercise**.

▶ Nurses play a vital role in health care in countries where there are few doctors.

Where you live

Many diseases are caused by the environment you live in. People living in poor conditions, especially in developing countries, have to work harder to stay healthy. The water they drink may be dirty, and medical care is often not as good as in developing countries.

The environment in developed countries can also be damaging to health. Poor housing, dirty air and high levels of stress can cause disease.

▼ Many people take up running to keep fit. These runners are taking part in the New York Marathon.

First aid

When someone has a heart attack, is suddenly taken ill or is hurt in an accident, first aid can save their lives. People who are trained in first aid learn the simple things they can do to keep the victim's condition from getting worse until expert help arrives.

find out more

Diseases
Food
Medicine
Sports and games

Heart and blood

The heart is a muscular pump that pushes blood around the body. Blood is the body's transport system. It carries food and oxygen to the body's cells, and takes away wastes.

All vertebrates (animals with backbones), and many invertebrates – for example, earthworms, snails and insects – have hearts. In people, the heart is made up of four muscular chambers: two **atria**, and two **ventricles**.

The heart pumps blood around the body through tubes called **blood vessels**. Oxygen and nutrient-rich blood is carried away from the heart by thick-walled blood vessels called **arteries**. Once the oxygen and nutrients in the blood have been removed, the blood returns to the heart through thinner-walled blood vessels called **veins**.

Blood is made up of two kinds of cell. **Red blood cells** carry oxygen and dissolved foods around the body. They also carry away wastes. **White blood cells** help the body fight off infection and injury.

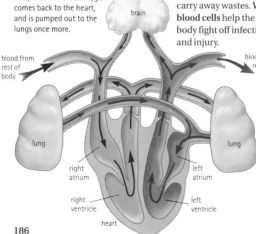

▲ Human blood, magnified many times.

▼ A human kidney. As the blood gives up oxygen and nutrients to the body's cells, the cells get rid of waste into the blood. The kidneys filter out the waste through tiny tubes called nephrons.

renal artery
'dirty' blood
'cleaned' blood
renal vein
ureter
nephrons
urine (goes to bladder)

▼ How the heart pumps blood round the body. In the lungs, the blood picks up oxygen from the air. The blood then goes to the heart, which pumps it to the brain and the rest of the body. Blood without oxygen comes back to the heart, and is pumped out to the lungs once more.

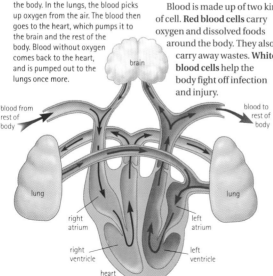

brain
blood from rest of body
blood to rest of body
lung
lung
right atrium
left atrium
right ventricle
left ventricle
heart

find out more

Breathing
Human body
Medicine

Heat and temperature

Heat is a kind of energy called thermal energy. It is the energy that an object has because the atoms and molecules that make it up are vibrating, or moving quickly back and forth.

If an object is heated, its atoms get more energy and vibrate faster. If it cools down, it loses energy and its atoms vibrate more slowly.

▶ Temperature is a measure of heat. It is measured using a thermometer. There are several different temperature scales. On the Celsius scale, shown here, ice melts at 0 °C and water boils at 100 °C.

Moving heat

Heat can travel through solids, liquids and gases. It can even travel through empty space.

Some materials, like metals, are good **conductors**, or carriers, of heat. In these materials energy is passed from fast-moving atoms in hot parts of the metal to slower-moving atoms in cooler parts. This warms up the cooler parts.

Substances like air are **insulators**: they are poor conductors of heat. Instead, they carry heat in another way – by **convection**. During convection a circulating current forms as hotter material moves away and cooler material moves in to take its place.

Heat energy can also travel as invisible waves by **radiation**. This is how the heat from the Sun reaches us here on Earth. All hot things lose heat through radiation. The hotter they are, the more they radiate.

◀ The stars shine with different colours depending on how hot they are. The hottest stars give off a blue-white light, while cooler stars are usually reddish. In this photo of the Butterfly star cluster, most of the stars are hot blue stars, but the brightest in the cluster is a cooler red giant.

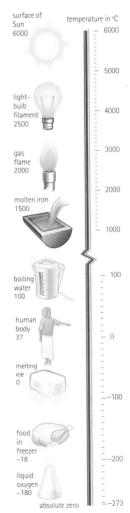

temperature in °C

surface of Sun 6000 — 6000

— 5000

light-bulb filament 2500 — 4000

gas flame 2000 — 3000

— 2000

molten iron 1500 — 1000

boiling water 100 — 100

human body 37 — 0

melting ice

— −100

food in freezer −18 — −200

liquid oxygen −180

absolute zero — −273

Heaven *see* Religions • **Heredity** *see* Genetics • **Himalayas** *see* Asia

Hindus

Hindus are people who follow Hinduism, a religion which began over 4000 years ago in India. Hindus themselves call it the *Sanatana Dharma*, which means 'everlasting truth'.

Hindus believe that everyone has his or her own way of finding a path to God. You can still be a Hindu if you do not believe in God, or if you think that God is not a person but a force called **Brahman**. On the other hand, you can worship God as male (Shiva or Vishnu), as female (Durga, Lakshmi or Saraswati), or even as a partly animal form (Ganesh or Hanuman).

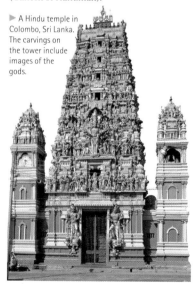

▶ A Hindu temple in Colombo, Sri Lanka. The carvings on the tower include images of the gods.

▲ Ganesh is an elephant-headed God. He is known as 'the remover of obstacles'.

Hindu beliefs

Hindus think that it is very important to teach others *dharma*, the truth about the way things are. Dharma is also the word used for doing your duty.

Reincarnation is the Hindu belief that your soul is reborn in another living thing when you die. It may start off in a plant, then move on to an animal, and then to a human. What you will come back as in the next life depends on what you do in this life. This is known as **karma**. Good karma will mean a good life next time.

In the hope of escaping this cycle of birth and death Hindus try to follow four ways or paths in life. These are to study their religion, to meditate, to worship well and to do their duty as best they can.

Hindu holy books

The Hindu holy books – the Vedas and the Upanishads – contain many great sayings about God and the world. The **Mahabharata** and the **Ramayana** are two very long poems that are part of the Hindu holy books. They tell stories about the gods and goddesses and teach important lessons about Hinduism.

Worship

Hindus may have a **shrine** for worship at home. A shrine is a special place with images of one or more of the Hindu gods and goddesses. The family places offerings of things like flowers and perfume in front of the images and repeats verses from the Hindu holy books.

Temple worship is special and some Hindu temples are huge and beautifully decorated. Each temple has at least one priest, who helps Hindus in their worship and looks after the building and the images of the gods and goddesses inside. Hindus also visit temples to celebrate the many Hindu festivals held throughout the year.

Some temples are sites of **pilgrimage**. A pilgrimage is a journey people make to a place because it is special to their religion. The many pilgrimage sites in India also include rivers and mountains.

▲ Sadhus are holy men who live on offerings given by ordinary Hindus.

• Some Hindus choose to live in religious communities or completely on their own, relying on other people for food. In India people feel that it is an honour to give to such holy people.

• Over 80 per cent of the population of India are Hindus. Other Hindus live in North America, Africa, Indonesia, Nepal, Sri Lanka, the Caribbean and Britain.

▼ Thousands of Hindu pilgrims travel to the holy cities along the banks of the sacred River Ganges every year. Visitors to Varanasi bathe in the river to make themselves pure.

find out more
India and Pakistan
Religions

Horses

For thousands of years people have used horses for riding, to pull heavy loads and for sport. There are seven different kinds of horse. Only two of these have been tamed.

All horses are **herbivores**. They feed by **grazing** on plants, such as grasses. In the wild they spend many hours each day eating.

Wild horses

Wild horses, such as **zebras** and **wild asses**, live in herds in the open grasslands of Africa, the Middle East and Asia. They have good senses of sight, hearing and smell, so they can detect hunting animals from a distance. When they are in danger, they can run very fast over long distances to escape.

Domestic horses

Horses were first **domesticated** (tamed) by people in central Asia over 6000 years ago. Because horses are strong and fast, they were used to pull chariots. Later they were used for riding or to pull wagons and carts.

There are now over 150 breeds of domestic horse, including **ponies**. Ponies are small horses that stand less than 142 centimetres high.

Today people use horses more for pleasure than for work. Many people like to ride and horse racing is a popular sport.

▲ Przewalski's horse is closely related to domesticated horses. Today it survives mainly in zoos.

HORSE RECORDS

Largest: One Percheron was over 2 m high and 5 m long

Smallest: In 1997 a miniature horse measured 53.24 cm

Fastest: 69.2 km/h over 400 m

Note: horse height is measured from the shoulders down.

find out more
Farm animals
Grasslands
Mammals

▼ Zebras live in family groups. An adult female usually leads the group. She is followed by her foals. Next come the other mares and their young. The stallion, the father of all the foals, follows.

Human beings

Today there are over 5.5 billion human beings on Earth. All humans belong to the same animal species – *Homo sapiens sapiens*. Like cats, apes and dolphins, humans are mammals.

The key to the success of human beings is our **intelligence**. We have made fire and tools, built shelters, grown food and clothed ourselves. We have changed our surroundings to suit our needs.

▼ Black and white children playing together. Skin colour is just one of the many possible variations in the human body. These variations often depend on where your ancestors came from originally. People with dark skin originally came from hot, sunny countries. Pale-skinned people came from colder countries.

These skills have made it possible for human beings to spread throughout the world, from dark forests and hot deserts to remote islands and the Arctic ice.

Social animals

Human beings are social animals – we live our lives in groups. Since prehistoric times we have banded together in **families** and **tribes** to share important tasks such as gathering food and caring for children.

About 10,000 years ago a few human beings discovered how to grow crops. Since then, human **settlements** have grown from simple villages to vast cities.

Our skill with **language** allows us to share knowledge and ideas. Different groups of humans have developed special ways of life and beliefs – **culture**. The food we eat, the clothes we wear, the music we listen to and the religion we follow are just some of the things that make up our culture.

▲ For most of our history human beings have been hunter-gatherers. Hunter-gatherers live by gathering wild foods and by hunting wild animals. This way of life still survives among a few groups of people. This man belongs to the Aeta people of the Philippines.

Human body

Like the bodies of all animals, the human body is made up of billions of tiny **cells**. Particular kinds of cells are grouped together to form **tissues**, and these in turn make up **organs,** such as the heart and the lungs.

Some groups of organs and tissues work together in **systems** to perform particular jobs. There are eight main systems in the human body.

▼ The human body.

The **nervous system** is made up of the brain, the spinal cord and a network of nerves. It is the body's communication and control system. See Brain and nerves, page 51.

In our **digestive system** the food we eat is broken down into liquid, and the nutrients that our body needs are absorbed into our blood. Our food gives us energy and makes it possible for us to grow and repair our bodies. See Digestion, page 107.

The **circulatory system** is made up of the heart, the blood vessels and the blood. The blood carries nutrients and oxygen to all the body tissues, and takes away waste materials. See Heart and blood, page 186.

The **reproductive systems** of males and females work together to produce new human beings. See Sex and reproduction, pages 332–333.

The **excretory system** gets rid of the body's waste. The kidneys filter the blood and remove the waste as urine, which collects in the bladder. This is then passed out of the body. See Heart and blood, page 186.

Human beings

The windpipe (trachea) and the lungs make up the **respiratory system**. This system enables us to take in oxygen from the air we breathe. Our bodies use oxygen to produce energy from our food. See Breathing, page 52.

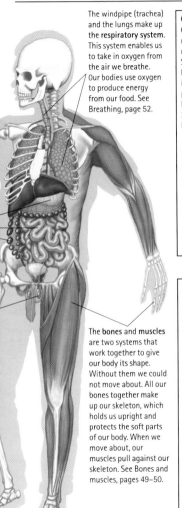

Glands

Glands are special organs that make chemicals that the body needs, such as sweat and saliva. Some produce chemicals called hormones that control important life processes. Humans have more than 25 different hormones.

The **pituitary gland** produces growth hormones.

The **thyroid gland** produces thyroxin, which increases activity.

Men's **testes** produce testosterone, which causes their voice to get deeper, their beard to grow and their sex organs to enlarge.

The **pancreas** produces insulin, which makes the liver absorb sugar from the blood.

Women's **ovaries** produce sex hormones that control their menstrual period and egg production.

▶ Some of the main glands of the body.

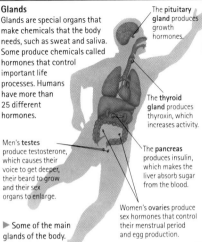

The **bones** and **muscles** are two systems that work together to give our body its shape. Without them we could not move about. All our bones together make up our skeleton, which holds us upright and protects the soft parts of our body. When we move about, our muscles pull against our skeleton. See Bones and muscles, pages 49–50.

Immunity

Immunity is the body's ability to defend itself against infection and fight disease. The parts of your body that enable it to do this make up the immune system.

Various parts of the body are involved in the immune system. **White blood cells** fight bacteria and viruses. The **thymus** is important in the development of the immune system. **Bone marrow** makes white blood cells. The **lymph nodes** get rid of bacteria and also make white blood cells. The **spleen** cleans the blood. The **tonsils** protect you from infection.

tonsils

lymph nodes

thymus

bone marrow

spleen

lymph vessels

▶ The human immune system.

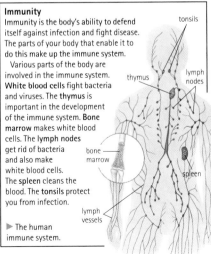

Ice

Ice is frozen water. It is a solid made up of tiny, six-pointed crystals. Icebergs, icicles, hail, snowflakes, and glaciers are all made of ice.

▲ Ice crystals on a window pane.

Water freezes at a temperature of 0 °C. Unlike any other substance, it expands when it freezes. Under a magnifying lens you would see that snowflakes are made up of six-pointed, star-like crystals. Bigger blocks of ice are also made up of ice crystals, but these are harder to see because they are so tightly packed.

▲ Icebergs floating in Jokulsarlon lake, Iceland. The icebergs have broken off from the nearby Vatnajokull glacier, one of the largest in Europe.

Ice-sheets, glaciers and icebergs

Large areas of ice and snow that cover the land permanently are called **ice-sheets**. The world's main ice-sheets are found in Antarctica and Greenland.

A **glacier** is a moving mass of ice. Glaciers usually form high in the mountains, when snow builds up over many years to form a thick layer of ice. The weight of the ice above makes the bottom of the glacier melt, and it begins to creep downhill.

Icebergs are huge lumps of ice that break away from the edges of ice-sheets (or glaciers, if they reach the sea) and float in the sea. Only about a ninth of an iceberg shows above the surface. Icebergs begin to melt as they drift away from the polar regions.

find out more

Antarctica
Arctic
Films
Solids, liquids and gases
Water
Weather

Incas

The Incas were native South Americans who had an empire in and around the Andes mountains. They were excellent organizers and engineers. But their harsh rulers were unpopular, and Spanish conquerors destroyed the empire in the 16th century.

◀ Five hundred years ago the Incas sacrificed this young girl to the mountain gods. She was buried at a great height, where the ice and snow preserved her body.

Warlike Incas came to Cuzco (modern Peru) about 1000 AD. Over the next 500 years they conquered an empire that stretched along the west coast of South America. Although they had no iron tools, they were clever builders. They made a network of roads 20,000 kilometres long.

The emperor of the Sun

Most ordinary people were farmers. They grew maize (corn), tomatoes and peanuts, and used canals and channels to water their fields. Their all-powerful ruler was known as the **Inca**. He said the Sun was his ancestor. Everyone had to live where he told them and do exactly as he said. As a result, the Inca was not very popular.

End of the empire

In 1532 Francisco **Pizarro** and a band of Spanish conquerors attacked the empire and captured the Inca, **Atahualpa**. Although his people fought back, they had little chance against Spanish guns. Forty years later the Inca empire was no more.

▲ The Inca empire in the early 16th century had about 12 million inhabitants.

Knot write!
The Incas did not have writing. Instead, they used a system of coloured cords with knots in them. A 'reader' picked up information from the choice of colour and the position of the knots!

find out more

Empire, Age of
Exploration, Age of
South America

▶ The Inca fortress city of **Machu Picchu** was built between two mountains.

India and Pakistan

India and Pakistan are neighbouring countries in South Asia. They were a single country until 1947 and are now great rivals. Well over a billion people live in the area. India alone has a population of almost a billion people – only China has more.

South Asia also includes Bangladesh, Sri Lanka, Nepal, Bhutan and the Maldive Islands.

The region has a rich history of ancient civilizations, cultures and religions.

INDIA AND PAKISTAN FACTS

India

Capital: New Delhi

Population: 980,000,000

Area: 3,166,829 sq km

Languages: Hindi, English and others

Religion: Hindu, Muslim

Pakistan

Capital: Islamabad

Population: 136,000,000

Area: 803,943 sq km

Languages: Urdu, Punjabi and others

Religion: Muslim

• You can see the flags of India, Pakistan and Bangladesh under Asia.

country boundary
disputed boundary
main roads
main railways
◆ capital city
■ ■ large cities
▲ high peaks (height in metres)
land height in metres

5000
2000
1000
500
200
sea level

Mountains and rivers

The Himalayas and Karakoram mountains separate the area from the rest of Asia. They contain the world's 20 highest peaks. They are cold and very little grows there.

Three of the world's mightiest rivers drain the mountains. The Indus flows through Pakistan, the Ganges through northern India and the Brahmaputra through north-east India and Bangladesh. The best farmlands are by these rivers. Farmers grow wheat, lentils and cotton.

The southern half of India is tropical, and summers are very hot. But between September and June a wind called the monsoon brings cooler weather and heavy rains. These rains allow farmers to grow rice and tropical fruits. The monsoon rains reach northern India, and are important for farmers there, too.

▲ Bus and truck drivers in Pakistan often take great trouble decorating their vehicles. This coach is travelling through mountainous northern Pakistan.

Peoples

Most Indians are followers of the Hindu religion and most Pakistanis are Muslims. But there are also Muslims, Buddhists, Christians, Sikhs and Jains in India. Three out of every four Indians live in villages and most villagers work the land. In the mountains people keep herds of sheep and goats. The populations of India and Pakistan are growing so quickly that it has been difficult to grow enough food. In the 1960s new types of rice and wheat were introduced to produce bigger crops, and today India grows enough grain for everyone. But the population is still growing very fast.

There are also great cities, such as Mumbai (Bombay) and Kolkatha (Calcutta) in India, and Karachi in Pakistan. Many poor farmers have moved to these cities in search of work. As a result the cities are overcrowded, and many people do not have homes or jobs.

Ancient history

The earliest civilization in this area grew up around the cities of Harappa and Mohenjo-daro in the Indus Valley around 2500 BC. About 1000 years later the Aryan people arrived from central Asia. They developed the Sanskrit language and Hinduism. Islam was introduced in the 8th century AD by Arab conquerors from the west. Mongol armies attacked in the 13th century, but the region remained under Muslim rule.

In 1526, Babur, prince of the city of Samarkand, founded the Mughal dynasty, which ruled north India and Pakistan for 200 years. The Mughal emperors were Muslims. They built beautiful palaces and places of worship, and laid out lush gardens. The most famous emperor was Akbar (1556–1605). Another Mughal emperor, Shah Jahan, built the Taj Mahal at Agra in memory of his wife.

Empire and independence

In the 18th century European trading companies came to India and were allowed to set up in business by local rulers. The British drove out the other Europeans and conquered the lands of the Indian rulers. In 1876 the British Queen Victoria became the Empress of India.

Indians began to resist British rule and demand more say in their own government. But some Muslims wanted a separate country for themselves. The problem was solved in 1947 by dividing the country in two. India became a largely Hindu country. The mainly Muslim country of Pakistan was divided into two parts, West and East. After a war, in 1971 East Pakistan became the independent country of Bangladesh.

Gandhi

Mohandas Gandhi (1869–1948), called the 'Mahatma' (Great Soul) was the leader of India's independence campaign against the British Empire. He and his followers chose non-violent means of protest. Gandhi was an inspiration to people around the world fighting for their rights. But he did not live long after his dream of independence came true. He was assassinated in 1948. Jawaharlal Nehru became India's first prime minister and Muhammad Ali Jinnah was Pakistan's first leader.

▼ Hinduism has many gods. Each part of the country has its own festivals and sacred places. The Rathyatra festival takes place at the temple of Jagannatha in Puri, eastern India. Thousands of people gather to haul heavy wooden chariots containing small images of the god Jagannatha and his brother and sister along a special route.

find out more ▶
Architecture
Asia
Buddhists
Dance
Empire, Age of
Hindus
Mongols
Muslims
Sikhs

Industrial Revolution

The Industrial Revolution started in Britain about 1750 and spread worldwide. It turned a land of farms and craft shops into one of towns, factories and railways. In the end this huge change made almost everyone better off.

Why **Britain**? Britain's population was rising fast. There were more people to make goods and to buy them. Britain was a rich, settled land. It had plenty of **raw materials** such as coal, wool and iron, and its overseas **colonies** supplied more.

Inventions such as weaving machines and **steam engines** meant that goods could be made faster and cheaper in **factories**. Barges, ships and **trains** took these goods all over the world.

Businessmen and landowners grew fabulously rich. **Towns** sprung up. Men, women and children flocked to these towns to find work in the factories. Conditions were terrible: noisy, dangerous and

▶ Power spinning. Richard Arkwright's water-powered spinning frame, invented in 1769, turned out strong cotton threads for weaving into cloth. By 1782 Arkwright employed 5000 workers in his 'manufactory'.

unhealthy. But many workers, especially women, were earning their own money for the first time. And very gradually conditions improved.

A worldwide revolution

During the 19th century the Industrial Revolution spread to northern Europe and the USA. Later, Russia and Japan began industrializing, followed by China and countries in the Americas and Africa.

KEY DATES

1713 Abraham Darby uses coke to make iron

1733 John Kay invents a weaving machine

1764 James Hargreaves invents a spinning machine

1775 James Watt's steam engines go on sale

1825 First public railway opens

1837 Alfred Krupp begins making arms in Germany

1843 First ocean-going iron ship launched

find out more

Engines and motors
Industry
Iron and steel
Transport

◀ The head of a British coal mine during the Industrial Revolution. The machine in the background is a steam pump used to stop the mine flooding.

Industry

Industry is any sort of activity that people do that produces goods or services. There are many different types of industry, including farming, mining, manufacturing, banking and tourism. Almost all industries are run with the aim of making money.

All industries belong to one of three different groups – primary, secondary or tertiary industry.

Primary industry

Primary industries extract natural materials from the Earth. They include quarrying, mining, farming, forestry and fishing. **Quarrying** extracts stone and breaks it up for use in building. **Mining** extracts metals and minerals such as coal, oil and copper. These may be taken to factories to be made into other products, or used to fuel power stations, where they are burned to produce energy.

Farming produces goods by planting and harvesting crops and managing animals. The **fishing** industry gets its produce from the sea, or from fish farms. Many of these goods are later processed in factories.

Most primary industries produce **raw materials** – materials that can be used to make other things, or can be eaten, or burned as fuel.

In poorer countries, primary industries are very important and most people earn a living by working in them. In richer countries only a few people work in primary industries.

• When people make things at home to sell through a local market stall or shop, it is called a **cottage industry**. Potters who sell their pottery through local outlets are running a cottage industry.

▼ Workers in a rock quarry in Karnatak, India. Workers can usually earn higher wages in the cities than on the land, and so people are moving from the countryside to the cities in search of jobs.

Secondary industry

Secondary industries change raw materials such as cereals, oil or timber into **products**. They are also known as **manufacturing industries**.

There are many different sorts of secondary industry. Some examples are food-processing, construction and car-making. Many companies usually operate in each industry. For example, Ford, Volkswagen, Renault and Honda are just a few of the world's car manufacturers.

When a company builds a new factory, it has to decide where to put it. It will probably choose a site that has good transport links.

It will also want to be sure that there are people living nearby to work in the factory.

Tertiary industry

Tertiary industries are about activities rather than products. They are also called **service industries**. Transporting goods to the people who will buy them, and selling them when they get there, are tertiary industries. Other examples are banking, insurance, health care, education, leisure and tourism.

Tertiary industries grew rapidly in most of the world's richer countries in the second half of the 20th century.

▲ Assembling pick-up trucks in a factory in Thailand. **Mass production** in factories means that more goods can be made using fewer people. Such goods are cheaper because the cost of machinery and labour is spread over more items.

• *Industrial countries* are those that have a lot of manufacturing, or secondary industry. Examples of these are Japan, Germany and the USA.

▼ **Trade unions** are associations of workers who campaign for better wages and working conditions. If they cannot come to an agreement with employers, they may strike (stop work). This photograph, taken in London in 1926, shows trade unionists marching in support of a general strike, in which workers from many different industries go on strike together.

find out more

Farming
Fishing
Industrial Revolution
Mining
Plastics
Tourism
Trade

Information technology *see* Computers

Insects

There are more insects than any other kind of animal. Insects are found almost everywhere on Earth. Around one million different kinds of insect have already been identified, and new ones are being discovered all the time.

▲ Ladybirds like these do a useful job in helping to control insect pests such as aphids.

▶ The body parts of a typical insect.

forewing

hindwing

compound eye

spiracles (for breathing)

ocelli (simple eyes)

antenna (feeler)

ovipositor (for laying eggs)

mouthparts

head   thorax   abdomen

Like crabs and spiders, insects are members of the **arthropod** group, a huge group of **invertebrates**. Invertebrates are animals that do not have backbones.

A skeleton outside

Like all arthropods, insects' bodies are protected by an **exoskeleton**. This hard case supports their bodies from the outside. All insects have to **moult**, or shed their exoskeleton, in order to grow.

Thanks to their tough, waterproof exoskeleton, insects can live almost anywhere in the world and under almost any conditions. There are insects living on high mountains, in hot, dry deserts – and a few even live in the sea!

Body parts

An insect's body is divided into three main sections: the head, the thorax and the abdomen. On its head are its mouth, eyes and antennae, or feelers.

INSECT RECORDS

Longest insect:
A stick insect from Borneo reaches 54.6 cm including its legs

Smallest insect:
A kind of beetle and a kind of fly are smaller than some single-celled animals

Heaviest insect: The male Goliath beetle of Equatorial Africa weighs 70 to 100 g

find out more

Animals
Bees and wasps
Butterflies and moths

The **thorax** is the central part of the insect's body. Most insects have three pairs of legs and two pairs of wings attached to their thorax.

The main part of the insect's gut and its digestive system are in the **abdomen**. So are its sex organs.

Insect groups

Insects that are related to each other are grouped together into large groups, or orders. Around three quarters of all kinds of insects belong to one of five main groups.

These five groups include: beetles, bugs, flies, wasps (including ants and bees), and butterflies and moths. Other smaller groups include cockroaches, earwigs, and grasshoppers.

Ants and termites

Ants and termites always live in huge groups or colonies. There are many thousands of individuals in each colony, but they all have the same mother: the **queen**.

Ants eat many kinds of food, including plants and other animals. Termites eat only plant food. Ants and termites are themselves eaten by many larger animals, such as aardvarks and anteaters.

Beetles

Beetles are easy to recognize because their thickened front wings make them look as if they are wearing heavy armour.

There are more types of beetle than any other sort of animal. So far scientists have discovered over 400,000 different kinds.

Many beetles are recyclers, helping to return dead matter to the soil, where it can be used for new plant growth. Others feed off other insect pests.

Fleas and lice

Fleas and lice do not have wings and live as parasites on other

▲ Beetles come in many shapes, sizes and colours. The violet ground beetle (1) cannot fly. The green tiger beetle (2) feeds mainly on other insects. The great diving beetle (3) lives in the water. The orange and black oil beetle (4) lives in the desert.

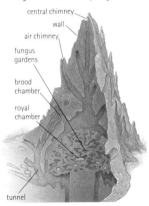

▼ Some kinds of termite build enormous nests, rising many metres above the ground. The queen and her mate live in a royal chamber inside the nest. The termite colony uses the nest to grow food and raise young.

central chimney
wall
air chimney
fungus gardens
brood chamber
royal chamber
tunnel

flea

louse

▲ Fleas have backward pointing hairs and sharp claws to help them cling onto their hosts. Lice use their gripping claws to cling on.

horsefly

mosquito

▲ Male horseflies suck nectar from plants. But females suck blood from horses, cattle and humans. Mosquitoes have slender, soft bodies.

adult

grasshopper

eggs

nymph

▲ Incomplete metamorphosis. There is a diagram showing complete metamorphosis under Butterflies and moths.

animals, such as mammals. **Parasites** live by feeding on the other animal (their **host**), and usually cause it harm in the process. Both fleas and lice often carry diseases.

Flies and mosquitoes

All flies have two pairs of wings. But only the front pair is used for flying. The tiny hind pair is probably used to help them balance.

Some types of fly do useful jobs, such as breaking down decaying plants and animals or carrying pollen from flower to flower. But others, like mosquitoes, carry diseases that they pass on to people and animals when they bite them.

Grasshoppers and crickets

Grasshoppers and crickets are insects that have existed since before the dinosaurs. They are among the insects that undergo

▲ A desert locust. 'Locust' is the name given to several large, short-horned grasshoppers. In the Middle East and Africa, locusts have been the most feared of all pests since farming began. This is because they can move together in huge swarms, destroying whole fields of crops as they feed.

a process called **incomplete metamorphosis**. When they hatch, the young have no wings. Each time they moult their wings grow bigger. Finally, when they are fully grown, they can fly. Other familiar insects, such as butterflies, beetles and flies, undergo **complete metamorphosis**. Their bodies change completely when they become adults.

◀ Bugs are a large and varied group of insects with one thing in common. They cannot eat solid food. All bugs have long, thin, sharp-tipped mouthparts to pierce the stems, leaves or fruit of plants to suck up the sap, or pierce the skin of animals to suck blood. This is a shield bug sucking sap from a flower.

Internet

The Internet is a huge computer network that makes it easy for people all around the world to exchange and share information.

The Internet, or the Net, works by linking together many small groups (**networks**) of computers belonging to organizations, universities and government departments.

To join the Internet you only need a personal computer, a modem and a telephone line. You can then send and receive electronic mail (**email**), get information about thousands of different subjects and transfer computer files.

▶ Special companies called Internet service providers link millions of personal computers all over the world to the Internet.

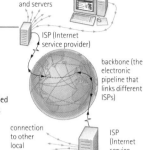

connection to other local computers and servers

local computer

ISP (Internet service provider)

backbone (the electronic pipeline that links different ISPs)

connection to other local computers and servers

ISP (Internet service provider)

local computer

The worldwide web

The worldwide web is part of the Internet. It is a collection of thousands of independent computers, called web servers, that are linked worldwide. These servers store information in special files called **web sites**. Programs called web browsers help people look through, or 'surf', the web sites. Many people and businesses set up their own web sites to give information about themselves or to sell products. The sites may contain video clips, animations, music and pictures. Anyone surfing the worldwide web can look at these sites and download information from them.

◀ Schoolchildren in the UK using the Internet. They can connect to web sites all around the world, and email children in other schools.

KEY DATES

1969 Internet first developed by scientists working at the US Department of Defense

mid–1980s around 1000 computer networks linked to the Internet

1990 Worldwide web developed at CERN (European Organization for Nuclear Research) in Switzerland

find out more

Communications
Computers
Telephones

Republic of Ireland

The Republic of Ireland is a country in north-west Europe. It is often called the 'Emerald Isle', because grass grows lush and green in the mild, moist climate.

The rugged Irish coastline is broken up by bays and sandy beaches. Most of the country's low mountains and moorlands are near the coast.

Agriculture and industry

Farmers raise beef and dairy cattle in large numbers, and cereals, potatoes and sugar beet are important crops. Other Irish products sold abroad include linen, crystal glass, whiskey and beer. Many people work in the electronics and computer industries, or in factories making plastics. Fishing and tourism are also important.

A troubled past

England took control of Ireland in the 1500s. The majority of people were Catholics, so when land was given to Protestants from England and Scotland, the Irish protested violently. In 1921 southern Ireland became an independent republic, while Northern Ireland remained part of the United Kingdom. But the division did not solve Ireland's problems. Riots, shootings and bombings troubled the country, but in 1998 the outlines of a peace plan were finally agreed.

▲ The Northern Ireland Peace Agreement was signed in Belfast in 1998 by the British and Irish prime ministers, and representatives of the main Northern Irish political parties.

IRELAND FACTS

Capital: Dublin

Population: 3,625,000

Area: 70,282 sq km

Language: English, Irish Gaelic

Religion: Christian

Currency: 1 Irish pound = 100 pence

Wealth per person: $14,710

▼ The lush landscape of the Ring of Kerry in Killarney National Park, Ireland.

find out more

Britain, History of
Celts
Europe
United Kingdom
Vikings

Iron and steel

Iron is the cheapest and most important metal on Earth. It is used to make all kinds of things, from needles and screws to ships and buildings.

Iron is so useful because it can be treated in different ways to have many different properties. Steel is the most useful form of iron. It is a mixture of iron and small amounts of other elements.

Out of the Earth

Iron is usually found in rocks. Rocks that are rich in iron are called **iron ores**.

After iron ore has been dug out of the ground, the iron is extracted using a chemical process called **smelting**. The crushed iron ore is mixed with coke and limestone and heated in a **blast furnace**, a tall oven made of steel and lined with fireproof bricks.

Iron into steel

Pure iron is not very hard. But by heating it and mixing in different elements, such as carbon, manganese or silicon, its properties can be changed.

To make steel, the iron is heated once again, to remove carbon and other impurities. Then small amounts of other metals can be added to make an **alloy** (metal mixture). Different alloys have different properties. Adding chromium to steel, for example, produces stainless steel, which does not rust.

▲ Inside this hot rolling mill at a steel foundry, red-hot slabs of steel are moved backwards and forwards under huge rollers to form sheets.

◀ A blast furnace. When crushed iron ore, coke and limestone are heated together, they react inside the furnace to form molten iron and a waste material called **slag**. The molten iron is drained from the furnace through one tap, the slag through another.

skip for carrying iron ore, coke and limestone

gas outlet

blast of hot air

slag

molten iron

tap for slag

tap for molten iron

• The three most important steel-producing countries are China, Japan and the United States. China produces over 100 million tonnes of steel each year.

find out more
Early people
Industrial Revolution
Metals

Islands

An island is an area of land surrounded by water. Islands are found in lakes or rivers, and also in oceans and seas. They come in many different forms and sizes. The world's largest island is Greenland.

rising sea level covers low-lying land

continental island

lava is deposited on the ocean floor

the lava builds up above sea level to form an island

▶ How different kinds of island are formed.

volcanic island

Islands can be formed in many ways. Some mountainous islands are the tops of **volcanoes** that have erupted on the ocean floor. Iceland, the Caribbean islands and the Aleutian Islands are all examples of volcanic islands. Other islands are small landmasses that have become separated from the mainland.

Islands are sometimes formed when the sea level rises after large ice-sheets have melted. Lowland areas are flooded, leaving the areas of land in between as islands. Many low-lying islands in warm seas are made of **coral**.

Island life

Coconut palms are the first plants to grow on many tropical islands. The coconuts are

carried to the islands by the sea. Other plants may arrive as seeds carried by migrating birds.

Many islands are home to kinds of plants and animals found nowhere else on Earth, for example the lemurs of Madagascar. On some islands there are no mammals, and other types of animal may flourish because they face less competition than they would on the mainland.

find out more

Caribbean
Continents
Pacific Islands
Volcanoes

▶ Low-lying islands are often made of **coral**, rock made from the skeletons of tiny animals. Sometimes coral forms a circular ring called an **atoll**, which encloses a lagoon. Kayangel Atoll is part of the Caroline Islands in the Pacific Ocean.

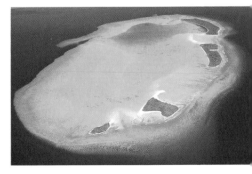

Israel *see* Middle East

Italy

It is no surprise that Italy is one of the most popular tourist destinations in the world. It is home to spectacular cities such as Florence, Rome and Venice, fine art, palaces, cathedrals and beautiful countryside.

Italy lies on a long strip of land sticking out below the Alps in Europe. It looks like a tall boot kicking the Italian islands of Sicily and Sardinia.

Fruit and vegetables grow on Italy's rich farmland. Its warm climate allows vines to grow everywhere, and Italy is one of the world's biggest **wine** producers. Its northern cities are world leaders in **design** and **engineering**, making cars, clothes, shoes and textiles.

Italy's history

Two thousand years ago, the **Roman empire** was vast and the people of Italy felt they ruled the world. Four centuries later barbarian tribes captured Rome and broke up the empire.

From the Middle Ages until the 19th century Italy was a jigsaw of small **city states**. Then, in 1860, a soldier, Giuseppe **Garibaldi**, and a politician, Camillo **Cavour**, managed to unite these states into a single country.

Between World War I and World War II Italy was under the control of the fascist dictator Benito **Mussolini**. But after World War II Italians voted to make Italy a republic.

ITALY FACTS

Capital: Rome

Population: 57,750,000

Area: 301,255 sq km

Language: Italian

Religion: Christian

Currency: 1 Italian lira = 100 centesimi

Wealth per person: $19,020

Small but beautiful!

The **Vatican City** in Rome, the headquarters of the Roman Catholic Church, is the world's smallest country. It is 0.44 sq km in area, and has a population of 1000 people.

find out more

Europe
Governments
Middle Ages
Painting and drawing
Renaissance
Romans

◀ Venice was once a great trading centre built on islands in a lagoon. It is now in danger of sinking into the lagoon.

Japan

Japan is a wealthy, bustling country of many islands in eastern Asia. Its industries make goods which sell all over the world.

Thickly wooded hills and mountains occupy two-thirds of Japan. The country has more than 60 active volcanoes and is often shaken by earthquakes. The highest mountain, **Mount Fuji**, is an old volcano. Northern Japan has cold, snowy winters and short summers. In the south, the climate is hot and humid.

Japanese life

The main island, Honshu, is where most people live. Because so much of Japan is mountainous, three-quarters of the people live in towns and cities near the coast. Many people live in suburbs and commute to work.

Each of Japan's islands has large areas of farmland. **Rice** is the main crop. Farmers use machines to plant the rice seedlings, but a great deal of the work has to be done by hand.

Japan has become a rich and powerful **manufacturing** country. It is a leading producer of cars, ships and television sets, and sells a great deal of electronic equipment. But it has to import nearly all its raw materials and its coal and oil.

Japan's history

Since the 6th century BC, Japan has been an empire, ruled by an **emperor**. But from AD 1160, real power was in the hands of warrior lords called **shoguns**, who ruled in the name of the emperor. The shoguns were supported by powerful knights known as **samurai**.

European traders arrived in the 16th century, but in 1637 the shoguns banned almost all foreign trade. Japan remained cut off from the rest of the world

JAPAN FACTS

Capital: Tokyo

Population: 125,900,000

Area: 377,728,000 sq km

Language: Japanese

Religion: Shinto, Buddhist

Currency: 1 yen = 100 sen

Wealth per person: $39,640

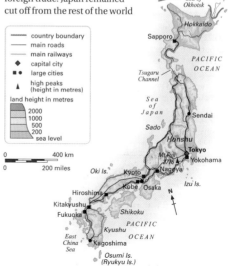

---- country boundary
—— main roads
—— main railways
◆ capital city
■ ● large cities
▲ high peaks (height in metres)
land height in metres

2000
1000
500
200
sea level

0   400 km
0   200 miles

◀ Tokyo is one of the world's largest, most modern cities. But car exhaust fumes have polluted the air so much that in the town centre there are oxygen supplies on the streets.

find out more

Asia
Food
Myths and folk tales
Religions
Volcanoes and
  earthquakes
World War II

until 1854, when the USA forced the Japanese to open their ports.

In 1867 the emperor Mutsuhito (Meiji) took over the rule of Japan from the shoguns. Japan quickly built up its power, and between 1894 and 1937, took control of Korea, Taiwan and large areas of China.

During World War II Japan fought with Germany against the USA and the Allies. Japan was eventually defeated, and US and Allied forces occupied Japan for seven years. Since then Japan has adopted a **democratic government** and built up its industries, but it still has an agreement not to develop its army and navy.

▼ This view of Mount Fuji is one of many painted by the Japanese artist Hokusai. He was perhaps the greatest artist of the *ukiyo-e* school – 'pictures of the floating world'.

Japanese arts
The traditional arts of Japan are very simple, elegant and formal. The Japanese pioneered **bonsai** (growing miniature trees). They also perfected **origami**, or paper folding. The favourite kind of poetry is the **haiku**, which is just 17 syllables long. Japan is also the home of many **martial arts**, such as judo, karate and sumo wrestling.

Jellyfishes and corals

Jellyfishes, corals and sea anemones all live in the oceans. Although they look very different, they are all related to each other.

All jellyfishes, sea anemones and corals have simple, circular bodies without a head or tail. They eat other animals, and catch their prey using stinging **tentacles**. They also all digest their food in a stomach with only one opening.

Jellyfishes move through the water with a pulsing movement, trailing their long tentacles behind them. These tentacles are covered with stinging cells, and the jellyfish uses them to stun prey such as fishes, shrimps and other sea animals, before eating it.

Sea anemones and **corals** have petal-like rings of short tentacles around their mouths. These make them look like plants, but in fact they are creatures called **polyps**. Their tentacles too are studded with stinging cells, and used to stun tiny creatures that touch them.

Sea anemones are soft-bodied animals. They live by attaching themselves to a hard surface in deep or shallow water.

Corals take minerals from the seawater and build them into a hard cup-like skeleton to support and protect themselves. Some corals live alone. But many live in large colonies, called **coral reefs**.

▲ Much of a jellyfish's bell-shaped body is made up of a stiff, jelly-like material.

• There are about 6500 different kinds of coral and sea anemone and around 200 different kinds of jellyfish.

Man-o-war
The Portuguese man-o-war looks like a big jellyfish, but it is really a floating colony. In the colony many polyps live and work together. Some of the polyps form long tentacles to sting and capture prey.

▼ Sea anemones and corals can often be found together. This sea anemone is living on a sea-fan coral.

> **find out more**
> Islands
> Oceans and seas
> Seashore

Jews

Jews are people who belong to the Jewish community. The religion of the community is Judaism, one of the oldest religions in the world. Jews live all over the world, but many think of Israel as their homeland.

▲ At the festival of **Passover**, Jews remember how God helped the Israelites to escape from Egypt. At a meal called the Seder, a plate of foods symbolizes the Israelites' experiences. For example, lettuce and radishes represent bitterness and a bowl of salt water represents tears.

Jews believe in one God who made, sees and knows everything. They believe they have a special relationship with God that began with Abraham, who is seen as the father of the Jewish people.

Abraham and Moses

Abraham lived in Mesopotamia (now Iraq) in about 1800 BC. He followed God's call to move with his family to a new land. Then one of Abraham's grandchildren, Jacob, was told by God that he would be known as 'Israel'. His descendants were called 'the children of Israel' or Israelites.

Later, the Israelites were slaves in Egypt. To persuade the Egyptians to free them, God sent plagues. The last plague killed all the first-born sons of the Egyptians, but 'passed over' the Israelites' houses. God then used Moses to lead the Israelites out of Egypt towards the 'promised land' of Israel. After 40 years they came to Mount Sinai, where God gave Moses the **Torah**. The Torah contains the teachings and laws of God (including the **Ten Commandments**) and forms part of the Jewish Bible.

◀ When Jewish boys are 13 and girls are 12, they come of age. A boy becomes a **Bar Mitzvah**, a 'son of the commandments', and a girl becomes a **Bat Mitzvah**, a 'daughter of the commandments'. At a special ceremony in the synagogue, the Bar Mitzvah recites a prayer and reads from the Torah.

Worship

The Jewish holy books or **Scriptures** are written in Hebrew. Jews learn Hebrew so they can study and discuss the Scriptures. Jews can worship anywhere, but they meet for study and prayer in **synagogues**. The focus of a synagogue is the handwritten Torah scroll, which is kept in a cupboard called the **Holy Ark**. The main services are led by a **rabbi** (Jewish teacher), or a person who has studied the scriptures for a long time.

▶ The Holy Ark containing the Torah inside a synagogue, the building where Jews go to worship.

The Sabbath

The focus of each week is the Sabbath. This is a day of rest, play and prayer lasting from dusk on Friday to dusk on Saturday. In Jewish homes on the Friday evening, two special candles are lit and the family sings a prayer called the 'kiddush' before supper.

find out more
Religions

● **David** and **Solomon** who lived in the 10th century BC, were two of Israel's most famous kings. David made Jerusalem the capital of Israel. His son Solomon built the Temple, which made Jerusalem a holy city.

● Throughout history Jewish people have been attacked (persecuted) as a group that stands out as being different. In Nazi Germany in the 1930s and 1940s, over 6 million Jews were killed. This is known as the **Holocaust**. In 1947 the United Nations decided there should be a Jewish state in Palestine. This was called Israel.

▼ The Western or Wailing Wall is the only part of the Temple in Jerusalem that survived after the Romans destroyed it in AD 70. These Jews have come to the Wall to pray.

Joan of Arc *see* France *and* Middle Ages

Kangaroos and other marsupials

Kangaroos, koalas, opossums, wombats and wallabies are all marsupials. Marsupials are mammals that raise their young in a pouch on the mother's belly.

When baby marsupials are born, they are very tiny. Some are the size of a grain of rice. Although they have hardly begun to develop, they have strong forelimbs and claws. They use these to crawl into a furry **pouch** on their mother's belly. There they find a teat and begin to feed and grow. They stay in the pouch until they are big enough to look after themselves.

Marsupials live only in Australia, New Guinea and South and North America. There are around 280 different kinds. Most eat plants, but some, like the opossums of the Americas, eat other animals.

MARSUPIAL
RECORDS

Largest: red kangaroo. Males up to 2.5 m long and weigh up to 90 kg.

Smallest: the Pilbara ningaui: adults can be 4.6 cm long and weigh 2 g.

The best-known Australian marsupials are kangaroos, koalas and wombats. **Kangaroos** have powerful back legs. The biggest kangaroos can cover more than 10 metres in a single bound. **Koalas** are climbers and live in trees. They eat mostly eucalyptus leaves and shoots, and sleep for about 18 hours a day. **Wombats** live in burrows in the ground. They come out at night to feed.

▲ A female red kangaroo with her young. The red kangaroo is the largest marsupial, and one of the most common.

find out more ▶

Animals
Australia
Mammals

Playing possum

If the Virginia opossum is caught or frightened, it tries to fool its enemy by pretending to be dead. This is known as 'playing possum'.

▼ Marsupials come in many shapes and sizes, and live in very different ways. Some are plant-eaters, others eat flesh. Some climb trees and others burrow underground.

koala

wombat

cuscus

American opossum

Knights

Knights were heavily-armed soldiers who fought on horseback. The most famous knights were those of medieval Europe. It was a great honour to be a knight.

Two inventions made knights the most powerful soldiers on the battlefield. One was stirrups. These gave riders more control over their horses and helped them stay in the saddle. The other invention was **steel armour**, which made a charging knight a sort of medieval tank.

As the knights' large war-horses, armour and weapons were very expensive, they were given lands to live off by their king. In return they had to serve the king by fighting for him. The idea of land in exchange for service was at the heart of Europe's **'feudal system'**.

▲ Ladies watch two knights fighting in a tournament. Tournaments followed strict rules. Even so, knights were often badly hurt or killed.

Chivalry

Because knights could be rough bullies, a code of knightly behaviour was drawn up. It was known as chivalry. It said that a knight should be brave but kind to the weak (especially women), strong but polite, determined but honest. The knights' importance on the battlefield soon disappeared after the invention of guns.

● Among the best known of all knights are **King Arthur** and the Knights of the Round Table. But the real King Arthur was not a knight. He was an English soldier who fought against the Anglo-Saxons. When the legend was retold in the 12th century, King Arthur became a medieval figure, and his followers chivalrous knights.

Heraldry

It was impossible to recognize a knight in his armour, so the problem was solved by 'heraldry' – a system of designs on a knight's shield and clothes. Each knight was known by his 'coat of arms'.

▼ The background colour of a shield is its **field**. A field can be divided up in various ways, called **divisions**. A **charge** is a picture or shape on the field.

Charges

Bend   Fess   Saltire   Chevron

Divisions

Quarterly   Paly

find out more

Castles
Crusades
Middle Ages
Normans
Weapons

Lakes

Lakes are large areas of water surrounded by land. They form when water collects in a hollow in the ground, or behind a natural or artificial barrier.

rift-valley lake

There are many different types of lake. They are named according to how they are formed. **Crater lakes** lie in the natural hollows of old volcanoes. Lake Bosumtwi in Ghana lies in a crater that was probably made by a meteorite.

Glacial lakes form where ice-sheets and glaciers have left the ground very uneven. They have scraped and hollowed out rock, or dumped sand, gravel and clay in uneven layers. Such lake districts are found in Finland and in northern Canada. Lakes may fill holes in the glaciated valley floor, as in the Lake District in England.

Rift-valley lakes are long thin lakes such as Lake Malawi, Lake Tanganyika and Lake Turkana in East Africa, and the Dead Sea between Israel and Jordan. When the Earth's crust slipped down between long fault lines, the water filled part of the floor of the valley.

Artificial lakes are created by humans, using earth, stone and concrete dams to hold back the river. The water in the lake is used for drinking, to irrigate (water) farmland, and to generate electricity.

glacial lake

▲ How glacial lakes and rift-valley lakes are formed.

▼ Crater Lake in Oregon, USA. About 6000 years ago the volcano Mount Mazama erupted, and the upper part was completely destroyed. Crater Lake formed in the crater that was left behind.

LAKE RECORDS

Largest lake: Caspian Sea, central Asia (371,000 sq km)

Largest freshwater lake: Lake Superior, Canada/USA (83,270 sq km)

Deepest lake: Lake Baykal, Russia (1741 m deep)

find out more

Ice
Mountains
Rocks and minerals
Water

217

Languages

We use languages to communicate facts and ideas, to ask questions, to explain things, to tell stories. Languages can be both spoken and written. We write things down when we want to keep them and use them again later, or when we want someone else to read them.

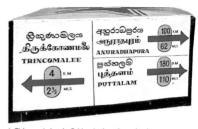

▲ This road sign in Sri Lanka is written in three languages: Sinhalese, Tamil and English. The English language spread around the world from the 17th century, when Britain began to create an empire. English is still spoken in many countries that used to be part of this empire.

There are well over 4000 languages in the world. In Africa alone there are about 1300.

Language families

Languages can be divided up into different families. Greek, Latin, English, French, Russian and Hindi all belong to the huge **Indo-European** family. One much smaller family includes Finnish, Hungarian and perhaps Turkish. Others include the Chinese languages and the languages of Japan and Korea. There are four families of African languages.

Languages today

Most people learn one language at home. This is their **mother tongue**. But some people are **bilingual** – they speak two languages equally well. They may have parents who speak different languages. In some countries it is normal to use a mother tongue at home and an official language in school or at work.

When people from different countries want to speak together they may use an **international language**. English and French are often used as international languages.

Writing

Writing is a way of storing words – and so recording information, ideas and stories. Books, laws, the news, and letters and cards to friends are all written down.

▼ The languages with most speakers.

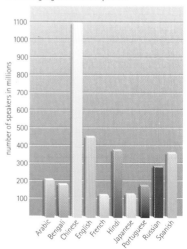

Writing developed from drawing. Two very early kinds of writing were pictograms and ideograms. In a **pictogram** a picture of something, such as a circle for the Sun, is used to mean the object itself. In an **ideogram** the whole idea of the word is explained in a shape. The Chinese writing system uses ideograms.

The earliest true writing was developed by the Sumerians in Mesopotamia (now Iraq) in about 3250 BC. It is known as **cuneiform** and was made up of wedge-shaped signs written on clay tablets. Cuneiform was used for about 3000 years.

Hieroglyphics

Hieroglyphics are a form of writing that uses pictures and symbols instead of words. The ancient Egyptians developed hieroglyphics about 3100 BC and used them for 3500 years. Egyptian hieroglyphic writing uses at least 700 different signs. The Maya people of Central America also used hieroglyphs for over 1000 years.

horse

to stand upright

Alphabets

Most languages today are written using an alphabet. The first alphabet was probably developed in the 15th century BC by the Canaanite people of Syria. It had 32 letters.

The Phoenicians reduced the Canaanite alphabet to 22 letters and spread it through the Mediterranean. The Greek, Roman, Arabic and Hebrew alphabets developed from the Phoenician.

The alphabet in which English and many other European languages are written is the one the Romans used. Today it is the most widely used alphabet in the world.

▲ Chinese ideograms. The earliest forms were simple drawings. Over the centuries they changed into shapes that are easy to write.

• If you want people to understand what you say, you have to use the right words and put them in the right order. The way we put a language together is called its **grammar**.

find out more

Ancient world
Communications
Egyptians, ancient

А Б В Г Д Е Ё Ж З И Й К Л М Н О П Р С Т У Ф Х Ц Ч Ш Щ Ъ Ы Ь Э Ю Я
а б в г д е ё ж з и й к л м н о п р с т у ф х ц ч ш щ ъ ы ь э ю я

अ आ इ ई उ ऊ ऋ ए ऐ ओ औ अं अः क ख ग घ ङ च छ ज झ ञ
ट ठ ड ढ ण त थ द ध न प फ ब भ म य र ल व श ष स ह

ص س ش ز ر ذ د خ ح ج ث ت ب ا
ي و ه ن م ل ك ق ف غ ع ظ ط ض

◀ The Cyrillic (top), Devanagari (middle) and Arabic (bottom) alphabets are three of about 50 different alphabets used in the world today. The Arabic alphabet is written from right to left.

Lasers *see* Light

Law

The law of a country is its system of rules. The law sets out how people in that country have to behave. People who break the law are punished. The police, courts and prisons carry out the law.

The law often gives people both **rights** and **duties**. For example, in many countries the law gives people a right to free education when they are children, but a duty to pay taxes on money that they earn when they are adults.

Each country has its own set of laws. In democratic countries, most new laws are made by **parliament**. In countries that are ruled by a **dictator**, the dictator makes all the laws himself.

▼ This scene from a US courtroom shows a criminal case being heard by a judge and jury. The woman at the centre is a lawyer. The jury must decide whether the person on trial is innocent or guilty.

International law

International law sets out how countries should behave in their dealings with each other. But one branch of international law sets out how governments should behave towards their own people. In 1948 the United Nations adopted the **Universal Declaration of Human Rights**. It says that everyone has the right to life, security, freedom and protection by the law. But countries are not legally bound to follow it.

▲ One of the oldest systems of law was created nearly 4000 years ago by Hammurabi, king of Babylon. He had 282 laws carved on this large block of stone.

Systems of law
In many European countries such as France, Germany and Italy, modern law is based on the system used by the Romans. In many English-speaking countries, modern law is based on English law. In some Muslim countries such as Iran the law is based partly on Islamic law.

Criminal law

When someone steals, or uses violence, they commit a **crime**. Criminal law defines what behaviour is a crime. For example, killing someone is almost always a crime.

When someone is accused of committing a crime, they go to **court** to be tried. At the **trial** one **lawyer** puts their case to the judge and jury, while a second lawyer puts the case against them. A **jury** is a group of ordinary people who listen to the evidence and decide whether the accused person is innocent or guilty. The **judge** controls the trial, advises the jury, and decides on the punishment.

Punishment may be a fine or an order to do community service, or, if the crime is serious, a **prison** sentence.

▲ The Mafia is a secret society. It is involved in organized crime around the world, for instance selling illegal drugs and kidnapping people. These Mafia suspects are on trial in Italy.

Civil law

Civil law sets out rules for everyday life and for business. It deals with matters such as housing, land, work, money and family life. For example, when two people divorce, they often go to court to decide who the children will live with, and how the money will be divided.

Police

The main job of policemen and women is to prevent, investigate and solve crimes. They also try to keep public order. Police forces around the world often work together.

◄ Everyone's fingerprints are different. After a crime is committed, the police try to match the fingerprints they find at the scene with those of people who might have committed the crime.

find out more
Governments

Lenses and mirrors

Lenses are specially shaped pieces of glass or plastic that bend a beam of light as it goes through them. Mirrors reflect, or bounce back, most of the light that falls on them.

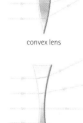
convex lens

Lenses and mirrors are used in many types of device that gather and **focus** light. Microscopes, telescopes and cameras are just a few of the devices that depend on lenses and mirrors. The lenses we use most often are the ones in our eyes.

Bouncing back or bending

Light travels in a straight line through empty space, but when it meets an object, it changes direction. Both lenses and mirrors take advantage of this.

When light hits the surface of a mirror, it is **reflected** back, like a ball bouncing off a hard wall. But when the light hits other materials, like glass or water, it is bent (**refracted**) as it travels through. This happens because the light travels more slowly through these materials than it does through air.

Light is bent (refracted) and reflected according to a few simple rules. These rules can be used to draw diagrams showing what happens when light passes through different shapes of lens or is reflected off different types of mirror.

▶ When a beam of light passes through a convex lens, the lens focuses the light down to a point. When a beam of light passes through a concave lens, it spreads out.

concave lens

▼ Telescopes that collect light are called optical telescopes. There are two main types: refracting and reflecting telescopes. A refracting telescope uses two lenses (the main lens and the eyepiece lens) to focus and magnify the image. A reflecting telescope uses two mirrors (the primary and secondary mirrors) instead of lenses. Most big telescopes are reflecting telescopes.

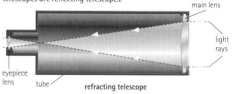

main lens / light rays / eyepiece lens / tube
refracting telescope

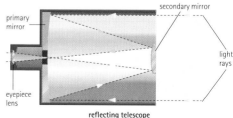

secondary mirror / primary mirror / light rays / eyepiece lens
reflecting telescope

Concave, convex and curves

Different kinds of lens can either focus light to a narrow point or spread it out. There are two main types of lens. A **convex** lens is thicker in the middle. If you look through it, things look bigger. A **concave** lens is thinner in the middle. If you look through one, things look smaller.

Mirrors can be concave or convex, too. Convex mirrors bulge outwards. They make things look smaller, but give a wider view. Concave mirrors curve inwards. They magnify things held close to them, but produce a tiny, upside-down image of things far away.

Using mirrors and lenses

Lenses and mirrors are used in cameras to collect light and focus it onto light-sensitive film. Most telescopes and microscopes uses lenses and mirrors to show us things that are too small or too far away to be seen with the naked eye. They

do this by making objects appear bigger and brighter.

In optical microscopes (ones that use lenses and mirrors) there are two lenses. The **objective lens** creates a magnified image of the object you are looking at. The **eyepiece lens** magnifies that image even further. The best optical microscopes can magnify up to 2000 times.

▲ With a flat mirror, the image of an object appears to be as far behind the mirror's surface as the object is in front of it. But the mirror reverses the image from left to right – so words look as if they were written backwards.

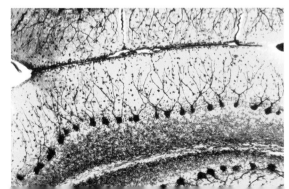

◀ This highly magnified picture of a tiny part of the brain was taken using a microscope. The individual nerve cells can be clearly seen.

find out more
Light
Senses

223

Life on Earth

Living things have several things in common: they grow, they reproduce, and they can react to changes in their surroundings. Life on Earth probably began more than 3500 million years ago. Scientists think that the first living things were creatures like bacteria, which lived in hot, muddy places under water warmed by volcanoes.

▲ Stromatolites are made up of layers of blue-green algae and rock. These living stromatolites are in Australia. The oldest known fossils are of stromatolites 3500 million years old.

After hundreds of millions of years, some living things began to use the Sun's energy to make food. In this process, called **photosynthesis**, they used carbon dioxide in the atmosphere and gave off oxygen. Plants still make food in this way today. Gradually oxygen became part of the Earth's atmosphere. All animals need oxygen to live.

▼ Evolution of life began more than 3500 million years ago. This timeline shows only the last 500 million years. Scientists can never be sure of the exact time an animal or plant evolved, so it shows only when something was living rather than when it first appeared. Some of the kinds of animals shown living 500 million years ago, such as starfishes, are still living today, but most are now extinct. (have died out). (These drawings are not to scale.)

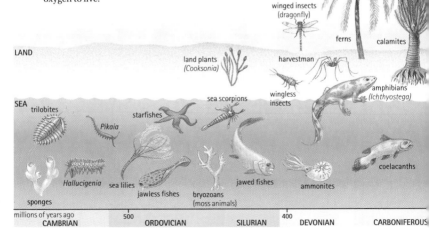

winged insects (dragonfly)

ferns   calamites

LAND

land plants (Cooksonia)   harvestman

sea scorpions   wingless insects   amphibians (Ichthyostega)

SEA

trilobites   starfishes

Pikaia   coelacanths

sponges   Hallucigenia   sea lilies   jawless fishes   bryozoans (moss animals)   jawed fishes   ammonites

| millions of years ago | | | | | |
| CAMBRIAN | 500 | ORDOVICIAN | SILURIAN | 400 | DEVONIAN | CARBONIFEROUS |

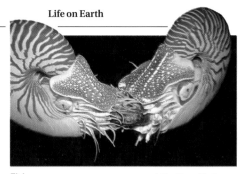

Animals

The first animals were probably like some single-celled creatures of today, such as amoebas, which live in all sorts of moist places. The first complex animals appeared over 600 million years ago – they included sponges, jellyfishes and worm-like creatures.

Life in the sea

About 570 million years ago many animals developed hard shells. These shells make good fossils, so we know quite a lot about them. Fossils of this age include corals, brachiopods, starfishes, snail-like animals and trilobites – armoured creatures related to crabs and insects.

Fishes

The first – heavily armoured – fishes appeared about 500 million years ago. Eventually many different kinds of fishes, including sharks and the ancestors of bony fishes, lived in the seas and fresh waters.

▲ Nautiluses like the two in this picture are sometimes called living fossils. Their relatives include ammonites, which were common 400 million years ago.

● Ninety-nine per cent of all the different kinds of animal that have ever lived are now extinct.

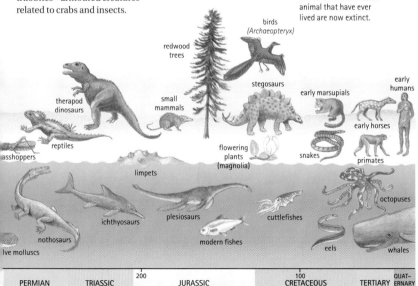

▲ Cooksonia, one of the first land plants. Cooksonia had a waxy outer layer (cuticle) to prevent it drying out, and tubes in the stems to transport its water and food.

Life on land

Gradually plants and animals began to invade the land. About 400 million years ago a few small plants, fungi, mites and insect-like creatures lived by the water. Some of the animals fed on the plants. In time plants grew larger and covered much of the land. They provided suitable habitats for many kinds of animal.

Lunged fishes

Unlike most modern fishes, many fishes at this time had lungs as well as gills, and could breathe air. Some lived on the river-beds, and used their fins like legs. They were all flesh-eaters, and probably they sometimes scrambled right out of the water to grab prey. In time, **amphibians** – animals that can survive out of water for part of their lives – developed from such 'walking fishes'.

Reptiles

The first reptiles lived about 280 million years ago. Their skin was probably hard, dry and waterproof, and their eggs probably had a shell like those of modern reptiles. Slowly the reptiles adapted to many different environments. Some, such as plesiosaurs and ichthyosaurs, returned to the water. Flying reptiles called pterosaurs soared above. Most **dinosaurs** were giant land-living animals.

▲ After insects, pterosaurs were the first animals to fly. Pterosaurs were reptiles that had gradually developed wings, and took to the skies over 200 million years ago. Birds were the next animals to fly, and finally bats, which are the only flying mammals.

Mammals and birds

The first mammals had developed – probably from fast-moving reptiles – by the time of the earliest dinosaurs, over 200 million years ago. Birds evolved later. The earliest bird that we know of lived about 147 million years ago. It was clearly related to small flesh-eating dinosaurs.

When the dinosaurs died out about 65 million years ago, mammals, birds and modern types of fishes and flowering plants survived. In time huge numbers of mammals and birds occupied much of the Earth. Mammals became the largest living creatures. One of the most recent mammals to evolve was humans.

▼ Early people shared their world with many animals that are now extinct. We know about these animals from cave paintings, fossils and other remains. Among the animals our ancestors hunted was the woolly mammoth.

Life on Earth

• Scientists have discovered more than 1.75 million different kinds (species) of living thing, and the total number could be about 13 million. The numbers of known species in the Monera and Protoctista kingdoms are probably only a tiny proportion of those that exist.

▶ When we think of living things we usually think first of **animals** and **plants**. But animals and plants are only two of the five **kingdoms** of living things. A kingdom is the name for a huge group of life forms. The other three are **Fungi**, **Protoctista** and **Monera**.

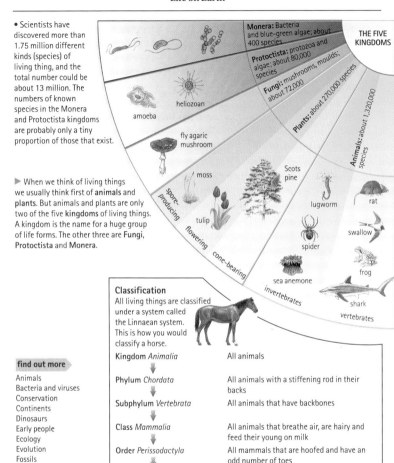

THE FIVE KINGDOMS

Monera: Bacteria and blue-green algae; about 400 species

Protoctista: protozoa and algae; about 80,000 species

Fungi: mushrooms, moulds; about 72,000

Plants: about 270,000 species

Animals: about 1,320,000 species

heliozoan

amoeba

fly agaric mushroom

moss

tulip

spore-producing

flowering

cone-bearing

Scots pine

lugworm

spider

sea anemone

invertebrates

rat

swallow

frog

shark

vertebrates

Classification

All living things are classified under a system called the Linnaean system. This is how you would classify a horse.

Kingdom *Animalia*	All animals
Phylum *Chordata*	All animals with a stiffening rod in their backs
Subphylum *Vertebrata*	All animals that have backbones
Class *Mammalia*	All animals that breathe air, are hairy and feed their young on milk
Order *Perissodactyla*	All mammals that are hoofed and have an odd number of toes
Family *Equidae*	All horse-like mammals, from about 60 million years ago
Genus *Equus*	All single-toed horses, from about 5 million years ago
Species *Equus caballus*	Domestic horse

Light

Light is a form of energy. Light usually comes from hot objects, like the Sun or flames, but it can also be made in other ways. We only see things if they give off light, or reflect light into our eyes.

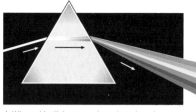

▲ When white light passes through a prism, the colours are bent by different amounts and you see a rainbow made up of all the colours of the spectrum.

We use light for many purposes. Light bulbs and torches help us see when it is dark. Solar power plants use light energy from the Sun to generate electricity. And tiny pulses of laser light travelling down optical fibres carry telephone calls, TV pictures and computer data around the world.

A family of waves

Light usually behaves like a wave. Light waves spread out from a light source in the same way that ripples on a pond spread when you drop a stone into the water.

The light we see is just one member of a whole family of **electromagnetic waves**. Others include ultraviolet light, radio waves and X-rays. Light and other kinds of electromagnetic wave travel at speeds of around 300,000 km per second. Nothing can travel faster!

Travelling light

Light normally travels in straight lines in empty space. It can travel through many types of

◀ Lasers produce a narrow beam of bright light that is made up of just one wavelength of light: a pure colour. They are used in many ways in our everyday lives – for instance, for reading bar codes at supermarkets, or playing compact discs. Here a laser is being used to perform eye surgery.

• The Sun, candles, fires and light bulbs all give out light because they are hot. If a material is heated to more than about 700 °C, it starts to glow. The light comes from the material's atoms, which give out energy in tiny bursts of light called **photons**.

Quick as a flash!

If you could travel at the speed of light, in just one second you would be able to go round the Earth more than seven times.

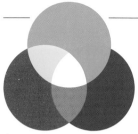

▲ You can make all the colours in the spectrum by mixing together beams of red, green and blue light. These three are called **primary colours**. When light of all three primary colours is mixed together, it produces white light.

▲ Mixing coloured paints or inks is different from mixing light. Each coloured paint absorbs some wavelengths of light, so when you mix different paint colours, the combination absorbs more light wavelengths. If you mix the three primary colours (for paints these are red, blue and yellow), you get black, not white.

materials. But if it is blocked, a shadow forms where the light cannot get through.

When a beam of light meets an object, it changes direction. When light hits a surface like a mirror, it is reflected, or bounced off, like a ball bouncing off a hard surface. When light enters materials like water or glass, it is **refracted**, or bent.

Seeing colours

White light is a mixture of all the colours. It contains the full **spectrum** of colours (all the colours of the rainbow).

Different colours have different **wavelengths**. The wavelength is the distance between the peak of one wave and the peak of the next. Red wavelengths are the longest. Violet waves are the shortest.

We see objects as coloured because their surfaces absorb some light wavelengths but not others. The colour we see is the light that is reflected back to our eyes. An object that absorbs all light wavelengths except red looks red; one that absorbs everything except blue light appears blue.

find out more

Lenses and mirrors
Radiation
Senses

Bright idea
For centuries people burned either gas or different types of oils and candles to get light. Then in the 1870s, the British scientist Joseph Swann and the American inventor Thomas Edison both had the same idea – to produce light by using electricity to make a thin wire, or filament, glow inside a glass bulb with the air pumped out of it. The breakthrough came when they found the right material to use for the filament (Edison used carbon). Most light bulbs we use today have a filament made from the metal tungsten.

Machines see Forces • **Magazines** see Newspapers • **Magnets** see Electricity

Mammals

Mammals are one of the main groups of animals with backbones. There are many different kinds. Whales, mice, elephants and bats are all mammals. People are mammals too.

Mammals are found almost everywhere in the world. You will find mammals in the freezing regions of the Arctic and in Antarctic seas, in hot deserts, in steamy rainforests and everywhere in between.

There are about 4000 different kinds of mammal. Monkeys and apes climb through trees. Deer and horses run across the plains. Moles burrow through the earth. Whales live only in the oceans. Bats fly through the air.

Some mammals, like rhinoceroses, eat just plants. Others, like lions and weasels, eat only meat. Still others eat both plants and meat.

▼ A grey seal cub suckling milk.

What makes a mammal?

Although they look very different, all mammals have some things in common.

- All mammals have bones, including a backbone.
- All mammals have lungs and breathe **air**.
- All mammals are **warm-blooded**.
- All mammals have some **fur** or **hair** at some stage in their lives.
- All female mammals feed their young on **milk**, which they produce in their mammary glands, or **breasts**.

The biggest living animals are mammals. The biggest animal of all is the blue whale, and the biggest land-living animal is the African elephant. Many large

▲ A male orang-utan. Orang-utans are apes that live in forests on the islands of South-east Asia. Like many large mammals, they are in danger of becoming extinct. This is mainly because humans have destroyed many of the places where they live.

mammals, such as rhinoceroses, tigers and gorillas, are in danger of dying out. This is mainly because people have taken over the land where they live.

Mammal groups

Mammals are divided into three main groups: **monotremes**, **marsupials** and **placental mammals**. Which group they belong to depends on how their young develop.

▲ A duck-billed platypus. Platypuses look like otters but have a beak like a duck, which they use to catch small water creatures like shrimps.

Monotremes

Monotremes are the only mammals that hatch from **eggs**. All other kinds of mammal are born live. There are only three kinds of monotreme: two kinds of echidnas, or spiny anteaters, and the duck-billed platypus. All three live in Australia or New Guinea.

Platypus eggs hatch after just 10 days. The young platypuses get their milk from pores on their mother's belly.

Marsupials

Kangaroos are the best-known marsupials. But there are many others, such as possums, koalas and wombats.

When marsupials are born, they are tiny and not fully developed. Some are no larger than a grain of rice. As soon as they are born, they crawl up to a pouch on their mother's belly. Here they latch onto a nipple and suck milk. They continue to grow and develop in their mother's pouch.

One hundred million years ago marsupials lived all over the world. But today they are found mainly in Australia and New Guinea. A few kinds, such as opossums, live in North and South America.

Placental mammals

Most mammals, including people, are placental mammals. The young of placental mammals grow inside their mothers. The developing babies are attached to their mother's womb by a spongy organ called the **placenta**

Live fast, die young!
Once a year all the males of a kind of marsupial mouse, the brown antechinus from eastern Australia, go on a rampage for two weeks. They rush around fighting and trying to mate with as many females as possible. Within about two weeks, all the males are dead from the stress of it all.

MAMMAL RECORDS

Largest mammals: Blue whales can grow up to 33 m long and weigh around 120 tonnes

Smallest mammals: Some shrews are less than 4.5 cm long and weigh only about 2 g

Tallest mammals: Giraffes can be up to 5.3 m tall

◀ Bats are the only mammals that can fly. This fishing bat hunts at night. It catches fish with its large hind feet, which have especially long, strong claws. Bats are placental mammals.

Marriage *see* Families • **Martial arts** *see* Sports facts, page 427

and a cord called the umbilical cord. The placenta supplies them with food and oxygen while they are growing.

Mammal hunters

Some of the best mammal hunters are cats and dogs. But many smaller mammals are hunters too. Weasels feed mainly on smaller mammals. Otters hunt for fish, frogs and other small water mammals in rivers and in the sea.

▲ Otters are excellent swimmers.

Plant-eaters

Many mammals are plant-eaters, or **herbivores**. They include some of the biggest mammals, such as elephants, antelopes and cattle. Many smaller mammals, for instance rabbits, are plant-eaters too.

Omnivores

Many mammals eat a mixture of both plant and animal food – they are called omnivores. Mice eat insects and other small creatures as well as plants.

Many small mammals eat insects. Hedgehogs, shrews and moles are insect-eaters, or **insectivores**. They are among the most active of all mammals. They need a lot of food to keep their small bodies warm.

◀ Weasels kill their prey with a bite to the base of the skull.

▲ Anteaters have no teeth. Instead they use their sticky tongues to lick up insects.

▲ Hedgehogs feed in the evenings.

▲ Shrews only grow to about 7 cm long.

find out more

Animals
Bears
Cats
Dogs
Elephants
Farm animals
Horses
Human beings
Kangaroos and other marsupials
Life on Earth
Mice and other rodents
Monkeys and apes
Sex and reproduction
Whales and dolphins

▼ The gaur is a type of wild cattle from South-east Asia.

▲ The elk (or moose) is the largest kind of deer. Like other deer it is a plant-eater. Males use their antlers to fight other males.

Marx, Karl *see* Communists *and* Philosophy • **Mathematics** *see* Numbers

Medicine

Medicine is the treatment of disease. It includes diagnosing the disease (identifying what is wrong), treating it with drugs, surgery or therapy, and even preventing it in the first place.

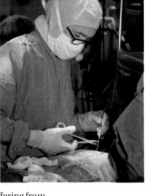

▶ This surgeon is suturing (sewing up) an incision (cut) after completing an operation.

Medicine has improved our lives in many ways. People in most parts of the world are much less likely to die of disease than they were 100 years ago.

People who work in medicine include doctors, nurses, surgeons, therapists and psychiatrists (who treat mental disease). All these people are involved with treating and caring for people suffering from disease. Some also carry out research into understanding and curing disease.

Doctors and nurses

Doctors and nurses are trained to prevent and cure illnesses. There are two main types of medical doctor: the family doctor or **general practitioner** (GP) and the specialist. If you are

Superdoc!
The most operations carried out in one day were 833 cataract operations performed by Dr M. C. Modi in India.

▼ This graph compares the number of people per doctor in countries around the world. In Niger, for example, there is one doctor for every 53,000 people, whereas Italy has one doctor for every 200 people.

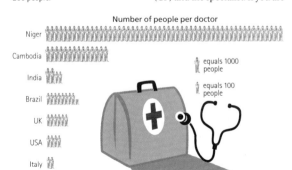

Number of people per doctor

Niger

Cambodia

India

Brazil

UK

USA

Italy

🧍 equals 1000 people

🧍 equals 100 people

find out more

Diseases
Drugs
Health and fitness
Radiation

ill, you usually go to your GP first. They diagnose the problem and decide if you need to see a specialist.

Specialists usually work in hospitals. They may work with a particular group of people, such as children or old people, or with particular diseases, for example cancer.

Nurses work with doctors to care for patients. Some also specialize in a particular area. Community nurses visit people in their homes, but most nurses work in hospitals.

Hospitals

Hospitals provide a wide range of treatments, including emergency care after accidents, surgery and drug treatment. Thousands of **drugs** are available today to treat illnesses, and scientists are developing new ones all the time.

Hospitals also carry out tests on patients. Machines called **scanners** show doctors images of the insides of the body. Some scanners pick up signals from the heart or brain. Others check that an unborn baby is developing properly. Some of these tests aim to identify diseases such as cancer early, so that they can be treated before they become dangerous.

Hospitals may also be centres for research, or teaching hospitals, providing training for doctors and nurses. There are

◀ Florence Nightingale became known as 'the lady with the lamp' while in charge of nursing injured soldiers during the Crimean War in 1854. She was one of the founders of modern nursing, and became an English national heroine.

also some specialist hospitals, including **maternity hospitals** for women giving birth, **psychiatric hospitals** for people who are mentally ill, and **children's hospitals**.

Complementary medicine

Some methods of curing illnesses do not use artificial drugs or surgery. Together they are known as complementary medicine.

Traditional **Chinese medicine** is based on complicated ideas about inner harmony. The different forms include **acupuncture** (below), and **moxibustion**, in which dried herbs are burnt next to the skin.

Osteopathy and **chiropractic** are ways of treating backache and other pains in the joints and muscles by pulling and pushing them to get them back into their proper positions.

In **homeopathy** patients are given a tiny amount of a substance that produces the same type of symptoms as the illness, to encourage the body's own natural healing processes.

▶ Acupuncture is used for relieving pain, curing disease and improving health. Needles are inserted into the body at points along 'meridians' (energy pathways) shown on this ancient study figure.

◀ Towards the end of the Middle Ages some doctors in Europe began to cut open human bodies to examine their structure (anatomy). As a result, understanding of anatomy grew rapidly. In this 16th-century painting a doctor is using a corpse to teach students.

Operations

An operation is the treatment of a disease or injury by going into the body and removing or repairing the damaged part. The doctors who carry out operations are called **surgeons**.

There are a number of different kinds of surgery. In **transplant surgery** the surgeon repairs or replaces a diseased part of the body, such as a kidney or the heart, with a healthy part from another person. In **keyhole surgery** a camera, and tiny cutting and gripping tools, are used to carry out operations through a very small cut.

Medicine in the past

People have been practising medicine for thousands of years. The ancient Greek doctor **Hippocrates of Cos**, who lived about 2400 years ago, has had a great influence on modern medicine. He argued that diseases could be explained if patients were examined carefully.

From the 9th century onwards, medical schools were founded in various parts of Europe. Medicine developed rapidly during the following centuries, with scientists making many important discoveries about disease and its treatment.

Famous scientists who had an impact on the history of medicine include the 17th-century English physician **William Harvey**, who accurately described the circulation of the blood, and the 19th-century English surgeon **Joseph Lister**, who introduced the idea of antiseptic (germ-free) surgery.

A hole in the head!

Operations have been carried out for thousands of years. Skulls more than 10,000 years old have been found with holes drilled in them. This operation, called trepanning, was probably done to release evil spirits from the patient's head.

Metals

Gold rings, drinks cans, car bodies, needles and steel girders – all these things are made from metals. Nearly three-quarters of the elements on Earth are metals. People have been using them to make things for thousands of years.

Some metals are bright, others are dull. Some are soft, others are hard. But all metals have some properties in common.

Except for mercury, all metals are solids at room temperature. Pure metals are shiny when they are polished, and they are all good conductors of electricity and heat.

Most metals are fairly strong. They can be crushed or stretched without breaking. Metals are malleable – they can be easily shaped by hammering or rolling. Many are also ductile. This means that they can be drawn out to make wires.

Where can you find them?

Most metals are found in rocks called **ores**. Ores usually contain a mixture of other substances along with the metal. It takes several steps to get the metal out from the ore.

First the ore is dug out of the ground. Next it is crushed to a powder. Then the tiny pieces of metal are separated out. Usually the metal pieces are found combined with other materials, so the metal has to be purified before it can be used.

Purifying

Metals such as iron and tin are purified by **smelting**. This means that they are heated to a high temperature in a furnace with coal or coke. Smelting separates the ore into molten metal and a solid residue or slag.

Metals such as aluminium are purified by **electrolysis**. In electrolysis the ore is first melted or dissolved in a liquid. Then an

▲ Although metals often look smooth on the surface, they are made up of crystals. This magnified photograph shows the tiny crystals on the surface of the metal palladium.

find out more

Atoms and molecules
Elements
Iron and steel

▼ These rusty cars show how metals can be attacked by air, water or other substances in their surroundings. This kind of damage is called **corrosion**. Many metals corrode. Rust is the type of corrosion that forms on iron and steel.

Properties and uses of some metals

Metal	Properties	Uses
Aluminium	Light and strong, especially in alloys. Good conductor of electricity and heat.	Principal building material for aircraft. Used for parts of cars, trains and ships, and in all kinds of machines. Soft drink cans, doors and window-frames, saucepans, electric cables.
Copper	Reddish-yellow, quite soft, easily shaped. Very good conductor of heat and electricity.	Electrical wires and cables; also for water pipes. Important alloys include bronze (copper and tin) and brass (copper and zinc).
Gold	Yellow, shiny metal. Excellent conductor of electricity. Does not corrode.	Main use as a precious metal in jewellery and coinage. Also used for electrical connections in electronics.
Iron	Pure iron greyish, malleable, easily magnetized. Alloys have wide range of properties.	Most widely used metal, mostly as its alloy, steel. Used for making huge range of products, from bridges, cars and machinery of all kinds, to needles and paper clips.
Silver	White, shiny metal; easily shaped. Best conductor of heat and electricity.	Used as a precious metal in jewellery, ornaments and coins. Chemicals made from silver form the light-sensitive coating on photographic film.

electric current is passed through the liquid.

Some metals, like gold and silver, do not need to be purified. They do not combine easily with other materials, so they are found in a pure state.

Mixing metals

Pure metals are not often used on their own. Usually they are mixed with other metals or with small amounts of non-metals. These mixtures are called **alloys**.

Alloys can have very different properties from the metals they are made from. For example, they are often stronger or harder. By combining different metals in different amounts, scientists can make alloys that have all sorts of useful properties.

▼ Copper is soft and easy to work even when it is cold. This coppersmith in Marrakesh, Morocco is finishing a copper bowl he has made by hand.

Meteors *see* Solar System • **Mexico** *see* North America

Mice and other rodents

Mice, rats, gerbils, squirrels, beavers and porcupines are all rodents. Forty per cent of all mammals are rodents. They live all over the world.

▲ Grey squirrel.

The name 'rodent' means **gnawing** animal. At the front of

▲ Wood mouse.

their mouths rodents have two long, razor-sharp teeth in their upper jaw, and two in their lower jaw. They also have grinding teeth at the back of their mouths.

Rodents feed mainly on plants, although some also eat insects and other small creatures.

All kinds of rodent

Mice are found all over the world. Some live in harsh deserts, others in lush rainforests.

Rats eat almost anything. Although some kinds make good pets, their wild relatives can be major pests to humans.

People often keep **gerbils**, **hamsters** or **guinea pigs** as pets. Wild gerbils live on the edge of deserts in Africa and the Middle East. Hamsters live in burrows in Europe and Asia.

Squirrels are most active during the day. They live in almost all parts of the world. Some squirrels are adapted to live in trees. They often store food, usually by burying it.

Porcupines are large rodents with sharp quills all over their bodies. Some types live mainly in trees. Others live on the ground.

• Rodents' front teeth never stop growing. Rodents wear these front teeth down to the right length by gnawing on hard things.

Kamikaze rodents?

Lemmings live in the cold tundra regions of the Arctic. Every few years their numbers increase dramatically. Many leave to find a new home – and some drown in rivers or the sea. Because of this people once thought that lemmings committed suicide.

◀ Porcupine.

find out more
Animals
Mammals

Microscopes *see* Lenses and mirrors

Middle Ages

The long period of European history from about AD 450 to 1500 is known as the Middle Ages. The first 500 years (sometimes called the Dark Ages) were full of turmoil. But later Europe settled down, and many of the countries of modern Europe came into being.

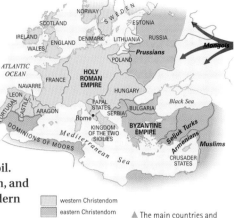

▲ The main countries and empires of Europe in about 1200.

When the Roman empire fell, Europe was invaded from all sides. First came warlike tribes such as the Goths, Vandals, Franks and Saxons. Then Muslims invaded from the south. Finally, the Vikings, Magyars and Saracens attacked.

It was the Christian Church that held European civilization together. It organized education, learning and arts. The memory of the Roman empire was also important. The Frankish king **Charlemagne** built up a Roman-style empire. Charlemagne's **Holy Roman Empire** fell apart, but a later empire that took its name lasted throughout the Middle Ages.

Christendom

Europe during the Middle Ages was known as 'Christendom' because Christianity was so important. The **Roman Catholic Church** dominated the lives of Christians in western Europe. The Church owned broad estates and magnificent buildings stuffed with treasures. Church officials ranged from mighty archbishops to humble monks, nuns and parish priests.

◄ The medieval splendour of Milan Cathedral (Italy). Such wonderful buildings, which took decades to build, remind us how important religion was in the Middle Ages.

On Sundays and 'holy days' everyone went to church. The Latin words sounded mysterious, almost magical. Going to church was the main way to avoid hell. People lived short lives, and diseases like the **Black Death** meant death was never far away.

Kings, knights and peasants

Europe was a patchwork of kingdoms and smaller dukedoms and cities. The different rulers often went to war. England and France fought the **Hundred Years War**. The most famous soldiers were **knights** in armour. The wealthy built huge stone **castles** for defence.

In the Middle Ages everybody had their place in a pyramid of importance, known as the **feudal system**. The king was at the top and the peasants at the bottom. Everyone served the person above them, in return for

KEY DATES

410 Visigoths attack Rome

711 Muslims invade Spain

800 Charlemagne crowned Emperor of the West

1095 First Crusade begins

1215 Nobles force King John to sign Magna Carta, England

1236 Mongols invade Russia

1337–1453 Hundred Years War between England and France

1348 Black Death reaches Europe

1358 Massive peasants' revolt in France

1450s Printing used in Europe

1469 Spain ruled under one crown

1483 Louis IX unites most of France

land and protection. **Kings** ruled with the help of the Church and their nobles. Women and peasants played little part in government.

Towns were few and far between. Most people were **peasants**, dwelling in village huts and scraping a living by farming. They could not read or write, and were desperately poor. Their masters demanded work and taxes. Occasionally, the peasants rose in revolt. They were crushed without mercy.

▲ Joan of Arc (1412–1431), the peasant girl who inspired the French to drive the English from her country. She was captured by the English and burnt at the stake.

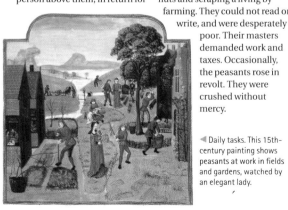

◀ Daily tasks. This 15th-century painting shows peasants at work in fields and gardens, watched by an elegant lady.

find out more

Black Death
Byzantine empire
Castles
Crusades
Europe
Knights
Normans
Vikings

Middle East

Three continents – Africa, Asia and Europe – join in the Middle East. Three great religions – Judaism, Christianity and Islam – had their beginnings there. For thousands of years the Middle East has been a crossroads for travellers and traders. It has also known great conflict.

The Middle East includes the whole of the Arabian Peninsula, Egypt, Israel, Iran, Iraq, Jordan, Lebanon, Syria and Turkey. The major natural resource is the vast deposits of **oil and natural gas** that were first discovered in the 1930s. They have brought great wealth to countries such as Saudi Arabia and Kuwait. But in less fortunate countries, such as Egypt and Jordan, there is still great poverty.

▼ An oil refinery in Saudi Arabia.

Geography

The climate is generally hot and dry. In the sandy deserts of Arabia, temperatures can soar to 50°C. People wear layers of loose clothes to protect themselves from the fierce sun. Snow falls in the mountains of Turkey, Iran and Iraq.

Water is scarce in the Middle East. But there are great rivers – the Nile, Tigris and Euphrates. The best farmlands are found along the banks of these rivers. In other places, people find

• The Middle East gets its name from Europeans, for whom it is half way to the 'Far East'. Sometimes it is named West Asia instead.

find out more

Africa
Asia
Christians
Jews
Muslims
Ottoman empire

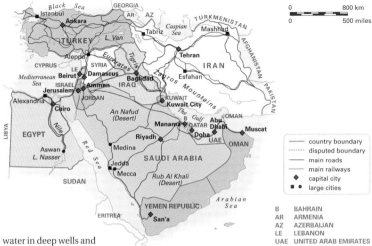

water in deep wells and **oases**. In Saudi Arabia there are **desalination** plants to turn sea water into fresh water for crops and for drinking.

People

Most people in the Middle East are **Arabs**. They speak Arabic and are mostly **Muslims**. There are also Iranians, Turks and Kurds, who are also mainly Muslims. Kurds and Palestinian Arabs do not have their own countries. They are scattered across the Middle East. In Israel most people are **Jews**.

Many people are farmers. Cotton, wheat, and fruit such as dates, grapes and olives are common crops. In drier and more mountainous areas there are **nomads**. They move from place to place with their herds of sheep, goats and camels.

There are important cities in the Middle East. Cairo (Egypt), Tehran (Iran) and Istanbul (Turkey) are the largest, with over

7 million inhabitants each. **Jerusalem** in Israel is a sacred city for Judaism, Christianity and Islam. **Mecca** in Saudi Arabia is the holiest site for Muslims.

History

Writing, farming and cities all began in the Middle East. The centre of many ancient civilizations was **Mesopotamia** (modern-day Iraq) around the Tigris and Euphrates rivers. The other centre was the Nile, where Egyptian civilization rose around 3000 BC.

The Jewish (or Hebrew) people lived at the eastern end of the Mediterranean. They believed in one almighty God. About 2000 years ago a Jew named Jesus claimed to be the son of God. His followers, the Christians, spread his teachings far and wide. Later an Arab named Muhammad began another new religion – Islam. By AD 750 Muslims (followers of Islam) had conquered a huge empire and spread Arab civilization from India to Spain.

Much of the Arab empire was taken over by the **Ottoman empire** in the 16th century. It eventually fell to French and British conquerors. After World War I the region was gradually divided into new independent countries.

Among the new countries was Israel, founded in 1948 as a homeland for the world's Jews. But the Palestinian Arabs claimed the land belonged to them. Other Arab countries supported the Palestinians. There were wars between Israel and its Arab neighbours in 1948–1949, 1967 and 1973. But Israel was undefeated and seized land from its enemies. The Palestinians fought back with acts of terrorism. In the 1990s some Arab states made peace

• In 1980 Iraq launched a war against its neighbour Iran. Hundreds of thousands died. In 1990 Iraq invaded Kuwait and was defeated by the more powerful forces of the United States and its allies. The US and its allies stopped buying oil from Iraq. Their air forces kept control of the skies over much of the country.

▲ The spiral minaret at Samarra, Iraq. A minaret is the name given to a tower next to a Muslim mosque. A man called a muezzin climbs to the top of the minaret to call worshippers to attend prayers. This minaret dates from the 9th century when Samarra was Iraq's capital.

with Israel, and Palestinians were able to govern some of the areas where they lived.

◄ These women are part of a group of nomads called Bedouin. They are sorting fleeces from their flock of sheep. Their home is a large tent made from strips of woven goat hair.

Migration

Migration is the regular movement of animals to and from a particular place. The most common type of migration is seasonal migration. Most animals that migrate seasonally spend the winter in one place and the summer in another.

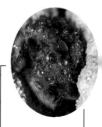

Some birds and other animals move away from their breeding areas in winter to places where the weather is warmer. Migrants in northern Europe include **starlings**, some kinds of **bat** and **reindeer**.

Some migrant animals make very long journeys indeed. The **Arctic tern** travels from the Antarctic to the most northerly parts of Europe, Asia and North America to breed. In contrast, some kinds of **hummingbird** move only a few hundred metres up and down a mountain slope.

Some animal migrations are only made once in a lifetime. For instance, **salmon** spend the first part of their lives in rivers, migrate to the ocean as adults, and then return to the rivers to breed. There they die, and their offspring begin the cycle again. **Eels** do the opposite – they hatch in the sea and migrate to fresh water to grow.

A few animals are on the move almost constantly. **Wildebeest** in Africa, and some kinds of **whale** in the oceans, make circular tours in the course of a year.

Hibernation

Instead of migrating, some animals, such as bats, hedgehogs and dormice, hibernate in winter. Hibernation is a kind of deep sleep. Most hibernating animals are small creatures that feed on insects, or other food that becomes scarce when the weather is cold. The only way they can survive is to hibernate. This bat is hibernating in a cave.

How do they do it?

How do all these animals find their way? Nobody really knows. Birds, dolphins and bees have magnetic particles in their brains, which may act like tiny compasses. Birds may also find their way from the position of the Sun and stars.

◀▼ Some green turtles migrate over 2000 km from their feeding grounds on the coast of Brazil to Ascension Island in the Atlantic Ocean to breed. This strange migration probably evolved over millions of years.

ATLANTIC

BRAZIL

Ascension Island

OCEAN

find out more

Animals
Birds

Milk *see* Food • **Milky Way** *see* Galaxies • **Minerals** *see* Rocks and minerals

Mining

Mining is the process of getting rocks and minerals out of the ground. Diamonds, coal and metal ores (rocks rich in a particular metal) are just some of the materials that are mined.

Some useful materials are deep underground. Others are near the surface. Different mining techniques have to be used, depending on where the material is found.

Digging in

Materials close to the surface can be mined from **quarries** or **opencast mines**. Coal, iron **ore** and aluminium are sometimes mined in this way. Huge power shovels and excavators are used to dig out materials and load them into trucks.

In **underground mines** miners dig shafts and tunnels to reach ores buried deep below the surface. The tunnels are held up with **props**. The ore is removed using explosives or drills. **Ventilation shafts** from the surface bring in air.

Mining dangers

Mining is a very dangerous job. Dusty air can damage miner's lungs, and explosives can cause accidents. There is also a risk of poisonous gases, flooding or fire. Occasionally the roof of an underground mine can collapse, trapping miners underground.

▼ Different methods of mining. In opencast, hydraulic mining and drift mining, materials are mined from near the surface. In hydraulic mining, high-pressure water is used. In underground mines, shafts and tunnels are dug to reach the ore layers.

> **Coal**
> Coal is the fossilized remains of plants from long ago. Millions of years ago plants died and piled up to form a spongy material called peat. Over the centuries the peat layers became buried in silt and sand. Gradually, the material above squashed the peat and turned it into coal.

find out more

Metals
Oil
Rocks and minerals

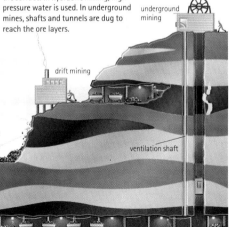

underground mining

drift mining

opencast mining

hydraulic mining

ventilation shaft

Mongols

The Mongols flashed through history like a meteor. Led by Genghis Khan, in barely 20 years they created the world's largest empire. Their power fell away in the next century. After another gleam of glory under Timur (Tamerlane), it vanished.

▲ Genghis Khan (1162–1227).

The Mongols were a nomadic people from central Asia. When they chose Temujin as their leader, he changed his name to **Genghis Khan** (Universal Ruler) and set out to conquer the world. His armies of fearless horsemen invaded China and took Beijing. In the west they swept through southern Russia, into the Crimea.

Genghis was not just a brilliant commander. He set up an excellent messenger system across his empire and carefully organized it into states.

Timur the lame

After Genghis' death, the empire grew larger still. The Mongols conquered Iran (Persia) and Iraq, and attacked Europe. **Kublai Khan**, Genghis' grandson, became emperor of China. He ruled with great skill, building roads and encouraging the Buddhist religion.

After the Mongols were driven from China, they found a new warrior leader, **Timur the Lame** (or Tamerlane). Once again the Mongol hordes went on the rampage, taking Northern India and defeating the Ottoman Turks. But Timur was no organizer, and his empire collapsed after his death.

▼ Timur's army invading India. The ruthless Mongol horsemen rarely took prisoners, and were feared the world over.

◻ empire of Genghis Khan 1227

◻ greatest extent of Mongol empire

find out more

Asia
China
India and Pakistan

KEY DATES

1206 Mongols choose Genghis Khan as their leader

1215 Genghis Khan captures Beijing

1220s Mongols advance to the Black Sea

1227 Death of Genghis Khan

1279–1294 Kublai Khan emperor of China

1368 Mongols driven from China

1398 Timur sacks Delhi

1402 Timur defeats Turks

1405 Timur dies

Monkeys and apes

Monkeys and apes are members of the primate group. Humans are primates too. All primates can grip things firmly with their hands. Many can also grip things with their feet.

Most primates have a poor sense of smell. Sight is their most important sense. Primates' eyes are at the front of their faces. This means they can judge distances accurately. Almost all primates can see colours.

Primates have large brains, so they are more intelligent than most other animals. They usually live in family groups.

Apes

Apes are the closest animal relatives of people. There are two main groups: the **great apes** and the **lesser apes**. Like people, apes live for many years, have big brains, and can walk upright. Like us, they have 32 teeth and no visible tail. The great apes, which include **gorillas**, **chimpanzees** and **orang-utans**, may live for about 50 years.

Monkeys

Monkeys are similar to apes, but tend to be smaller. Most monkeys have tails. A few live on the ground, but most jump or swing through the trees. South American monkeys have **prehensile** (gripping) tails, which they may use like an extra arm to hold on to the branches.

▲ Spider monkeys live in South America. Their strong prehensile tails have a sensitive tip.

▲ Colobus monkeys live in Africa. In the past many were killed for their beautiful coats.

find out more

Early people
Human beings
Mammals

▶ Chimpanzees live in the forests of central and western Africa. Like people, they use gestures and facial expressions to communicate. They also use tools.

◀ Gorillas are the largest of the great apes. They live in the forests of central Africa, in family groups.

Moon

The Moon is the Earth's closest neighbour in space. But it is not a planet. Instead it is a natural satellite of the Earth.

▶ Craters cover the surface of the Moon. Early astronomers thought the dark areas were oceans.

The Moon is only about a quarter the size of the Earth. It is made of rock, and its surface is covered with huge round depressions, called **craters**. Many of these are over 100 kilometres across. The craters were made when giant lumps of rock, called **meteorites**, crashed into the Moon.

Because it is so small, the Moon has only a weak pull of gravity. This means that the Moon cannot hold any air, or atmosphere. But in 1998 the space probe *Lunar Prospector* found water ice on the Moon.

Moonshine

The Moon does not give out its own light. It only shines because it reflects light from the Sun.

The Moon circles round the Earth, while the Earth travels round the Sun. As it circles, the Moon also spins round slowly. It takes about a month for the Moon to travel around the Earth. During this time it looks as if the Moon changes from a thin crescent to a flat disc, and back again. These different shapes are called the **phases of the Moon**.

find out more
Earth
Satellites
Solar System
Space exploration
Sun

▶ The phases of the Moon. It takes around 14 days to go from a Full Moon (top) to a New Moon (bottom), and another 14 days to get back to a Full Moon again.

▼ An Apollo astronaut drives the Lunar Rover ('Moon Buggy') as he explores the surface of the Moon. The Lunar Rover was used, in 1971 and 1972, by the last three Apollo missions to the Moon – *Apollos 15, 16* and *17*.

Mountains

Mountains are high peaks of land. They are formed by movements of the Earth's surface, and shaped by rain, sun, ice and wind.

Mountains are formed in different ways. **Fold mountains** are created when two pieces of the Earth's crust very slowly collide. Over millions of years, the rocks of the crust crumple and are pushed upwards to form mountains. The world's biggest mountain ranges were all formed in this way.

Block mountains form when huge blocks of rock are tilted or lifted up along lines of weakness, called faults. **Dome mountains** form when molten rock pushing up from below meets strong rocks at the surface. The strong rocks bulge upwards to form a dome.

Shaping mountains

As mountains rise above the surrounding land, they are attacked by rain, wind, rivers and ice. **Valleys** are formed when rivers or glaciers (rivers of ice) wear away the softer rocks, carving out deep channels in the mountainside and leaving ridges of rock on either side. Young mountains have high, steep-sided peaks and deep valleys. In time, the mountain tops are worn away and become more rounded, while the valleys become wider.

Mountain life

Conditions on mountains are harsh and difficult. As you climb up a mountain, the temperature gradually falls. There is snow on the top of high mountains even at the Equator. Winds are often very strong, and the weather can change very quickly. Plants have

▲ Small settlements in a mountain valley in the Swiss Alps. Farmers here move their dairy cattle to high pastures in spring, and bring them back to the sheltered valleys in the autumn.

● Mauna Loa, a volcanic island in Hawaii, is 9350 m high – taller than Everest. However, more than half of this height is under the sea.

▼ The different ways that mountains can form.

fold mountains

block mountains

dome mountains

Mozart *see* Classical music • **Muhammad** *see* Muslims

▲ Mount Everest in the Himalayas (on the left), is 8848 m tall – the highest mountain in the world. The Himalayas, the Karakoram mountains and the Hindu Kush together form a 3800-km mountain chain, the longest and highest in the world.

to grow in very thin soil, because much soil is washed away down the slopes. The lower slopes of a mountain are often covered with forests, but above a certain height, called the **tree line**, trees can no longer grow.

Valleys are the main areas where people live, because the climate is sheltered and the soils are more fertile. Valleys also provide routes for roads and railways. Many mountain people make a living from farming. There is also mining in mountain areas, and activities such as skiing and climbing.

Mountain climbing
The sport of climbing and exploring mountains became popular after the successful ascent of Mont Blanc, in the European Alps, in 1786. In 1953 Edmund Hillary, a New Zealander, and Tenzing Norgay, a Sherpa tribesman from Nepal, were the first people to climb Mount Everest. On very high mountains there is so little oxygen that climbers must wear breathing apparatus.

find out more

Continents
Lakes
Rocks and minerals
Volcanoes and earthquakes

▼ The world's greatest mountain ranges.

ARCTIC OCEAN

Mt McKinley ▲ 6194

NORTH AMERICA

ROCKY MTS

▲ Mt Elbert 4402

NORTH ATLANTIC OCEAN

PACIFIC OCEAN

EUROPE

Mt Blanc ▲ ALPS 4808

Atlas Mts

AFRICA

Ural Mts

Altai Mts

▲ Mt Elbrus 5642

Zagros Mts

ASIA

HIMALAYA

▲ Mt Everest 8848

PACIFIC OCEAN

Ethiopian Highlands

Equator

A N D E S

SOUTH AMERICA

Brazilian Highlands

Aconcagua ▲ 6960

SOUTH ATLANTIC OCEAN

Kilimanjaro ▲ 5895

INDIAN OCEAN

Mt Wilhelm ▲ 4509

Great Dividing Range

Mt Cook ▲ 3754

height of land (metres)

5000
2000
1000

▲ mountain peak
☐ permanent ice

Mushrooms and toadstools

Mushrooms and toadstools are the above-ground parts of some kinds of fungus. Fungi are an important group of living things. They get their food by breaking down the tissues of living or dead plants or animals.

There is no scientific difference between mushrooms and toadstools, although often the word toadstool is used for kinds that cannot be eaten. It is not easy to tell a poisonous mushroom from an edible one, so it is safest to eat only ones bought in the shops.

Under the ground

Only a small part of a mushroom or toadstool is above ground. Under the ground is a tangled network of tiny threads called **hyphae**. These hyphae absorb food from the material on which the fungus is growing.

Fungi reproduce by way of microscopic **spores**, which act like tiny seeds. The part of a mushroom or toadstool that we see is the **fruiting body**, the part that produces these spores.

The fruiting body of a mushroom or toadstool is usually umbrella-shaped, with a thick stalk and a broad cap. Beneath the cap are **pores** or hanging curtains called **gills**. Spores develop in the gills and are then carried off by the wind.

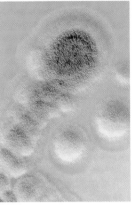

▲ Many kinds of fungus are much simpler than mushrooms and toadstools: just single cells. Some are useful to humans. The photo shows the fungus *Penicillium*, which produces the antibiotic penicillin. (Antibiotics are drugs that attack bacteria harmful to humans.)

High-speed hyphae!

Some fungi grow so fast that a single spore can produce more than 1 km of hyphae in 24 hours.

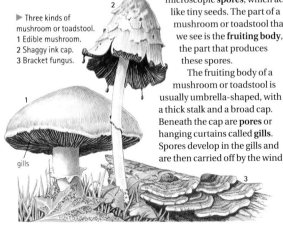

▶ Three kinds of mushroom or toadstool.
1 Edible mushroom.
2 Shaggy ink cap.
3 Bracket fungus.

gills

find out more

Algae
Drugs
Life on Earth

Music

Music is a powerful thing. It can tempt you to dance, or make you cry. It can calm you down or cheer you up. Music is sometimes called a world language because it helps people to express their thoughts and feelings without using words.

Music is as old as human beings. Prehistoric people chanted and made simple music by clapping their hands or hitting two sticks together. Later they made flutes from bones and drums from animal skins.

Making music

All music is made up of **notes**. These notes have different **pitches** (they are either high or low). Notes of different pitch can be played at the same time (in **harmony**) or one after another (in a **melody**). Longer and shorter notes are put together in a pattern called a **rhythm**. Almost all music is made up of a combination of these three elements – harmony, melody and rhythm.

▲ This Swahili drummer from Kenya is playing several kinds of drum. Drums are very important in African music.

Some of the earliest music of all is religious music. People have always used music and singing to honour their gods. In Europe, church songs were the first pieces of music to be written down.

Music around the world

Music is played all around the world, and comes in a huge variety of **styles**. Some regions, such as Europe, India and Japan, have traditions of **classical music**. This is serious, often complex music that was originally played in temples or at royal courts. And every part of the world has its

◀ These Quechua Indians from Peru are playing violins and harps – instruments brought to Peru by the Spanish.

own variety of **folk music** – music written and played by ordinary people.

In Europe two of the most famous kinds of folk music are **Irish music** and **flamenco** from Spain. In North and South America in the 20th century musical styles from different continents – particularly Africa and Europe – have merged to create new styles that are extremely popular today, including **pop**, **rock**, **jazz**, **country-and-western**, **reggae** and **salsa**.

In India you can hear classical Indian music as well as lively pop songs by famous Indian movie singers. Chinese **Beijing opera** mixes speech, song, acting and acrobatics to make a very exciting performance. In South-east Asia percussion music is very popular.

▲ These musicians are from Rajasthan, India. In Indian music, players often take a *raga* (series of notes) and *tala* (rhythm) and play around with them to create a new sound every time.

In Africa many pieces of music begin gradually as voices or instruments join in one by one. They often accompany dance. Popular instruments are **drums**, the xylophone and the *mbira*, on which metal keys are plucked by the thumbs and fingers.

• The words and music to folk songs are passed down over many years. Folk songs often began in country areas. Some were made up to help the day's work along, or tell of events in people's lives. Modern folk groups often use traditional instruments to give their music an authentic style.

Jazz music

Jazz is a musical form that is bursting with life. This is because the musicians who play or sing it make up all or part of it as they go along (they improvise). They often use set melodies, but a piece of jazz music is never quite the same twice.

◀ Billie Holiday was the greatest jazz singer of the 1930s, and her recordings are still popular today.

find out more

Classical music
Musical instruments
Orchestras and bands
Pop and rock music

Writing music

In most parts of the world, music is never written down. It is learned and passed on as it is played. In Europe in the 9th century AD, monks were the first people to write music down. Since then a special system for writing music has developed called **music notation**.

Notes are written on a set of lines called a **stave**. The higher a note is on the stave, the higher is its pitch. Each pitch is named after a letter from A to G, where A is lower than B, and so on. After seven letters the sequence begins again. This sequence of notes is called an **octave**.

▼ The notes of the **treble clef** and the **bass clef**.

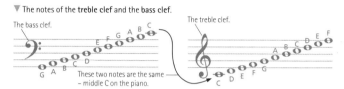

The bass clef.

The treble clef.

These two notes are the same – middle C on the piano.

▼ The length of a note is shown by its symbol. As you can see, some notes have different symbols depending on whether they are alone or in groups.

semibreve (4 beats) minim (2 beats) crotchet (1 beat) quaver (half-beat) semiquaver (quarter-beat)

▼ Part of the music for the Toreador Song from *Carmen*, an opera by Georges Bizet.

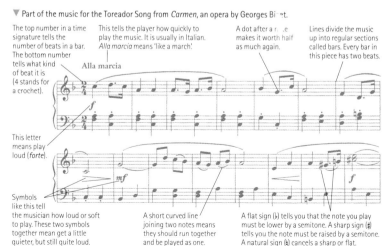

The top number in a time signature tells the number of beats in a bar. The bottom number tells what kind of beat it is (4 stands for a crotchet).

This tells the player how quickly to play the music. It is usually in Italian. *Alla marcia* means 'like a march'.

A dot after a note makes it worth half as much again.

Lines divide the music up into regular sections called bars. Every bar in this piece has two beats.

This letter means play loud (*forte*).

Symbols like this tell the musician how loud or soft to play. These two symbols together mean get a little quieter, but still quite loud.

A short curved line joining two notes means they should run together and be played as one.

A flat sign (♭) tells you that the note you play must be lower by a semitone. A sharp sign (♯) tells you the note must be raised by a semitone. A natural sign (♮) cancels a sharp or flat.

Musical instruments

The booming of a big bass drum, the tinkling of a triangle, the rich tones of the cello – these are all sounds made by musical instruments. There are all sorts of musical instruments across the world. But all make sounds in one of only a few different ways.

Hit a bell, blow on a trumpet or pluck a guitar string – all of these actions set up **vibrations** in the air which we hear as musical sounds. Musical instruments are divided into different groups depending on the way they make sounds. The four main groups are: wind instruments, stringed instruments, keyboard instruments and percussion instruments.

Wind instruments

Wind instruments are tubes or pipes which you blow. Some **woodwind** instruments have a hole you blow through (like a **recorder**) or across (like a **flute**). Others (like **clarinets** and **saxophones**) have reeds that vibrate when you blow through them. A reed is a thin piece of wood. You make different notes by covering holes in the tube with your fingers.

Brass instruments, such as **trumpets** and **trombones**, are long funnel-shaped tubes with a special piece for the mouth. To play one you make your lips vibrate in the mouthpiece – it's a bit like blowing a raspberry!

Stringed instruments

Stringed instruments make sounds when the player makes one or more strings vibrate. Some are plucked with fingers or a special plucker called a plectrum. When you play a **guitar**, one hand plucks the

▲ This ancient Assyrian carving dates from the 7th century BC. It shows musicians playing various wind and string instruments.

find out more

Classical music
Music
Orchestras and bands
Pop and rock music

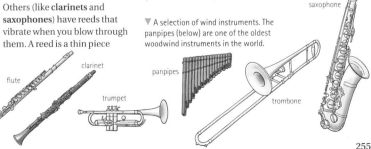

▼ A selection of wind instruments. The panpipes (below) are one of the oldest woodwind instruments in the world.

flute

clarinet

trumpet

panpipes

trombone

saxophone

violin

sitar

sarangi

samisen

spike fiddle

guitar

◀ Stringed instruments are found all over the world. They include the Turkish spike fiddle, the Indian sitar and sarangi, and the Japanese samisen.

strings while the other stops (presses on) the strings in different places to make different notes. Other stringed instruments, such as **violins**, use a bow pulled across the strings to make the sound. The other hand fingers the strings in the same way as a guitar.

Keyboard instruments

A keyboard is a row of **keys**. Usually some are black and some are white, as on a **piano**. When you press a piano key a small wooden hammer hits one, two or three strings. This makes them vibrate to make a note. When you take your finger off the key, a special pad called a damper touches the strings to stop them vibrating.

Percussion

Percussion instruments are banged, shaken, clicked, scraped or rasped to make sounds. Some, like **xylophones**, have different notes and can play tunes. Others, like **drums**, **maracas** and **cymbals** do not play particular notes. But they make different sounds. A **tambourine** can be either shaken or hit.

▲ A harpsichord is a keyboard instrument in which the strings are plucked by a quill rather than hit by a hammer. Harpsichords were popular in Europe from the 15th to the 18th centuries.

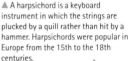

maracas

cymbal

tom-tom barrel drum   bass drum

Electronic instruments
Electronic instruments can make an amazing range of sounds. In some, like the electric guitar or violin, the sound of an instrument is altered and made louder electronically. Others, like synthesizers, can make totally new sounds.

Muslims

Muslims are people who follow the religion called Islam. Islam began about 1300 years ago in the part of the world we now call the Middle East. Today there are Muslims living all over the world.

▲ The Dome of the Rock in Jerusalem is built on the spot from where Muslims believe Muhammad rose to heaven.

Muslims worship and believe in one God, whom they call **Allah**. They believe that Allah made, sees and knows everything. Islam means 'to obey Allah'. Muslims believe that Allah sent messengers, called **prophets**, to tell them how he wants them to live.

Muhammad

Muslims believe that the last and greatest prophet was Muhammad. Muhammad was born in a city called **Mecca** in what is now Saudi Arabia. Muslims believe that Allah

▼ Children learning how to read the Koran in Arabic.

sent an angel to give messages to Muhammad. These messages were later written down in the **Koran**, the Muslim holy book.

Mosques

Muslims can worship anywhere, but there are special buildings called mosques for worship. Mosques usually have a dome and a tall tower called a **minaret**. Inside most

The Five Pillars of Islam

These are five things all Muslims try to do:

1 To accept the truth that there is no God except Allah and that Muhammad is the messenger of Allah.

2 To pray five times a day.

3 To give money to people who are poor or in need.

4 To fast (avoid food and drink in the daytime) during the festival called Ramadan, to show that they are living their lives the way Allah wishes.

5 To make a pilgrimage (journey) to Mecca.

257

mosques is a small arch to show the direction of Mecca, because Muslims face this holy city when they pray.

There are prayers in a mosque every day, but the most important time is Friday lunchtime. This is when the **imams** (Muslim teachers) give special talks and prayers. Mosques are also used as meeting places, and young people come to the mosque to be taught the Koran and Arabic, the language in which it is written.

Way of life

Muslims believe that Islam affects everything they do. **Islamic law** tells them the right way to live. Religious leaders base Islamic law on the Koran and the Hadith, a book about the life and sayings of Muhammad.

Islam teaches what foods are allowed and how some should be prepared. Alcohol is forbidden and Muslims are not supposed to smoke. Islam also tells Muslims how to dress decently. Men should always be covered from waist to knees. Women and older girls should dress so that only their hands and face can be seen.

▲ Muslims stand, kneel and bow in a certain order as they say their prayers.

find out more
Middle East
Religions

• There are two main groups of Muslims. Sunni Muslims do things in the most traditional way, based on the Hadith. Shi'ah Muslims live mainly in Iran and Iraq. They are very strict about their beliefs. Their leaders are called Ayatollahs.

▼ Muhammad is buried at this mosque in Medina, Saudi Arabia.

Mussels and oysters

Mussels and oysters are bivalve molluscs. Their soft bodies are protected by a shell made of two parts joined by a hinge of elastic tissue.

Some types of mussel live in rivers and lakes, but most kinds of oyster and mussel are found in the sea. All live by eating tiny bits of food that they filter out of the water. They mostly feed on tiny floating plants and animals called **plankton**.

A common mussel filters about 1.5 litres of water an hour to get its food. The water also holds oxygen, so they breathe and feed at the same time.

Hold fast

Many types of bivalve mollusc can burrow and move about. A few, like the scallop, can even swim. But mussels and oysters are different. They live attached to rocks. When in danger, they pull their shells closed.

Mussels attach themselves to rocks using strong threads called **byssus** threads. Oysters cement themselves to rocks.

If a grain of sand gets inside an oyster's shell, the animal covers it with layers of material to get rid of the irritation. This can turn the grain into a **pearl**.

▲ Common mussels can often be found attached to rocks along the seashore.

Grow slow!
The North Atlantic deep-sea clam grows very, very slowly. It is thought to take about 100 years to grow 8 mm.

▲ A freshwater mussel. Freshwater mussels live in rivers, lakes and ponds in most parts of the world.

◀ One side of an oyster's shell is bigger and rounder than the other. The oyster lives in the larger shell. When danger threatens it snaps shut its smaller, flatter shell.

find out more
Animals
Life on Earth
Oceans and seas
Seashore
Slugs and snails

Myths and folk tales

All around the world people tell stories to make sense of the things that happen to them, and to entertain each other. People were telling stories long before books, or even writing, existed.

Today people may read stories in books or magazines, watch them on television, or listen to them on the radio.

Myths

Myths are stories that are part of the culture and sometimes the religious beliefs of a people. They may provide answers to such questions as 'How was the Earth formed?' or 'Why does spring follow winter?' Many myths tell of gods and

▶ In an ancient Japanese myth, the twin gods Isanagi (right) and Isanami (left) created the world from a sea of lifeless mud by stirring the mud with a spear. Many myths tell of how the Earth was formed and how the human race began. These myths are known as **creation myths**.

goddesses, or of strange creatures – monsters, giants and dragons – with magical and sometimes terrible powers.

Legends

Legends are stories about real people that have become exaggerated over time. They usually tell of the adventures of especially brave or clever people. The story of David and

◀ In the legend of the Pied Piper of Hamelin, the town of Hamelin is overrun by rats. A young man offers to get rid of the rats – for a price. The people agree and the young man plays his pipe. When he plays, the rats follow him out of the town. But when he claims his fee, the people refuse to pay up. So he plays his pipe again. This time all the children of the town follow him – never to return.

• Greek myth tells of a time when only gods and giants, called Titans, lived in the Universe. One day one of the Titans, Prometheus, sat idly making tiny models of gods out of clay. The goddess Athene came along and breathed life into these dolls, and the human race was born.

find out more

Egyptians, ancient
Greeks, ancient
Poetry
Religions
Romans
Vikings

Goliath, in the Bible, is a legend. It tells of the young David who slays the giant Goliath with a stone from his sling. Goliath was probably a champion warrior who fought against the Israelites.

◄ The Asante people of West Africa tell stories about the trickster-god Anansi, who could take any shape he liked. Here Anansi (the spider) is talking to the Banana Bird, whom he tricks into letting him have all the bananas in a big plantation.

Folk tales

Some of the oldest stories are folk tales. The characters in folk tales are usually ordinary people who have extraordinary adventures. Some tell of poor people who become rich through their cleverness or bravery. Others are about wicked people who are punished, or foolish people who are made fun of.

Some of the same tales are told all over the world, although the details may change. One type of story tells of a person who meets a trickster in disguise. The ordinary character usually ends up tricking the trickster.

A **fable** is a type of folk tale that is short and teaches us a lesson. Fables often have one stupid and one clever animal in them.

Fairy tales

Fairy tales are stories in which magical things happen. In fairy tales, people who are kind or brave usually win through in the end, and live 'happily ever after'.

Many fairy tales were originally folk tales, told in different versions in different countries. They became fairy tales when someone wrote them down, often specially rewritten for children. The story we know as 'Cinderella' was written down by the French writer Charles Perrault in the 17th century. The original English version was called 'Cap o' Rushes'.

◄ This is an illustration from 'Aladdin and his Lamp', one of the tales of the *Arabian Nights*. It shows the genie that appeared from the lamp.

SOME FAMOUS STORYTELLERS AND STORY BOOKS

Over 100 fables were probably written down by **Aesop**, a Greek slave who lived in the 6th century BC. They include the story of 'The Tortoise and the Hare'.

The **Fables of Bidpai**, which were written down in India in the 3rd century AD, are the earliest known collection of fairy stories.

The Arabian Nights' Entertainment is a famous series of stories, first told in the Middle East 1000 years ago.

The German brothers **Jakob** and **Wilhelm Grimm** collected European fairy stories, including 'Snow White' and 'Rumplestiltskin', in the 19th century.

Nerves *see* Brain and nerves

Newspapers

Millions of people enjoy reading newspapers and magazines. These help them to keep up with the news, and are a good source of entertainment.

There are many different kinds of newspapers and magazines to appeal to people of all interests and ages. New ones are appearing all the time.

Gathering the news

All newspapers employ some of their own **reporters** to collect and write about the news. They also buy news reports from news agencies. These agencies gather news items from all over the world, then sell their reports to the newspapers.

Most newspapers and magazines also carry **advertisements**. Businesses and shops pay for these adverts; the money helps to pay for producing the newspaper or magazine. Some local papers make all their money from adverts and are given away free.

The editor's job

Newspapers usually have an editor-in-chief to oversee the production of the paper. There are also several other editors who look after the different sections. They are in charge of deciding what stories the paper will print and how the stories will appear. The news editor, for example, decides which news stories will appear. The picture editor is responsible for choosing the right pictures to use with each story.

▲ There are many different newspapers. Some appear every day, others every week. Some have local news, others write about stories of national or international interest.

◀ When the newspaper is ready for press, huge machines print the pages, put them in order, cut them and fold them ready for sale. People buy newspapers from shops and newsagents, or have them delivered to their homes.

find out more
Communications
Writing

Newts *see* Frogs and other amphibians

New Zealand

find out more

Australia
Empire, Age of
Exploration, Age of
Pacific Islands

The Maori people discovered New Zealand over 1000 years ago. They called it Aotearoa, which means 'Land of the Long White Clouds'. When the Dutch explorer Abel Tasman reached the islands in 1642, he named them New Zealand.

New Zealand is made up of two main islands in the Pacific Ocean. Both islands lie on an earthquake zone and the North Island has many volcanoes. The South Island has a spectacular mountain range.

Land and people

With warm weather and good soil, New Zealanders grow all kinds of fruit, vegetables and flowers. **Sheep farming** is also important. New Zealand sells lots of its produce abroad, for example lamb and butter. New Zealanders spend lots of time outdoors, sailing, fishing, playing rugby and walking.

History

Maori people came to New Zealand from the tropical islands of Polynesia. British farmers and whalers arrived in the late 18th century. Arguments over land led to fierce wars, which the Maori lost.

New Zealand became an independent dominion of Britain in 1907. Since then it has built up strong links with Australia and nearby Asian countries. Today Maori culture is growing strong again.

NEW ZEALAND FACTS

Capital: Auckland

Population: 3,650,000

Area: 268,812 sq km

Language: English, Maori

Religion: Christian

Currency: 1 NZ dollar = 100 cents

Wealth per person: $14,340

▼ Hiking around Milford Sound in the South Island is one of the loveliest walks in the world. Milford Sound is a fjord, a steep-sided valley flooded by the sea.

North Island

Whangarei
Auckland
Manukau
Bay of Plenty
Hamilton
New Plymouth
Rotorua
Gisborne
Ruapehu 2797
L. Taupo
Napier

Tasman Sea

Nelson
Cook Strait
Wellington

Greymouth

Mt Cook 3764
Southern Alps
Canterbury Plains
Christchurch

PACIFIC OCEAN

South Island

SOUTH PACIFIC

Milford Sound
Dunedin

Invercargill

Stewart I.

0	300 km
0	150 miles

◆ capital city
● large city
▲ high peaks (height in metres)

— main roads
— main railways

Nicaragua *see* North America • **Nigeria** *see* Africa • **Nomads** *see* Deserts, Early People

Normans

The first Normans were Vikings from Scandinavia, who came to northern France in search of land and wealth. In 911 they became Christians and the king of the Franks granted them land – the region of Normandy.

Normandy was a fertile land, with many good harbours. The Normans could trade and travel easily. They soon became rich. And they were excellent fighters, especially on horseback. **Knights** carried long, heavy lances, so when they charged, their enemies faced a line of deadly spikes.

Travels and conquest

The Norman **adventurers** Robert and Roger Guiscard took control of most of southern Italy in AD 1042, and captured Sicily from the Muslim Saracens.

Norman knights joined the first Crusade to win back Jerusalem from the Muslims in 1095.

Norman England

In 1066 Duke William of Normandy claimed the **English throne**. He invaded England, and defeated Harold, earl of Wessex, at the **battle of Hastings**.

Norman rule brought great changes in England. Many farmers lost their land, and had to work for Norman lords. Most people still spoke English, but educated people learned French and Latin.

▲ The Normans built hundreds of **castles**. They dug high mounds *(mottes)* on top of which they built a tower *(keep)*. Next to the motte was a yard *(bailey)* for people, animals and stores.

• In 1085 William ordered his barons to record who owned the English land, how much it was worth and who lived there. This huge survey, called the *Domesday Book*, still exists today.

find out more

Anglo-Saxons
Castles
Middle Ages
Vikings

◀ The **Bayeux Tapestry** tells the story of the Norman invasion of England. It is over 70 m long. This section shows William before the battle of Hastings.

North America

North America is the third largest continent in the world. It stretches from Canada in the north to the Caribbean in the south. Mountain ranges run like a giant backbone down the western side of the continent. In the east lie the smaller Appalachians, some of the oldest mountains on Earth. Between these mountain ranges are huge plains, across which the Mississippi and Missouri rivers run.

Almost all parts of the continent have warm or hot **weather** in summer. In winter the northern and central parts of the continent are bitterly cold, because there are no mountains to stop icy Arctic air blowing south. The coastlines on the Gulf of Mexico and the Caribbean Sea often suffer from hurricanes.

North America is rich in timber, oil, gas, gold and many other **natural resources**.

North American history

North American history began when the first **settlers** arrived from Asia, about 15,000 years ago. They lived by hunting, fishing and farming. In what is now Mexico, the **Maya** and **Aztec** peoples built up great civilizations around huge stone cities.

▲ A Native American totem pole from Vancouver, on Canada's west coast. The pole is carved with sacred symbols known as totems.

KEY DATES

about 13,000 BC	First settlers cross from Asia to North America
about AD 600	Mayan civilization flourishing
1607	British settle in Jamestown, Virginia
1776	USA declares independence
1821	Mexico becomes independent from Spain
1846–1848	Mexico and USA fight to control Texas
1867	Canada begins governing itself

▶ The Pilgrim Fathers were a group of English settlers who wanted the freedom to worship God in their own way. They sailed to America in 1620. In the first winter, nearly half the settlers died of disease. But in the spring, friendly Native Americans taught them how to grow corn (maize) and catch local fish, and the colony survived.

265

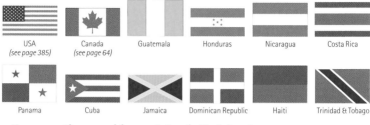

USA
(see page 385)

Canada
(see page 64)

Guatemala

Honduras

Nicaragua

Costa Rica

Panama

Cuba

Jamaica

Dominican Republic

Haiti

Trinidad & Tobago

European settlers crossed the Atlantic about 500 years ago. Spaniards moved into the south, while British, French, Dutch and others took over the north. The **Europeans** had guns and other advanced weapons. They killed huge numbers of **Native Americans** (American Indians) and took their land. For a time North America was like an overseas branch of Europe.

In time the North Americans tired of being under European control. First the USA, then Mexico and Canada broke free and became **independent** countries. As millions more people arrived from Africa, Europe and Asia, the countries of North America became a unique mix of races, customs and cultures. Parts of the region became very wealthy.

NORTH AMERICA FACTS

Number of countries: 25

Population: 456,375,000

Area: 24, 249, 000 sq km

Highest peak: Mount McKinley, Alaska, 6194 m

Lowest point: Death Valley, California, 86 m below sea level

Largest lake: Lake Superior, 83, 270 sq km, is the largest freshwater lake in the world

Mexico
Population: 91,120,000
Area: 1, 978, 800 sq km
The central area of Mexico is a high plain surrounded by mountains. To the north are dry deserts; in the south-east is tropical jungle. The capital, Mexico City, is one of the largest cities on Earth. Mining is an important industry, especially silver-mining. There are also oil wells off the coast. Most farms are small, but fishing and timber are big business.

▼ Mexico City.

find out more

Aztecs
Canada
Caribbean
Continents
Mountains
South America
United States of America

Nuclear power *see* Atoms and molecules *and* Power stations

Numbers

We use numbers in almost everything we do. We count the number of children in a class, look for a house number in a street or find a page number in a book.

1	2	3	4	5	6	7	8	9	10
11	12	13	14	15	16	17	18	19	20
21	22	23	24	25	26	27	28	29	30
31	32	33	34	35	36	37	38	39	40
41	42	43	44	45	46	47	48	49	50
51	52	53	54	55	56	57	58	59	60
61	62	63	64	65	66	67	68	69	70
71	72	73	74	75	76	77	78	79	80
81	82	83	84	85	86	87	88	89	90
91	92	93	94	95	96	97	98	99	100

Early people probably recorded numbers with stone counters or by making marks on a stick or in a piece of clay. This is called keeping a tally. Each counter or mark stands for one thing. In time, shorter ways of writing numbers developed.

Hindu–Arabic numbers

The system we use for counting and writing numbers is called the Hindu–Arabic number system. It was first used in the 6th century in India, then later in Arabia. The system is very clever. With just 10 number symbols (0, 1, 2, 3, 4, 5, 6, 7, 8, 9), it allows us to write down any number we want. This is because the same symbol stands for different amounts depending on its place in the number. In the number 765, for instance, the 5 stands for five units, the 6 for six tens and the 7 for seven hundreds.

The Hindu–Arabic number system is called a **decimal** or base 10 system, because it counts in groups of 10. The **binary** system used by a computer has base 2. It uses just two symbols, 0 and 1, to count in units, twos, fours, eights and so on.

◀ The symbols used to write numbers are called **numerals**. Different number systems use different numerals for the same number. In the Hindu–Arabic system the numeral for one thousand is 1000; in Roman numerals it is M.

▲ The numbers in the red squares are called **prime numbers**. Prime numbers cannot be made by multiplying smaller whole numbers together. The numbers in the white squares can all be made by multiplying two or more prime numbers together: for example, 26 = 2 x 13. These are called **composite numbers**.

Odds on evens!

If you add or multiply two even numbers, the answer is always even. If you add two odd numbers, the answer is always even. But, oddly enough, if you multiply two odd numbers, the answer is always odd.

symbols (numerals)

Arabic	Hindu	Roman
1	९	I
2	२	II
3	३	III
4	४	IV
5	५	V
6	६	VI
7	७	VII
8	८	VIII
9	९	IX
10	९०	X
15	९५	XV
50	५०	L
100	९००	C
500	५००	D
1000	९०००	M

find out more

Graphs

Oceans and seas

The Earth is a watery planet. Seas and oceans cover more than two-thirds of its surface. Most seas are parts of oceans.

The five oceans are the Pacific, Atlantic, Indian, Arctic and Southern oceans. The largest enclosed seas are the Mediterranean and the Baltic.

Waves, currents and tides

The water in the oceans is always on the move. It is driven by winds, tides and currents.

▼ Around the edges of the continents the oceans are shallow. Away from the continents there are many underwater volcanoes. Huge volcanoes, called seamounts, rise up from the sea-bed. Other volcanoes appear beside trenches and near the mid-ocean ridges.

Winds whip up waves, but these only stir up the surface of the water. The ocean water itself is moved by currents and tides.

Currents carry water from one part of the world to another. Some flow deep along the sea floor. Others flow near the surface.

The level of the oceans rises and falls because of the tides. Tides are caused by the pull of the Moon's gravity on the Earth as the Earth spins.

▲ Millions of tiny zooplankton (animal plankton), like these young crustaceans, live near the surface where it is light. Tiny plant plankton (phytoplankton) live here too, because they need the light to grow and make food. Many animals in the oceans live by eating plankton.

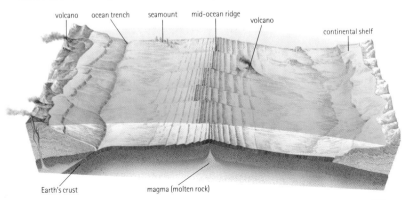

volcano   ocean trench   seamount   mid-ocean ridge   volcano   continental shelf

Earth's crust   magma (molten rock)

The ocean floor

There are long mountain chains and deep valleys on the ocean floor. The mountain chains are called mid-ocean ridges.

The surface of the Earth is made up of 13 huge pieces of crust, called plates. The mid-ocean ridges form when molten rock wells up between two plates and pushes them apart. Sometimes the mountains along the mid-ocean ridges are so tall that they break through the ocean surface to form islands. Deep valleys, or trenches, form where one plate dives beneath another.

Life in the oceans

Most of the animals and plants in the ocean live in fairly shallow waters near the coast. It is light here, so plants can grow and provide food for animals. But some types of fish and a few large mammals, such as whales, dolphins and porpoises, live in the middle of the oceans. Here they find fish or tiny plants and animals called **plankton** to eat.

Below 200 metres, there is not much light, so there are no plants. Fewer animals live here. They eat each other, or food falling from above.

Even fewer live in the very deep waters below 1000 metres. Food is very scarce in these cold and dark waters. Many of the fishes that live here have huge mouths, so they can eat animals larger than themselves.

THE WATERY WORLD

Area of Earth covered by oceans:
360 million square km (71% of Earth's surface)

Volume of water in oceans:
about 1370 million cubic km (over 97% of all water on Earth)

Average water depth: 4000 m

Deepest parts: 11,000 m in some ocean trenches.

Average water temperature:
4°C, dropping to 2°C in deep water.

▼ The Great Barrier Reef, off the coast of Australia, is the largest coral reef in the world. It is over 2000 kilometres long, and can be seen from space. Thousands of different creatures live on coral reefs, including parrot fishes, sea cucumbers and tiger sharks.

• The deepest ocean trench is the Marianas trench, near Japan. It is 11 kilometres deep – much deeper than Mount Everest is tall.

find out more

Continents
Earth
Fishes
Seashore
Water

Octopuses and squids

Octopuses and squids are invertebrates (animals without backbones) that live in the sea.

Squids, octopuses and their close relatives, cuttlefishes, belong to a group of **molluscs** called **cephalopods**. There are more than 500 different types of cephalopod. Most molluscs have a shell to protect their soft bodies. Only a few cephalopods have shells outside their bodies. Instead squids and cuttlefishes have an internal support system. Octopuses have two tiny cartilage-like rods for support.

Skilful hunters

Octopuses and squids are hunters. Octopuses catch their prey using their eight arms, which are covered in **suckers**. Squids and cuttlefishes, too, have eight short arms covered in suckers. But they also have two long **tentacles**, which they use to catch their prey. All cephalopods bite their prey and inject a poison that stops their victims from moving.

Octopuses and squids move through the water by **jet propulsion**. They squeeze water out through the end of their bag-like bodies to propel themselves forward.

Cephalopods have large brains and sensitive eyes, so they can spot danger quickly. They can hide themselves by changing colour. If an enemy comes too close, they release a cloud of black ink, which makes them even harder to find.

▲ Squids swim in the open seas. The giant squid is the largest of the invertebrates. It can grow to be a gigantic 20 metres long.

◄ Octopuses live mostly in shallow waters. They hide in rocky dens.

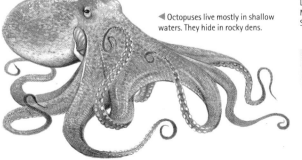

find out more

Animals
Life on Earth
Mussels and oysters
Slugs and snails

Clever 'pus!
Octopuses are probably the most intelligent of the invertebrate animals. They can remember shapes and colours.

Oil

Oil is one of the most important substances we use today. We use it to make petrol and other fuels. It is also important for making products such as plastics and chemicals.

Oil is sometimes called **petroleum**. It is the remains of dead plants and animals that sank to the sea floor millions of years ago. They were gradually covered by mud and sand, which turned to rock. Heat, bacteria and the weight of the rock slowly changed the remains into oil. The oil was trapped in spaces in certain types of rock.

Like coal and natural gas, oil is a **fossil fuel**. Once it has been used up, it cannot be replaced. Also, gases from burning oil can damage the atmosphere, and oil spills can cause pollution.

The search for oil

Once geologists have found rock layers that are likely to trap oil, oil companies drill deep narrow holes, called **oil wells**, to test for oil. These wells can be drilled on the land or on the sea floor.

The oil flowing from a well is called **crude oil**. Before it can be used, crude oil must be cleaned and processed at a **refinery**. Crude oil is transported to refineries by pipelines, tanker ships, rail or road.

▶ **Oil rigs** are large platforms used for drilling oil. A large tower, called a derrick, supports a long hollow pipe with a huge drill on its end. The well is drilled by turning the drill using an engine. As the well gets deeper, more pipe is added. Here a rig worker, called a roughneck, is connecting a new piece of pipe.

find out more ▶

Energy
Plastics
Pollution
Power stations

▶ At the refinery a fractional distillation tower is used to separate the oil into different products. The crude oil is heated until it boils and turns into vapour. The vapour rises up the tower, cooling as it rises. Different parts of the vapour become liquids at different temperatures, so they flow out of the tower at different levels.

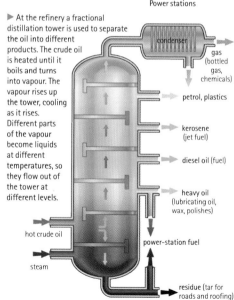

- condenser
- gas (bottled gas, chemicals)
- petrol, plastics
- kerosene (jet fuel)
- diesel oil (fuel)
- heavy oil (lubricating oil, wax, polishes)
- hot crude oil
- power-station fuel
- steam
- residue (tar for roads and roofing)

Olympic Games

The Olympic Games are an international festival of sports that are held once every four years. For athletes, swimmers, gymnasts and many other sports people, winning a gold medal at the Olympics is the ultimate dream.

▲ The five rings of the Olympic flag represent the five continents (Africa, Asia, Europe, North America and South America) joined together in the Olympic movement.

More than 200 countries take part in the Olympics, in over 270 events. The competitions are between individuals and teams representing their countries. There is no prize money for winning an Olympic event, only a medal: gold for the winner, silver for second place, and bronze for third.

The first Olympics

Today's Olympics are based on an ancient Greek festival, first held over 2700 years ago in Olympia. The early Olympics were religious festivals in honour of Zeus, the most powerful Greek god. At the first Games, in 776 BC, the only sporting event was a running race, but gradually more events were added.

Modern Olympics

The modern Olympic Games were first held in Athens in 1896. Since then, a different city has

• The Olympic Games are held in a different city each time – for example Seoul, South Korea, in 1988; Barcelona, Spain, in 1992; Atlanta, USA, in 1996; and Sydney, Australia, in 2000.

◀ Michael Johnson of the USA setting a world record time of 19.32 seconds in the 200 metres at the 1996 Atlanta Olympics. Over the history of the Olympics, record times have gradually improved. In 1896, the winning time for the men's 100 metres was 12.0 seconds. In 1996, the winning time was 9.84 seconds – over 2 seconds faster.

► Jesse Owens of the USA winning a gold medal in the 1936 Olympic Games, held in Berlin. Adolf Hitler, the leader of Nazi Germany, hoped to use the Games to prove that white Europeans were superior to all other people. Jesse Owens – a black athlete – proved Hitler wrong, winning gold medals in four athletics events.

hosted each Olympics (although a few cities, such as Los Angeles, have hosted the Games more than once). The main Olympics are held every four years, in the summer. The many different sports include over 40 athletics events, gymnastics, swimming, yacht racing, boxing, judo, tennis, hockey and cycling. There is also a separate Winter Olympics, held in the middle year between two summer Olympic Games. Events in the Winter Olympics include ice skating, skiing and sled events. Shortly after the main summer Olympics there are the Paralympics, for disabled competitors.

Women at the Olympics

Women were not allowed even to watch the ancient Olympic Games, and there were no women's events in the 1896 Olympics. However, at the 1900 Paris Olympics, women competed at golf and tennis. Since then, the number of women's events at the Olympic Games has gradually increased.

▼ Women's judo at the 1996 Atlanta Olympics.

• At every Olympics, a flame is lit before the Games at Olympia, in Greece. Runners then carry the flame to the city where the Olympics are being held. Then a huge torch is lit at the opening ceremony and burns day and night until the Games end. This is the Olympic flame.

find out more

Sports and games
See also Sports facts, pages 426–429

► Speed-skaters at the 1994 Winter Olympics in Lillehammer, Norway. As well as various skating and skiing events, the Winter Olympics include the biathlon, which combines skiing and shooting, and tobogganing, in which competitors slide down ice-covered tracks at speeds of more than 135 km/h.

Operas *see* Classical music • **Operations** *see* Medicine

Orchestras and bands

When musicians play together in an orchestra or band, it is not just good luck that makes their music sound good. All orchestras and bands are made up of instruments from different families, each of which adds to the music they produce. And the musicians have to spend hours practising together before they perform.

▲ The first steel bands were from Trinidad in the Caribbean. The players play tuned oil drums, called 'pans'.

Orchestras usually include stringed, woodwind, brass and percussion instruments. **Chamber orchestras** are made up of about 20 people. **Symphony orchestras** may have as many as 120 players. Orchestras play mostly classical music, but they also play music for television, films and pop songs.

Bands are usually made up of woodwind, brass and percussion instruments. Lots of bands are named after the kinds of instrument they play, such as **brass**, **pipe** and **steel bands**. Others are named after the kind of music they play, such as jazz, dance or **marching bands**. Pop groups are also often known as bands.

find out more

Classical music
Music
Musical instruments
Pop and rock music

• A **gamelan** is an Indonesian orchestra. The special sound of a gamelan comes from its instruments – gongs, bells, cymbals, drums, flutes and metallophones, which are like xylophones, but with metal bars.

• **Gagaku** is an old form of Japanese orchestra. Gagaku music is probably the oldest kind of music for orchestras in the world.

first violins	flutes	trumpets
second violins	oboes	trombones and tubas
violas	clarinets	percussion
cellos	bassoons	harp
double-basses	horns	piano

▲ Musicians in a symphony orchestra are arranged around the conductor. The conductor directs the musicians holding a small stick called a baton.

Ottoman empire

The Ottoman (or Turkish) empire lasted for 600 years. Its Muslim sultans had their capital in Constantinople (Istanbul) and ruled lands in three continents. Their empire stretched from Hungary in Europe, to Algeria and the Sudan in Africa, and the Persian Gulf in Asia.

The Ottoman empire was named after its Turkish founder, **Uthman I**. In 1453 the Turks captured the Christian city of **Constantinople**. From here their merchants and warships sailed into the Mediterranean. Twice the Turks besieged the Austrian capital, Vienna.

The sultans had enormous power. Their courts were a mixture of culture and cruelty. In the 16th and 17th centuries, they were famed for their poetry, art and fine buildings. The sultans even had their own personal troops, the **Janissaries**. These were boys taken from Christian families. They were not allowed to marry.

The sick man

The Ottoman empire fell apart slowly. By the late 19th century, when the Balkans broke away to become independent countries, it was known as the 'sick man of Europe'. The Arab parts of the empire rebelled during World War I, and the last sultan fled.

▲ The greatest sultan of all, Suleiman the Magnificent (1494–1566). He was a fine general who expanded his empire into Hungary and Mesopotamia (Iraq). He was also a wise and able ruler.

find out more

Byzantine empire
Middle East
World War I

KEY DATES

1258–1326 Uthman I

1453 Ottomans capture Constantinople

1529 Turks besiege Vienna

1571 Battle of Lepanto

1683 Turkish armies driven back from Vienna

1918 Turks defeated in World War I

1923 Turkey becomes a republic

▼ A useless victory. When the Turks captured Cyprus in 1570, the Christians formed a league to get it back. A huge fleet defeated the Turks in the naval battle of Lepanto. But the Turks kept Cyprus.

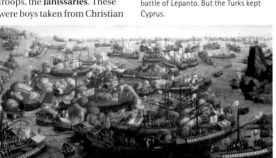

Owls see Birds • **Oxygen** see Elements • **Oysters** see Mussels and oysters

Pacific Islands

There are about 10,000 islands in the Pacific Ocean, spread over a very wide area. Some of the islands are so remote that they were among the last places on Earth to be settled by people.

Most of the islands in the Pacific are either coral reefs or volcanic peaks. The people who live there depend on fishing, farming and tourism. Coconut palms provide copra (dried coconut flesh) and coconut oil. These are important exports. Bananas, pineapples and other tropical fruits are also grown.

The islands were first settled about 5000 years ago. People sailed from South-east Asia in ocean-going outrigger canoes. As they gradually spread across the islands, they developed hundreds of different cultures and languages.

Europeans first came to the area in the 18th century. They introduced Christianity. But the diseases and weapons they brought with them killed many of the islanders. During World War II there was fierce fighting between the USA and Japan across the Pacific.

In the 1960s and 1970s most of the islands became independent countries. But some are still governed by foreign powers.

Splat!
Nauru's main export is phosphate. Phosphate comes from guano, or ancient bird droppings. It makes good fertilizer.

find out more
Australia
Japan
New Zealand
Population and settlement

◀ Polynesian children in their outrigger canoe hold up the fish they have caught. The outrigger is a small float fastened by two poles to one side of the canoe, to help stabilize it. Polynesians are the most numerous of the peoples in the southern Pacific. The other peoples are the Melanesians and the Micronesians.

Painting and drawing

About 30,000 years ago prehistoric people were painting scenes of animals on rocks and cave walls. Since then people around the world have used paintings and drawings to decorate temples, palaces and other buildings. In these pictures artists have told stories of gods, goddesses, heroes, battles and celebrations.

The tools of the artist's trade include pens, pencils, brushes, paints, paper, canvas – and more recently computers.

Artists can paint on almost any surface, but the traditional surfaces are canvas, wood, paper and plaster (walls). **Canvas** is a rough cloth made of cotton. Painting on **silk** is very popular in China and India. Most drawing is done on paper.

Artists use many different kinds of paint. Since the 15th century a lot of painting has been done in **oils**, a kind of paint in which the **pigment** (colour) is mixed with oil. Two other painting techniques have been important in the history of art. **Fresco** involves painting quickly on wet plaster. It has often been used for painting walls. **Watercolour** is usually used for fairly small pictures on paper. In the 20th century artists began using a new type of paint called **acrylic**.

The pigments used in paint have traditionally been made from many substances, including clays, rocks, metal ores and minerals. In the 20th

▲ The ceiling of the Sistine Chapel, Rome. From 1508 to 1512 Michelangelo worked on top of a high scaffold to paint a massive series of ceiling frescos. The painting turned out to be one of the most astonishing creations in the history of art. And Michelangelo was recognized as an artist of genius as well as a great sculptor. This panel tells the story of Adam and Eve's expulsion from Paradise.

◄ This delicate painting on silk shows a tiger hunt in Rajasthan, northern India.

century many bright new colours were made from artificial dyes.

Artistic styles

Every society has its own artistic styles. In China there is a long history of delicate landscape painting. Islamic (Muslim) art uses beautiful and intricate patterns, but very rarely shows things, people or animals. But styles also change over time. The history of a society's art is called its artistic **tradition**.

The European (Western) tradition is unusual in that the individual artist is considered very important. Most artists whose names are well known today are European.

European art

The development of European art has been strongly influenced by two things: classical Greek art and Christianity. Christianity was practically the only subject of painting from the 5th century AD to the Renaissance in the 14th century. People painted the walls of churches with scenes from the Bible. At a time when most people could not read, these paintings helped them to understand Christian teachings.

During the **Renaissance**, which began in Italy in the 14th century, artists became very interested in the art of ancient Greece and Rome. Learning from ancient artists, they developed a more realistic style of painting. They began to paint **portraits** and scenes from Greek mythology. Sandro

▲ The German artist Albrecht Dürer (1471–1526) was one of the great Renaissance artists. He is particularly famous for his woodcuts, such as *The Rhinoceros*. A woodcut is made by drawing a detailed design onto a piece of wood, cutting it out, and then printing the image from the wooden plate.

◀ *Rouen Cathedral* by Claude Monet (1840–1926). Monet was one of the greatest French **Impressionist** painters. Instead of showing things in great detail, these painters tried to give an impression of what the eye sees at any particular moment. Impressionist paintings are now among the most popular of all paintings.

▲ *Child Holding a Dove* by Pablo Picasso (1881–1973). Picasso is considered by many people to be the greatest artist of the 20th century. This painting dates from his 'blue' period. Perhaps his most famous style was *cubism*, in which objects or people are broken up into small geometrical shapes.

Botticelli (1445–1510) painted fresh, colourful and graceful mythological scenes. In the 17th century **landscape** and **still life** became popular in Europe. Canaletto (1697–1768) is famous for his scenes of Venice.

In order to make a living, artists had to paint pictures that they thought would appeal to other people. But some artists began to see painting as a way of expressing their feelings about the world. The personalities of great painters had always come through in their work, but the desire for intense self-expression ('expressionism')

FAMOUS PAINTERS

Giotto (about 1267–1337) was a very influential Italian painter. In his frescos he painted people in a much more natural way than other artists of his time.

Leonardo Da Vinci (1452–1519) was an Italian artist and inventor of genius, who lived during the Renaissance. His painting the *Mona Lisa* is perhaps the most famous painting in the world.

The Dutch painter **Jan Vermeer** (1632–1675) painted scenes of everyday life. His use of light and colour gave calm and serenity to his paintings.

Vincent van Gogh (1853–1890) was a Dutch painter who painted scenes from nature and ordinary life. His bold, excited brushstrokes show deep emotion.

did not become common until the early 19th century. The deserted, romantic landscapes of Caspar David Friedrich (1774–1840) were among the first paintings in this style.

Since then, the subject of painting has gradually come to be seen as less important than an artist's personal treatment of it. This trend finally led to **abstract** art. In this kind of art, lines, colours, shapes, patterns and textures exist for their own sake. The first purely abstract pictures were painted in about 1910, and abstraction has been one of the most important approaches to art ever since.

find out more

Cartoons and animation
Early people
Renaissance
Sculpture

▶ This watercolour, *Swinging*, is by Vassily Kandinsky, one of the first artists to paint totally abstract pictures.

Philosophers

What is true and what is false? What is real and what is not real? What is right and what is wrong? Why are we alive and how should we live our lives?

▲ This is the yin-yang, the symbol of the ancient Chinese belief that a balance of opposites makes all life possible. The Chinese philosopher Lao-Tzu (4th century BC) set out the way (the Tao) to maintain this balance.

These are questions that many people ask at some time in their lives. But a few people have put a lot of work into trying to understand and answer questions like these. These people are philosophers.

The Greeks

European – or Western – philosophy began with the ancient Greeks. The Greek philosopher **Socrates** (469–399 BC) was the first to use a set of

▼ This detail from 'The School of Athens' by Raphael (1510) shows Plato (left) and Aristotle walking together in Plato's Academy in ancient Greece.

rules, or **logic**, to discuss important matters. Socrates' pupil **Plato** (429–347 BC) believed that the right way to teach is to ask questions. And **Aristotle** (384–322 BC) wrote about many subjects – politics, logic, biology, mathematics and ethics. His ideas have been very important in Europe.

Philosophy today

Most philosophers today no longer work with such big questions. Instead they concentrate on trying to understand how we use language.

Take the word 'fair', for example. Does being fair mean treating everyone the same? Or does it mean treating people in a way that is right for them? Should everyone get the same-sized slice of cake, or should bigger people with bigger appetites get more?

▶ Karl **Marx** (1818–1883) was a German philosopher and political thinker. He wrote the *Communist Manifesto*. His ideas – known as Marxism – were very influential in the 20th century.

find out more

Governments
Greeks, ancient
Religions

• The French philosopher René **Descartes** (1596–1650) decided that there was only one thing he could know for sure. This was that he himself existed. 'I think, therefore I am', he said.

Photography

Photography is the art of taking pictures with a camera. It includes everything from deciding on a subject to developing and printing the finished photograph. Many people take photographs for pleasure, often to create a record of holidays or family occasions. But photography is also used in newspapers, magazines and books, and in advertisements.

To take a good photograph, you need to think about how to **compose** it. The composition of a photograph includes how the subject is arranged, how it fills the frame, what shapes and colours are present, and how light is used. But the quality of your photograph also depends on the **camera** you use and how you use it.

▲ The British photographer Julia Margaret Cameron (1815–1879) was one of the earliest and greatest portrait photographers. This photograph of Alice Liddell, (the original 'Alice' for whom Lewis Carroll wrote *Alice in Wonderland*), taken in 1872, is typical of her powerful, close-up style.

The main parts of a single-lens reflex (SLR)

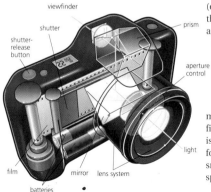

viewfinder

shutter

shutter-release button

prism

aperture control

light

film

mirror   lens system

batteries

How cameras work

When you take a photograph, the camera's **shutter** opens for a split second, to let light in. Most cameras have an **aperture** (opening) which lets more or less light through the lens. The **lens** collects the light and focuses it onto the **film**, where it makes an image. In most cameras the lens can be adjusted to sharpen the image. This is called **focusing**. Many cameras today focus automatically. Light-sensitive chemicals on the film record the image.

To take a good photograph, the camera must let just the right amount of light hit the film. This is called the correct **exposure**. If it is very bright, the shutter needs to be open for less time and the aperture should be small. When it is darker, a slower shutter speed and a larger aperture are needed.

Types of camera

Disposable cameras are the simplest and cheapest type of camera. **Compact** cameras are popular because they are light and easy to carry, but have useful features such as automatic focus, exposure and flash. **Single-lens reflex (SLR)** cameras are the type of camera used by most professional photographers. In most cameras the viewfinder is very close to the lens. In an SLR camera, when you look through the viewfinder you are looking through the lens itself. **Digital cameras** have no film. The picture is recorded by a special microchip and can then be viewed on a computer.

Developing and printing

After you have taken a photograph, the film has to be

▶ The cluster of stars shown here would be hardly visible in a normal photograph – they do not give out enough light. However, they give out very powerful X-rays, so scientists used a special X-ray camera to take this photograph.

developed to make the image appear. Washing the film in chemical solutions changes the colour of the film where it has been exposed to light. Usually the developed film is a **negative**. This means that areas that were light in the original image are dark on the film, while dark areas appear light. To make a positive image, you shine light through the negative onto a piece of light-sensitive paper. This is then developed to produce a **print**.

find out more ▶
Films

PHOTOGRAPHY FIRSTS

16th century The camera obscura makes upside-down images, which are then traced onto paper.

1826 The Frenchman Joseph Niepce takes the first photograph. It has an eight-hour exposure, and is very faint.

1837 Louis Daguerre invents the first practical camera. It takes pictures in which the light parts become dark and the dark light. This kind of negative image is known as a daguerrotype.

1839 William Fox Talbot discovers how to make multiple positive prints from a negative.

▼ This photograph of a tiger in water has been taken using high-speed photography.

Physics

Physics is a science that studies the basic forces and laws that control how the Universe works. It is sometimes called the 'science of everything'.

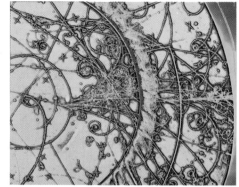

Physicists try to understand and explain how matter (the material things are made from) behaves. They study forces and motion, electrical and nuclear energy, heat, the behaviour of light and sound, and the structure of atoms and molecules.

The study of physics has led to many important new developments. These range from electricity and more efficient machines, to lasers, electronics, nuclear power and space exploration.

From motion to quantum theory

The first real physicist was the Italian **Galileo Galilei**, who worked in the early 1600s. His ideas helped the British scientist Isaac **Newton** work out the laws of gravity and motion in the late 1600s. In the 19th century, British physicists Michael **Faraday** and James **Clerk Maxwell** discovered the laws of electricity and magnetism. Later, other physicists observed

radioactivity and subatomic particles for the first time.

At the start of the 20th century, Albert Einstein's theories of **relativity** gave us a new understanding of time and space. Another theory, **quantum mechanics**, explained how matter behaves at the scale of the atom.

▲ Bubble chambers show the tracks of the particles that make up atoms, such as protons, electrons and quarks. They are an important tool for physicists studying these subatomic particles.

Albert Einstein
Albert Einstein was born in 1879 in Germany. In 1913 he moved to the United States and spent the rest of his life there. His theories about relativity and the relationship between time and space changed the way that scientists think. Without his ideas lasers, television, computers, space travel and many other things that are familiar today might never have been developed.

find out more

Atoms and molecules
Electricity
Energy
Forces
Light
Radiation
Sound

Pirates

Where there are ships, there are bound to be pirates, or sea-robbers. The most famous pirates lived around 1550–1720. None was worse than the dreaded 'Blackbeard' (Edward Teach), whose name filled every honest sailor's heart with terror.

◀ Beware the corsair! The Muslim corsair pirates of North Africa used their speedy galleys to capture Christians, whom they sold as slaves.

Greek and Roman pirates were a real menace. Once they even captured Julius Caesar!

The 'golden age' of piracy began when Europeans started trading around the world. Stately treasure galleons, sailing back from America, were a tempting target. Pirates, like the **buccaneers**, hid among the Caribbean islands and took passing ships by surprise. Many victims gave in without a fight. To encourage this, pirates built up terrible reputations. **Blackbeard** hung lighted fuses about his head and cut off people's fingers to get their rings.

Pirates of the East

The Indian Ocean was also thick with pirates. The **Gujarati Rovers** patrolled India's west coast. Henry Avery, the most successful European pirate, captured a ship loaded with diamonds, then vanished with his loot. Chinese pirates were even better organized. The husband and wife team, **Ching Yih** and **Ching Shih**, had a private pirate navy of 1800 vessels and 30,000 men.

find out more ▶

Empire, Age of
Exploration, Age of

Not so Jolly Roger!
Chinese pirates were famously nasty. Ching Shih rewarded everyone who brought her a severed head. Other captains were said to nail their prisoners' feet to the deck, then beat them to death.

◀ Terrible two: the famous women pirates Anne **Bonny** and Mary **Read**. Dressed as men, they were as hardy as any who sailed under the skull and crossbones. They were captured in 1720. The other members of their gang were hanged, but Anne and Mary were spared because they were pregnant.

Plants

Plants range in size from giant trees to tiny mosses. They include the largest and the oldest living things. Unlike animals, plants do not usually move around or eat. They grow rooted in the ground, and make their own food in special 'chemical factories' in their leaves.

The most important difference between plants and animals is how they get their food. This also helps to explain why plants are green. Like all living things, plants are made up of microscopic 'building blocks' called cells. They are green because their cells contain a green chemical called **chlorophyll**. The chlorophyll is bundled into packages called **chloroplasts**, which are the plant's food factories.

Green factories

To make its food, a plant needs two 'raw materials' – the gas carbon dioxide, which it gets from the air, and water from the soil. The plant takes up carbon dioxide through special pores in its leaves, while water is taken up by the plant's roots.

The chlorophyll in the plant's cells absorbs energy from sunlight. The chloroplasts use this energy to turn carbon dioxide and water into sugars,

▼ Photosynthesis happens in two stages. First, the plant uses light energy to split water into hydrogen and oxygen. This is the **light reaction**. Second, the hydrogen combines with carbon dioxide to make sugars. This reaction does not need light and is called the **dark reaction**.

▲ A flowering head of cocksfoot grass. Grass flowers use the wind to spread pollen from plant to plant. Grasses are the most successful group of flowering plants. Many are annual: they live for a season, produce a large quantity of seeds, and then die.

▼ Cross-section of a leaf, showing how sunlight and carbon dioxide reach the photosynthesizing cells. Also, the xylem tubes bring water to the cells, while the phloem tubes carry sugars to other parts of the plant.

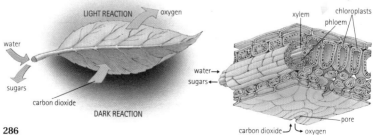

LIGHT REACTION

oxygen

water

sugars

carbon dioxide

DARK REACTION

sunlight

xylem

chloroplasts

phloem

water→

sugars←

pore

carbon dioxide ↳ oxygen

which are the plant's food. The whole process of making food using sunlight is called **photosynthesis**.

Plant variety

A typical plant (a tree, for example) has roots that anchor it in the ground and absorb water and minerals. Its stem or trunk holds up the leaves, so they can take in sunshine for photosynthesis. Tube-like cells (**xylem**) in the stem carry water from the roots to the leaves. Other tubes (**phloem**) transport sugars to wherever the plant needs them for energy.

Plants such as mosses and liverworts are much simpler, but they still photosynthesize and fit the basic pattern of a plant. Other plants, however, are not green: they get their food in different ways. Plants such as mistletoe live partly as parasites, which means they 'steal' food from green plants. Other plants, such as toothwort, get all the goodness they need from dead plant material in the soil.

Seeds and spores

Because plants do not move about, they cannot meet and mate with others of their kind. They therefore reproduce and spread themselves in other ways.

Flowering plants produce male and female sex cells in their flowers. They rely

▲ Venus fly-traps live on soils poor in nitrogen. To get extra nitrogen, they catch insects in their spring-trap leaves and absorb nutrients from them.

either on the wind or on animals to carry the male sex cells (called pollen) to the female sex cells of another flower. There, the sex cells join to produce seeds (**fertilization**). Seeds are usually enclosed in a fruit, which is designed to carry the seed away to a new place to grow. Other plants spread in slightly different ways. **Conifers**, for example, also have tiny flowers that spread pollen. But their seeds are usually produced on a woody cone. The seeds are then spread by the wind.

Ferns, mosses and **liverworts** have more complicated life cycles. Instead of seeds, they spread by spores – dust-like particles that are spread by the wind. These spores grow into plants that are quite unlike the adults; they are tiny green flaps that can only survive in damp places. These green flaps produce male and female sex cells in tiny pockets on their underside. The male sex cells swim to other pockets, where they fertilize the female sex cells. An adult fern, moss or liverwort grows from the fertilized cells.

◀ Plants often store food in their roots or in underground stems. Sometimes we eat these food stores: carrots, for example, are swollen roots, and potatoes are swollen underground stems. Plants also need other chemicals called minerals. They take in these minerals through their roots, dissolved in water.

287

Plants

▼ The plant kingdom includes mosses, liverworts, ferns, conifers and flowering plants. The groups are divided according to how they reproduce. Some other groups of living things are plant-like, but are not regarded as true plants. Many algae, for example, can photosynthesize, but some algae move about like animals. Mushrooms and toadstools also look like plants, but they are actually a type of fungus.

find out more

Algae
Flowers and fruits
Food
Grasslands
Mushrooms and toadstools
Trees

▲ Mosses have a simpler structure than flowering plants. They have no proper roots, and collect all the water and minerals they need from the rain that falls on them.

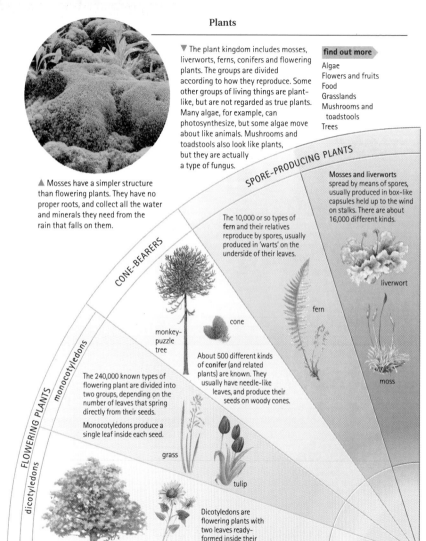

SPORE-PRODUCING PLANTS

Mosses and liverworts spread by means of spores, usually produced in box-like capsules held up to the wind on stalks. There are about 16,000 different kinds.

The 10,000 or so types of **fern** and their relatives reproduce by spores, usually produced in 'warts' on the underside of their leaves.

liverwort

fern

moss

CONE-BEARERS

monkey-puzzle tree

cone

About 500 different kinds of **conifer** (and related plants) are known. They usually have needle-like leaves, and produce their seeds on woody cones.

FLOWERING PLANTS

monocotyledons

The 240,000 known types of flowering plant are divided into two groups, depending on the number of leaves that spring directly from their seeds.

Monocotyledons produce a single leaf inside each seed.

grass

tulip

dicotyledons

Dicotyledons are flowering plants with two leaves ready-formed inside their seeds.

oak tree

sunflower

Plastics

Plastics are artificial materials made from chemicals. They can be easily shaped to make many different kinds of thing. Telephones, computers, toothbrushes, clothes and countless other things are made from plastics.

Plastics are made by linking together small molecules called monomers into long chains called **polymers**. The raw materials for the monomers usually come from crude oil. It is possible to make plastics with different characteristics by making the polymers form in different ways.

Using plastics

Plastics are among the most useful modern materials, because they are so versatile. They can be transparent, like glass, or made in any colour. They can be formed into ultra-light solid foams, or made into flexible **synthetic fibres** that can be woven into cloth. Plastics can also be used in **composites** – materials in which strong, stiff fibres are embedded in a tough plastic resin.

▼ Blow moulding and extrusion are just two of the many ways that plastics can be shaped. Blow moulding is used to make plastic bottles, and plastic pipes are made by extrusion.

▲ This roller-blade racer is wearing a helmet and protective clothing made from a tough plastic called polycarbonate.

find out more

Atoms and molecules
Oil

What makes what?
- Plastic bags and drinks bottles are often made of polythene.
- Disposable cups for hot and cold drinks are often made of a lightweight polystyrene foam.
- The carpet you walk on may be made of nylon, a polymer fibre.
- Fleece jackets are made of another kind of polymer fibre, polyester.

Blow moulding

1 hot plastic put in mould

compressed air

2 air forced in, shaping plastic to mould

3 finished bottle

Extrusion

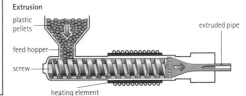

plastic pellets

feed hopper

screw

heating element

extruded pipe

Poetry

Poetry is using words in unusual and exciting ways – making patterns, rhythms and pictures out of words. The poet Samuel Taylor Coleridge described poetry as 'the best words in the best order'.

The word poetry comes from a Greek word that means 'to make'. When you write poetry, you are making something – a pattern, a picture – out of words. Sometimes the pattern is a shape. This poem is by Keith Bosley:

SNAKE

Snake glides
    through grass
       over
      pebbles
    forked tongue
  working
never
speaking
   but its
     body
    whispers
  listen

The pattern of words is usually a pattern of sounds as well. In good poetry the words and sounds fuse together to make a picture and a rhythm.

How like a winter hath my absence
  been
From thee, the pleasure of the
  fleeting year!
What freezings have I felt,
  what dark days seen!
What old December's
  darkness everywhere!

▶ The 18th-century English poet and artist **William Blake** made etchings of his poems, and then printed and coloured the pages himself. This is a print of his famous poem 'The Tiger'.

In these lines from one of his sonnets, William Shakespeare uses **rhyme** ('been' in line 1 rhymes with 'seen' in line 3) and **rhythm** (a regular beat) to give the poem shape. He also uses **imagery**. He tells us how he is feeling by creating a picture of something else – of winter.

Two kinds of imagery are used a lot in poetry: similes and metaphors. In a **simile** the poet says something is *like* something else: 'how like a winter hath my absence been'. In a **metaphor** something is described as if it *is* something else: 'thee, the pleasure of the fleeting year'.

Another technique used in poetry is **alliteration**. This is when two or more words close to each other begin with the same sound, for example 'freezings' and 'felt', and 'dark days'.

• Poetry existed even before writing. Early people probably told each other stories in the form of long poems. Some of the oldest surviving poems, such as the ancient Greek poems *The Iliad* and *The Odyssey*, are long stories, with casts of gods and heroes. Before Homer wrote them down, they were passed on by word of mouth from generation to generation.

find out more

Drama
Myths and folk tales
Writers

Pollution

We cause pollution when we do damage to our surroundings. Litter is one form of pollution. But chemicals and waste from factories, farms, motor cars and even houses cause much more serious pollution.

Over the years, laws have been passed to reduce pollution, and many people are working to limit the damage it does to our **environment**. However, pollution remains a big problem.

Air pollution

Factories, power stations and motor vehicles make waste gases, soot and dust, which all get into the air. The polluted air damages people's lungs. Some kinds of air pollution can even cause brain damage. Waste gases in the air can also cause **acid rain**, which damages trees, lake and river life, and buildings.

Ozone is a gas produced naturally from oxygen in the upper atmosphere. A thin layer of ozone surrounds the world, and protects us from the harmful ultraviolet rays in sunlight. Ozone is being

▲ This satellite picture taken above the Antarctic shows how pollution is causing thinning of the ozone layer, especially over the Poles. The colours indicate ozone levels in the upper atmosphere. In the red and grey area at the centre there is virtually no ozone at all.

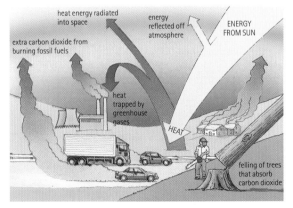

heat energy radiated into space

energy reflected off atmosphere

ENERGY FROM SUN

extra carbon dioxide from burning fossil fuels

heat trapped by greenhouse gases

HEAT

felling of trees that absorb carbon dioxide

◀ Some of the gases in the Earth's atmosphere act like the glass in a greenhouse, trapping heat from the Sun. Exhaust gases from vehicles and power stations have greatly increased the amounts of carbon dioxide, the main greenhouse gas, in the air. Scientists believe that this greenhouse effect is causing the world to become warmer. This is known as global warming.

destroyed by pollution from burning fuels and by some chemicals. Damage to the ozone layer means that more people get skin cancer.

▲ In some large cities, the air is so polluted that people wear face masks to filter out dust and soot from the air.

Water pollution

Acid rain can pollute lakes and rivers. But there are many other kinds of water pollution. Some towns and villages pump untreated sewage into rivers or the sea, while factories sometimes release poisonous chemicals and wastes. These pollutants can kill fishes and other water animals and plants. Farmers use **fertilizers** and

chemical **pesticides** that can also be washed into rivers and streams after heavy rainfall. The sea can also be polluted by spillages of oil from oil tankers and oil rigs.

Pollution of the land

People cause pollution when they thoughtlessly dump their rubbish. Some kinds of rubbish rot away quite quickly, but many plastics will never decay.

Radioactive waste from nuclear power stations could also cause serious pollution. Nearly all nuclear waste is safely contained, but small amounts do sometimes escape. Many scientists are worried about the long-term effects of this type of pollution, because nuclear waste can stay radioactive for thousands of years.

find out more ▶

Air
Conservation
Farming
Industry
Radiation

Black seas

On 25 March 1989, the oil tanker *Exxon Valdez* ran aground in Alaska, USA, spilling over 30,000 tonnes of oil into the sea. Over 2400 km of coast were polluted and thousands of seabirds died as they tried to clean the oil that clogged their feathers. A hugely expensive clean-up operation followed, and the environment is still recovering.

▶ The beautiful Annapurna Valley is the most popular trekking destination in Nepal. But the booming tourist trade has brought problems. In this picture you can see how rubbish left by campers pollutes the environment.

Pop and rock music

Pop music is a powerful part of popular culture today. It is played on radios everywhere. Lots of people have CD, tape and record collections of their favourite music. There are many different styles of pop music. Rap, hip-hop, soul, heavy metal, drum 'n' bass, disco, jungle and trance are just a few.

What these styles have in common is that they all have their roots in **rock 'n' roll** – a type of music that developed in the southern USA in the 1950s.

Rock 'n' roll roots

In the 1940s and 1950s, black musicians in southern USA started to play a style of music that had a strong rhythm. It had developed out of blues, country and western, and jazz. They called it **rhythm and blues**. When white DJs started to play this music on the radio, they called it rock 'n' roll.

The black artist **Chuck Berry** was one of the first great rock musicians. Many players have copied his ringing guitar sound. But the most popular early rock star of all was **Elvis Presley**. He is still known as the 'King of Rock 'n' Roll'.

The sixties

The biggest rock 'n' roll group of the 1960s was the British group the **Beatles**. They had their first hit in 1962 with 'Love Me Do'. Another world-famous British group is the **Rolling Stones**. Like the Beatles, the Stones wrote

▲ By 1956 Elvis Presley had become a star, with hits such as 'Hound Dog' and 'Blue Suede Shoes'. He sold 500 million records in his lifetime.

◀ At the root of the Beatles' success was the song-writing partnership of John Lennon (second left) and Paul McCartney (right). The band's lively songs, their wit and their rebellious attitudes won them millions of fans.

their own songs, but their music was more influenced by American soul and blues.

Pop and politics

During the 1960s pop musicians began to use their music to say something political. The anti-war songs of **Bob Dylan** and **Joan Baez** expressed the feelings of many young people at the time of the Vietnam War.

Since then many pop records have contained a political message. In the 1970s **reggae** artists such as **Bob Marley** wrote songs promoting the dignity of black people.

Meanwhile **punk** burst onto the British music scene in 1976. Bands like the **Sex Pistols** used aggressive music and lyrics, and outrageous dress and behaviour, to rebel against authority.

Rap and **ragga** appeared in the 1980s, and became popular ways of expressing political views. Rap uses rhyming lyrics spoken or sung fast against a fixed beat.

Dance and glamour

All sorts of styles developed in the 1970s. **Glam rock** artists like **David Bowie** created a theatrical style. Rhythm-based **soul** and **disco** music, with their strong dance beats also emerged. In the 1980s stars such as **Madonna**, who combined catchy melodies with a dramatic image and performance, became world superstars. And new dance styles, including **techno**, **hip-hop** and **jungle**, were hugely popular in the 1990s.

◀ The British group the **Spice Girls** were enormously successful in the late 1990s. This was partly because their image was carefully designed to appeal to teenagers. They appeared continually on television, and in newspapers and magazines.

◀ By the 1990s many bands were using computers to produce their music. **Oasis** was the most successful of a group of bands that went against the trend. They reminded people that it was possible to create great rock with a few guitars, a drum-kit and the ability to write good songs.

TOP 10 BEST-SELLING SINGLES

1 'Candle In the Wind 1997' – Elton John

2 'White Christmas' – Bing Crosby

3 'Rock Around the Clock' – Bill Haley and the Comets

4 'I want to hold your hand' – The Beatles

5 'It's Now or Never' – Elvis Presley

6 'I Will Always Love You' – Whitney Houston

7 'Don't Be Cruel/Hound Dog' (double A side) – Elvis Presley

8 'Diana' – Paul Anka

9 'Hey Jude' – The Beatles

10 'I'm a Believer' – The Monkees

find out more

Music
Musical instruments

Population and settlement

The world's population has been through massive changes in the past century. The number of people in the world reached 6 billion in 1999. By 2010 half of the world's population will live in cities.

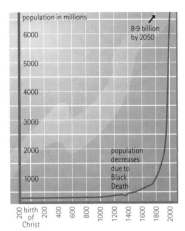

population in millions

8·9 billion by 2050

population decreases due to Black Death

200 birth of Christ 200 400 600 800 1000 1200 1400 1600 1800 2000

Although the world's population has been growing for many centuries, it has grown much more quickly in the past hundred years. Between 1880 and 1960 the world population doubled to 3 billion. Over the next 40 years the population doubled again.

Some experts say that the world cannot support and feed more people. Others argue that numbers will level off in the next 50 years or so, and improvements in farming will provide enough food for everyone.

Patterns of change

The study of population is called **demography**. Demographers have shown how countries have followed the same pattern of population change. Before modern times, countries had high birth rates and death rates. Then, because of improvements in medicine, diet and hygiene, death rates fell. After a time,

families wanted fewer children, so birth rates also fell. In developed countries these changes have taken place over one or two hundred years. They are now happening in developing countries, at a much faster rate.

Developed countries usually have populations with more elderly people and fewer children. In some countries,

▲ This graph gives an idea of how the population of the world has grown over the past 2000 years.

▼ A small village just below the high mountains of the Himalayas in Nepal.

295

▶ Land and housing are expensive in big, fast-growing cities. Poor people have to build shelters from whatever material they can find. These shanty towns in São Paulo, Brazil, are called favelas.

such as Germany and Italy, so few people are born each year that their populations will soon start shrinking.

Developing countries have high birth rates, so there are more children per adult. In countries with young and growing populations it is difficult for the government to feed and house everyone.

Settlements

Except for nomads (travellers), most people live in a settlement of some sort. **Villages** are usually found in rural areas, where farming is the main way of life. Places with markets, shops, schools and other services are **towns**. They usually have a few thousand inhabitants. **Cities** are large centres of population, often with cathedrals,

▼ Centres of population are visible at night from space because of their street lights. Parts of North America have so many cities so close to one another that the term megalopolis has been used to describe them. You can see a megalopolis along the north-eastern coast of the USA.

universities, factories, offices and airports. The largest cities spread across hundreds of square kilometres. These **metropolitan regions** may be home to 10 or even 20 million people. Examples include Tokyo, New York, Los Angeles and Mexico City.

Over the last century the fastest-growing cities have been in the developing world. Sometimes they grow so quickly that people have to build their own homes and provide their own water, heating and light. These places are usually called squatter settlements or **shanty towns**.

From the country to the city

In the past, towns became cities because people moved there from the country. When modern machines were introduced into farming, fewer people were needed in the fields. At the same time, factories in cities needed workers. This movement of people took place in Britain in the 19th century, and continues in countries such as Mexico, Brazil, India and China today. More recently, improvements in transport have encouraged people in developed countries to leave crowded cities for the countryside.

Moving across the world

Throughout human history people have moved from one part of the world to another. But from the 18th century, when population – especially in Europe – began to grow rapidly, people moved in larger numbers. In the 19th century millions left Europe, China and India to settle in the Americas, Australia and Africa. Millions now migrate to North America, Europe and the Middle East. Today around 100 million people live in a different country from the one they were born in. Some settle permanently in a new country. Others go just to work and earn wages to send to their families.

Wars, famines and natural disasters often force people to leave their home countries against their will. There are between 20 and 30 million such **refugees** across the world.

▼ This map shows the main movements of peoples over the past 2500 years.

Underground towns

In the remote Australian mining town of Coober Pedy it is so hot that homes, shops and churches are built underground.

In the Cappadocia region of central Turkey, people live inside homes carved out of volcanic rock formations.

find out more

Archaeology
Families
Human beings
Transport

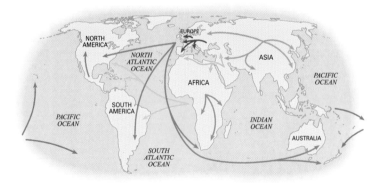

→ Germanic tribes spread into western Europe, 5th century AD
→ Arabs conquer North Africa and Middle East, 7th century AD
→ Polynesians colonize the islands of the eastern Pacific and New Zealand, 300 BC–AD 750
→ southern migration of Bantu peoples in Africa, 2000–1500 years ago

→ Mongol armies push into eastern Europe, Middle East, China and India, 13th–16th centuries
→ Europeans migrate to the Americas (from 16th century), South Africa (from 17th century) and Australia and New Zealand (from 19th century)
→ African slaves taken to the Americas, 16th–19th centuries
→ Latin Americans migrate to the USA, 20th century

Ports *see* Ships and boats • **Portugal** *see* Europe

Pottery

Pottery is the art of making things out of baked clay. It is also the name for the things that are made this way. Pottery (or ceramics) is used to make many things as well as pots – for instance crockery such as mugs and plates, tiles, sinks and spark plugs.

Clay looks and feels like mud, but when it is wet, it can be shaped. And when it is baked, it becomes hard. Different kinds of clay are used to make different types of pottery. The roughest clays make **earthenware** (for instance flowerpots), which is not waterproof. Finer clays make **stoneware**, which is waterproof. The finest clays are used to make **porcelain**.

How pottery is made

The first pots were made by hand, and many are still made this way by craftspeople around the world. Individual pots are also often made using a **wheel**. But most pottery today is made in factories, from moulds.

Most potters fire their pots in a **kiln** (an oven that reaches very high temperatures). They then glaze the pot. A **glaze** is a thin layer of melted glass, which covers the pot. This makes it smooth and waterproof, and can add colour.

◀ Porcelain is made out of fine white clay. It is fired at very high temperatures and produces strong and delicate china, like this 17th-century Chinese vase.

▲ This Indonesian potter is decorating a wheel-made pot before firing it. Methods of decorating pots include marking them when they are still soft, 'trailing slip' (liquid clay) over them and cutting patterns into the slip, and colouring the pots with glazes.

• Pottery is one of the oldest technologies of all. The first pots were probably made in the Middle East about 9000 years ago. The potter's wheel was invented about 3500 years ago.

• Ceramic materials are very strong. They are also good insulators. This means they keep heat in well. Ceramic tiles are used on the Space Shuttle to protect the metal skin of the craft from heat.

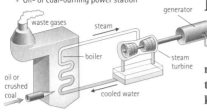

▼ Oil- or coal-burning power station

generator

waste gases

steam

boiler

steam turbine

oil or crushed coal

cooled water

Power stations

The electricity you use whenever you plug into the mains comes from a power station that may be hundreds of kilometres away.

One way of producing electricity is to move a wire in a magnetic field. In a power station, machines called **generators** contain large coils of wire between two rotating magnets. Turbines – like huge fans with many blades – turn these magnets to make electricity.

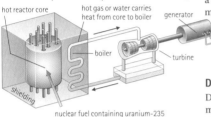

▼ Nuclear power station (pressurized water reactor)

hot reactor core

hot gas or water carries heat from core to boiler

generator

boiler

turbine

shielding

nuclear fuel containing uranium-235

Different fuels

Different power stations use different methods to produce the power for driving the turbines. About two-thirds of the electricity generated today is produced in power plants that burn **fossil fuels** such as oil, gas and coal. In these plants the fuels are burned to heat water in a boiler and turn it into steam. Jets of steam then drive the turbines.

▼ This tidal power station was built across the River Rance near St Malo, France. It harnesses the power of the tides to generate electricity. Inside the dam and below the water level are rows of turbines. As the tides flow in and out, the moving water turns the turbine blades. The turbines drive the generators that produce the electricity.

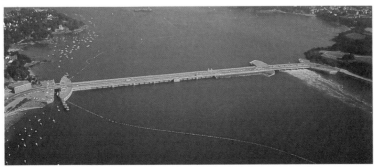

Nuclear power stations also heat water to make steam, but the heat is created when radioactive fuels, such as uranium, are split apart in a process called fission.

The pollution problem

The fossil fuels we burn to generate electricity cause pollution. Gases released into the air can cause acid rain, which damages plants and pollutes lakes. Burning fossil fuels also produces carbon dioxide, a 'greenhouse gas' that adds to global warming. Another problem is that we are running out of fossil fuels. Once they are used up, they cannot be replaced.

Nuclear power stations do not produce pollution, but they do create radioactive waste. This must be stored safely for thousands of years until it is no longer dangerous. Many people also worry that accidents at nuclear power plants could release radioactivity.

Alternative answers

One way to solve these problems is to use **alternative energy**

sources to generate electricity. In hydroelectric plants, the energy from fast-flowing water from rivers, waterfalls or dams is used to turn turbines to generate electricity. In wind farms, wind energy turns the blades of windmills to generate electricity. In solar cells, heat from the Sun is converted directly into electricity.

Alternative energy sources won't run out. But they are usually more expensive, and they cannot yet produce enough electricity to meet all our needs.

Lots of watts!

Large power stations can generate up to 2000 megawatts of power. This is enough electricity to power about 200 million light bulbs!

find out more

Electricity
Energy
Light

▶ Combined-cycle power stations have two turbines. The first, like the one shown here, is a gas turbine – a type of jet engine which uses gas as its fuel. It provides the power to drive one generator. The heat from the jet engine exhaust is used to make steam. This steam is used to turn another turbine, which drives a second generator.

Pregnancy *see* Sex and reproduction

Printing

Printing is a way of making many identical copies from one original.

With modern printing methods thousands of copies of anything from an encyclopedia to a soup packet can be produced quickly and cheaply.

The print revolution

The big breakthrough in printing words came around 1450, when the German printer Johann **Gutenburg** invented letterpress printing. Each letter was cast separately in metal (**moveable type**). This made it possible for letters and numbers to be re-used and re-arranged again and again to form new pages of print.

The invention of printing gave many more people the chance to read and learn about

▲ A print worker checks a sheet of colour printing as it comes off the printing press. Printed colour pictures are made up from tiny dots of just four colours: magenta (a bluish red), yellow, cyan (a greenish blue) and black. When the tiny dots are printed very close to each other, your eyes blend them together so that you see a full range of colours.

new things. It also helped to spread ideas quickly around the world.

Modern methods

Lithography is the most common method of printing used today. In lithography, the letters and pictures to be printed are copied on to a special printing plate. The ink sticks to those areas of the plate that are to be printed, but not to other areas.

find out more
Newspapers
Writing

Type and images
Printed pages are made up of type (letters and numbers) and images (drawings and photographs). Today, pages are usually made up on a computer. The computer files are used to make photographic film, from which printing plates can be made.

▼ Lithography is the printing process used most widely today. In this process a picture or image of the page that is being printed, including the words and any drawings or photos, is made in a special coating on a metal plate.

The image on the plate is greasy, and attracts ink.

A roller spreads water over all the plate except the greasy parts.

A second roller spreads ink, which sticks to the greasy image.

The inked image is transferred on to the paper.

Racism

Racism means judging someone by their race rather than by who they are as an individual. Throughout history racism has led to great injustice and cruelty. Today many governments recognize that racism is evil.

All human beings look different. But particular groups of human beings (known as **races**) have certain physical characteristics in common. People from sunny lands, for instance, tend to be darker-skinned than those from cold climates. When differences of language, religion and customs are added, we have separate '**ethnic groups**'.

▲ South Africa's Archbishop Desmond Tutu, a leading campaigner against racism. When his country's racist system (apartheid) was abolished, he headed a Truth and Reconciliation Commission that tried to heal old wounds.

Causes of racism

Racism can occur when different ethnic groups live in the same area. They may be afraid or jealous of each other. Sometimes one group thinks itself superior to another. Many 19th century Europeans, for example, thought they were better than Africans.

Horror and hope

Racism has scarred modern times. European Americans persecuted Native Americans (the 'Indians') and African Americans. There have been horrible racist massacres in Cambodia, Rwanda and the Balkans. Worst of all was the Nazi massacre of some 6 million Jews in World War II.

The United Nations is completely opposed to racism. Many countries have made it a crime.

▼ During World War II the Nazis rounded Jewish people up into huge camps called concentration camps, where millions were killed. This picture of starving children in Auschwitz was taken in 1945.

Unfair play

A South African law of 1950 said that all citizens had to belong to one of three groups: White, Black or Coloured (mixed race). Only those registered as White were allowed to vote for the government or represent their country at sport.

find out more

Human beings
South Africa
United Nations
World War II

Radar

Radar is a way of using radio waves to 'see' things and to find out which way they are moving. Radar can tell us the position of a moving or a still object, even if it is far away or in dark or foggy conditions.

Radar is short for **RA**dio **D**etection **A**nd **R**anging. It is used for many things. For example, ships and planes use radar to look out for other ships, planes or hazards nearby. Air traffic controllers use radar to tell the position of aircraft around busy airports. Weather forecasters use radar to 'see' approaching storms or hurricanes. Scientists use radar to study the atmosphere and to track spacecraft. The police use radar to help them catch speeding motorists.

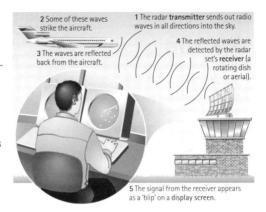

2 Some of these waves strike the aircraft.

1 The radar **transmitter** sends out radio waves in all directions into the sky.

3 The waves are reflected back from the aircraft.

4 The reflected waves are detected by the radar set's **receiver** (a rotating dish or aerial).

5 The signal from the receiver appears as a 'blip' on a display screen.

▲ How a radar system detects a flying aircraft.

Bouncing beams

Radar works by sending out **radio waves** called **microwaves** and measuring how they return. A **transmitter** first sends radio waves into the sky. If the waves hit a solid object, some of them bounce back. These reflected waves are picked up by a **receiver** (a rotating aerial). When an object has been detected, a 'blip' appears on the radar screen. The radar works out how far away it is by measuring how long it took for the radio wave to travel to the object and back.

• Radar was invented by the British scientist Robert Watson-Watt in 1935. It was first used for detecting enemy aircraft.

find out more

Radiation
Weapons

◀ 'Stealth' aircraft are designed to be very difficult to detect. F-117A Stealth fighters (left and right) have flat surfaces at many angles, which scatter radar beams. The B-2 Stealth bomber (centre) is made from special plastics that absorb radio waves.

Radiation

Radiation is energy on the move. To radiate means to give out heat, light or other energy.

There are two main types of radiation. In **wave radiation**, energy travels as invisible electromagnetic **waves**. In **particle radiation** the energy is in the form of tiny particles that shoot out from atoms at enormous speeds. Radioactive materials, like the fuels used in nuclear power plants, produce both types of radiation.

Radiating waves

There are many types of electromagnetic wave. Radio signals, light and heat are just some examples. They are all produced in different ways and have different wavelengths and frequencies.

The **wavelength** of a wave is the distance between any two wave crests. Its **frequency** is the number of wave crests that pass a particular point every second. Frequency is measured in hertz, or vibrations per second.

Higher-frequency (shorter wavelength) waves, such as X-rays and gamma rays, carry

▲ The wavelength and frequency of a particular kind of radiation are closely related. Longer waves have a longer wavelength and a lower frequency: fewer wave crests pass a particular point every second. Shorter waves have a shorter wavelength and a higher frequency.

▼ We use electromagnetic waves in many ways, from radio broadcasts and microwave cooking to killing cancer cells. Some types of radiation warm things, others allow us to see things. The electromagnetic spectrum, shown below, includes all kinds of electromagnetic waves arranged according to their wavelengths and the amounts of energy they carry.

wave crest — *wave crest*
wavelength — Longer waves
wave crest — *wave crest*
wavelength — Shorter waves

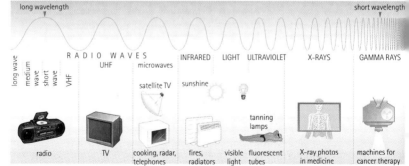

long wavelength   short wavelength

| long wave / medium wave / short wave / VHF | R A D I O   W A V E S UHF microwaves | INFRARED | LIGHT | ULTRAVIOLET | X-RAYS | GAMMA RAYS |

satellite TV — sunshine — tanning lamps

radio — TV — cooking, radar, telephones — fires, radiators — visible light — fluorescent tubes — X-ray photos in medicine — machines for cancer therapy

more energy than lower-frequency waves. The most energetic waves, such as gamma rays, can penetrate most solids. They are only stopped by thick layers of lead, steel or concrete.

Shooting particles

There are two types of particle radiation: alpha and beta radiation. **Alpha radiation** is made up of particles that contain neutrons and protons. This form of radiation travels fairly slowly and can be easily stopped. It cannot pass through paper or skin.

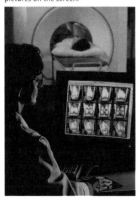

▼ Doctors use many kinds of radiation to help them find out what is wrong with someone. Magnetic resonance imaging (MRI) uses magnetism and radio waves to look at soft tissues such as the brain. Here a technician is using an MRI scanner. A computer turns the information from the scanner into the pictures on the screen.

Beta particles are electrons travelling at high speeds. They have more energy than alpha particles and can penetrate further. But they can be stopped by a sheet of metal.

Radiation all around us

Every day we are all exposed to some kinds of radiation. Natural radiation is all around us in the air, in rocks, and coming from the Sun and machines such as televisions and photocopiers. So long as it is in small doses, this radiation is not dangerous. But radiation in large amounts can be damaging, so it must be used very carefully.

RECOGNIZING RADIATION

Many important ideas about radiation were developed by European physicists in the late 1800s.

1873 The Scotsman James Clerk Maxwell predicted that there were other kinds of invisible radiation similar to light.

1887 The German Heinrich Hertz confirmed Maxwell's ideas when he discovered radio waves.

1895 The German Wilhelm Röntgen discovered another form of radiation, X-rays.

1896 The Frenchman Henri Becquerel discovered that uranium gives off invisible radiation. He called this effect radioactivity.

▲ This computer picture shows how radioactivity spread across the northern hemisphere following an accident in April 1986 at the Chernobyl nuclear power plant in the former Soviet Union. The bright pink areas show where levels of radioactivity were highest. The radioactivity caused cancer in many people, and made many others very ill.

find out more

Atoms and molecules
Energy
Heat and temperature
Light
Power stations
Radio
Sound
Stars

Radio

Radio uses invisible waves to let you hear sounds broadcast from thousands of kilometres away.

▲ This little boy in Beijing, China is listening to a portable radio. The first small, portable radios appeared in the 1950s.

• An American station, KDKA started the first regular public broadcasting in 1920.

find out more
Communications
Radiation
Television

Radio waves belong to a whole family of waves called electromagnetic waves. Like other electromagnetic waves, such as light and X-rays, radio waves can travel very long distances very quickly – 300,000 kilometres in one second.

Waves for communication

Radio waves are used by radio stations for **broadcasting**, or sending out, radio programmes. These can be music, news, chat shows or plays.

Before being broadcast, the sounds are first changed into electric signals. These signals are then sent (**transmitted**) through the air using radio waves. When they are picked up by a radio

receiver, the radio waves are changed back into copies of the original sounds so you can hear them.

Radio waves are also used for many types of **communication**. Ships and aircraft use radio to communicate and for **navigation**. Television also uses radio waves to transmit pictures and sound. Police, fire, taxi and ambulance crews sometimes use **two-way radios** to send and receive messages. Mobile phones are linked to the main telephone network by radio.

Gugliemo Marconi
A young Italian, Gugliemo Marconi, was the first person to see the potential of radio. In 1896 he built a 'wireless apparatus' that could send Morse code messages, and in 1901 he sent the first radio message across the Atlantic Ocean. The message was sent from Poldhu in Cornwall, England to St John's, Newfoundland, Canada.

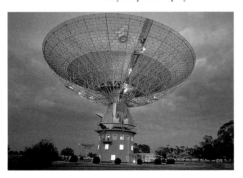

◀ Radio waves are also used by scientists to study outer space. Radio telescopes, like this one at Parks, New South Wales, Australia collect radio waves from distant stars and galaxies. They have big dishes to collect very faint radio signals. Radio telescopes can be used in daylight as well as at night.

Recording

Recording is a way of keeping sounds or video pictures so that you can hear or see them later.

When we record something, the sounds and pictures are turned into **electrical signals**. These are then used to make the recording. A microphone can turn sounds into electrical signals; a video camera can do the same with pictures. A tape player, disc player or video player turns the recording back into sounds or pictures.

Analogue and digital

Any recording can be made either in analogue form or in digital form. An analogue recording is a direct copy of the electrical signal produced by the microphone or camera. Analogue recordings suffer from the problem that they can become distorted as they are copied or played back.

To make a digital recording, the signal is coded by turning it into a long list of binary numbers (numbers made up of only 0s and 1s). The long list of numbers is called a **digital signal**. Once a recording has been digitized, it can be copied exactly time after time.

▲ A portable MiniDisc player. The recordings on a minidisc can be combined and rearranged, rather like the information on a computer disk.

find out more

Sound
Music
Television

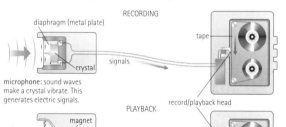

RECORDING

microphone: sound waves make a crystal vibrate. This generates electric signals.

diaphragm (metal plate)

crystal

signals

tape

record/playback head

cassette recorder: electric signals through the recording head put a magnetic pattern on the tape.

PLAYBACK

magnet

coil

cone

loudspeaker: electric signals make a coil vibrate. The coil's vibrations move the cone, which gives out sound waves.

signals

cassette player: the magnetic pattern on the tape generates electric signals in the playback head. The signals are boosted by an amplifier.

◀ Recording and playback using a cassette tape.

Patterns on tapes and discs

The **recording head** of a tape or disc recorder is what turns electrical signals into patterns on a tape or disc.

In a cassette or video recorder, sounds and pictures are recorded as **magnetic patterns** on a tape. Every cassette or video tape is coated with millions of tiny magnetic particles. The recording head magnetizes these particles weakly or strongly, depending on the strength of the electrical signal.

On a CD, the information is recorded digitally. A laser beam burns a pit into the surface of the CD for every '1' in the digital signal; where there is a '0' in the signal, the surface is left smooth. On the underside of the disc, the pattern of pits comes out as a series of 'steps' and 'flats' (meaning no step).

Flashback

The first successful sound-recording machine was built in 1878 by the American inventor Thomas Edison. The machine, called a phonograph, recorded sound by making a groove on a cylinder covered in tin-foil or wax. Flat discs (**records**) were first used for recording in 1888. The earliest recordings were made mechanically. Electrical recordings, using microphones and amplifiers, were first made in the 1920s. Magnetic tape was

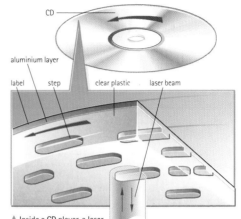

▲ Inside a CD player, a laser beam reads the pattern of steps and flats on the underside of the CD. Electronic circuits turn this pattern into electrical signals, which are used to form the sounds you hear or the words and pictures you see on the screen.

developed in the 1930s, videotape in the 1950s and compact discs in the early 1980s.

CD TRACKS

The sound patterns on a CD are recorded in a spiral track. This track is extremely narrow – you could fit 200 of them in the width of a human hair.

Recording studios

Most music recordings are made in a recording studio. In the studio, different voices and instruments are picked up by different microphones and recorded separately. Each recording is called a *track*. The tracks are mixed together to make the final recording.

Recycling *see* Energy

Reformation

For centuries the Christians of western Europe all belonged to the Roman Catholic Church. The head of the Church was the pope. During the Reformation, Protestants (protesters) left the Catholic Church and set up their own independent churches.

In the Middle Ages the **Catholic Church** was very rich and powerful. Some churchmen led very grand lives, while many ordinary priests were ignorant and poor. Men and women of faith felt the Church let them down. They couldn't even understand its services, which were in **Latin**.

Several believers, such as John **Wycliffe**, urged reform, but little happened. Then, in 1517, the German monk Martin **Luther** started a revolt. He criticized the pope, monasteries, the use of Latin, and many Church teachings. Thousands joined his Protestant movement because they liked its ideas. Others wanted to seize the Church's wealth.

▲ Martin Luther (1483–1546). The Reformation began when Martin Luther pinned a list of 95 complaints against the Roman Catholic Church onto the door of his local church at Wittenberg, Germany.

War and division

Protestantism spread around northern Europe, led by teachers like John **Calvin** and John **Knox**. England's Henry VIII put himself at the head of the new Church of England. France, Germany and the Netherlands saw bitter religious wars.

Presbyterians in Scotland
Puritans in England
Calvinists in the Netherlands
Huguenots in France
Church of England 1559
Roman Catholic Church
Calvin from 1541
Lutherans in Germany and Scandinavia
Luther from 1517
Catholic Church in western Europe
Eastern Orthodox Church in Greece, Balkans and Russia

◄ This diagram shows how the new Protestant Churches split off from the Catholic Church. There was no Reformation in the Eastern Orthodox Church.

A cover-up!

The insides of medieval churches were covered in colourful paintings. Protestants said these images got in the way of true prayer. When they took control of a church, they whitewashed over the pictures.

find out more
Christians
Europe

Religions

A religion is a set of beliefs and a way of life that a group of people follow. The six major world religions are Buddhism, Christianity, Hinduism, Islam (Muslims), Judaism (Jews), and Sikhism, but there are many other religions around the world.

The followers of most religions believe in a great power for good, sometimes called **God**. Some religions believe in many **gods** and **goddesses**, with different roles and characters.

The teachings of most religions set out how people should behave in their daily lives. These teachings are written in special books – the **scriptures**. Most religious beliefs also include ideas about what happens to people's spirits, or souls, when their bodies die.

SOME RELIGIONS AROUND THE WORLD

Confucians follow the teachings of Confucius (or Kongzi), who lived in China in the 6th and 5th centuries BC.

Jains belong to an ancient Indian religion. They try to avoid harming any form of life.

Rastafarianism is a religion that started in the 20th century. Rastafarians believe that emperor Haile Selassie of Ethiopia was a living god.

Taoists follow the ancient Chinese religion of Taoism.

Zoroastrians follow the teachings of Zoroaster, who lived in Persia (Iran) in about 1500 BC.

▲ Confucius.

Worship

Many religions have special buildings where people meet to pray and worship together. An official minister, a **priest**, often leads the worship. Many religious groups sing and play music, and most hold **festivals** to celebrate important days or times of the year.

• Monks and nuns are men and women who devote their lives to their religion. They spend their time in prayer and worship, or helping others.

◀ This boy is taking part in a special ceremony to show that he wants to be a Zoroastrian. Many religions hold such 'initiation' ceremonies, in which young people become full members of the religious group.

find out more

Buddhists
Christians
Hindus
Jews
Muslims
Sikhs

Renaissance

Renaissance means 'rebirth'. It is the name for a period of great progress and achievement in European art, architecture and learning. The Renaissance began in Italy in the 14th century and, over the next 200 years, spread through the whole of Europe.

The Italian artist **Giotto** (about 1266–1337) started to paint in a more lifelike way, and other **artists** and **sculptors** followed his example. **Architects** designed buildings based on the simple, grand styles of ancient Greece and Rome. **Scholars** took a fresh interest in the ideas of the Greeks and Romans. In general, the men and women of the Renaissance were more open-minded than those of medieval Europe. A daring few challenged traditional ideas about science, the Universe and even religion.

During the Renaissance, learning and art were very fashionable. Rulers, nobles and merchants spent fortunes on the finest poems, paintings, sculptures and buildings. Many new schools and universities were set up.

▶ Classical architecture reborn. The great dome of Florence Cathedral (1436), designed by Filippo **Brunelleschi**. He got the idea for the dome by studying the buildings of Ancient Rome.

find out more

Architecture
Astronomy
Europe
Italy
Painting and drawing
Sculpture

Lying for his art!

In 1508 the pope ordered the sculptor, painter and architect Michelangelo to paint the new Sistine Chapel. Michelangelo had to lie on his back on a high platform to paint the ceiling. The job took him four years.

◀ *The Grand Duke's Madonna* (1504) by **Raphael**, one of the great Italian Renaissance painters. The picture shows how artists had learned to use light and shade to make their pictures appear realistic.

◀ Leonardo da Vinci's design for a giant catapult. Leonardo (1452–1519) was the ideal 'Renaissance man' – painter, sculptor, architect, engineer and inventor.

Reproduction *see* Sex and reproduction

Reptiles

Crocodiles, tortoises, snakes and lizards are all reptiles. Most live in the warmer parts of the world. They have a tough, dry, scaly skin, and they breathe through lungs. Like birds, they lay eggs.

▲ Chameleons are a kind of lizard. They can camouflage themselves by changing colour, sometimes very quickly.

After mating, female reptiles lay their **eggs** in a sheltered, dry place. Reptile eggs have a papery or leathery shell. Most reptiles leave their eggs to hatch by themselves, but female crocodiles watch over their eggs, and guard the young after they hatch. Sea snakes keep their eggs inside their bodies until they are ready to hatch.

Keeping warm

Mammals and birds can make heat within their bodies, so that even when the air is cold, their body stays warm. Reptiles cannot do this – they are 'cold-blooded'. If the air around them is cold, they cool down too, and their bodies do not work properly. So they do things to keep warm. In the morning, reptiles bask in the sun to warm up as quickly as possible. They then go off to feed. Moving about helps them to keep warm.

Because they are cold-blooded reptiles need very little food for their size. Some snakes can go up to two years without eating! Birds and mammals need more food because they use a lot of energy keeping their bodies warm.

▲ Geckos are lizards that have suction pads on their feet. These help them to climb walls or walk on ceilings.

Open wide!

Snakes swallow their food whole. To take such a mouthful they have to unhinge their lower jaws at the centre and the sides.

▼ Nile crocodiles are the largest kind of crocodile. They may grow over 8 m long, and can live 200 years.

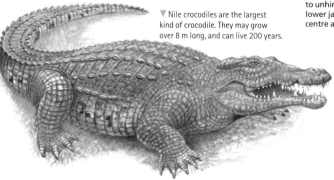

Types of reptile

Long ago there were many different kinds of reptile. The best known of these were the **dinosaurs**. For over 150 million years they were the biggest and most important land animals. Today, there are only four main groups of reptiles left.

Crocodiles and **alligators** are ferocious hunters that live in water. Their huge jaws and sharp, pointed teeth are ideal for holding fish. Big adult crocodiles can tackle larger creatures – they sometimes eat humans. Crocodiles and alligators have few natural enemies, but some have been hunted for their skins.

Snakes are reptiles that have no legs. All snakes are flesh-eaters. They track their prey by smell – a snake's 'nose' is its forked tongue. Snakes such as pythons loop themselves round their prey and suffocate it. Other snakes catch their food by grabbing and swallowing it. Some snakes have poison fangs to paralyse their prey.

Lizards are generally small, agile reptiles that feed on insects and small animals. They have many enemies. They protect

▲ The boa constrictor squeezes its prey to death. It can grow to over 9 m long.

themselves by moving quickly and by **camouflage** – they match their environment and so are difficult to see. Some types can shed their tail if an enemy grabs it.

Turtles, **tortoises** and **terrapins** all have armour-like, horny shells, and sharp-edged, horny jaws instead of teeth. Tortoises are mainly plant-eaters, terrapins feed on small creatures and turtles eat sea plants and some animals.

▲ Cobras have poison fangs. They can spread the ribs in their neck to form a hood.

find out more

Animals
Dinosaurs
Life on Earth

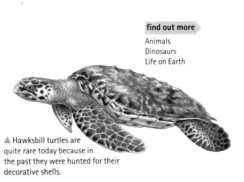

▲ Hawksbill turtles are quite rare today because in the past they were hunted for their decorative shells.

Rivers

When rain falls or snow melts, trickles of water run off the land. The trickles join to form small streams, which merge to form a river. A river becomes deeper and broader as more and more streams join it. Eventually, the river flows into the sea.

RIVER RECORDS

Longest river: Nile, Africa, 6673 km

Biggest river: Amazon, South America, 6570 km. Carries about a quarter of all the water that runs off the Earth's surface.

Near its source, a river is small but fast-flowing. In its middle course, the river is fuller. It flows more slowly in a series of bends. Towards its mouth, a river becomes wide and sluggish. Where the river enters the sea, sediment (pebbles, sand and soil) builds up in a fan-shaped **delta**.

Shaping the land

Rivers cut into the land as they flow over it, creating **valleys** and **gorges**. Sediment is swept along by the water, scouring away the river bed.

If a river flows over hard rock followed by softer rock, the softer rock wears away more quickly and a **waterfall** is formed. Mountain rivers often have many waterfalls.

River life

Rivers and streams provide many different habitats for plants and animals. People have always settled along rivers too. River valleys have good soil and are good transport routes. The river provides water for farming, drinking and washing, and dams that can generate electricity.

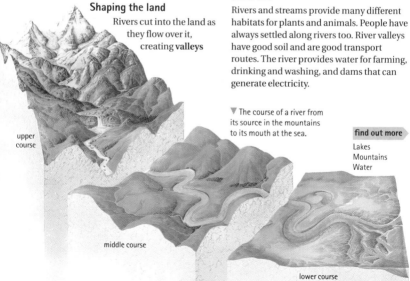

▼ The course of a river from its source in the mountains to its mouth at the sea.

upper course

middle course

lower course

find out more

Lakes
Mountains
Water

Rocks and minerals

Rocks are all around you. You walk on them, see them in cliffs, along the seashore and in holes in the ground. The soil in your garden comes from rocks too.

▲ Here is copper in another disguise. This mineral is called chalcopyrite. It contains copper mixed with iron and sulphur.

Rocks are the hard, solid parts of the Earth. All rocks are made up of chemical compounds called minerals.

Mineral mosaic

Minerals come in many different forms. Each form has its own characteristics. These include its colour, hardness, crystal shape and the way it reflects light.

There are more than 2500 different kinds of mineral. Gold, silver, diamonds and rubies are all minerals. So are the clays used to make pottery, and the graphite in your pencil lead.

Some rocks are made up of one mineral. But most are made up of several different kinds. If you look carefully at a rock you can see the different minerals in it.

There are three main types of rock – igneous, sedimentary and metamorphic. Each is formed in a different way.

Igneous rocks

Igneous rocks form when a hot mass of molten material,

▲ Azurite, a mineral that contains copper, gives this rock its beautiful deep blue colour. Sometimes you can use colour to help you guess the elements that make up a mineral. But beware! Elements like copper can appear as other colours too.

▼ The sedimentary rocks that form these cliffs at Eleonore Bay, Greenland, were laid down in layers called strata.

find out more

Elements
Life on Earth
Metals
Volcanoes and
  earthquakes

from beneath the Earth's crust (**magma**), cools and solidifies.

Sometimes the magma forces its way up from deep below the Earth's crust and flows from a volcano as lava. The lava cools quickly to form rocks with very small crystals. **Basalt** is an example of this type of rock.

Other times the magma collects underground. Here it cools more slowly to form rocks with larger crystals. **Granite** is a rock that forms in this way.

Sedimentary rocks

Sedimentary rocks are made up of sediments – small particles of mud or sand, or broken bits of other rocks. **Sandstone**, **shale** and **limestone** are examples of sedimentary rocks.

When sedimentary rocks are formed, the layers of sediment, called **strata**, are pressed down by the weight of material above. Minerals dissolved in the water between the sediment particles form crystals. These crystals cement the sediments together.

Metamorphic rocks

Metamorphic rocks form when igneous or sedimentary rocks are heated and put under pressure (squeezed). This causes them to change.

Marble is a metamorphic rock that is created when limestone is heated. **Slate** is another type of metamorphic rock. It is dark and shiny, and splits easily into sheets.

On the surface
In many places the Earth's surface is covered by soil. Soil is made up of rock particles and decayed plant and animal matter.

Soil begins to be formed when rocks are slowly broken down into small particles by the action of wind, water and ice. When plants and animals living in this rocky soil die, their remains are broken down, adding to the soil.

▼ How different types of rock are formed, plus examples of the three rock types.

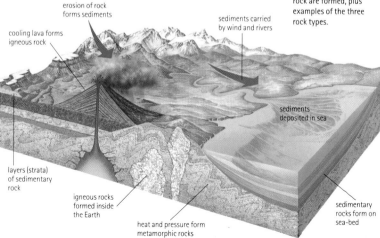

erosion of rock forms sediments

cooling lava forms igneous rock

sediments carried by wind and rivers

sediments deposited in sea

layers (strata) of sedimentary rock

igneous rocks formed inside the Earth

heat and pressure form metamorphic rocks

sedimentary rocks form on sea-bed

Romans

The Romans were an ancient people who created a huge empire, the capital of which was Rome. At its height the Roman empire surrounded the Mediterranean and stretched from Britain to Syria.

The **Roman empire** was very well organized. This is one of the reasons it was so successful. Paved stone **roads** connected all parts of the empire with Rome. Wherever the Romans went, they took their way of life and their language (**Latin**) with them.

The Roman army

The Roman army was the most skilful and disciplined fighting force in the ancient world. It played a vital role in the creation of the empire. The army conquered peoples, built forts and roads, and kept Roman lands safe from attack.

Soldiers were organized into units called **legions**, made up of about 5000 men. The men trained and fought in groups of 80 with a **centurion** (an officer) in charge of each. The legionary soldiers fought on foot. Each soldier carried two javelins for throwing, and a sword and a

KEY DATES

about 753 BC First settlement built at Rome.

509 Latini people drive Etruscans out of Rome and establish Roman republic.

264 Romans rule all Italy.

146 Romans defeat Carthage and rule Spain and North Africa.

51 Julius Caesar conquers Gaul (France).

44 Caesar assassinated.

27 Augustus becomes first emperor.

AD 43 Claudius conquers Britain.

117 Empire reaches its greatest extent.

330 Emperor Constantine moves capital to Byzantium.

395 Empire divides into western and eastern halves.

410 Goths destroy city of Rome.

◄ The Roman empire in the 2nd century AD. The names of many modern countries and even continents come from the names of Roman provinces.

317

shield for close fighting. Other units, called **cavalry**, fought on horseback.

The provinces

The Romans divided the lands they had conquered into large areas called **provinces**. They encouraged the local people to live like Romans, and built temples to Roman gods and goddesses. Although many local customs survived, a Roman way of life spread throughout the empire.

Everyday life

Roman towns were usually well planned, with straight streets and a central meeting place (**forum**). Many people lived in blocks of apartments, often built above shops or workshops. Richer people had private houses, with gardens and rooms for slaves. Some houses had mosaic floors and underfloor heating.

▶ Julius **Caesar** was a brilliant and powerful Roman general. In 49 BC he turned his army on Rome and started a civil war, which he won. He appointed himself **dictator** (sole ruler) for life. Less than a year later, Caesar was stabbed to death by a group of conspirators.

Roman towns usually had regular supplies of water and an efficient sewage system. Pipes brought water from aqueducts to private houses, businesses, fountains and public baths.

From republic to empire

At first Rome was a **republic**. Some people (men who owned property) were allowed to vote for the politicians who formed the government. At the head were two men, called **consuls**. A sort of parliament, called the **senate**, discussed state business and made new laws.

• The Latin language developed into many European languages spoken today, including Italian, Spanish and French. The alphabet used in English is Roman and Roman numerals are often used.

◀ The Romans loved bathing and all Roman towns had at least one bath house. These fine baths, in present-day Bath, England, were built in the 1st century AD.

Roosevelt, F. D. *see* United States • **Rowing** *see* Sports fact file

The first century BC was marked by a series of **civil wars**, in which rival politicians fought for power. The struggle continued until 27 BC, when Octavius, the adopted son of Julius Caesar, defeated his rivals and made himself emperor. He took the name **Augustus**.

This was the end of the republic. It was also the beginning of the most peaceful and prosperous period in Rome's history. This was known as the **Pax Romana** ('Roman Peace'). It lasted for about 200 years.

The end of empire

In the 3rd century AD weak emperors and internal fighting left the empire open to attack. In AD 324 the Emperor Constantine

▶ This Roman mosaic of fishermen comes from Utica, a Roman settlement in North Africa. It dates from the 4th century AD.

moved the capital east to **Byzantium** (present-day Istanbul in Turkey) because it was easier to defend. The western part of the empire was gradually invaded by tribes from the north, the Goths, Huns and Vandals, and in 410 Rome fell. The eastern part became the Byzantine empire.

find out more

Ancient world
Byzantine empire
Greeks, ancient
Slaves

▼ The Forum Romanum (Roman forum) at the time of Augustus. Augustus put a great deal of money into making Rome a great city. He is said to have claimed that he found Rome a city of brick and left it a city of marble.

1 Basilica Julia (courthouse)
2 rostra (the speaker's platform)
3 Temple of Castor and Pollux
4 Basilica Aemilia
5 Curia Julia (senate house)

Russia

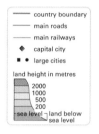

Russia is the largest country in the world. It stretches across two continents, from central Europe to the eastern tip of Asia.

The low **Ural Mountains** separate European and Asian parts of Russia. To the east of these mountains is **Siberia**, a cold, mostly forested area where few people live. Not many people live in the north either, because here much of the land is tundra – bare, frozen ground.

People

Most Russians live in the west of the country. Three-quarters of them live in cities – Moscow and St Petersburg are two of the biggest cities in Europe.

Most of the population is Russian, but there are over 100 other nationalities, many of whom try to keep alive their traditions, languages and religions. In the far north people live a more traditional life. Some keep reindeer herds, or live by fishing. Most farmers live in the west, which has the best farmland. They farm mainly cattle, potatoes and wheat.

AZ AZERBAIJAN
EST ESTONIA
GE GEORGIA
LAT LATVIA
LI LITHUANIA
MOL MOLDOVA

country boundary
main roads
main railways
♦ capital city
■ ● large cities
land height in metres
2000
1000
500
200
sea level ┐ land below sea level

RUSSIA FACTS

Capital: Moscow

Population: 147,800,000

Area: 17,075,400 sq km

Language: Russian, 100 others

Religion: Christian

Currency: 1 rouble = 100 kopecks

Wealth per person: $2240

Resources and industry

Russia is rich in minerals. It mines oil, natural gas, coal, copper, iron ore, gold, silver, platinum, lead and nickel. Factories get power from hydroelectric power stations on the Don and Volga rivers. Russia's rivers are also used by ships to transport goods around the country. Timber is one of Russia's most important exports, as more than one third of the country is covered by a vast forest called the *taiga*.

Russia's history

Early rulers of Russia were called tsars (emperors). **Ivan the Terrible** crowned himself tsar in the capital city, Moscow, in 1547. Under his rule Russia expanded into Siberia and along the River Volga. In 1613 Mikhail Romanov was made tsar. The Romanov family ruled Russia until 1917. Mikhail Romanov's grandson, **Peter the Great**, made Russia a world power and created a new capital city, St Petersburg. He also conquered new land. This expansion was continued in the late 18th century by Catherine the Great.

But by the middle of the 19th century, Russia was in trouble. A costly war had been fought against Britain and France in the Crimea and most Russians were very poor and unhappy.

▶ St Basil's Cathedral, a Russian Orthodox church in Moscow. Most Russian Christians belong to the Russian Orthodox Church.

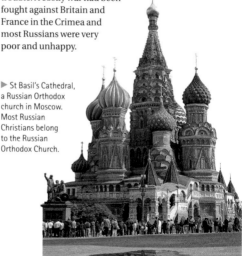

Russia

find out more

Asia
Christians
Communism
Europe
Governments
Mongols
World War I
World War II

Russia in the 20th century

Russia's entry into World War I increased people's hardship and anger. In 1917 there was a revolution, and the tsar was forced to give up his throne. Russia became a republic, but eight months later the Bolsheviks (Russian communists), led by Vladimir **Lenin**, took power.

In 1922 Lenin established the Union of Soviet Socialist Republics (USSR, or Soviet Union), which covered almost all of the old Russian empire. When he died in 1924, power passed to Josef **Stalin**. Under Stalin's rule, which lasted until 1953, millions of people starved on the state-owned farms, and anyone who opposed him was imprisoned or killed.

Communist rule remained strong until 1985. Then a new leader, Mikhail **Gorbachev**, tried to reform the Soviet Union. In

▲ The Winter Palace in St Petersburg was taken by the Bolsheviks in 1917. The Russian Revolution brought the Romanov family dynasty to an end.

1991 the Communist Party was disbanded and the Soviet Union collapsed. Boris **Yeltsin** became the first president of the new Russian Federation. Since that time the country has suffered serious economic difficulties.

The longest day

From east to west Russia is about 8000 km wide and it crosses 11 time zones. This means that while people are eating their breakfast in the European part of Russia, in the Asian Far East they are sitting down to supper at the end of the same day!

▼ President Boris Yeltsin talking with coalminers in 1991. Yeltsin was the first Russian leader to be elected by the people.

Satellites

When we think of a satellite, we imagine a communications satellite sending TV pictures across the world, or a weather satellite taking pictures of the Earth. But a satellite can also be a natural object, like the Moon.

◀ One of the 12 NAVSTAR satellites that make up the GPS navigation system. The satellite's 'wings' are actually solar panels, which it uses to generate power.

A satellite is an object that travels around a larger body. Many of the planets have natural satellites, called **moons**. Our Moon is a natural satellite that travels around the Earth. Artificial satellites also travel around the Earth.

Into orbit

Artificial satellites are launched into space by **rockets** such as the Space Shuttle. Once in space they travel along a circular or oval path called an **orbit**. A satellite is held in orbit by the gravity of the planet it is travelling around.

Artificial satellites do many different jobs. **Communications satellites** pick up radio, television and telephone signals and send them back down to Earth. **Weather forecasting satellites** collect information about the weather. The **Global Positioning System** (**GPS**) is a network of satellites that is used for navigation. A GPS receiver on Earth gets signals from three satellites, and compares the arrival times of the three signals. From this it can calculate its position to within 100 metres.

find out more ▸
Communications
Space exploration

▶ The planet Jupiter has 16 natural satellites, or moons, going round it. This is a picture of one of them, Calisto.

◀ Communications and GPS satellites travel in geostationary orbits. They seem to stand still over the Earth's surface because they orbit at the same speed as the Earth. Other satellites travel in a polar orbit. A satellite in fast polar orbit passes over the whole Earth once each day.

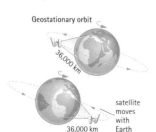

Geostationary orbit

36,000 km

36,000 km

satellite moves with Earth

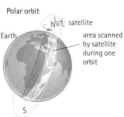

Polar orbit

satellite

Earth

area scanned by satellite during one orbit

N

S

Schools and universities

Almost all children go to school, where they learn useful skills such as reading and writing. They also learn about the world.

In rich countries many children stay at school until they are 18, and then go on to college or university. In very poor countries some children, particularly girls, may not get the chance to go to school at all. Those who do may stay there for a few years only.

Primary schools

A primary school is the first school a child goes to. In Britain children start school at 5, in the USA at 6 and in Russia at 7.

Secondary schools

Children go to secondary school from the age of 11 or 12 until they are 16 to 18. Here they study subjects such as science, maths, computers, history, geography and languages. Before they leave they may take public examinations. These can lead to qualifications that will help them get a job or a place at a college or university.

Universities and colleges

At university students study to get a higher qualification called a **degree**. At college many students learn skills to prepare them for a particular career, such as car mechanics, hairdressing or electronics.

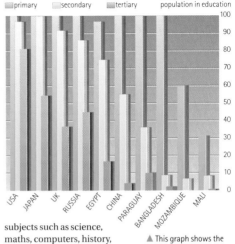

percentage of the population in education

☐ primary　☐ secondary　■ tertiary

USA　JAPAN　UK　RUSSIA　EGYPT　CHINA　PARAGUAY　BANGLADESH　MOZAMBIQUE　MALI

▲ This graph shows the percentage of people in primary, secondary and tertiary education (universities and colleges) in 10 different countries. In the USA most people go to a university or college, but in Mali fewer than a third even go to primary school.

• What is taught in schools is known as the **curriculum**. In some countries the government sets the curriculum.

find out more

Children

◀ In this village school in Nepal children of different ages are being taught in one class.

Scientific Revolution

Between about 1543 and 1687, European thinkers created a scientific way of thinking about things. We call this change the Scientific Revolution.

Before the Scientific Revolution, people had ideas and used facts to back them up. For example, as the Bible said God made the Earth first, it must be at the centre of the Universe.

The thinker Francis **Bacon** (1571–1626) rejected this way of reasoning. He said we should start with facts that could be *proved*, then make rules that agreed with these facts. The astronomer Nicolas **Copernicus** (1473–1543), for example, had spent years observing how the stars and planets moved. He had used his observations to show that the Sun, not the Earth, was at the centre of the Universe.

Using the new scientific approach, scientists began to make sense of the world. Astronomers Tycho Brahe, Johannes Kepler and **Galileo Galilei** (1564–1642) backed up Copernicus' ideas. Galileo also improved the telescope. William **Harvey** (1578–1657) proved that blood went round the body. But the greatest figure of the Scientific Revolution was Isaac **Newton** (1642–1727). Newton discovered the laws of gravity and movement. He also showed that white light is made up of the different colours.

▲ Robert **Hooke** (1635–1703) invented a very powerful microscope that made it possible for him to see tiny objects, for instance fleas, in minute detail. He is also famous for working out how materials stretch.

Getting in a flap!
Although Isaac Newton was the greatest genius of his day, he could miss some very obvious things. For example, it is said that he made a small cat-flap for his cat and a larger one for his dog – when one large flap would have done for both!

find out more
Astronomy
Exploration, Age of
Forces
Solar System

◀ Isaac Newton.

Sculpture

Sculptors create works of art that are three-dimensional – they are solid instead of flat like a painting. A piece of sculpture may be free-standing, so that you can walk around it. Sometimes you can touch it and feel its texture and shape.

Sculpture has been made from all sorts of materials, including plastics, bricks and even ice. However, traditional materials are wood, clay, stone and metal.

Carving or moulding

There are two ways of shaping material in sculpture: **carving** and **moulding**. The first method is to take a block of stone or wood and carve into it to create a shape.

The second way is to mould a lump of soft clay or wax into a shape. This is then fired in a kiln, like pottery, to make it hard. Alternatively it can be used to make a mould from which a cast (an exact copy) is made, usually in metal.

Modern sculptors have added a third method. They sometimes create a sculpture by welding, glueing, or simply grouping different objects and materials together.

Materials

Wood is the most popular material for sculpture in many parts of the world, including Africa and Oceania. Many woods, especially hardwoods, have beautiful colours and markings, which can be seen when the wood is worked. But wood eventually rots, so most of the ancient sculpture that has survived is made of other materials. **Clay** and **stone** produce sculpture in many

▲ Sculpture is an ancient art. This clay bison was sculpted in France about 20,000 years ago. It is about one-sixth life size. The oldest known sculptures are small stone figures of women, made about 25,000 years ago.

▲ This statue of David, by the Italian sculptor Michelangelo (1475–1564), is perhaps the most famous sculpture in the world. Michelangelo is often considered to be the greatest sculptor who ever lived.

find out more
Painting and drawing
Pottery

Phidias was a Greek sculptor who lived in the 5th century BC. He designed much of the sculpture that decorated the Parthenon in Athens.

The French sculptor Auguste **Rodin** (1840–1917) created powerful, realistic sculptures, such as *The Thinker*. They often portray a single action or emotion.

The 20th-century British sculptor Henry **Moore** (1898–1986) is famous for his massive figures that simplify the human form into smooth shapes.

different textures and colours. Granite is the hardest and most weatherproof stone, but many sculptors' favourite stone is **marble** because it produces an extremely beautiful surface.

Bronze is the most popular metal for sculpting. It can be worked easily, and it is attractive and lasts well. Some of the most striking bronze sculptures have been produced in Africa and China. Gold, silver, iron, steel and aluminium are other metals that sculptors use.

© Christo

▲ Surrounded Islands (1980–1983), by Christo and Jeanne-Claude, is not really a sculpture, it is an 'installation'. An installation is a large-scale work of art built in a particular place, and designed to be temporary.

◄ This bronze sculpture of the head of a young man was made by the Edo people of Benin in West Africa in about 1550. It was cast from a wax mould.

Kinds of sculpture

Sculptures have been made for many different purposes – for instance to create memorials to the dead, and to decorate buildings. In almost all civilizations important buildings have been decorated with carvings. Among the most breathtaking examples are the ancient Hindu temples in India. Many artists have used sculpture to express themselves and to experiment with materials, shapes and ideas. In the 20th century, some sculptors have even made sculpture out of junk.

Sea *see* Oceans and seas ● **Sea birds** *see* Birds ● **Seals** *see* Mammals

Seashore

The seashore is the part of the coast where the ocean or sea meets the land – from low-tide mark to just above high-tide mark. Some seashores are sandy or muddy. Others are rocky.

Lots of animals and plants live on the seashore.

On the rocks

Rocky shores have many pools. Each has its own community of animals and plants. Most of the animals breathe oxygen from the water, using gills. They only come out to feed when the tide is in.

Sandy and muddy shores

Although sandy and muddy shores often look empty, there may be as many as 100,000 animals per square metre there. Most of these animals live by burrowing beneath the surface. There they are out of sight of predators and protected from the sun and wind.

▲ Take care not to tread on a sea urchin at the seashore. They belong to the echinoderm ('spiny skin') group of animals and it can be very painful to have a spine in your foot!

find out more

Coasts
Crabs and other crustaceans
Fishes
Jellyfishes and corals
Mussels and oysters
Oceans and seas

▼ Different kinds of plants and animals live at different levels of a rocky shore.
Animals like sea anemones, starfishes (1), sea urchins and small fishes live in rock pools on the lower shore. They are covered with water most of the time. Seaweeds that need wet conditions, such as sea kelp (2), serrated wrack (3) and thong weed (4), live here too.
Further up the shore seaweeds like bladder wrack (5), knotted wrack (6) and spiral wrack (7) cling to the rocks. So do animals like mussels (8) and barnacles (9). Crabs and shrimps live here too.
Seaweeds like channel wrack (10) and plants like lichens (11) live high up, where it is dry for much of the time.

Walking on balloons?

On the underside of starfishes are hundreds of little, soft bumps called tube feet. Each one is like a balloon, filled with sea water. Most have a sucker on the end, so the starfish can grip onto the sea-bed to walk!

Seasons

The seasons change throughout the year. Daylight changes according to the seasons. So does the weather. These changes affect the way we live.

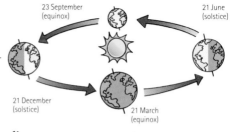

23 September (equinox)

21 June (solstice)

21 December (solstice)

21 March (equinox)

▲ How the tilted axis of the Earth affects the seasons.

The Earth takes one year to travel round the Sun. The seasons happen because the Earth is tilted along an imaginary line, the axis, as it travels. This axis runs through the North and South Poles.

From March to September, the North Pole is tilted towards the Sun. Places in the northern hemisphere enjoy longer days, so they get more sunshine and the weather is warmer. Meanwhile, in the southern hemisphere the days are shorter and the air is cooler.

From September to March the South Pole is tilted towards the Sun. Then the south enjoys warmer weather, while in the north it is cold.

The changing year

The seasons are different in different parts of the world.

At the **Equator** the temperature and daylight stay nearly the same all year. The Equator has four seasons: two wet seasons and two dry ones. The **tropics** (near the Equator) have only one wet season and one dry one.

In the **temperate** regions between the tropics and the Poles there are four seasons – spring, summer, autumn and winter.

Near the **Poles** it is cold all year round. But in the summer season the days are very long, while during the dark winter the Sun never rises above the horizon.

• The **equinoxes**, on 21 March and 23 September, are the two days each year when the hours of darkness and light are equal. The days with the longest and shortest hours of daylight are called the **solstices**.

find out more

Climate
Earth
Time
Weather

▼ These pictures were taken every hour on midsummer's day near the North Pole. They show the Sun's position. Though the Sun dips, it never actually sets.

Senses

Your senses tell you what is going on in the world around you. All animals need this information to survive – to move and communicate, to find food and to escape from danger.

Different animals have developed senses that equip them for their surroundings. Humans have five main senses – sight, hearing, touch, smell and taste.

All sense organs turn the information they gather about the outside world into nerve impulses, which go to the brain. The brain processes this information and turns it into recognizable sights, sounds, smells, tastes and touches.

Eyes

Eyes focus light from surrounding objects to form a picture of the outside world.

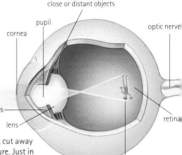

lens muscle: changes shape of lens, to focus close or distant objects

pupil

optic nerve

cornea

iris

lens

retina

▲ The human eye, cut away to show its structure. Just in front of the lens is a sheet of muscle called the iris. This is the coloured part of the eye. It has a round hole at its centre called the pupil. In bright light the iris muscles contract. This shrinks the pupil and stops too much light getting to the retina. In dim light the iris relaxes and the pupil widens.

image is upside down: brain turns it right way up

The human eye focuses light through a **lens** onto a layer of light-sensitive cells at the back of the eye called the **retina**. The retina cells send messages along nerves to the brain. Other mammals have eyes similar to the human eye. Octopuses and squids also have this kind of eye. Other animals – for instance many insects, and crustaceans such as crabs – have **compound eyes**. These are made up

▲ Blind people can use their sense of touch to read a special kind of writing called Braille. Braille letters are printed in patterns of small dots, which stick up from the surface of the paper. The letters can be read by brushing the tips of the fingers lightly across the dots.

◄ Dragonflies have very large compound eyes. Each eye is made up of thousands of light-sensitive tubes, called ommatidia.

of lots of narrow, light-sensitive tubes. Each tube shows only a tiny area, but the information from all the tubes together makes up a picture.

Hearing

All animals with backbones (vertebrates), and some insects, have ears. We use our ears to detect sound. In vertebrates, the ear also controls the sense of balance. In the human ear, sounds are focused by the outer ear onto the **eardrum**, which vibrates. This makes tiny bones inside the ear (the **ossicles**) vibrate, and these make sensory hairs in the inner ear (the **cochlea**) vibrate, too. The sensory hairs are attached to nerves, which send messages to the brain.

▲ Fennec foxes live in deserts. They hunt at night, using their acute sense of hearing to detect movements of the lizards and insects that they eat. Their huge ears also act as radiators, to help keep them cool during the day.

Smell and taste

Humans and most mammals smell through the nose. The nose is lined with special nerve cells that can detect odours (very tiny amounts of chemicals in the air). In humans and other animals, smell and taste are closely linked. The tongue detects basic tastes such as sweet, salt and sour. But many food 'tastes' are actually detected by the nose.

Touch

Touch tells an animal what things feel like. The main organ of touch in humans is the skin. Some nerve endings in the skin are sensitive to pressure, while other nerves are sensitive to heat and cold. Some animals (for example, cats) also have long whiskers on their snouts that are very sensitive to touch.

▲ Shrews have poor eyesight, but have an excellent sense of smell, and communicate with one another by scent.

Super sonar!

Bats are active at night, and find their way in the dark using **echolocation**. As it flies, a bat makes short, very high-pitched squeaks. Echoes from the squeaks bounce back from surrounding objects to the bat's ears, giving it information about the things around it. A bat's echolocation system is so good that it can catch insects on the wing.

find out more

Animals
Disabilities
Human beings
Skin and hair

Sex and reproduction

In many animals, including people, there are two sexes, males and females. In these animals males and females mate and reproduce sexually.

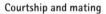

▲ A human sperm penetrates an egg.

In **sexual reproduction** a **sperm** cell from the male joins with an **egg** cell from the female. As a result, the young receive genes from both parents. **Genes** carry information that makes a new living thing grow to be similar to its parents. But because it inherits some characteristics from one parent and other characteristics from the other, each new individual is a mixture of both parents.

Not all living things reproduce sexually. Amoebas, for example, reproduce asexually – by splitting in two. And many plants can be grown from cuttings taken from a bigger plant. Plants and animals that reproduce **asexually** have young that look just like them.

Courtship and mating

Before they can produce young, all animals that reproduce sexually have to attract a mate. This process is called courtship. Many male birds perform amazing displays to attract a female. Other animals use

▼ Japanese cranes perform a complicated courtship dance. The male and female strut around each other with quick, stiff steps, and half-spread wings.

Safe sex
Some animals only have sex when the female is ready to become pregnant. But others, including people, can have sex at any time.

For people, having sex, or making love, often involves very powerful feelings. It is important to think carefully about who you have sex with, and when. It is also important to take precautions – such as wearing a condom – against spreading diseases or causing an unwanted pregnancy.

find out more

Animals
Cells
Genetics
Growth and development
Human beings
Plants

special calls to let others know they are ready to mate.

Mating is the act in which the male fertilizes the female. Some animals, such as frogs, fertilize the eggs outside the body (**external fertilization**). But most land-living animals – insects, reptiles, birds and mammals – use **internal fertilization**. In internal fertilization the male sperm are squirted into an opening in the female's body.

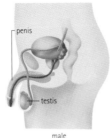
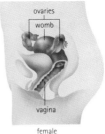

▲ The human male and female sexual organs.

Human sexual reproduction

Like all human beings, you began when your parents made love, and a sperm cell from your father joined with an egg inside your mother's body.

The sperm cells were produced in your father's **testes**. The egg that developed into you was produced inside your mother's **ovaries**. The ovaries release one egg into a woman's **womb** about every 28 days.

When a man and a woman make love, the man puts his **penis** into an opening in the woman's body called the **vagina**. Some of the sperm that he squirts out of his penis may swim into the woman's womb. If one of these sperm joins with the egg, it fertilizes it.

The fertilized egg attached itself to the wall of the womb, and your mother became **pregnant**. This means she began to carry a growing baby inside her.

• Sexuality is the word we use to describe sexual feeling and behaviour. When people are attracted to people of the opposite sex, they are heterosexual. But some people are homosexual – they are attracted to people of their own sex.

▼ How a human baby develops in the womb.

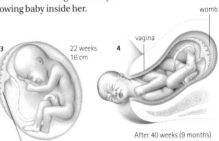

1

2 9 weeks 1.7 cm

6 weeks 0.5 cm

3 22 weeks 16 cm

4 womb

vagina

The **umbilical cord** carries nutrients to the baby in the mother's blood, and carries away waste.

The baby floats inside a bag of fluid called the **amniotic sac**.

The **placenta** roots the baby to the wall of the womb.

After 40 weeks (9 months) the baby is big enough to be born. The mother pushes the baby out head first through her vagina.

Shakespeare, William *see* Drama

Shapes

Every object has a shape. Some shapes, such as an oak leaf or a rock, are irregular. But other shapes, such as triangles, squares, cubes and spheres, are regular shapes with special mathematical properties.

The edges of a shape may be straight or curved. **Plane shapes** are two-dimensional; they have length and width but no thickness. Triangles, squares, circles and ellipses are all plane shapes. **Solid shapes** are three-dimensional. They have length, width and height. Cubes, cones and spheres are examples of solid shapes.

Naming shapes

The features of a shape that give it a name include the number of sides, the lengths of the different sides, and the angles between the sides.

triangle
(3 sides)

pentagon
(5 sides)

decagon
(10 sides)

circle (infinite
number of sides)

A plane shape with straight sides is called a **polygon**. A solid shape with straight edges is called a **polyhedron**. The flat parts of a solid shape are called its faces. A cube is a regular polyhedron with six identical square faces.

cube

sphere

cone

The circle is sometimes called a perfect shape because every part of its circumference or edge is exactly the same distance from the centre. The sphere is the solid shape with the same property.

◀ Polygons are plane shapes with straight edges. They are named according to the number of sides.

▲ Angles are measured in degrees. A complete turn of a circle is 360°. A quarter turn is 90° (a right angle). A half-turn is 180°.

find out more ▶

Numbers
Graphs

◀ Some three-dimensional (solid) shapes.

Symmetry

If a shape can be divided by lines to produce two or more exactly similar parts, it has **symmetry**. When a shape can be split into two parts that are the same shape and size, this is known as **bilateral** ('two-sided') symmetry. A circle has bilateral symmetry. It also has **rotational** symmetry, because it looks the same however you rotate it.

Sharks *see* Fishes • **Sheep** *see* Farm animals • **Shinto** *see* Religions

Ships and boats

For thousands of years, ships and boats have been used to carry people and cargoes on rivers and across oceans. Today most people travel long distances by air, but ships still carry cargo.

Ships are large, sea-going vessels; boats are much smaller. Most modern ships have engines that power underwater propellers. Some boats have engines, but they may also be driven by sails, oars or paddles.

Sailing

Sailing vessels use the force of the wind to push them along. Most modern sailing vessels are **yachts** – boats or small ships used for racing or leisure.

A sail acts rather like the wing of an aircraft. As the air flows across it, pressure builds up on one side. By angling the sail, sailors can use this pressure to make their boats move in almost any direction. By **tacking** (zigzagging), they can even sail against the wind.

Cargo and passenger ships

Most modern cargo ships are specially designed to carry one particular kind of cargo. **Container ships** carry hundreds of standard-sized containers. **Tankers** and **bulk carriers** carry

▼ An aerial view of the harbour of Salerno Campania, Italy. Loading equipment, storage space, cargo containers and vehicles cover a huge area. Special cranes and loading equipment on the dockside load the containers from trains and lorries on and off the container ships. Road and rail links are also needed to deliver the containers overland to and from the port.

▲ Kayaks were wooden-framed canoes covered with sealskin, made by the Inuit people of North America. Today, kayaks made from modern materials are used for sports such as white-water racing.

Giants of the sea

The biggest ships of all are oil tankers, which can be up to 450 m long – enough room for four football pitches! An oil tanker can take over 10 km to stop, even with the engines in full reverse.

cargoes such as oil or grain, which can be pumped on board through a pipe. Most passenger ships are either **ferries**, which make short trips, or luxury **liners**, which take people on holiday cruises.

Navies and warships

Naval ships are used in times of war to hunt and destroy enemy ships, submarines and aircraft, and for launching missiles. Small, mobile ships such as **destroyers** and **frigates** carry guided missiles. **Aircraft carriers** can carry over 90 aircraft, plus helicopters. Most naval vessels are packed with radar and other electronic equipment, to detect missiles launched against them.

▶ FLASHBACK ◀

The ancient Egyptians built boats from reeds as early as 4000 BC. The Greeks and Romans used long narrow **galleys** powered by lines of rowers. Between about 700 and 1000 AD, the Vikings built slim longships

Lifeboats

Lifeboats are specially built for saving people who are in difficulty at sea. They are self-righting – if they capsize, they will turn the right way again by themselves. They have powerful engines and are strong enough to withstand stormy seas. Many big lifeboats have now been replaced by small inflatable rubber boats, better suited to rescue work close to the shore.

Catamarans, hydrofoils and hovercraft

Ship's hulls (frames) are streamlined to cut down water resistance, but new kinds of craft are designed to reduce water resistance in other ways. Catamarans are wide vessels supported on two very narrow hulls. Hydrofoils have aircraft-like 'wings' attached to the hull, which lift it out of the water at speed. Hovercraft float above the water on a cushion of air.

for warfare, and sturdier boats called *knarrs* for long voyages. In the 16th century sailing ships called **galleons** were used to carry cargoes and as fighting ships.

Steamships (ships driven by steam engines) started to replace sailing ships in the early 1800s. The first steamships were propelled by large paddle wheels, but these were soon replaced by propellers. In the 20th century diesel engines largely replaced steam power.

find out more
Engines and motors
Fishing
Oceans and seas
Submarines

▼ Some common ships and boats.

speedboat

hovercraft

sailing yacht

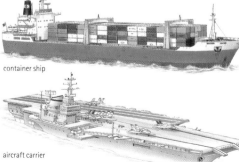

container ship

aircraft carrier

Sikhs

Sikhs are people who follow the religion called Sikhism. Most Sikhs live in the Punjab in northern India, where the Sikh religion started. But there also Sikhs in Britain, North America and other countries.

Sikhs believe in one God, who is everywhere in the Universe. And they believe that God created one humanity, and so all human beings – male and female, and those of all races and religions – are equal.

The Gurus

Sikhism was started by **Guru Nanak**, who lived in the Punjab from 1479 to 1539. In Punjabi, 'Guru' means 'teacher' and 'Sikh' means 'learner'.

Guru Nanak appointed a second Guru to continue his teaching after he died. After this, each Guru appointed the next one, until there had been ten Gurus.

In 1604 the fifth Guru, **Guru Arjan**, collected all the Gurus' teachings together to make the Sikh holy book.

The tenth guru, **Guru Gobind Singh**, said that, after his death, Sikhs should use the holy book as their Guru. Therefore the book is called the **Guru Granth Sahib**.

Before he died, in 1708, Guru Gobind Singh also started the **Khalsa**, the Sikh community. Sikhs join the Khalsa at a ceremony called **amrit**.

▲ Guru Nanak had friends from other religions, including Mardana, a Muslim (left), and Bala, a Hindu (right).

• Most Sikhs wear the **Five Ks**: *kes* (uncut hair); *kangha* (comb); *kara* (bracelet); *kachera* (undershorts); and *kirpan* (sword). All these remind Sikhs of the ways in which they should behave as members of the Khalsa.

find out more
Hindus
Religions

◀ The Sikh place of worship is called a **gurdwara**. Women and men can lead worship, and all worshippers sit on the floor.

Skin and hair

Skin is an outer protective layer that covers the bodies of most types of animal. Some animals have scaly skin, others are smooth. In mammals, the skin is covered with hair.

Skin stops your body from losing water. It also protects it against infection and is an important organ of touch.

The outer layer of skin is called the **epidermis**. It is made up of dead skin cells. The layer below, the **dermis**, contains blood vessels, nerves, hair roots, nerves and sweat glands.

Some skin cells also contain a dark pigment called **melanin**.

This pigment protects the skin from dangerous ultraviolet rays in sunlight. People with dark skins have more melanin than those with lighter skins.

All mammals, including people, have hair on their skin. On many animals, the hair forms a thick coat called fur.

Hair helps to control the animal's body temperature. It also gives an animal its characteristic markings. These markings can help the animal attract a mate. They may also provide it with **camouflage** to help it hide from its enemies. Some special types of hair, like **whiskers**, act as sense organs. An animal's whiskers are very sensitive to touch.

▲ The thick, white winter coat of the Arctic fox keeps out the cold and camouflages the fox in the snowy Arctic landscape. Even the soles of the fox's feet are covered with fur.

• Hair can grow in several different ways. The type of hair depends on the shape of the follicle it grows out of. Round follicles produce straight hair; oval follicles produce wavy hair; and flat follicles produce curly hair.

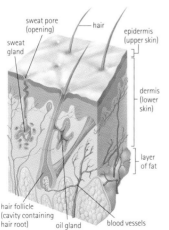

sweat pore (opening) — hair
epidermis (upper skin)
sweat gland
dermis (lower skin)
layer of fat
hair follicle (cavity containing hair root)
oil gland
blood vessels

◀ This diagram shows what a small piece of skin looks like. The thin upper layer of dead skin (the epidermis) wears away every time you touch something. But it is replaced from the layer of living cells below (the dermis) as fast as it is removed.

find out more
Human beings
Mammals

Skyscrapers see Buildings *and* Construction

Slaves

A slave is a person who is treated like a 'thing' rather than a human being. A slave is owned by someone else, and has to do what they want. Nowadays, slavery is banned throughout the world. But for thousands of years it was common.

Gladiators!
In Ancient Rome, male slaves were sometimes trained as professional fighters, or 'gladiators'. They then fought each other – often to the death – to entertain large crowds.

Slavery existed throughout the ancient world. In Greece and Rome slaves did all the tough jobs. The worst work was in the mines, where few slaves lived long. Household slaves were better off. Some were treated almost as members of the family, and well-behaved slaves could be set free.

The ordinary farmers of Medieval Europe (known as **serfs**) were little better than slaves. Their lord owned their land, and they needed his permission to travel and even to get married.

▼ African slaves harvesting sugar cane in the Caribbean. While the unpaid slaves work in the blazing sun, their master sits on his horse in the shade.

The slave trade

Perhaps the worst slavery in modern times took place in the southern USA and the Caribbean. Because there were not enough European settlers to work the land, millions of **Africans** were brought over to work as slaves.

The slaves could be bought and sold, and were treated very badly. Eventually, in 1861, US president Abraham **Lincoln** went to war to abolish slavery. Even after this, African-Americans were treated as second-class citizens.

▲ A diagram of a slave ship in which Africans were jammed like sardines. Crushed together like this, many died before they reached America.

• The former slave Harriet **Tubman** (1820–1913) spent 10 years helping over 300 African-American slaves escape to Canada, where slavery was illegal. The escape route was known as the 'Underground Railway', and she was its most famous 'conductor'.

find out more

Africa
Caribbean
Empire, Age of
Greeks, Ancient
North America
Romans
South America
United States of America

Slugs and snails

Slugs and snails are a type of mollusc. They are found living on land, in lakes, rivers and ponds, and in the sea. They move around by using a large muscular 'foot' to walk or swim.

▲ Garden snails eat mostly decaying plants. Gardeners do not like them because they also eat young shoots.

There are more than 35,000 different kinds of slugs and snails. All are **gastropods**. The name gastropod means 'stomach-foot'. Land snails and slugs make a trail of slime to ease themselves along.

Like other molluscs, snails have shells to protect their soft bodies. When they are threatened, they hide inside their shells. Some slugs have a tiny shell inside their bodies. Snails have their shells on the outside.

Slugs and snails have a mouth on the underside of their heads. Inside their mouth they have a ribbon-like tongue, called a **radula**, covered with thousands of tiny teeth. They use their radula to scrape away at food.

Most land snails and slugs eat plants. But some types of slugs and snails that live in the sea feed on other animals.

Lager louts!
Slugs can be serious garden pests. But one way of getting rid of them is to put out a saucer of beer. The slugs will crawl in for a drink. They quickly become so drunk they drown.

▲ Welks are snails that live in the sea. They feed on barnacles and mussels.

• Many slugs and snails are **hermaphrodite**. This means that they have both male and female sex organs. So any member of a species can mate with any other member of the same species.

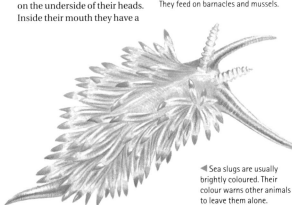

◀ Sea slugs are usually brightly coloured. Their colour warns other animals to leave them alone.

find out more

Animals
Mussels and oysters
Octopuses and squids

Solar System

The Solar System is made up of the Sun and all the things that orbit around it. Although the Solar System seems very important to us on Earth, it is just a tiny speck compared to the rest of the Universe.

▲ The US space probe *Pathfinder* landed on the surface of Mars in July 1997. Inside was a 63-cm long robot vehicle called *Sojourner*, designed to study the rocks on Mars. This photo shows *Sojourner* emerging from its packing after landing. In the background is the Martian landscape.

• Astronomers think that the Solar System was formed around 5 billion years ago when a huge cloud of gas and dust fell together, pulled by its own gravity.

The Sun is the largest body in the Solar System. Like all stars, the Sun gives off huge amounts of heat and light.

Nine **planets** – Mercury, Venus, Earth, Mars, Jupiter, Saturn, Uranus, Neptune and Pluto – orbit (travel around) the Sun. Mercury is nearest to the Sun, Pluto is furthest away. Mercury, Venus, Earth and Mars are small rocky planets. Jupiter and Saturn are giant balls of gas. Uranus and Neptune are large planets made of gas and ice.

◀ The surface of Venus is always covered by thick layers of clouds. In this picture radar was used to 'see' through the clouds and take pictures of the surface below.

▼ The planets of the Solar System. The planets are drawn to scale, so you can compare their sizes. The Sun is larger than all the planets put together.

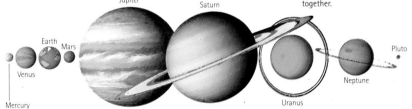

Jupiter

Saturn

Earth

Mars

Venus

Mercury

Pluto

Neptune

Uranus

Solar System

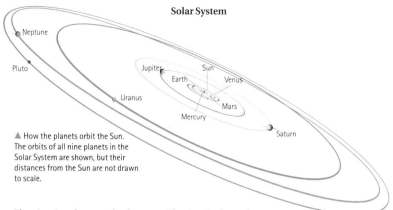

▲ How the planets orbit the Sun. The orbits of all nine planets in the Solar System are shown, but their distances from the Sun are not drawn to scale.

Pluto is a tiny planet made of rock and ice. **Space probes** carrying cameras and scientific equipment have visited all the planets except Pluto.

Orbits round the Sun

The Sun's powerful gravity keeps the planets from whizzing off into outer space. The planets orbit the Sun, following an oval-shaped path called an ellipse. The further a planet is from the Sun, the longer the time it takes to complete an orbit.

The time it takes a planet to make one orbit is equal to one year on that planet. A year on Mercury, which is nearest the Sun, is just 88 days. A year on Earth is around 365 days. But on Pluto, the planet which is furthest from the Sun, a year lasts for over 90,000 days!

Moons and asteroids

Moons are natural **satellites** – things that orbit round planets. All the planets except Mercury and Venus have moons orbiting

Mini-moon!
On its approach to Jupiter, the space probe *Galileo* photographed a small asteroid, about 52 km long, called Ida. Orbiting Ida at a distance of about 60 km was a tiny 'moon', only about 1.5 km across. Scientists called the mini-satellite Dactyl.

◀ This picture of Saturn and its rings was taken using an infrared telescope. The rings are made up of particles of ice, orbiting Saturn like tiny moons. Saturn has at least 18 larger moons. The largest, Titan, is bigger than the planet Mercury. Two moons, Tethys (green) and Dione (yellow) are arrowed on the picture.

them. The Earth's Moon is one of the biggest – only Jupiter and Saturn have bigger moons.

As well as the planets, millions of chunks of rock, called asteroids, orbit the Sun between Mars and Jupiter. Some scientists believe asteroids are fragments of a planet that was unable to form because of Jupiter's gravity.

Asteroids may be little more than specks of dust, or they may measure up to 940 kilometres across. Sometimes lumps break off from them and fall to Earth as **meteorites**.

▲ In 1997 many people in the northern hemisphere enjoyed the spectacular sight of the comet Hale-Bopp. It was one of the brightest comets ever to reach the inner Solar System. Hale-Bopp last approached the Sun about 4200 years ago, and is expected to return in about 2380 years.

Comets

Comets are giant lumps of ice and frozen gases mixed with bits of rock and dust. There are billions of comets, forming a cloud that extends far beyond the Solar System.

Most of the time, comets travel far from the Sun. If a comet gets close to the Sun, it begins to melt. Gas and dust boil away, forming a long, trailing tail that points away from the Sun.

Some comets take thousands of years to orbit the Sun, but a few take much less time. Halley's Comet, for example, can be seen from Earth every 76 years. It last appeared in 1986.

find out more
Earth
Moon
Radar
Satellites
Sun

Nicolas Copernicus

The Polish astronomer Nicolas Copernicus was the first person to work out that the Sun lies at the centre of our Solar System and that all the planets orbit around it. He published his theory in a famous book, *De revolutionibus orbium coelestium*, in 1543. Copernicus's ideas challenged the Church's belief that God created the Earth at the centre of the Universe. His book was regarded as evil, and was banned by the Roman Catholic Church in 1616.

▶ An astrological map of the world from Copernicus's *Harmonia Macrocosmica*, published around 1530.

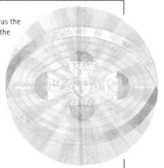

Solids, liquids and gases

Everything around us is either a solid, a liquid or a gas. These are the three states of matter. Whether something is a solid, liquid or a gas depends on how the particles in it (the atoms or molecules) are linked together.

Some materials change from one state to another when they are heated or cooled or when the pressure changes.

Atoms make the difference

The atoms or molecules that make up solids are closely linked together and do not move around much. This means solids can keep their shape without a container.

Liquids cannot hold their shape. You have to put liquids in a container to keep them from flowing away. This is because the particles in liquids are not so closely linked.

In gases the particles are not linked to each other at all. They shoot about in all directions. This is why gases spread out to fill whatever space they are in.

Three in one

Water is the only substance that is found as a solid, a liquid and a gas under normal conditions here on Earth.

At room temperature, water is a liquid. At temperatures below 0 °C, it freezes to become a solid – ice. If you heat water to 100 °C, it will boil and start to **evaporate**. It then turns into a gas called water vapour. If you cool water vapour down, it will **condense** and turn into a liquid again.

▲ Atoms in a solid, a liquid and a gas.

◀ Carbon dioxide is a gas at room temperature. But when you freeze it, it turns into a solid called dry ice. At room temperature, dry ice turns from a solid directly into a vapour – and makes a spooky-looking fog. The vapour is heavier than air, so you can pour it.

find out more

Atoms and molecules
Elements
Heat and temperature
Ice
Water

Songbirds see Birds

Sound

Sounds are caused by vibrations. They travel to our ears as waves. You cannot see sound waves, but when they enter your ears, they make your eardrums vibrate and you hear a sound.

Sounds can be high or low. These differences are because of the speed at which the sound wave vibrates (its **frequency**). Frequency is measured in hertz (Hz), or vibrations per second. The higher a sound's frequency, the higher-pitched the sound.

Most people can hear sounds between about 20 Hz and 20,000 Hz. Sounds above the range of our hearing are called **ultrasonic** sounds. Some of these can be heard by dogs, cats and bats.

find out more

Aircraft
Musical instruments
Radiation
Recording
Senses

Travelling sound

Sound waves can travel through solids, liquids and gases. But they cannot travel through space. In air, sound waves travel at a speed of about 330 metres per second. This is nearly a million times slower than light – but still pretty fast!

When sound waves hit hard surfaces, they are reflected back. This causes **echoes**. If you stand in an underpass and shout, you will hear many echoes all around you as the sound waves reflect off the sides of the tunnel.

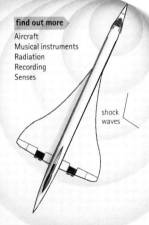

◀ **Supersonic** aircraft, like Concorde, travel faster than the speed of sound. When an aircraft breaks the sound barrier, it squashes the air in front of it and creates shock waves. You hear a loud noise, called a sonic boom, as each shock wave passes you.

shock waves

▶ Big vibrations make the air vibrate more and cause a louder sound. Noise levels need to be checked because very loud sounds can permanently damage your ears. Scientists measure sound levels in **decibels** (dB). Some typical sound levels are shown here.

noise level in decibels

space shuttle lift-off

very loud personal stereo

damage to ears

road drill

♪♫ rock concert

some discomfort to ears

telephone ringing

normal conversation

leaves rustling

South Africa

South Africa is the country at the southern tip of Africa. South Africa is the richest country in Africa because it has many valuable minerals, including gold and diamonds.

South Africa is a land of deserts, high mountains and grasslands, where elephants, lions, zebras and other animals still roam. The climate is warm, with hot, dry summers and mild, wet winters. Farmers grow maize (corn), fruit, wine and other foods.

South Africa's history

The ancestors of most black South Africans arrived about 1600 years ago. In 1652 the Dutch built a settlement at the Cape, which the British took over in 1815. There were fierce wars between the Europeans and the black people, especially the **Zulus**.

▲ The city and port of Cape Town, at the foot of Table Mountain.

South Africa became self-governing in 1910, and an independent country in 1961. In the new country, only whites could vote, or join the government. In 1948 the ruling whites passed **apartheid** ('apartness') laws, which were even more unfair to blacks. The **African National Congress** (ANC) fought apartheid. In 1962 their leader Nelson **Mandela** was imprisoned. He was released in 1990 and went on to win South Africa's first democratic elections in 1994.

◄ As president of South Africa from 1994 to 1999 Nelson Mandela tried to reconcile all South Africans.

S. AFRICA FACTS

Capitals: Pretoria, Cape Town, Bloemfontein

Population: 42,300,000

Area: 1,233,404 sq km

Language: English, Afrikaans, Xhosa, Zulu

Religion: Christian, trad. African religions

Currency: 1 rand = 100 cents

find out more
Africa
Racism

South America

South America is the fifth biggest continent. It has some of the world's largest cities, but there are also wild and remote regions where few people live. Its rainforests and mountains contain a fantastic range of wildlife.

Amazing Amazon!
The Amazon is not the longest river in the world, but it is the biggest in every other way. Nearly a quarter of all the water that runs off the Earth's surface flows down the Amazon, and it is more than 240 km wide at its mouth. The Amazon has more than 1000 tributaries, seven of them more than 1600 km long.

South America is sometimes grouped with Central America and called Latin America. This is because most people there speak Spanish or Portuguese, languages that grew out of Latin. Other people speak Native American languages such as Quechua and Aymará.

Geography

Almost every kind of climate is found in South America. The equator runs through the north of the continent. Here it is hot, humid and wet all year round. The rainforests of **Amazonia** surround the Amazon, the world's second longest river. Along the Pacific coasts of Chile and Bolivia there is the **Atacama desert**, the world's driest place.

▼ The village of Maras in the Peruvian Andes. The Andes mountains start near the Caribbean Sea in the north and end in Tierra del Fuego in the far south. They run through Colombia, Ecuador, Peru, Bolivia, Chile and Argentina.

South America

country boundary	land height in metres
◆ capital city	5000
■ large city	2000
▲ highest peaks (height in metres)	1000
	500
	200
	sea level

0 ——— 1000 km
0 ——— 500 miles

Caribbean Sea

Barranquilla
Valencia
Maracaibo
Caracas
VENEZUELA
Medellín
Georgetown
Paramaribo
GUIANA HIGHLANDS
Cayenne
French Guiana
(France)
Cali
Bogotá
COLOMBIA
Quito
Cotopaxi 5896
Equator
ECUADOR
Chimborazo 6310
Negro
Amazon
Guayaquil
Manaus
Belem
Fortaleza
Tapajos
Xingu
Madeira
BRAZIL
Recife
A N D E S
PERU
Mato Grosso
São Francisco
Lima
Salvador
L. Titicaca
La Paz
Brasília
BRAZILIAN HIGHLANDS
BOLIVIA
Belo Horizonte
PACIFIC OCEAN
O C E A N
Atacama Desert
Paraguay
Paraná
BRAZIL PLATEAU
Tropic of Capricorn
PARAGUAY
São Paulo
Rio de Janeiro
Nova Iguaçu
Gran Chaco
Asunción
Curitiba
Aconcagua 6960
Pôrto Alegre
Córdoba
Rosario
URUGUAY
ATLANTIC
Santiago
Montevideo
C H I L E
A N D E S
A R G E N T I N A
Buenos Aires
Rio de la Plata
Pampas
Patagonia
Falkland Islands
(UK)
Tierra del Fuego
Cape Horn

Peru

Bolivia

Chile

Ecuador

Colombia

Venezuela

Guyana

Suriname

348

Brazil

Population: 159,500,000
Area: 8,511,965 sq km

Brazil is the biggest and most populated country in South America. It is almost twice as big as Europe. Over 160 million people live there, half of all South Americans. Most Brazilians live along the Atlantic coast where the biggest cities, São Paulo and Rio de Janeiro, are located. The lowlands of the **Amazon** basin are covered with dense rainforest, with a great variety of animals, birds, insects and trees. Several hundred thousand Native Americans live in the remoter forest areas. But their lives, and those of the wildlife, are threatened by the spread of the timber industry, mining, ranching and dams.

SOUTH AMERICA FACTS

No. of countries: 13

Population:
317,846,000

Area:
17,832,000 sq km

Highest peak:
Aconcagua (6969m):
the highest mountain outside Asia

Highest active volcano: Ojos de Salado (6887 m):
highest in world

Longest river: the Amazon (6400 km):
second longest in world.

▲ Many petrol stations in Brazil sell alcohol made from sugar cane as an alternative fuel to petrol.

which taught respect for nature. But they were not powerful enough to stop the European invaders who arrived after 1492. Spanish **conquistadors** (conquerors) led by Francisco Pizarro came to Peru in 1532 and quickly defeated the Incas.

Cape Horn in the far south is the closest land to Antarctica. Here it is cold and the seas are famous for being stormy and dangerous.

The Andes mountains extend for over 7100 kilometres alongside the continent's western edge and contain many active volcanoes.

Early history

Modern-day South Americans are descended from Europeans, Africans and Native Americans. The Native Americans of the Andes, such as the Nazcas, Chimus and Incas, developed great empires. They had their own governments and religions

Argentina

Population: 35,400,000
Area: 2,780,092 sq km

Argentina won independence from Spain in 1816. Thousands of migrants from Italy, Germany, Britain and other European countries moved there to make their fortunes. Some settled in the capital, Buenos Aires. Today it is home to two out of every five Argentines. Other settlers headed for the rich farmlands that cover most of the country. These are called the Gran Chaco in the north and the **Pampas** in the south. They produce beef, wheat and maize for export to the rest of the world. In Patagonia, in the far south, there are rich oil and natural gas fields.

Paraguay

Uruguay

The Spanish and the Portuguese divided South America between them. Portugal ruled Brazil, and brought in millions of slaves from Africa to work on farms growing sugar, cotton and tobacco. The Spanish forced the Native Americans to work in their silver mines. Many slaves and Native Americans died as a result of the harsh conditions forced upon them, but also from diseases brought by the Europeans. Much of the continent's wealth was taken back to Europe.

Independence

In the 1800s the new societies of South America grew tired of European rule and the Wars of Independence began. Led by two great generals, José de San Martín and Simón Bolívar, South American countries won their freedom one by one. San Martín liberated Argentina, Chile and Peru, while Bolívar won freedom for Bolivia, Colombia, Ecuador and Venezuela.

The continent developed farms, mines and factories. Much of the world's copper, tin, zinc, coffee, cocoa, and fruit now comes from South America. This has brought wealth to the region, but there is great inequality between rich and poor.

▼ Aymará Indians from Bolivia. More than half of all Bolivians are Native Americans. Bolivia was once part of the Inca empire, and Quechua, one of the languages spoken there, was the language of the Inca people.

▲ Simón Bolívar was a brilliant general who led the struggle against the Spanish rulers of South America. In 1825 he helped defeat the Spanish armies in upper Peru. A new country, called Bolivia, was named in his honour.

South-east Asia

South-east Asia is a region of dense forests, tropical islands and remote mountains. Over the centuries it has been a meeting place for traders, religions and cultures. In recent years South-east Asia has enjoyed rapid economic growth.

Indonesia is the world's largest island chain. It is made up of over 13,000 islands. The Philippines has over 7000 islands. Cambodia, Vietnam, Laos, Thailand and Burma (Myanmar) are all on the Asian mainland. Malaysia includes lands on the mainland and on the giant island of Borneo.

Singapore and Brunei are small but wealthy countries.

Landscape and climate

The tropical climate is hot and very wet. Java gets 2000 millimetres of rain every year. **Monsoon** winds bring heavy rains to the Philippines in the summer. Fierce storms called

find out more

Asia

Empire, Age of

------ country boundary

land height in metres

5000
2000
1000
500
200
sea level

BA BANGLADESH
BR BRUNEI DARUSSALAM
PNG PAPUA NEW GUINEA

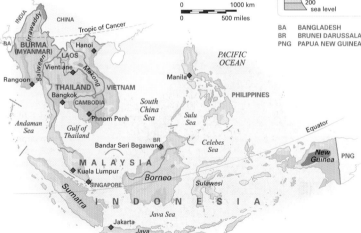

351

typhoons often cause flooding and damage. There are also hundreds of **volcanoes**, especially in Indonesia and the Philippines.

Vast areas are mountainous and covered in **tropical forests**. These forests have more different kinds of plants, animals and insects than any other place in the world. Thousands of species are not found anywhere else.

People

Many different peoples live in South-east Asia. Indonesia and Malaysia are mainly Muslim countries. Thailand and Burma are Buddhist. The Philippines is mainly Christian. In remote mountains there are hundreds of small tribes. They have their own religions and languages.

The traditional ways of life were based on farming **rice** and **fishing**. In recent years oil and natural gas have been found. Countries such as Malaysia and Singapore have developed factories making clothes, cars and computers. The new wealth

can be seen in modern cities such as Kuala Lumpur. But in 1997 the region was struck by economic troubles.

History

For thousands of years South-east Asia was settled by waves of different peoples from Asia. Traders from around the world came to buy **spices** such as nutmeg and pepper. First came Arabs in the 13th century. Later Dutch, Portuguese and British ships fought with each other to control the prized spice trade.

From their trading posts the Europeans gradually took over and ruled the area. After World War II European rule was challenged. The Vietnamese fought their French rulers, who turned to the USA for help. Vietnam became divided between the communist North and the pro-Western South. The USA sent troops to help the South. The **Vietnam War** ended in 1973, when the US troops withdrew. In 1976 North and South Vietnam were united under a communist government.

▲ Angkor Wat is an ancient complex of Hindu temples and buildings in the jungle of Cambodia. It was the country's capital between the 9th and 12th centuries.

• In 1975 the people of East Timor declared themselves independent of Portugal. But the Indonesian army immediately invaded the territory and made it part of Indonesia. In 1999 democratic elections were finally held, and the people voted overwhelmingly in favour of independence.

Space exploration

The Space Age began in October 1957, when the Soviet Union launched the satellite *Sputnik 1* into orbit. Since then, human beings have walked on the Moon and robot spacecraft have explored our Solar System.

▲ The X-33 unmanned test rocket is the prototype (trial model) of a completely reusable spaceplane, the VentureStar.

After the launch of *Sputnik 1*, both the USA and the Soviet Union began planning to send astronauts to the Moon. Both countries launched many space missions, sending astronauts into orbit around the Earth and unmanned **probes** to the Moon. Then in July 1969 three US astronauts – Michael Collins, Neil Armstrong and Edwin Aldrin – flew to the Moon in the *Apollo 11* spacecraft. Over the next three years there were five further Moon missions.

The Space Shuttle

The Space Shuttle was the first spacecraft that could fly into space many times. Only the huge main fuel tank is new for each flight. The Shuttle is now the USA's main launch vehicle. Its large cargo bay can carry satellites into orbit, or it can hold a space laboratory, where astronauts can do scientific experiments. In 1990 the Shuttle *Discovery* launched the space

▼ The Space Shuttle *Discovery* blasts off from the Kennedy Space Center, Florida, USA. The first Space Shuttle was launched in April 1981. The Shuttle takes off like a rocket, but lands like a glider.

probe *Ulysses*, which flew over the north and south poles of the Sun. In the same year the Shuttle placed the Hubble Space Telescope into orbit.

Space stations

A space station is a home in space where astronauts can live and work. The first space station was *Salyut 1*, launched by the Soviet Union in 1971. Then in 1986 a larger Russian space station, *Mir*, was launched. *Mir* was gradually extended by adding on extra sections.

In 1998, the first pieces of a new space station, the ISS (International Space Station), were assembled in space. It will be four times larger than *Mir* and will contain six laboratories.

Missions to the planets

Since the Moon missions, most space exploration has been carried out by unmanned space probes travelling to other planets. They take photographs and use radar and other

◄ Astronaut Bonnie J. Dunbar in the Space Shuttle's Spacelab science module. Once in space, the astronauts are weightless. They must sleep strapped into sleeping bags, eat and drink from special containers, and exercise hard to keep fit.

▶ Outside the spacecraft astronauts must wear a protective spacesuit. The backpack carries the astronaut's oxygen supply and a manned manoeuvring unit (MMU). This fires jets of gas to help the astronaut move around. Astronauts study the Earth, the stars and galaxies, and the space around them. They also make things, such as some medicines, that would be difficult to make on Earth.

Problems of space travel

To launch a satellite or astronauts into space, a spacecraft must overcome the pull of the Earth's gravity. This requires powerful engines that burn many tonnes of fuel. If the spacecraft is carrying astronauts, it also has to carry all the food, water and air they will need on the trip. When the spacecraft returns to Earth, friction from the Earth's atmosphere makes it extremely hot. The spacecraft itself and the astronauts inside must be protected from this heat.

instruments to collect information, which they send back to Earth by radio. Space probes have landed on Mars and Venus, and have travelled deep into Jupiter's atmosphere. They have flown past Saturn, Uranus and Neptune, and visited the Sun and Halley's comet.

find out more

Astronomy
Engines and motors
Moon
Satellites
Solar System

▼ A Voyager space probe. The two Voyager probes took pictures of Jupiter and Saturn, and *Voyager 2* went on to Uranus and Neptune.

Spain

Spain is a country in southern Europe with a varied landscape and climate. The high central plain of the Meseta is dry, with cold winters and hot summers. Northern Spain is wet and lush, while in the south, Almeria is hot and very dry.

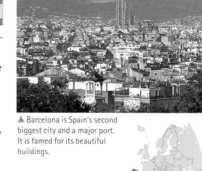

▲ Barcelona is Spain's second biggest city and a major port. It is famed for its beautiful buildings.

Spain has a mix of people. Most are Roman Catholics, and many towns have large churches. In the north there are factories, producing cars, or making electrical goods or books. Oranges, olives, wheat and barley are the main farming crops. **Tourism** is also important in many areas.

Spain's history

Before Spain became part of the **Roman empire** in 300 BC, Phoenicians, Greeks and Celts had settlements there. In AD 718, **Moors** and other Muslims conquered all but the north. They ruled until the late 15th century, when the Christian kingdoms of the north took control once again.

In the 16th century Spain conquered a vast empire in Central and **South America**, and became rich and powerful. However, in the 19th century most of these colonies were lost.

In 1931 Spain became a republic. But after a civil war (1936–1939) the fascist dictator General Francisco Franco ruled Spain. Today, Spain is a monarchy again, under King Juan Carlos.

SPAIN FACTS

Capital: Madrid

Population: 39,300,000

Area: 504,750 sq km

Language: Spanish, Catalan, Galician, Basque

Religion: Roman Catholic

Currency: 1 peseta = 100 céntimos

Wealth per person: $13,580

find out more

Empire, Age of
Europe
Exploration, Age of
Muslims
South America

◄ Small, traditional farms still exist in many parts of Spain.

Species *see* Life on Earth

Spiders and scorpions

Spiders and scorpions are different from insects. They have eight legs, and their bodies are divided into two main parts. Both live by catching small prey.

There are over 30,000 kinds of spider known, and more are still being discovered. But there are fewer than 1000 different types of scorpion known.

Spiders are found in most parts of the world. All can make several kinds of **silk**. They use the silk to make **webs** and traps, to tie up their prey and to protect their eggs.

▼ Garden spiders are common web-building spiders.

▲ Tarantulas live in the south-west USA, Mexico and South America. They hunt mainly at night, and are not dangerous to humans.

▼ Spiders, like this orb-weaver spider from Trinidad, are born knowing how to build the complicated webs they use to catch food. They produce the silk to build the web through the spinnerets at the end of their abdomen.

Male spiders are usually smaller than females. When they mate, the female often eats the male. But she takes good care of their eggs and the young.

Scorpions live in the warmer parts of the world. They feed mainly on insects which they kill quickly using the poisonous sting at the tip of their tail. They hide in the day and come out at night to hunt.

Female scorpions produce living young. They carry their babies on their back for about two weeks.

Less than bite-size!

In some kinds of golden-orb spider, the female weighs more than 1000 times as much as her mate. He is smaller than her normal prey, so she does not bother to eat him.

find out more
Animals

▶ A brown scorpion. Scorpions have jointed tails and front legs with pincers. They use these to grab and hold prey.

Spinning *see* Textiles • **Sponges** *see* Oceans and seas

Sports and games

One of the best ways to keep fit and healthy is by doing sports. Sports are competitions of fitness and skill, either between individuals or between teams. Millions of people enjoy sports, both by taking part and by watching them live or on television.

▲ Darts is an indoor game particularly popular in pubs and clubs. On the standard clock board, a dart in the centre, the bull's-eye, scores 50 points.

There are hundreds of different sports, ranging from simple running races to adventure sports like hang-gliding and round-the-world sailing. Sports such as squash or gymnastics test both skill and fitness. Others, such as chess and snooker, are skilled but not so strenuous.

Athletics

Athletics includes running, jumping and throwing events. These are probably the oldest forms of sport. Modern athletics events take place in a large stadium, with a 400-metre oval track for running, and areas within the track for field events such as the pole vault, long jump, javelin and discus.

Team games

Many of the world's most popular sports are played in teams. They are usually ball games, such as football, basketball, baseball and cricket. Most team sports are played on a large field or on a court. In football and cricket there are 11 players on each team, while in baseball there are nine. Basketball teams have five players. In all these sports, substitutions are allowed during the game.

Racket sports

Tennis, squash, badminton and table tennis are the most

The sports industry

Modern sport is big business, and an important part of the entertainment industry. Millions of people around the world watch major sports competitions such as the football World Cup and the Olympic Games on television. Advertisers pay top sports stars large amounts of money to advertise their products.

◀ Michael Jordan of the Chicago Bulls, probably the greatest basketball player of all time, was also one of sport's top earners. Baseball, basketball and football are among the most highly paid sports.

Tennis player Martina Navratilova of the USA winning the last of her record nine Wimbledon singles titles in 1990. Wimbledon is one of the four 'grand slam' events, which are the most important competitions in the tennis year.

and events such as yacht racing, canoeing and water-skiing, which take place on rivers and lakes or at sea. Swimming events were included in the first modern Olympic Games, in 1896, and today they still form an important part of the Olympic programme.

popular racket sports of all. Most racket sports involve hitting a ball (or shuttlecock) over a net, but in squash the ball is hit against the walls of a court.

Combat and target sports

Like athletics, combat sports such as boxing, fencing, wrestling and judo are very ancient. There were boxing and wrestling matches at the Greek Olympic Games 2500 years ago.

Target sports such as archery and shooting involve firing weapons at a target. Golf is also a target sport. It was first played in Scotland in the 15th century.

Water sports

Water sports include swimming and diving competitions, which are held in a swimming pool,

Winter sports

Winter sports take place on ice or snow. The most popular are skating, skiing and ice hockey, but there are others such as

Jack Nicklaus of the USA at the 1991 US Masters golf tournament. Golf is a truly international sport. Huge TV audiences follow the major tournaments, and millions of people of all ages play the game. A golfer uses a set of clubs to hit a ball towards a hole cut in the ground. Over a set number of holes, the winner is the player who takes fewest strokes in total to get the ball into every hole.

Squids *see* Octopuses and squids • **Starfish** *see* Seashore

◀ Windsurfing (sailboarding) was pioneered in the USA in the 1960s. Its popularity spread so quickly that it was accepted as an Olympic event in 1984. A sailboard is similar to a surfboard but with a mast and a triangular sail.

find out more
Football
Olympic Games
See also Sports facts,
    pages 426–429

are many different events. Cycling, for example, includes sprinting and other track events, road racing, and mountain bike racing on steep downhill or rough tracks.

Check it out

tobogganing and ice yachting. The main competition for winter sports is the Winter Olympics.

Wheeled sports

There are races for just about every type of vehicle with wheels, but the main wheeled sports are motor racing, motorcycle racing and cycling. For each of these sports there

Other sports

There are many other types of sport. Animal sports include angling, horse racing, show jumping and greyhound racing. Aerial sports include hang-gliding, ballooning and skydiving. And there are many different kinds of indoor sport – snooker, chess, bridge, and other card and board games.

The origin of chess is believed to be an ancient Indian game called 'chaturanga'. This had pieces representing the king, his wise men, and the four sections of the army – elephants, chariots, horsemen and infantry.

◀ A young child plays draughts against his father. Like many other indoor games, draughts requires concentration and thought rather than physical fitness.

Stars

Stars like our Sun are huge glowing balls of tremendously hot gas. They are so far away that light from even the nearest stars takes many years to reach us.

Stars come in many sizes. Our Sun is a fairly small star. Red giants, the largest stars, are several hundred times bigger than the Sun. White dwarfs, which are the smallest stars, have diameters less than one-hundredth that of the Sun.

Starlight, star bright

Most stars are made up mainly of two gases, hydrogen and helium. The gases are squashed together by gravity. The outside of a star is very hot, but at the centre it is much, much hotter.

Inside the star, particles of hydrogen crash into each other and fuse, or join together, giving off huge amounts of nuclear energy.

The colour of a star's light gives an idea of how hot the star is. Blue-white stars are the hottest, with surface

▼ The birth and death of a medium-sized star like our Sun. The star begins as a cloud of gas in a nebula, and will end up as a white dwarf. The blue arrows show how the material blown off from stars is recycled into nebulas, which become future stars.

▲ Most stars are born in groups, or **clusters**, rather than one by one. This 'jewel box' cluster of young stars is about 40 million years old. It is in the Large Magellanic Cloud, a small galaxy close to our own.

• Stars look like they are standing still, but really they are always on the move. Barnard's star, for example, moves about 3500 km every 180 years.

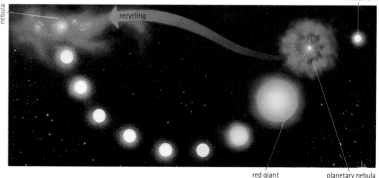

nebula

recycling

white dwarf

red giant

planetary nebula

▲ Stars are created in clouds of gas and dust called **nebulas**. The columns of dark gas in the Eagle Nebula, shown here, are called the 'pillars of creation' because stars are forming in them.

temperatures of around 20,000 °C. White stars are a bit cooler. Our Sun is a yellow star, with a surface temperature of around 6000 °C. The coolest stars are red stars.

Clustering together

Some of the brightest stars in the night sky are **double stars**. These are made up of two stars held together by the force of gravity. Sirius, the brightest star in the sky, is a double star.

Many other stars are parts of star **clusters**. Clusters are made up of stars of the same age which were born from the same cloud of gas and dust.

Birth and death

Stars are being born all the time. They begin as clumps of gas and dust in space. Gravity helps to pull this material together. A new star is born when the gas gets so hot and squashed up that the hydrogen in the star starts to fuse together.

Most stars live for billions of years, but not forever. When the hydrogen gas in a star is used up, it begins to change, and finally it dies. Small stars like the Sun first swell up into giant red stars (red giants), then shrink into white dwarfs and fade away. More massive stars die in a tremendous explosion called a **supernova**. The cores of these exploded stars sometimes turn into **black holes**. Black holes are so dense that nothing, not even light, can escape from their gravity.

▼ This star, Eta Carinae, is one of the biggest stars known. It is about 4 million times brighter than the Sun. In 1843 a massive explosion created the huge clouds of gas seen around the star.

find out more

Energy
Galaxies
Sun
Universe

▲ As a yellow star dies, it throws off great clouds of gas to create beautiful coloured patterns. This dying star is called the Cat's eye nebula. At the centre of the swirl of gases is a white dwarf.

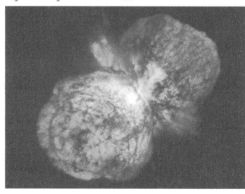

Submarines

Submarines are sea-going vessels that can dive below the waves or travel on the surface.

Navies use submarines to patrol the seas. **Naval** submarines carry powerful missiles and torpedoes. **Submersibles** are small submarines, used for exploration and research.

How submarines work

Submarines have large, hollow **ballast tanks**, which can be filled with air or with water. To dive, a submarine fills its ballast tanks with water. The submarine gets heavier, and it sinks. To surface, compressed air is used to blow water out of the ballast tanks. This makes the submarine lighter and it rises again.

Submarines cannot use diesel or petrol engines underwater, because these need air to work.

Instead, they mostly use **electric motors**. Most large submarines are **nuclear-powered**.

Submersibles

Submersibles are used for such jobs as exploring the sea bed and repairing oil rigs. Some submersibles have no crew: they are operated by remote control from the surface.

▲ The remote-controlled submersible *Nautile*. It was used to find and explore the wreck of the liner *Titanic*, which sank in 1912 when it hit an iceberg.

▼ How a submarine dives underwater and surfaces. Fins called hydroplanes on the sides of the submarine tilt to help it steer downwards or upwards.

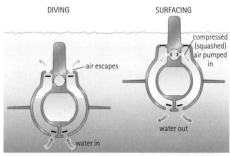

DIVING

air escapes

water in

SURFACING

compressed (squashed) air pumped in

water out

hydroplanes

hydroplanes

find out more

Ships and boats
World War II

SUBMARINE FIRSTS

1620 First underwater vessel built by Dutch inventor Cornelius Drebbel

1775 First true submarine, the *Turtle*, built by US engineer David Bushnell

1875 Ancestor of modern naval submarine built in USA by John Holland

1958 World's first nuclear submarine, USS *Nautilus*, travelled under North Pole

Sun

The Sun is our nearest and our most important star. Without the Sun there would be no life on Earth.

Like all stars, the Sun is a giant ball of hot gas. With a diameter of around 1,392,000 kilometres, the Sun takes up more than 1 million times as much space as the Earth.

For us on Earth, the Sun is a very important star. It provides us with heat and light to stay alive. This energy is created in the core of the Sun. Temperatures there reach 16 million °C, and atoms of hydrogen are squeezed until they fuse, or join together, releasing huge amounts of energy. This is the energy that makes the Sun shine.

The swirling surface

At the surface of the Sun temperatures are around 6000 °C. Twisting streamers of hot gas shoot out into space and then fall back again. In some places, cooler, darker patches called **sunspots** appear. These come and go in an 11-year cycle.

Solar **flares** near the sunspots send out bursts of magnetic particles. When these reach the Earth they cause beautiful displays, called auroras. But they also disrupt communications and power lines.

▲ Sometimes the Moon lines up between the Earth and the Sun, and blocks out the sunlight. This is called a **solar eclipse**. During a total solar eclipse it is possible to see the corona, a faint ring of gases around the Sun, spreading out into space.

Sun, Sun and more Sun
Ninety-nine per cent of all the matter in the Solar System is in the Sun.

◀ During a solar prominence great fountains of flaming gas shoot out and loop back to the stormy surface of the Sun.

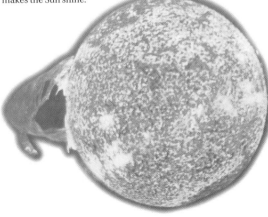

find out more

Energy
Heat and temperature
Plants
Solar System
Stars

Teeth

Teeth are used for holding, cutting and chewing food. Teeth are very strong, but they will decay if they are not cared for.

Most vertebrates (animals with backbones) have teeth. Different sizes and shapes of teeth are adapted to do different jobs. Meat-eating animals have sharp, pointed teeth that are useful for tearing off bits of meat. Plant-eaters have teeth with broad, flat surfaces that are better for grinding tough food like grass.

Humans have a mixture of types of teeth. The teeth at the front of our mouths are called **incisors**. They have straight chisel-shaped edges for biting off mouth-sized bits of food. On each side of the incisors is a single pointed tooth, called a **canine** tooth. Our back teeth, called **molars**, are broad and bumpy. We use them to grind food into small pieces before swallowing.

Healthy teeth

It is important to keep your teeth healthy. You can do this by cleaning them every day and visiting a **dentist** regularly. The dentist's job is to look after your teeth and treat them if they become diseased.

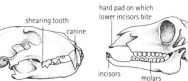

▲ Some people have to wear braces on their teeth to straighten them. Here a dentist is using ultraviolet light to harden the cement fixing the braces to a girl's teeth.

find out more

Bones and muscles
Digestion
Human beings

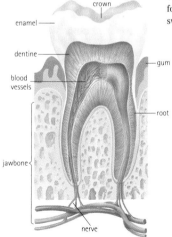

▼ Most of a tooth is made out of a hard material called **dentine**. The top part, called the crown, is coated with an even harder material called **enamel**. Inside the tooth is a hollow area filled with pulp, made up of blood vessels and nerve fibres. The tooth is fixed firmly into the jawbone by the tooth root.

crown
enamel
dentine
blood vessels
gum
root
jawbone
nerve

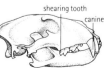

▼ Carnivores (meat-eaters) like the lion (left) have long canines to kill and tear up their prey. They use their big shearing teeth to crack bones and cut flesh. Herbivores (grass-eaters) like the sheep (right) bite off grass with their incisors, then grind it up with their molars.

shearing tooth
canine

hard pad on which lower incisors bite

incisors
molars

Telephones

A telephone is a device that lets you talk to other people almost anywhere on Earth, simply by pressing a few buttons.

Telephones use tiny pulses of electric current or light to send sounds over the worldwide **telecommunications network**.

Making a call

Pressing the number buttons on your telephone sends signals to your local **telephone exchange**. The exchange uses these signals to direct your call through the telecommunications network so that it reaches the telephone you are calling.

In the telephone handset, a microphone, called the **transmitter**, changes the sound you make with your voice into electric signals. These signals are carried through the telephone network. An earphone, called a **receiver**, then changes any electrical signals it receives back into sounds.

Mobile phones work by sending radio signals to a radio

mast. From there the signals are fed into the telephone network.

Using the network

Fax machines and computer **modems** can be connected to the network too. Fax machines can send pictures over the telephone lines. Computer modems send and receive information (data) over the network to other computers.

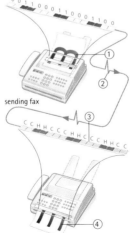

► Facsimile, or fax, machines can send copies of pages of text or pictures over telephone lines to another fax machine. To send a fax the machine that is sending first dials the receiving machine. When the receiving machine answers, the sending machine begins to scan the document.

sending fax

receiving fax

▲ Alexander Graham Bell invented the telephone in 1876. In this photograph, taken in 1892, he is making the first phone call from New York to Chicago, USA.

find out more
Communications
Internet
Recording

1 Light sensors sense the pattern of light and dark on the page and turn it strip by strip into digital signals (a series of electrical 0s and 1s)

2 The digital signals are sent very rapidly through the telephone network

3 At the receiving fax, the pattern of 0s and 1s is turned into a series of hots and colds in a heating element

4 Heat-sensitive paper passes through the elements. It turns black where it is heated, to reveal the pattern of light and dark on the original document

Telescopes *see* Astronomy, Lenses and mirrors, Radio

Television

Television is a way of sending moving pictures from one place to another. It lets us watch events from around the world as they happen.

For many people around the world television is the main way of getting news and entertainment. In developed countries, almost every home has a **television set**. In less developed countries the number of television sets is growing too.

Worldwide watching

Millions of people around the world enjoy watching soap operas, situation comedies, adventure programmes, plays and game shows on television. Because many **television programmes** are made in the United States, Europe and other developed countries, television is helping to spread Western culture to all parts of the world. Not everyone thinks this is a good thing.

Pictures into signals

Just like an ordinary camera, a **television camera** collects light from a moving scene. Inside the

▲ The Scottish engineer John Logie Baird was one of the pioneers of television. In 1926 he gave the first public demonstration of television in England. In 1929 his equipment was used to make the first television broadcast of pictures.

▼ Television news programmes keep us informed about what is happening in the world. Millions of people around the world watched the funeral of Princess Diana on their television sets in September 1997. Thousands watched on giant TV screens in Hyde Park, London.

● In **digital television**, television signals are made up of a list of numbers. This gives clearer pictures because less information is lost in transmission. In the future, all television will be digital. It will also be in wide-screen format, just like movie pictures.

find out more
Communications
Drama
Radio

camera a light-sensitive device scans the pattern of light strip by strip and changes this information into electrical signals. Sound is added to the signals later.

The signals are sent to your television set by radio waves via satellites, or through cables underground. Signals from many different television stations arrive at your television set. The first thing it does is pick out the signal from the station you want. This is called **tuning**. Next, it takes the signal apart to make signals for red, green and blue, and for sound. It uses these signals to recreate the picture on its screen and to make sound.

▼ Cutaway of a television set. The signal that arrives at your television set contains information about both pictures and sounds. The sound signal is sent to an amplifier and a speaker. The red, green and blue picture signals go to three electron guns inside the television. These fire electron beams at a phosphor coating on the inside of the screen. The coating is made up of a huge number of coloured strips, which are lit up by the electron beams. The shadow mask makes sure that each beam only hits strips of the right colour.

▲ Popular television dramas can make their actors world famous. Here the actress Gillian Anderson stars as FBI Agent Dana Scully, in a scene from the hit American science-fiction series *The X-Files*.

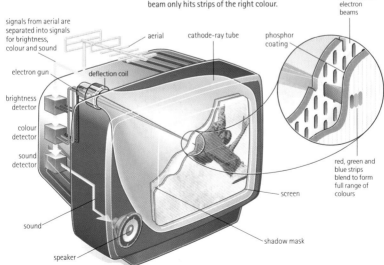

signals from aerial are separated into signals for brightness, colour and sound

aerial

cathode-ray tube

phosphor coating

electron gun

deflection coil

shadow mask guides electron beams

brightness detector

colour detector

sound detector

red, green and blue strips blend to form full range of colours

screen

sound

shadow mask

speaker

Textiles

A textile is a cloth or fabric made from fibres. The fibres may be natural materials that come from plants or animals, or they may be synthetic fibres. Many textiles contain a mixture of natural and synthetic fibres.

Textiles can be made to have many different properties so they can be used for many things. Textiles are used in car tyres, in parachutes and sails, and for bandages and other medical uses. The clothes you wear are often made of textiles. So are things in your home, like carpets, towels, sheets, curtains and furniture covers.

▲ In this close-up of a rough kind of cloth called 'burlap', you can see the way the vertical and horizontal threads (the warp and the weft) cross under and over each other.

Textile properties

The properties of a finished textile depend partly on the fibres from which it is made. Textiles made from natural fibres, such as cotton, silk, flax or wool, are generally softer, absorb moisture better and are more heat-resistant than textiles made from synthetic fibres.

Synthetic fibres, such as nylon, polyester or acrylic, are often stronger and more hard-wearing than natural fibres.

shearing
fleece
washing
carding
spinning
sliver
yarn

◀ Woollen yarn is made from fibres from a sheep's fleece. Before the fibres can be spun, the fleece must first be washed. It is then carded to form a sheet of fibres, then twisted into a thick rope called a 'sliver'. Next, the wool is stretched and spun into yarn. The yarn is usually dyed before being sold as balls of wool, or woven into cloth, or knitted into jumpers, scarves and other clothing.

find out more
Clothes
Plastics

▶ To make clothes, cloth is cut into shapes and the pieces are sewn together. Here a woman working in a jeans factory in Poland is using a heavy-duty sewing machine to sew together pieces of denim to make jeans.

The fibres are made by forcing chemicals through tiny holes in a nozzle, called a spinneret.

Modern textiles are often made from a mixture of natural and synthetic fibres to give the best combination of properties for a particular product.

Making textiles

People have been making and using textiles since prehistoric times. Most methods of making textiles were invented thousands of years ago. At first textiles were made by hand. Then machines were invented to carry out the different tasks. Now most textiles are made by machine.

The first step is to make the fibres into yarns or long threads. Natural fibres like cotton or wool are first washed, then combed in a process called **carding**. In the next step, **spinning**, the natural or synthetic fibres are twisted together to make long threads or yarns.

The yarns are often then **dyed** before being made into textiles by **weaving**, **knitting** or **felting** them. In weaving, lengths of yarn are criss-crossed on a loom. In knitting, the yarn is linked together in loops. In felting, the fibres are pressed and become matted together.

Once the textile has been made, it is often washed. Sometimes it is coated to make it waterproof or fireproof. And sometimes patterns are printed onto its surface.

MANY TYPES OF TEXTILE

There are hundreds of different types of textile. Here are a few of the most common ones.

Denim: a strong woven cotton cloth used for jeans and other tough garments.

Linen: a strong fabric made using fibres from the flax plant.

Tweed: a heavy cloth with a rough surface, woven from wool.

Silk: a smooth, strong and lightweight cloth made from fibres produced in the cocoons of insects called silkworms.

Nylon: a fabric made from threads of nylon, a strong, stretchy synthetic fibre.

◀ This Guatemalan woman is using a backstrap loom to weave cloth. It is called a backstrap loom because the lengthwise, or warp, threads are kept tight by a strap that runs around the weaver's back.

Time

Years, days, hours, minutes and seconds – time can be measured in many ways.

In the past, the ways people measured time were based on movements of the Earth, the Sun and the Moon. Days lasted for the time it takes the Earth to spin once on its axis. Months lasted for the time it takes the Moon to orbit around the Earth. Years were measured by the time it takes for the Earth to orbit around the Sun.

A solar year is actually 365 days, 5 hours, 48 minutes and 46 seconds long. But the calendar by which we measure the days of the year has only 365 days. To keep the calendar in step with the seasons, we add an extra day, 29 February, to the calendar every four years. Years

◀ This 18th-century pendulum clock uses a swinging pendulum to keep the time. The small wrist watch next to the clock face keeps time much more accurately. It is controlled by radio signals from an atomic clock kept in Frankfurt, Germany. This atomic clock is one of the most accurate in the world.

with this extra day are called leap years.

Time ticks by

Clocks help to measure time more precisely by counting a regularly occurring event, like the swinging of a **pendulum** – a rod or rope with a weight on the end. Many modern clocks and watches work by measuring the natural vibrations of atoms in a **quartz crystal**.

The most accurate clocks are **atomic clocks**. These work by measuring the vibrations of certain atoms. Atomic clocks are accurate to less than a millionth of a second every year.

● To find out about time zones, see page 420.

◀ At any one time half of the Earth is lit by the Sun, while the other half is in darkness. In the part of the Earth facing the Sun, it is daytime. In the other part of the Earth, it is night. Here, India can be seen at the top of the lit part of the Earth.

find out more
Earth
Seasons

Toads *see* Frogs and other amphibians ● **Tortoises** *see* Reptiles

Tourists

People who travel for pleasure – to enjoy a relaxing holiday by the sea, to walk in mountains, or to visit a beautiful old city – are called tourists. Many tourists travel abroad. Others visit different areas of the country where they live.

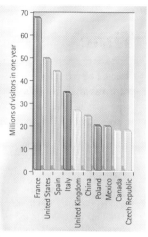

▲ This graphs shows the 10 most popular tourist destinations. Top of the list are France, the USA and Spain.

Most tourists come from richer, developed countries such as the USA and Australia. Most also visit developed countries. Europe and North America are the most popular destinations. But today more and more people are going on adventure holidays in more remote parts of the world. For example, walking holidays in Morocco and Nepal are becoming very popular.

Tourism has led to the development of **tourist industries** in the countries that tourists visit. These industries provide services such as hotels, restaurants, guided tours, taxis and souvenir shops.

Although tourists help create jobs, they can also bring problems. Many countries spend a lot of money building roads, airports and hotels in the tourist areas. This may mean that they spend less on important services for their own people.

Tourists frequently cause pollution. Traffic fumes are damaging the ancient monuments of Egypt, which attract many millions of visitors every year. Tourists also sometimes upset local people by not respecting their customs and culture.

find out more
Industry
Pollution
Transport

◀ Many tourists go on holiday just to relax on sandy, sunny beaches. This beautiful palm-fringed beach is on the island of Antigua in the Caribbean. The tourist industry in the Caribbean has grown fast in the last few decades.

Trade

The simplest form of trade is to swap something that you have for something that someone else has. If I give you a bag of rice and, in exchange, you give me a bunch of bananas, we are trading with each other.

Trade involves the buying and selling of **goods (products)**, such as chocolate bars, televisions or oil. People also trade in **services** – for example, a window cleaner sells the service of cleaning windows.

The people who buy goods and services are called **consumers**. We are all consumers. Most of us are also **producers** – we work to make a product or provide a service, for which we get paid **money**. The money we earn makes it possible for us to buy the products we need and want.

Money

Exchanges that do not involve money – like rice for bananas – are called **barter**. But today almost all trade involves money. We use money to pay for things we buy and we receive money when we sell things. Money can be coins or notes, or be held in a bank account. Each country has its own type of money, called its **currency**.

The economy

The system of buying and selling goods and services is known as the **economy**. A healthy economy is one where plenty of products

▲ A lot of everyday trade takes place in **markets** and **shops**. Most market stalls, like this one in Tunisia, sell goods that have been produced locally. Shops can range in size from one person selling things they produced themselves to huge supermarkets and hypermarkets. Some shops sell just one thing, such as shoes or books.

find out more

Europe
Industry

people work for businesses

businesses pay wages to workers

people buy goods and services from businesses

businesses produce goods and services to sell to people

◀ The economic cycle of producing and consuming goods and services.

Trade unions *see* Industry

are being produced and people have enough money to buy them. Economies work at many levels. Every household has its own small economy. Each country has a national economy. And all the countries together make up the **global economy**. The global economy depends on the health of international trade.

International trade

Goods and services sold to customers in foreign countries are known as **exports**. Goods and services bought from another country are known as **imports**. Together the trade in imports and exports make up international trade.

International trade is very important because different countries produce different things. A country can buy goods from abroad that it is unable to

produce at home. In Britain it is too cold to grow oranges, so they are imported from hotter countries like Spain. Japan has few energy sources of its own, so it has to buy supplies of coal and oil from other countries.

Free trade

Free trade is where a group of countries agree to import each other's goods and services freely. However, countries sometimes fear that imports of cheaper goods will mean that people making similar goods at home will lose their jobs. Some countries try to stop the import of foreign goods by placing a tax on them. This is known as **protectionism**, because its aim is to protect the home industries from competition.

◀ In stock markets, shares are bought and sold. People who buy shares are buying a part of (a share in) a company or commodity (such as oil). This is the famous New York Stock Exchange on Wall Street.

• Advertising is an important part of trade. Companies advertise their goods and services to persuade people to buy them.

▲ In November 1996 French lorry drivers striking for better working conditions blockaded motorways, ports and airports all over France. Their action disrupted trade all over the country, stopping supplies such as fuel and food from reaching their destinations.

Trains

Trains are the fastest and most efficient kind of land transport. High-speed passenger trains can carry up to 800 passengers at speeds of nearly 300 kilometres per hour. Freight trains are slower, but can carry thousands of tonnes of goods such as oil, chemicals and cars.

▲ The famous steam locomotive 'The Rocket' was designed by George Stephenson and built by his son Robert. In 1830 it was chosen to be the engine on the first public main line railway, the Liverpool and Manchester Railway.

The **locomotive** is the powerhouse of a train. Early locomotives were powered by **steam engines**, but modern locomotives are usually diesel- or electric-powered. **Diesel locomotives** have diesel engines, like those in trucks or cars. **Electric locomotives** get the power to drive their motors from

▼ 'Maglev' stands for magnetic levitation. In a maglev train, powerful magnets on the train and on a guide rail below are used to make the train 'float' above the track. There is no contact with the track and so no friction to slow the train down. This German test train can reach speeds of 400 km/h.

overhead wires, or from an electrified rail on the track. In **diesel-electric locomotives** a diesel engine turns a generator, which makes electricity to power the motors.

Tracks and signals

Railway track is made of steel rails laid on concrete or wooden blocks called sleepers. Modern rails are heated and stretched as they are laid down. This stops them warping in hot weather.

The track has to be as level as possible, with no tight curves. **Viaducts** (high bridges) carry the railway across valleys, while

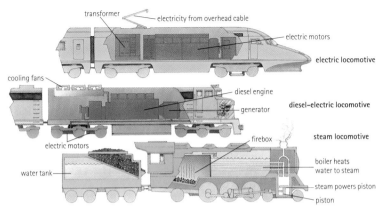

transformer — electricity from overhead cable

electric motors

electric locomotive

cooling fans

diesel engine

generator

diesel–electric locomotive

steam locomotive

electric motors

firebox

boiler heats water to steam

water tank

steam powers piston

piston

tunnels carry it through hills.

A railway line is divided into sections, with a signal at the beginning of each section. Only one train is allowed in each section, to avoid collisions. A train can pass a signal only if it shows 'go'.

The signals are operated from a **signal control centre**. A computer makes sure that there is only one train travelling on each section of line. Some locomotives have on-board computers that stop the train automatically if a signal shows 'stop'.

Railway history

The first steam locomotive was built by Richard Trevithick in 1804, but the railway age did not truly begin until 1830, when the Liverpool and Manchester Railway was opened. Over the next 20 years, many other countries began building their own railway networks.

By 1917, there were about a million miles of railway track worldwide. But this was the peak of railway development. People began to use cars instead of trains, and railways became gradually less important.

▲ Diagrams showing how different kinds of locomotive work.

find out more

Engines and motors
Industrial Revolution
Transport

Underground railways

The first underground railways were shallow tracks not far below street level. The first part of the London Underground was opened in 1863. Engineers later developed techniques of tube-tunnelling at 25 to 28 metres below ground. In the USA, the first stretches of the New York subway opened in 1904.

The London Underground has the most track (over 400 km). New York has the most stations (466), and Moscow carries the most passengers (over 6 million a day).

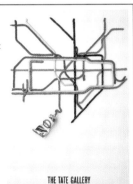

THE TATE GALLERY
by Tube

▲ This unusual poster of the London Underground shows the network of lines that make up London's underground railway system.

Transformers *see* Electricity

Transport

Transport is the carrying of people or goods (things) from one place to another. Ships, trains, cars and aircraft are all types of transport. Without transport there would be no trade, tourism or industry – and many of us would not be able to get to work or school.

◀ Polynesians were using canoes like this one to travel across the Pacific over 5000 years ago.

The invention of new kinds of transport through the centuries has changed the way people live. But these new inventions have also led to problems such as pollution.

Early types of transport

People started to use horses and donkeys for transport about 7000 years ago. The next big breakthrough was the invention of the wheel, about 5500 years ago. Horses and other animals could now pull wheeled carts.

But for thousands of years there were very few good roads.

It was often much easier to go by boat, and rivers became important highways. In prehistoric times, people used dugout canoes and rafts. Later they built larger boats and ships. By the 16th century, large sailing ships could travel right round the world.

The transport revolution

A revolution in transport began in the 18th century. Many canals were built, so that horse-drawn barges could move heavy loads. People also started to build better roads. But the most important thing was the invention of the steam engine.

The first steam-powered railway engines were built in the early 19th century. Trains carried

▲ A balloon built by the Montgolfier brothers of France. In 1783 it made the first ever human flight.

▶ One of the most successful early steam locomotives was the British *Rocket*, built by Robert and George Stephenson in 1829.

◀ The Grand Canal in China is one of the oldest canals in the world. Work started on it in the 6th century BC. Today, the canal is 1794 km long.

▲ The first aeroplane was built and flown by the American Wright brothers in 1903.

people and goods farther and faster. At the same time, steam engines began to be used in ships. In time, steam ships were built that were bigger and faster than sailing ships.

Cars and aircraft

The petrol engine was invented in the late 19th century, and petrol-driven cars followed soon after. Over the next hundred years millions of cars, buses and lorries were built, as well as roads for them to drive on. Eventually road transport became as important as the railways.

The first aeroplane flew in 1903, but it was not until the 1950s that airliners began to carry large numbers of people. Air travel is fast, so more and more people are now able to visit faraway places. However, it is too expensive to carry large amounts of goods in aeroplanes.

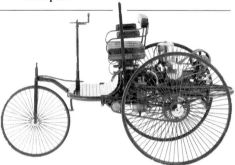

▲ A copy of the three-wheeled vehicle built by Karl Benz in 1886 in Germany. Many people consider this to be the first true motor car.

Transport and the environment

Some kinds of transport can have a bad effect on our environment. Traffic jams are a common problem in cities. The fumes from cars, lorries and buses pollute the air and damage people's health. They are also a major cause of global warming. The noise the vehicles make is a kind of pollution. Building new roads often destroys the places where wild animals and plants live.

To avoid these problems, more people could walk or cycle, or use public transport. Some cities now ban private cars from their centres.

● After walking, cycling is probably the most common form of transport in the world. Bicycles are very adaptable – they can cope with heavy loads. They are also cheap and do not cause any pollution.

find out more

Aircraft
Bicycles
Bridges
Cars
Pollution
Trains
Ships and boats
Space exploration
Submarines

◄ Many cities suffer from frequent traffic jams.

Trees

Trees are tall, straight plants with strong, woody trunks, supporting a mass of branches. The biggest plants of all are trees. And trees also live longer than any other living things.

Trees belong to two main groups of plants. Trees with cones and needle-like leaves belong to the group of **conifers** or cone-bearing plants.

Broadleaf trees are a type of flowering plant. They usually have wide, flat leaves. Common broadleaf species include the oak, ash and holly, and the many species of palm.

Trees that shed all their leaves for part of the year are called **deciduous**. Shedding leaves helps protect the tree from frost or drought. Most deciduous trees are broadleaves. **Evergreen** trees keep their leaves all year.

◀ Many conifers grow faster than broadleaves, and produce a fairly soft type of wood.

▶ A cross-section through a tree trunk. A ring of living cells outside the sapwood (called the cambium) produces new xylem and phloem. Xylem tubes carry water and minerals up the tree from the roots. Phloem tubes carry the food made in the leaves to other parts of the tree. The xylem grows at different speeds at different times of the year. This produces rings in the wood. By counting these rings you can tell the tree's age.

Labels on cross-section: bark — phloem — cambium — sapwood (living xylem) — heartwood (dead xylem) — annual ring (the 14 rings show that the tree is 14 years old) — bark cambium

Tree structure

The main parts of a tree are the roots, trunk, branches and leaves. Most trees have huge **root systems**. They spread through the soil like underground branches. The roots absorb water and minerals from the soil. They also stop the tree from blowing over.

The **trunk** of the tree is made up mostly of dead wood, which is hard and strong. However, immediately beneath the bark is a zone of living cells. In this zone, called the **sapwood**, a band of tube-shaped cells carries water

TREE TOPS

Oldest living tree
A bristlecone pine called 'Methuselah' in California, USA, is 4765 years old

Tallest tree
'Mendocio Tree', a Californian coast redwood, is 112 m tall and is still growing

Most massive tree
'General Sherman', a giant sequoia in California, is 83.82 m tall, has a diameter of 11.1 m and a girth of 31.1 m

find out more

Flowers and fruits
Forests
Plants
Wood

and food up and down the tree. **Bark** is the rough layer of dead, corky wood that covers the outer surface of the tree.

The **leaves** of trees form a leafy crown. In forests, the crowns of many trees join together into a continuous **canopy**. Each leaf plays its part in making food for the tree by **photosynthesis**. Light energy from the Sun powers this process, so the leaves are arranged to receive as much light as possible.

Tree reproduction

Trees reproduce from seeds, which grow and spread in different ways. The seeds of conifers grow in **cones**. The ripe

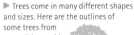

▶ Trees come in many different shapes and sizes. Here are the outlines of some trees from around the world.

Banyan

Horse chestnut

Baobab

Silver birch

seeds are shaken out and spread by the wind.

Like other flowering plants, broadleaves produce **flowers**. After fertilization the flowers form **fruits**, which contain the seeds. The fruits can be berries or nuts, or dry, papery fruits that are spread by the wind.

▼ Broadleaved trees like oak and ash grow quite slowly. The wood of broadleaves is generally harder than conifer wood.

Spruce

Trees and people

People everywhere use wood from trees to build and make things, and as fuel for fires. Tree fruits provide a rich source of food. Trees also help to keep the air fresh. Like all plants, trees absorb carbon dioxide and release oxygen when they photosynthesize.

Palm tree

United Kingdom

The United Kingdom (UK) is a country in north-west Europe. Its people have settled and conquered many parts of the world. The English language is now spoken across the globe.

The UK is surrounded by the Atlantic Ocean to the west and the North Sea to the east. The narrow English Channel separates it from France.

Geography

The UK's weather is mostly influenced by winds from the Atlantic. They bring heavy rains and winter snows to the more mountainous areas of the west, such as the Scottish Highlands and the Lake District in England.

The southern and eastern parts of the UK have more lowland areas, and the climate is drier. Lowland England, Northern Ireland and central Scotland have good farmlands and green hills.

Peoples

Over the centuries, the English, Irish, Welsh and Scots nations have mixed together so that many British people have

Devolution

The Scottish Nationalist Party in Scotland and Plaid Cymru in Wales have demanded independence from the UK for many decades. In the 1990s, the Scottish and Welsh voted to have their own elected assemblies. Although they remain part of the UK, this gives them more control over their economies and their cultures.

▼ Tourists from around the world visit London because of its historic buildings, including The Houses of Parliament and the Tower of London. The Houses of Parliament were built in the mid-19th century, after fire destroyed the original medieval palace.

United Kingdom

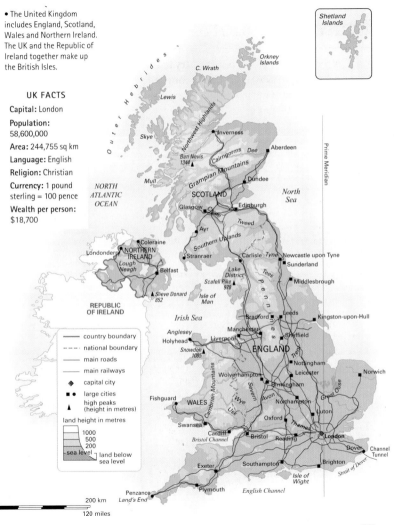

• The United Kingdom includes England, Scotland, Wales and Northern Ireland. The UK and the Republic of Ireland together make up the British Isles.

UK FACTS

Capital: London

Population: 58,600,000

Area: 244,755 sq km

Language: English

Religion: Christian

Currency: 1 pound sterling = 100 pence

Wealth per person: $18,700

Shetland Islands

C. Wrath

Orkney Islands

Outer Hebrides

Lewis

Skye

Northwest Highlands

Inverness

Ben Nevis 1344 ▲

Cairngorms

Dee

Aberdeen

NORTH ATLANTIC OCEAN

Mull

Grampian Mountains

Dundee

SCOTLAND

North Sea

Prime Meridian

Glasgow

Edinburgh

Ayr

Tweed

Southern Uplands

Coleraine

Londonderry

NORTHERN IRELAND

Lough Neagh

Belfast

Stranraer

Carlisle

Tyne

Newcastle upon Tyne

Sunderland

REPUBLIC OF IRELAND

▲ Slieve Donard 852

Lake District

Scafell Pike 978

Tees

Middlesbrough

Isle of Man

Pennines

Irish Sea

Anglesey

Holyhead

Bradford

Leeds

Kingston-upon-Hull

Manchester

Liverpool

Sheffield

Snowdon 1085

ENGLAND

Trent

Cambrian Mountains

Wolverhampton

Nottingham

Leicester

Norwich

Birmingham

Severn

Wye

Avon

Northampton

Great Ouse

Fishguard

WALES

Usk

Luton

Swansea

Cardiff

Oxford

Thames

London

Bristol Channel

Bristol

Reading

Dover

Channel Tunnel

Exeter

Southampton

Brighton

Isle of Wight

Strait of Dover

Penzance

Land's End

Plymouth

English Channel

country boundary
national boundary
main roads
main railways
◆ capital city
■ ● large cities
▲ high peaks (height in metres)

land height in metres

1000
500
200
sea level   land below sea level

0   200 km

0   120 miles

ancestors from more than one nation. English is the official language of the UK, but about half a million people speak Welsh and around 80,000 speak Scots Gaelic.

British people have settled many other parts of the world and immigrants from the British empire have come to the UK. British cities such as London and Birmingham have large communities from South Asia and the Caribbean.

Cities and industries

The UK contains some of the most crowded regions in the world. A great chain of cities stretches from Liverpool to London. Along with Glasgow in Scotland, Belfast in Northern Ireland and parts of South Wales, these cities were the first centres of modern factories in the world. They grew rapidly in the 19th century, using the country's deposits of coal and iron ore for industry. In the 20th century the UK became an important producer of chemicals, medicines, cars, aircraft and computer products.

The region around **London** is home to about one in five of the UK's people. It is a world centre of banking, publishing, tourism and other industries.

▲ Glencoe is a beautiful area of rugged peaks in the Scottish Highlands. The Highlands are a region of ancient mountains and long narrow lakes, called lochs.

find out more

Anglo-Saxons
Britain, History of
Empire, Age of
Europe
Industrial Revolution
Ireland, Republic of
Normans

Northern Ireland

Until the 1920s the whole of Ireland was part of the UK. In 1921 the Republic of Ireland became a separate country, leaving Northern Ireland as part of the UK. Protestants in Northern Ireland (sometimes called Unionists) wanted to stay in the UK. Catholics, sometimes called Nationalists, wanted to join the Republic of Ireland.

Between 1969 and 1998 there were many shootings and bombings, as extremists from both sides fought for their cause. Then in 1998 talks between Unionists, Nationalists, the UK government and the Republic of Ireland led to a peace plan. This stated that Northern Ireland would remain part of the UK as long as the majority of people wanted it to do so. But the plan also involved closer links between Northern Ireland and the Republic.

▲ A political mural (wall painting) in Belfast supporting the Irish nationalist party, Sinn Féin.

United Nations

The United Nations (UN) is an international organization whose purpose is to maintain peace all over the world. It also tries to help solve economic and social problems.

The United Nations was set up after World War II by 51 countries. Together they drew up the **Charter of the United Nations**, which sets out its aims and rules. Today nearly all the countries in the world are members of the UN. It had 185 members in 1999.

The General Assembly

Every member state sends a representative to the **General Assembly**. They discuss world problems such as pollution, poverty and disarmament. The **Security Council** has representatives from 15 countries. They always include the USA, China, Russia, France and Britain – the permanent members. The Security Council meets when there is a crisis, for example when one country invades another.

Peace-keeping

When war breaks out, the UN sometimes sends a **peace-keeping force**. The force is made up of troops from different member countries. Their task is very difficult and they do not always succeed.

▲ The first meeting of the General Assembly in 1945, at which the UN Charter was drawn up.

▼ Bosnian Serbs welcome a battalion of UN peace-keepers in February 1994. The UN troops are Russians.

UN AGENCIES

UNHCR: UN High Commission for Refugees

UNICEF: UN International Children's Emergency Fund

FAO: Food and Agriculture Organization

WHO: World Health Organization

WB: World Bank

UNESCO: UN Educational, Scientific and Cultural Organization

find out more

Governments
Law
World War II

United States of America

The United States of America (USA) is the world's richest and most powerful country. American products, from bubble-gum to computers, sell around the world. Hollywood films have helped spread the American way of life to many countries. And the USA has the most advanced armed forces in the world.

There are 50 states in the USA, 48 of which are joined together. Alaska is separated from the other states by Canada, while Hawaii is in the middle of the Pacific Ocean.

Land and climate

The USA is so big that it has a wide range of climates, from the freezing, snowy climate of Alaska to the tropical weather of Florida. The south-west is very dry, but the north-west has heavy rainfall.

The west coast of the USA suffers many **earthquakes**. The worst ones happen along the San Andreas fault, a huge crack in the Earth's surface that runs

▼ The Grand Canyon is 350 km long, and at its deepest point the Colorado River flows nearly 2 km below the surrounding landscape. In some places the gorge is 29 km wide.

United States of America

Seattle
WASHINGTON
Portland
OREGON
IDAHO
MONTANA
Fort Peck Res.
NORTH DAKOTA
MINNESOTA
WISCONSIN
MAINE
VT
NH
Boston
MS
NEW YORK
CT
RI
New York
NJ
Philadelphia
DE
Baltimore
MD
Norfolk
Missouri
Great Plains
Rocky Mountains
WYOMING
SOUTH DAKOTA
NEBRASKA
IOWA
Minneapolis
Milwaukee
Chicago
Detroit
Cleveland
Pittsburgh
PA
OHIO
Columbus
Cincinnati
WV
VA
Lake Superior
Lake Michigan
Lake Huron
Lake Erie
Lake Ontario
Buffalo
Snake
Sacramento
Oakland
San Francisco
NEVADA
Salt Lake City
UTAH
Denver
COLORADO
KANSAS
Kansas City
St Louis
Indianapolis
IN
IL
MISSOURI
KENTUCKY
Ohio
Sierra Nevada
Colorado
Las Vegas
CALIFORNIA
Los Angeles
San Diego
Grand Canyon
ARIZONA
Phoenix
NEW MEXICO
OKLAHOMA
ARKANSAS
TENNESSEE
NORTH CAROLINA
Charlotte
SOUTH CAROLINA
Appalachian Mountains
Dallas
TEXAS
San Antonio
Houston
LA
New Orleans
MS
ALABAMA
GEORGIA
Atlanta
Mississippi
Washington D.C.
CANADA
MEXICO
Rio Grande
Gulf of Mexico
Tampa
FLORIDA
Miami
ATLANTIC OCEAN
THE BAHAMAS
CUBA

CT	CONNECTICUT
DE	DELAWARE
IL	ILLINOIS
IN	INDIANA
LA	LOUISIANA
MD	MARYLAND
MA	MASSACHUSETTS
MS	MISSISSIPPI
NH	NEW HAMPSHIRE
NJ	NEW JERSEY
PA	PENNSYLVANIA
RI	RHODE ISLAND
VA	VIRGINIA
VT	VERMONT
WV	WEST VIRGINIA

0   500 km
0   250 miles

— country boundary
--- state boundary
◆ capital city
■ ● large cities

land height in metres
2000
1000
500
200
sea level
land below sea level

close to San Francisco and Los Angeles.

Western USA is mostly mountainous. The **Rocky Mountains** are the largest, but there are many other mountain ranges. Large rivers such as the Colorado and Snake have cut deep gorges and canyons through the mountains. In places the rivers have been dammed to provide hydroelectric power for cities and water for irrigating fields.

East of the mountain ranges lie the **Great Plains**, vast areas of rich grassland. The Plains are one of the world's most important areas for growing wheat and raising cattle.

The Mississippi, the Missouri and the Ohio rivers drain water from most of central and eastern USA. The rivers are useful for transport, but floods can cause great damage. East of the Mississippi are the Appalachian Mountains. In the past, these mountains were an important coal-mining area. East of the Appalachians is the **eastern seaboard**. Many of America's great cities, such as New York, Washington DC and Philadelphia, are found here.

People and cities

The USA has the third largest population of any country – over 250 million people. Most of them live along the east coast, or in west-coast cities such as San Francisco and Los

385

Angeles. Outside these cities there are still areas with few people. Wyoming, for instance, is about the same size as the UK, but only 100,000 people live there.

Most of today's Americans are descended from people who arrived within the past 400 years. They include many Europeans, Africans who originally came as slaves, and people from South America and South-east Asia.

Farms, mines and factories

The USA has rich farmlands, producing maize (corn), soya beans, tomatoes, oranges, peaches, cheese, beef, chickens and many other foods. There are also large amounts of oil and gas, metals such as iron and copper, and minerals such as salt. And US factories produce many different kinds of goods, from clothing and food to cars and computers.

The USA has also made some of the most important **inventions** and discoveries of the last 150 years. Telephones, electric lights, aeroplanes, nuclear weapons and the silicon chip were all invented in the USA.

History of the USA

The United States of America was born on 4 July 1776, when the 13 British **colonies** in North America became an independent country. The original USA was only a small part of the country we know today, but in less than 100 years it had expanded across North America.

The frontier and war

The US was soon expanding its frontier westward. It bought huge areas from France and Spain, and seized still more from Mexico. This led to bitter fighting with the Native Americans (also known as Indians), who lost most of their land.

© Disney

▲ The most successful films have always come from Hollywood. Film stars such as Marilyn Monroe, Harrison Ford and the cartoon character Mickey Mouse are known worldwide.

▼ The Statue of Liberty stands at the entrance to New York Harbour. It was given by France to the American people in 1886. Her torch represents freedom and her book the law.

US government

Each US state has its own state government. Over them all is the federal government, which organizes the whole country. The federal government's parliament is called Congress. It has two houses, the Senate and the House of Representatives.

The US president is elected by all the people. He has great power, but he has to work with Congress.

KEY DATES

1776 Britain's North American colonies declare their independence

1803 US buys most of midwest America from France

1848 US gets California from Mexico

1861–65 American Civil War

1917 US enters First World War

1929 Great Depression begins

1941 US enters Second World War

1969 Americans land on the Moon

Americans also disagreed about **slavery**. The issue was settled by a long and bloody civil war between the north, who wanted to abolish slavery, and the slave-owning south. The south lost and slavery was abolished.

Industry and immigrants

After the American Civil War, the USA became an **industrial country**. Thousands of factories and mines opened. Railroads criss-crossed the country. Towns grew into vast cities. This made the US very powerful. It helped win the First and Second World Wars, and led the fight against communism.

Meanwhile, millions of new settlers (immigrants) were arriving, changing the American way of life. The different races and cultures normally lived together in peace, but the unfair treatment of African-Americans occasionally led to serious violence.

▲ President John F. Kennedy, one of America's best-loved modern presidents, travelling through Dallas, Texas. Tragically, he was shot dead seconds after this picture was taken.

USA FACTS

Capital: Washington D.C.

Population: 265,620,000

Area: 9,160,454 sq km

Language: English, Spanish

Religion: Christian

Currency: 1 US dollar = 100 cents

Wealth per person: $26,980

◀ Chief Sitting Bull of the Sioux people, one of the most famous Native American leaders. In 1876 he defeated General Custer at the Battle of Little Bighorn.

find out more

American Revolution
Empire, Age of
Films
North America
Slaves

Universe

The Universe includes everything that exists – from the Earth to the most distant parts of space. The distances are so vast that it takes billions of years for light to reach us from the edges of the Universe.

Scientists think that the Universe began 15 billion years ago with a huge explosion called the **Big Bang**. This explosion created all the **matter** (the 'stuff' that everything is made of) and energy in the Universe and was the beginning of time and space.

Just after the Big Bang the Universe was incredibly hot and dense. But it quickly began to expand, or spread out, and cool down.

At first all the matter in the Universe was made up of vast numbers of fast-moving **particles**. Three hundred thousand years later it had cooled down enough for **atoms** to form. A billion years after that, huge clouds of gas began to collect together, and **galaxies** started to form.

The Universe is still expanding, and no one knows when it will stop – if ever. But some scientists think that eventually the force of gravity will pull all the galaxies together in a giant collision, called the '**big crunch**'.

▲ This image shows some of the most distant galaxies in the Universe. Because their light takes so long to get to us, the picture looks back through time as well as space, at galaxies formed when the Universe was still young.

find out more

Astronomy
Atoms and molecules
Galaxies
Solar System
Space exploration
Stars

◄ This picture tries to give some idea of the scale of the Universe.

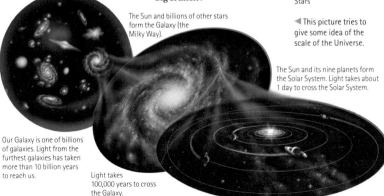

The Sun and billions of other stars form the Galaxy (the Milky Way).

The Sun and its nine planets form the Solar System. Light takes about 1 day to cross the Solar System.

Our Galaxy is one of billions of galaxies. Light from the furthest galaxies has taken more than 10 billion years to reach us.

Light takes 100,000 years to cross the Galaxy.

Vikings

For about 200 years the Vikings terrified western Europe. From the 8th century onwards, Viking war parties left Scandinavia (Norway, Sweden and Denmark) and sailed south looking for plunder. Some went as far as the Mediterranean. In time they settled all around the North Sea and North Atlantic.

▲ The happier side of Viking life. A leather boot fixed to a skate carved from animal bone. Archaeologists found it among the remains of a house in York, England.

Viking **raids** were sudden and violent. They first hit Britain around AD 793. Over the next 100 years the Vikings conquered north-west Scotland and settled in Ireland. They came to live in north-east England, too. In 1016, England had a Viking king (Cnut or Canute). The Vikings also settled in Normandy, Germany and Russia.

Further north, Viking adventures were even more amazing. They went to Iceland in the 860s. From here they set up bases in Greenland and North America.

The centre of every Viking **settlement** was a wooden hall. Here Viking men and women feasted and told fantastic stories of gods and heroes.

The Vikings were **farmers** and **traders** as well as warriors. Their merchants travelled through Russia to Constantinople (Istanbul) and Baghdad. **Women** ran the farms when their husbands were away. One tough Viking woman even captained her own ship across the Atlantic.

Thundering Thursday!

Thor, the thunder-god, was one of the Vikings' favourite gods. Thursday (Thor's day) is named after him. He carried a huge hammer, which he used to strike his enemies with thunder and lightning.

▶ A Viking **longship** (warship) as it may have looked. Longships were powered by a sail or by oars. They could ride out the roughest storms.

find out more
Anglo-Saxons
Europe

Viruses *see* Diseases • **Vitamins** *see* Food

Volcanoes and earthquakes

Hot lava, ash and smoke pouring out of volcanoes cause damage in many parts of the world. The shaking of the ground in an earthquake can destroy cities.

▲ A thick cloud of smoke, gas and ashes rose above the snowy slopes of Mt Ruapehu, New Zealand, when it erupted in September 1995.

Both earthquakes and volcanoes are affected by the movement of the **plates** that make up the Earth's crust. These plates are always on the move. Learning about the behaviour of the plates helps scientists to guess when volcanoes will erupt and where earthquakes will happen.

Big bang

Volcanoes form when molten rock, called magma, from beneath the Earth's crust pushes its way up through cracks in the surface. When the magma reaches the surface the volcano erupts, sending out clouds of **ash** and gases. Red-hot molten

▼ An erupting volcano. Most of the magma bursts out through the main vent, creating a fiery cloud of ash, smoke and lumps of lava (volcanic bombs). Flows of lava build up the sides of the volcano, then cool to form solid rock.

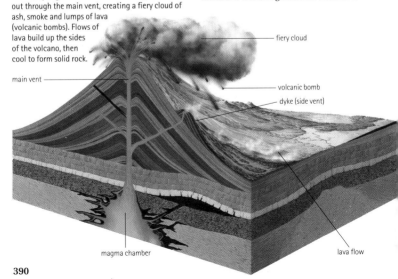

main vent

fiery cloud

volcanic bomb

dyke (side vent)

magma chamber

lava flow

rock, called **lava**, can also pour out.

As the lava cools, it hardens to form solid rock. The lava and ash can build up to form a cone. Large volcanic mountains can build up very quickly this way.

Volcanoes are not active all the time. When a volcano has not erupted for a while, it is said to be dormant, or sleeping.

All shook up

Big earthquakes – the kind that can cause a lot of damage – only usually happen where two plates meet and rub against each other.

Many earthquakes happen at sea in ocean trenches. These are places where one plate dives beneath another. These

earthquakes cause huge waves, which can cause great damage when they reach the shore. On land, earthquakes kill people when they destroy buildings and roads or cause landslides.

Strong earthquakes are common in places like Japan and California. These areas are located near the edges of plates. In countries that are far from a plate boundary, such as Britain, earthquakes that take place are mostly too weak to feel.

The earthquake **focus** is the point below ground where an earthquake begins. But when people describe where an earthquake takes place, they usually refer to the point on the Earth's surface that is directly above the focus. This is called the **epicentre**.

◄ Powerful earthquakes are very dangerous because they damage roads and buildings. When these collapse many people can be killed or injured. This section of road was broken up during the earthquake that damaged the Japanese city of Kobe in 1995.

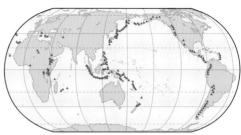

▲ This map shows a 'ring of fire' – a pattern of active volcanoes – around the Pacific Ocean. The pattern helps to show the boundaries of some of the plates that cover the Earth's surface.

• The **Richter scale** is used to measure the size of earthquakes. A very small earthquake will measure 1 on the Richter scale. But an earthquake that measures 10 causes total devastation. The 1908 earthquake that destroyed San Francisco in the USA measured 8.3 on the Richter scale.

> **find out more**
> Continents
> Earth
> Islands
> Rocks and minerals

Water

Water is the most important liquid on Earth. We cannot live without it. Three-quarters of our planet is covered by water. Most is in oceans, seas and rivers. Some is frozen and forms ice caps at the North and South Poles.

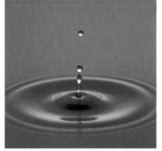
▲ Water forms into round droplets as it falls to the Earth as rain.

Water goes round and round in a process called the **water cycle**. Clouds in the sky contain water as a gas – **water vapour**. This gas condenses (becomes a liquid) and falls to Earth as rain or snow. The rain brings water to seas, rivers and lakes. Water also goes into the soil, and is taken up by plants.

Heat from the Sun evaporates water from the Earth's surface (turns it back into water vapour). The water vapour rises up through the atmosphere and forms clouds again.

Water for life

There is more water in you than any other substance. Around 70 per cent of your body is water.

Like all animals, you need water to stay alive. Your body loses water when you

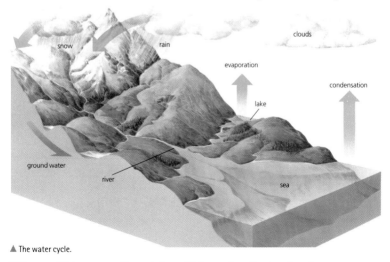

snow rain clouds

evaporation

condensation

lake

ground water

river

sea

▲ The water cycle.

breathe, sweat and go to the toilet. You can go for many weeks without food, but if you go for three or four days without water, you could die. Plants, too, need water to live. They usually take water in through their roots.

Taps and drains

The tap water you use for drinking and washing is rainwater. This **water supply** is sometimes taken from rivers. It can also come from large storage lakes called reservoirs. Sometimes water is drawn from deep holes in the ground, called wells.

Before water can be used, it must be cleaned at a water treatment plant. The cleaned water is then pumped through

◀ In some parts of the world water is not piped to houses. People have to get their water from wells. Here, oxen help to draw up buckets of water from a well in India.

pipes to storage tanks, ready for when it is needed.

Used water from houses and offices is called **sewage**. It is carried by drains to a sewage treatment plant, where it is cleaned before it is returned to a river or the sea.

• Water is a molecule that contains two atoms of hydrogen and one atom of oxygen. The chemical formula for water is H_2O.

find out more ▸

Ice
Rivers
Solids, liquids and gases
Weather

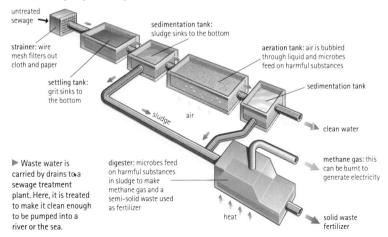

untreated sewage

strainer: wire mesh filters out cloth and paper

settling tank: grit sinks to the bottom

sedimentation tank: sludge sinks to the bottom

aeration tank: air is bubbled through liquid and microbes feed on harmful substances

sedimentation tank

sludge

air

clean water

▶ Waste water is carried by drains to a sewage treatment plant. Here, it is treated to make it clean enough to be pumped into a river or the sea.

digester: microbes feed on harmful substances in sludge to make methane gas and a semi-solid waste used as fertilizer

heat

methane gas: this can be burnt to generate electricity

solid waste fertilizer

Weapons

Prehistoric people made the first weapons to help them kill wild animals. But they also used these weapons to attack other people – their enemies – and defend themselves when other people attacked them.

The first weapons were sharp stones and pointed sticks. Long-range attacks were made with stone-throwing **slings**, and with bows and arrows.

Bows, arrows and swords

Bows and arrows were popular weapons for thousands of years. Over time bows became longer and more powerful, and fired metal-tipped arrows. The **crossbow** shot heavy bolts, but it was awkward and took a long time to load.

The first **swords**, the most common weapon of all, were made over 5000 years ago. They came in all shapes and sizes, from the short, stabbing swords of the Romans to the huge two-handed broadswords of medieval warriors. Metal was also used for axes, spear and lance heads, and shields. Metal rings and plates were shaped into **body armour**.

Guns

The invention of guns in 14th-century Europe changed

▲ A Roman catapult that launched huge stones at enemy forts. Machines like this were the largest weapons of their time.

▶ The longbow could fire an arrow that pierced armour at 100 paces.

weapons completely. Early **cannons** fired metal or stone balls. They were unreliable and slow to use. Some even blew up in the firer's face. In time they became stronger and lighter, and were fitted with wheels. They were taken on board ships, too. By the early 19th century, a

▶ An early handgun (musket) and its firer. He is holding a burning fuse used to fire the gun.

broadside of ship's cannon was terrifyingly powerful.

Early **handguns** were also heavy, slow to use and inaccurate. They were useless in the rain because wet gunpowder wouldn't fire. The invention of **shells** (metal cases holding the bullet and the charge that fired it) solved this problem. Shell-firing guns were loaded at the back (breach loading). This speeds up firing. A spiral groove in the barrel (the rifling) improved accuracy.

Modern weapons

Modern weapons are more powerful than ever. **Machine guns**, so deadly in World War I, fire a rain of bullets. Massive guns hit targets many miles away. **Tanks** combine speed, armour and heavy guns.

In World War I aircraft and airships took guns and bombs into the air. The first **long-range missiles** (the V1 and V2) were launched in World War II.

Today we have '**smart bombs**', which use computer technology to reach targets with pin-point accuracy, and **laser-guided weapons**, which are guided by lasers.

Horrible new ways of killing people include hidden **mines**, which explode when trodden on, **poison gas** and even deadly **bacteria**. Scientists have invented explosives, like **dynamite** and TNT, many times more powerful than gunpowder. Finally, in 1945, came the most terrible weapon of all – the **nuclear bomb**.

▲ The US Apache attack helicopter can carry a whole arsenal of weapons.

Big Bang!

To attack Constantinople (Istanbul) in 1453, the Turkish leader Mehmet used the biggest cannon the world had ever seen. It took 100 oxen and 2000 men to pull it into position. When it fired (only seven times a day), its 500 kg ball went about two kilometres.

find out more

Atoms and molecules
Ships and boats
World War I
World War II

▶ A modern warship. The missile cruiser is really a floating platform for weapons.

Weather

Wind, rain, clouds and sun – they all combine to make up our weather. Weather is the state of the atmosphere around us.

The weather can change very quickly. Weather forecasts help us to know what the weather will be like hours or days from now.

Air on the move

All weather conditions happen because heat from the Sun warms the surface of the Earth. This warming keeps the air in the atmosphere constantly on the move. This flowing air is called **wind**.

As the Earth's surface is heated by the Sun, it heats up the air. Winds are stirred up when warm air rises and cooler air moves in to take its place.

The area where two different bodies of air meet is called a **front**. Where a body of warm air meets a body of cold air, an area of low pressure called a **depression** often forms. Depressions can bring strong winds and stormy weather. In

▼ A satellite view of Hurricane Fran approaching the US mainland from the Caribbean in September 1996. Hurricanes are very violent storms with winds blowing up to 300 km/h. In a hurricane, swirling masses of winds circle around a calm 'eye' at the centre of the storm.

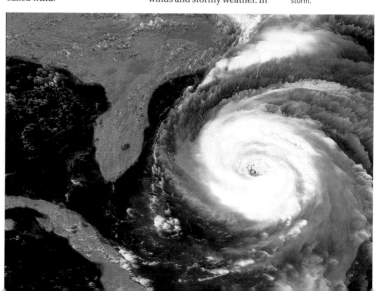

◀ During a depression warm air is pushed upwards, and large clouds are formed. These clouds often bring heavy rain.

• The usual weather of a place from year to year is called its **climate**. Climate depends mainly on how far north or south of the equator a place is, and on how much sun it gets. Unlike weather, climate changes very slowly.

Weather watching

Weather forecasting is a very difficult job! Many things can affect the weather. In order to forecast the weather in one area, meteorologists (scientists who study the weather) have to know what the weather conditions are over the whole Earth. Some of this information is collected at weather stations on the ground. Information can also be gathered by instruments carried on satellites that orbit the Earth or by weather balloons.

some parts of the world large depressions, called cyclones, form. These can develop into very strong storms such as hurricanes.

Clouds and rain

Heat from the Sun also evaporates water from the oceans. This forms clouds. When the clouds cool down, their moisture falls to the ground as rain. If the air gets very cold, the moisture then freezes, and snow falls instead of rain.

Rain and snow are the Earth's most important sources of water. Without them all the world's rivers, lakes and soils would dry up.

Clouds form in different shapes and at different heights in the sky. Looking at the clouds can give some clues about what the weather will be like.

▼ A weather balloon being launched in New Mexico, USA. Weather balloons and satellites carry instruments that measure temperature, air pressure and wind speeds. Plotting the information on a weather map makes it easier to see the weather patterns.

find out more

Air
Climate
Seasons
Water

Wetlands

Wetlands are damp, boggy areas such as lakes, ponds, marshes or swamps. They support huge numbers of plants and animals. Two-thirds of the fish caught around the world began their life in wetlands.

Wetlands provide rich feeding for animals. The abundance of insects and small animals living in the soft ground provides food for a huge variety of birds and mammals. Wetlands are also important stopover places for millions of migrating birds.

Wetlands are valuable for humans, too. They soak up water during storms and let it out into streams gradually. Saltwater **mangrove swamps** help to protect tropical coastlines, by forming a natural barrier against storms and hurricanes. They are also important to the fishing industry, as many commercially caught fish breed in them.

Types of wetland

There are many different kinds of wetland. Some are formed naturally, while others result from human activities.

Where rivers meander slowly over large flat flood plains, the slow-moving water drops the fine particles of soil and rock (sediment) to the bottom, and mud banks gradually build up. River bends may get separated off, and form marshy pools or lakes. Mud also builds up on the shores of estuaries, where rivers

▶ Mudskippers are small fishes that live in mangrove swamps, scuttling over the mud on their front fins. They can stay out of water for long periods, breathing a mixture of air and water stored in their gill chambers.

• People are slowly learning the usefulness of wetlands. In some places, beds of reeds are being planted to act as a natural filter for sewage, instead of building expensive treatment works.

◀ Some of the many types of animal and plant found in ponds. A pond is a small, shallow body of water. Ponds attract animals to drink, and birds come to look for food in them.

yellow iris
damselfly
pond skater
whirligig beetle
coot
water boatman
mallard
young pike
tadpoles
pond snail
common newt
great diving beetle
dragonfly nymph
caddis larva
duckweed
stickleback

meet the sea. At the mouth of the largest rivers, this mud forms vast fan-shaped deltas. Plants grow in muddy areas beside the sea, forming **salt marshes**, which are home to many wading birds and other animals.

The coasts of some tropical seas are fringed with mangrove swamps. (Mangroves are trees that are adapted to live in wet, salty places.) Mangrove swamps are home to many different animals, such as fiddler crabs, the young of many ocean fishes, crocodiles, alligators and birds such as storks, ibises and herons.

Large areas of the cooler parts of the world are covered in **peatlands**. These are formed by plants called bog mosses, which can grow in waterlogged areas. As they die, the remains of bog mosses form a spongy material known as peat. Peatlands are important areas for many breeding birds and insects.

Some wetlands are made by human activity. Disused gravel pits fill with water, and marshes develop around the edges of reservoirs. Many of these make valuable nature reserves. And flooded rice fields are home to fishes, egrets and herons.

▲ Lesser flamingos on Lake Nakuru, a salty lake in Kenya. Millions of birds come to the lake because the shallow water is full of the tiny insects, worms and crustaceans that they feed on.

Saving wetlands
Humans have destroyed about half the wetlands that once existed, and many more are under threat. Many have been drained to be built on or for farming. Others have been filled in as rubbish dumps. Many wetlands have become polluted, and peatlands are being destroyed by the harvesting of peat for gardening.

◄ Common hippopotamuses are the largest wetland animals: they can weigh up to 4.5 tonnes. Hippos are found in swamps and rivers from Egypt to South Africa.

find out more
Conservation
Ecology
Rivers

Whales and dolphins

Whales and most dolphins live in the oceans. Although they look like fishes, they are mammals and breathe air – just like us.

There are two main types of whale: toothed whales and baleen whales.

Toothed whales include giants like the sperm whale. Sperm whales feed mainly on squid. They can dive down to 1000 metres to find their prey. Sperm whales have the biggest brains of any animal.

Baleen whales include huge animals like the right whale and the blue whale. Baleen whales have no teeth. Instead they use huge fringed plates to sift tiny animals (**plankton**) out of the water. The plates are made of baleen, a material similar to our fingernails.

Like all mammals, whales and dolphins are **warm-blooded**. They give birth to live young and feed them on milk. They must come to the surface to breathe air.

Dolphins and porpoises

Dolphins and porpoises are small types of toothed whale. They usually swim in the open sea, although some come into inshore waters. They use their many small pointed teeth to catch fish.

Dolphins are very intelligent. They are sometimes trained to do tricks or to help people work underwater.

Hear my song!
Sound travels very well underwater, and whales communicate with each other using sound. The 'songs' of blue whales and fin whales may be the loudest sounds made by any animal. They have been detected over 850 km away.

• The blue whale is the largest animal in the world. It can grow to around 30 metres long and weigh over 100 tonnes.

find out more
Animals
Mammals
Oceans and seas

▼ A sperm whale (1), a right whale (2), a dolphin (3) and a porpoise (4), drawn to scale.

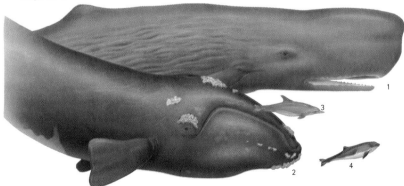

Witches

Witches in stories have pointed hats and black cats, and ride broomsticks through the sky. They chant magic spells. Most are wicked, frightening women, until the hero or heroine tricks them and escapes.

In the past people in most parts of the world believed that witches really existed. They thought these witches cast magic spells – usually to do harm to their neighbours. Today people in some parts of the world still believe in witches.

Witch-hunts

In Europe from the late Middle Ages belief in witchcraft spread rapidly. Many Christians thought that witches were possessed by the devil. So it was right, they thought, to hunt them down and kill them.

Witch-hunting became a mania. It was usually poor, old women who were accused. In parts of Germany a hundred women were burned a year. In England over 200 women were hanged in just two years. Altogether hundreds of thousands, possibly millions of women died.

As scientific knowledge grew, belief in witchcraft faded. There were few trials after 1700. In Salem in the USA, 30 people were executed for witchcraft in 1692. Five years later, the judge and jury admitted their mistake.

▲ This painting shows the three witches who appear in *Macbeth*, a play by William Shakespeare, written in 1606. They are described as old women 'withered and wild'. They chant spells, foretell the future and draw the hero into a web of evil.

• There are tales of witches in the Bible and in ancient Greek myth, for instance Medea who helps Jason steal the Golden Fleece.

find out more

Middle Ages
Myths and folk tales
Britain, history of

◀ In most of Europe witches were burned. In England they were hanged. This German woodcut of 1555 shows three women being burned at the stake.

Women's rights

In most traditional societies it was men who had the power and made the important decisions. They also owned almost all the property. Women spent most of their time preparing food and looking after children. They had little freedom.

In the last two hundred years many women have fought for their rights, and have achieved much greater equality.

In the 19th century, in Britain and the USA, women began to demand more freedom. They

▼ The suffragette leader Emmeline Pankhurst is arrested for an attack on Buckingham Palace in 1914. The suffragettes used dramatic publicity stunts as part of their campaign.

▶ In countries that live under Muslim law, such as Afghanistan, women are not allowed to show any part of their body in public. Some women agree with this law, but all women must obey it whether they agree with it or not.

wanted to work in professions, for instance as doctors. They also fought for the right of married women to own property.

The biggest campaign of all was for the **vote**. Without the vote, women had no political power. In Britain this fight was led by a group known as the **suffragettes**. By the end of the 1920s, women in many countries had won the vote.

But women still did almost all the housework and childcare. And they were often paid less than men at work. In the 1960s a second campaign began – the **women's liberation movement** – which demanded equal pay and equal opportunities. But at the end of the 20th century women in many parts of the world still lacked rights.

KEY DATES

1792 Mary Wollstonecraft publishes *A Vindication of the Rights of Woman*

1848 First Women's Rights conference, USA

1893 Women in New Zealand gain vote

1918 British women over 30 gain vote

1920 US women over 30 gain vote

1963 US Equal Pay Act

1970 Equal Pay Act in Britain

1979 United Nations outlaws discrimination against women

▶ **find out more**

Britain, History of
Law
United States of America

Wood

Wood is the material that makes up the trunks of trees and shrubs. It has many uses. It can be easily cut and carved into shapes. It can also be burnt as a fuel or used to make paper and other products.

Most wood is strong and hard-wearing. There are two main types: softwood and hardwood. **Softwood** comes from fast-growing trees like pine and spruce. It is useful for building, for making chipboard and for papermaking. **Hardwood** comes from slower-growing trees like oak and mahogany. It is often used to make good-quality furniture, boats and musical instruments.

Using wood

After trees have been cut down, they are taken to sawmills. Here large power saws cut them up into planks. Sometimes thin layers of wood called **veneers** are shaved off the tree trunk to decorate furniture or to make products like **plywood**. The waste wood from the sawing can be used to make **chipboard**.

Some wood products are made by breaking down the wood using chemical processes. Lignin is a chemical from wood that is used for plastics and road-building materials. Wood pulp is used for making paper and fabrics like viscose and rayon used in clothes.

▼ Paper is made from wood pulp. This is produced by stripping off the bark, cutting the wood into chips and then breaking the chips down into fibres using chemicals. The pulp then passes into giant machines, which spread out the pulp, drain out the water, then press it and dry it.

▲ Wood is often used in buildings. This house in Montana, USA, has a frame made of wood. The walls are also made of wood planks.

find out more
Construction
Forests
Trees

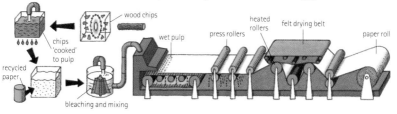

recycled paper
chips 'cooked' to pulp
wood chips
bleaching and mixing
wet pulp
press rollers
heated rollers
felt drying belt
paper roll

World War I

World War I lasted from 1914 to 1918. It changed the course of history. Fighting was worldwide on land and sea and, for the first time, in the air. Empires were destroyed and Europe lost a whole generation of young men.

Britain and Allies

Germany and Central Powers

neutral country

After the creation of the mighty German empire in 1871, France, Russia and Britain allied to defend themselves. Germany allied with Austria-Hungary, and by 1908 Europe was divided into two 'armed camps'. Rivalry over trade, colonies and the size of armed forces increased the tension.

War came when Austria-Hungary attacked Serbia, a Russian ally. Germany backed Austria-Hungary (the **Central Powers**), and France stood by Russia (the **Allies**). Before long, Britain, the Ottoman empire (Turkey) and Italy were also involved. The fighting spread to the Middle East and beyond.

▼ British troops going 'over the top' of their trench during the Battle of the Somme. They ran across open ground laced with barbed wire – known as 'no-man's land' – towards machine-gun fire.

Death in the trenches

Machine guns dominated the fighting. To shelter from bullets and shells, troops dug hundreds of miles of **trenches** (the **Western Front** and the **Eastern Front**). In these dirty and unhealthy holes they lived like rats. Attack was virtually suicide. Around Verdun some three-quarters of a million men died fighting over a few kilometres of earth.

In vain, commanders tried to end the deadlock with artillery bombardment, **mines**, and **poison gas**. Only when reliable **tanks** appeared in 1917 was the stalemate broken. By then millions had died.

Total war

The war affected everyone. Men had to join the armed forces, and women had to take

over their work in fields, offices and factories. Industry was geared to making armaments and supplies.

Both sides tried to cut off their enemies' food supplies. Britain blockaded German ports, German **submarines** torpedoed ships travelling to Britain. Many of these ships were American, and in 1917 the USA joined the war against Germany.

Russia came under communist rule and withdrew from the war in 1917. But, backed-up by American power, the Allies gained ground. By mid-1918 the Central Powers were in retreat, and in November the gunfire finally stopped.

The war to end all wars

The war cost some 10 million lives and destroyed the Russian, German, Austro-Hungarian and Ottoman empires. Britain and France were exhausted. When the peacemakers met in 1919, they agreed the conflict had been a 'war to end all wars'. But sadly, they did not sow seeds of friendship, but punished the losers. Twenty years later Europe was at war again.

▶ Posters like this one called on women to go to work in the arms factories. After the war, governments could not ignore the vital role that women had played – and in many countries women at last gained the vote.

THESE WOMEN ARE DOING THEIR BIT

LEARN TO MAKE MUNITIONS

KEY DATES

1879 Germany and Austria-Hungary become allies

1904 Britain and France sign *entente cordiale* (agreement)

1907 Russia joins *entente*

1914 Austria-Hungary attacks Serbia: beginning of war
Trench warfare starts

1915 Poison gas used
Submarine attacks on merchant ships

1916 German attack: Battle of Verdun
British attack: Battle of the Somme

1917 Revolution in Russia
USA enters war
British attack: Battle of Ypres
First successful use of tanks

1918 Russia makes peace
German spring offensive
'Black day of the German army' (8 August)
Armistice (ceasefire: 11 November)

find out more

Britain, History of
France
Germany
Ottoman empire
Russia
United States of America
Weapons
World War II

▼ One of the early British tanks. Although slow and unreliable, tanks made a breakthrough on the Western Front possible.

World War II

World War II was several overlapping wars, all fought at the same time. Just about everyone in the world was affected by the conflict. The casualties, particularly among civilians, were horrific, and it ended with the greatest nightmare of all – nuclear attack.

Allies and neutral countries
German conquests and allies
Japanese conquests and allies
— limit of Japanese conquests

▲ The war in Europe (left) and in the Pacific (right).

Japan's warlike leaders secretly planned to take over South-east Asia. They began in 1937 with an attack on China. Meanwhile in Europe the German leader Adolf **Hitler** was also planning to conquer an empire. Many Germans supported him. They liked his strong leadership. Too late, they realized their mistake. Hitler's Nazi Party destroyed all opposition and persecuted minority

▼ The pain of war. Russians searching for their missing loved ones in the city of Kursk. Before leaving the city, the Germans had carried out a dreadful massacre of civilians.

groups, especially Jews. After rounding up every Jew they could find, the Nazis began exterminating them (the **Holocaust**).

Abroad, Hitler joined Austria to Germany, broke up Czechoslovakia and, in 1939, invaded Poland. This launched a general European war. In alliance with the Italians, the German armies swept through mainland Europe. Their **Blitzkrieg** tactics – swift strikes with aircraft and armour – seemed unstoppable.

Only Britain and the neutral countries escaped. Britain was saved by the **battle of Britain** in 1940. It then faced years of bombing and attacks on vital supply ships.

Russia and America

In 1941 the war spread across the world. Hitler launched a huge attack deep into Russia. He was finally stopped by the sieges of Leningrad (St Petersburg) and **Stalingrad** (Volgograd). The German defeat at Stalingrad was a turning point in the war.

▲ The Yanks are coming! American troops wading ashore in Normandy, northern France, on D-Day, 6 June 1944.

Another turning point had come in December 1941, when the Japanese made a surprise air raid on **Pearl Harbor**, a US naval base in the Pacific Ocean. America immediately entered the war against both Japan and Germany. By mid-1942 they

▼ Total destruction. The Japanese city of Hiroshima after being hit by the world's first atomic bomb. 80,000 died at once, and 60,000 more within a year.

were fighting back across the Pacific, freeing the empire that Japan had conquered. The next year they spearheaded an invasion of Italy.

Victory

The Americans, British and their allies invaded north-west Europe on **D-Day** 1944, and began the long push towards Germany. In the east, the Russians slowly drove the enemy from their country and continued into Germany itself.

In May 1945 Germany surrendered. The Japanese had now lost all their conquests. Rather than invade Japan, the Americans wiped out the Japanese cities of **Hiroshima** and Nagasaki with atomic bombs. Six days later Japan surrendered, and the war was finally over. It had cost an incredible 50 million lives.

find out more

Europe
France
Germany
Japan
Racism
United Kingdom
United States of America
World War I

Worms

Worms have long bodies but no backbone or limbs. There are three main types: segmented worms, roundworms and flatworms.

find out more

Animals
Life on Earth

Earthworms and leeches are **segmented worms**. Their bodies are made up of a series of similar segments, or parts. Their head contains a brain, and their mouths have tiny horny jaws.

Earthworms burrow in the ground. They eat soil to get tiny scraps of food. This helps to turn over the soil and keep it fertile.

Leeches may live in ponds or streams, in the sea, or in hot, humid places. Their saliva contains a chemical that prevents blood from clotting. Many feed by sucking blood from other animals.

Flatworms do not have segmented bodies. They usually live in water. One type of flatworm, the tapeworm, lives as a **parasite** in the guts of vertebrates, such as pigs, mice, whales and people.

▲ Leeches have a sucker at both ends of their body, which they use to hang onto plants or rocks. Many eat only once every few months.

◄ An earthworm.

Roundworms, or nematodes, are usually less than 2 millimetres long. Huge numbers live in the soil, in the sea and in fresh water. Some live as parasites in people and animals, and can cause diseases.

Blood-suckers!
In the past doctors in Europe believed that many illnesses were located in the blood. They used leeches to suck blood from their patients – to cure them.

▼ Three different kinds of flatworms. Flatworms usually live in water or moist places.

▼ A roundworm.

liver fluke (flukes are a type of flatworm)

planaria – a non-parasitic flatworm

tapeworm – a parasitic flatworm

Writers

Lots of people write all sorts of things every day – from letters and postcards to shopping lists and emails. But we usually use the word 'writer' to describe someone who writes to entertain us, often by telling us some kind of story.

A writer is popular if lots of people read what they write. But a writer is great if people continue to read them for many generations – for hundreds or even thousands of years.

Fashions in writing change. They also vary around the world. There are many different kinds of writing: poetry, plays and novels are three of the most important. Today many writers write for film, television or radio.

Early writers

Much of the earliest writing that survives is in the form of **epic poetry**. Epic poems often tell long stories of gods and goddesses, heroes and heroines, monsters and dragons. Many were probably passed on by word of mouth before they were written down. The earliest-known epic poem is *Gilgamesh*, a Babylonian tale of an ancient hero-king. The longest is the Indian epic the *Mahabharata*, which tells of civil war between two branches of the same family.

The most famous ancient epics in the West are Greek poems, *The Iliad* and *The Odyssey*. They tell stories of war, adventure, love and betrayal.

The oldest surviving plays are ancient **Greek tragedies** – in which noble men and women

▲ The Russian novelist Leo Tolstoy at work in his study.

● We usually call someone a writer if their writing is published, and if we, the audience, pay to read what they have written. Some writers publish novels, others poetry or plays. People who write for newspapers and magazines (journalists) are also writers.

▼ In *The Odyssey* the Greek hero Odysseus tells how the Greeks finally defeated the Trojans after 10 years of war. They built a wooden horse and left it outside the city of Troy. The Trojans accepted the horse as a peace-offering, and took it inside the walls. But hidden inside were Greek soldiers, who opened the gates to the Greek army. This story and many others from *The Iliad* and *The Odyssey* have been used again and again in Western writing and art.

are destroyed by fate, and by weaknesses in their own characters. One of the greatest writers of Greek tragedies was **Aeschylus**.

The Indian writer **Kalidasa**, who lived during the 5th century, wrote plays and long poems. He took his stories from Hindu mythology.

The Middle Ages

One of the earliest English poems to have survived is the 8th-century Anglo-Saxon epic *Beowulf*, the tale of a hero who kills a monster but who is himself later killed by a dragon.

The Italian poet **Dante Alighieri** wrote his *Divine Comedy* in the 13th century. This beautiful poem describes his journey through Hell, Purgatory and Paradise.

▼ Dante Alighieri with a copy of *The Divine Comedy*. Dante was one of the first great writers to write in the language of ordinary people, rather than in Latin.

◀ Jane **Austen** was writing in England at the beginning of the 19th century. Her six witty novels, which include *Pride and Prejudice* and *Emma*, gently mock the behaviour of her day.

Two other medieval Italian writers, Francesco **Petrarch** and Giovanni **Boccaccio**, had a powerful influence on later writers, including Shakespeare. Petrarch is famous for his love sonnets, while Boccaccio wrote the *Decameron* – 100 tales of adventure, trickery and love.

Theatre's golden age

The most famous playwright of all time is William **Shakespeare**. He was writing in England in the 16th century, at the time of Elizabeth I – when the theatre was hugely popular.

A century later, at the court of Louis XIV, French drama was flourishing. **Racine** was a powerful writer of tragedies, while **Molière** wrote witty comedies.

The Romantic poets

Some of the best-known poets belong to a movement called **Romanticism**, which emerged in the late 18th century. The Romantic poets wrote about nature. They believed that individual experience and the imagination were very important. The German poet Johann Wolfgang von **Goethe** was one of the leaders of Romanticism. British Romantic poets include William **Wordsworth** and John **Keats**.

Novelists

A novel is a long story written in everyday language (prose). It often paints a realistic picture of everyday life. The first novel of all was probably *Don Quixote*, written in 17th-century Spain, by **Cervantes**. It tells the story of a foolish man who thinks he is a knight in the days of chivalry, and his sensible squire.

The popularity of the novel spread. French writers such as Gustave **Flaubert** and Emile **Zola** wrote detailed portraits of life in 19th-century France. In Russia Leo **Tolstoy** wrote *War and Peace*, which tells the story of three families in Russia at the time of the Napoleonic wars. In the USA Mark **Twain** wrote tales of adventure set along the Mississippi River.

◄ When Charlotte **Brontë** published her novel *Jane Eyre* in mid-Victorian England, she used a made-up name, Currer Bell. Many women wrote novels, but some thought they would be taken more seriously if people thought they were men. *Jane Eyre* is the story of an orphan girl's search for independence and happiness.

Modern writers

Novels continued to be popular in the 20th century. But many novelists, such as James **Joyce** and Virginia **Woolf**, concentrated on what goes on inside their characters' heads rather than on exciting plots.

The popularity of the novel spread to countries outside Europe too, particularly places that had been part of European empires. The Colombian writer Gabriel **García Márquez** wrote stories about family life and politics in South America that were realistic, but also partly magical. And the black American writer Toni **Morrison** wrote powerfully about black women's experiences during and after slavery.

Writing for children

Some writers have written specially for children. Lewis **Carroll** wrote *Alice in Wonderland* to entertain some children that he knew. A writer who is very popular with children today is Roald **Dahl**, who created some lively children in adventure stories such as *Charlie and the Chocolate Factory*.

◄ Charles **Dickens's** novels are full of larger-than-life characters, caught up in fast-moving plots. Dickens was probably the most popular novelist in Britain in the 19th century. This is an illustration from *David Copperfield*, Dickens's own favourite.

find out more

Drama
Myths and folk tales
Poetry
Television

Zoos

Zoos are places where people can go to see wild animals from many parts of the world.

The earliest zoos were collections of animals made by kings and noblemen. Today there are many types of zoo. One type is the **oceanarium**, which keeps dolphins and other sea creatures. Another is the **safari park**, in which the visitors stay in their cars while the animals roam in large enclosures.

What zoos do

Modern zoos do not keep animals just for visitors to look at. They also study the animals to find out as much as possible about them, and breed animals to return to the wild.

Breeding is an important part of the work of zoos. Many kinds of animal are very rare in the wild. If enough animals can be bred in zoos, groups can be returned to the wild in areas where they have become extinct.

Running a zoo

Even today, animals in zoos are often kept in bad conditions and are given poor food. But the best zoos have realized the importance of putting the needs of the animals first. Each anim gets the right kind of food, and enclosures are designed as far as possible to be like the animal's natural home. Many animals kept in zoos now live far longer than they would in the wild.

▲ In this oceanarium, a transparent tunnel allows visitors to walk right through a tank containing sharks and other ocean animals.

◄ The calf of this Arabian oryx was born in a zoo. In the early 1970s, the only Arabian oryx in the world were in zoos. They were successfully bred in captivity, and in 1982 a herd of animals was reintroduced into Oman.

Ancient zoos

The Roman emperor Nero is said to have kept a tame tigress called Phoebe. The French emperor Charlemagne kept many animals. His favourite was an elephant called Abul Aba.

---

find out more

Animals
Conservation

Data file

▶ The *Apollo 11* Moon launch.

Map of the world

This map shows all the sovereign countries of the world, as listed on page 416. A sovereign country is a territory with its own government. Grid references, which help you find countries on the map, are also listed on page 416.

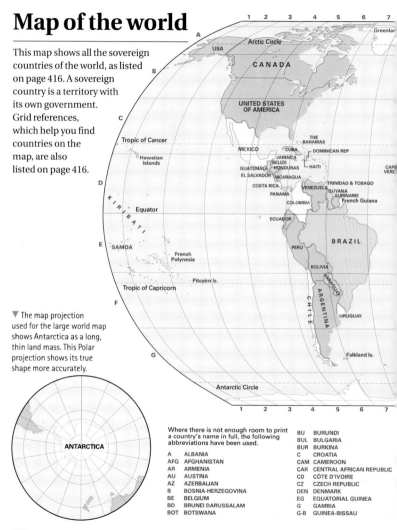

▼ The map projection used for the large world map shows Antarctica as a long, thin land mass. This Polar projection shows its true shape more accurately.

Where there is not enough room to print a country's name in full, the following abbreviations have been used.

A	ALBANIA
AFG	AFGHANISTAN
AR	ARMENIA
AU	AUSTRIA
AZ	AZERBAIJAN
B	BOSNIA-HERZEGOVINA
BE	BELGIUM
BD	BRUNEI DARUSSALAM
BOT	BOTSWANA
BU	BURUNDI
BUL	BULGARIA
BUR	BURKINA
C	CROATIA
CAM	CAMEROON
CAR	CENTRAL AFRICAN REPUBLIC
CD	CÔTE D'IVOIRE
CZ	CZECH REPUBLIC
DEN	DENMARK
EG	EQUATORIAL GUINEA
G	GAMBIA
G-B	GUINEA-BISSAU

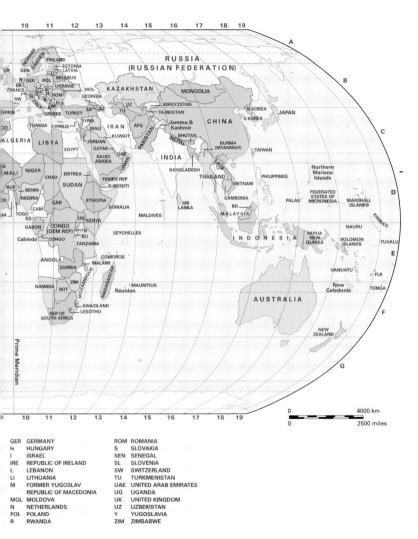

GER	GERMANY
H	HUNGARY
I	ISRAEL
IRE	REPUBLIC OF IRELAND
L	LEBANON
LI	LITHUANIA
M	FORMER YUGOSLAV REPUBLIC OF MACEDONIA
MOL	MOLDOVA
N	NETHERLANDS
POL	POLAND
R	RWANDA

ROM	ROMANIA
S	SLOVAKIA
SEN	SENEGAL
SL	SLOVENIA
SW	SWITZERLAND
TU	TURKMENISTAN
UAE	UNITED ARAB EMIRATES
UG	UGANDA
UK	UNITED KINGDOM
UZ	UZBEKISTAN
Y	YUGOSLAVIA
ZIM	ZIMBABWE

Countries of the world

After each country name is a grid reference relating to the world map on pages 414–415. The letter refers to the letters down the side of the map, the number to the numbers top and bottom of the map.

Afghanistan C13
Albania B10
Algeria C9–10
Andorra B10
Angola E10
Antigua & Barbuda D6
Argentina F6–G6
Armenia B12–C12
Australia F15–17
Austria B10
Azerbaijan B12–C12
Bahamas C6
Bahrain C12
Bangladesh C14
Barbados D7
Belarus B11
Belgium B10
Belize D5
Benin D10
Bhutan C14
Bolivia E6
Bosnia & Herzegovina B10
Botswana F11
Brazil E7–F7
Brunei Darussalam D15
Bulgaria B11
Burkina D9
Burma (Myanmar)
  C14–D14
Burundi E11
Cambodia D15
Cameroon D10
Canada B3–7
Cape Verde D8
Central African Rep. D10–11
Chad D10–11
Chile E6–G6
China C13–15
Colombia D6
Comoros E12
Congo, Democratic Rep.
  D10–E11

Congo, Rep. D10–E10
Costa Rica D5
Côte d'Ivoire D9
Croatia B10
Cuba C5–6
Cyprus C11
Czech Rep. B10
Denmark B10
Djibouti D12
Dominica D6
Dominican Rep. D6
Ecuador E6
Egypt C11
El Salvador D5
Equatorial Guinea D10
Eritrea D11
Estonia B11
Ethiopia D11–12
Fiji E18
Finland A11
France B10
Gabon D10–E10
Gambia D9
Georgia B12
Germany B10
Ghana D9–10
Greece C11
Grenada D6
Guatemala D5
Guinea D9
Guinea-Bissau D9
Guyana D7
Haiti D6
Honduras D5
Hungary B10–11
Iceland A9
India C13–D13
Indonesia E15–17
Iran C12
Iraq C12
Ireland, Rep. B9
Israel C11
Italy B10–C10
Jamaica D6
Japan C16–17
Jordan C11
Kazakhstan B12–13
Kenya D11–E11
Kirgyzstan B13
Kiribati D18–E18
Kuwait C12
Laos D15

Latvia B11
Lebanon C11
Lesotho F11
Liberia D9
Libya C10–11
Liechtenstein (see Europe
  map, pages 142–143)
Lithuania B11
Luxembourg B10
Macedonia (FYROM) B11
Madagascar E12–F12
Malawi E11
Malaysia D15
Maldives D13
Mali C9–D9
Malta C10
Mauritania C9–D9
Mauritius F12
Mexico C4–5
Moldova B11
Monaco B10
Mongolia B14–15
Morocco C9
Mozambique E11–F11
Namibia F10
Nauru E18
Nepal C14
Netherlands B10
New Zealand F18–G18
Nicaragua D5
Niger D10
Nigeria D10
North Korea B16–C16
Norway A10
Oman C12–D12
Pakistan C13
Palau D16
Panama D5–6
Papua New Guinea E17
Paraguay F7
Peru E6
Philippines D16
Poland B10–11
Portugal C10
Qatar C12
Romania B11
Russia B11–A19
Rwanda E11
St Kitts-Nevis D6
St Lucia D6
St Vincent &
  the Grenadines D6

Samoa E1
San Marino (see Europe
  map, pages 142–143)
São Tomé & Príncipe D10
Saudi Arabia C12–D12
Senegal D9
Seychelles E12
Sierra Leone D9
Singapore D15
Slovakia B10–11
Slovenia B10
Solomon Islands E18
Somalia D12
South Africa F11
South Korea C16
Spain B9–C9
Sri Lanka D14
Sudan D11
Suriname D7
Swaziland F11
Sweden A10–B10
Switzerland B10
Syria C11
Taiwan C16
Tajikistan C13
Tanzania E11
Thailand D14–15
Togo D10
Tonga E19–F19
Trinidad &Tobago D6
Tunisia C10
Turkey C11–12
Turkmenistan C12–13
Tuvalu E18
Uganda D11–E11
Ukraine B11
United Arab Emirates C12
United Kingdom B9
United States of America
  B4–C4
Uruguay F7
Uzbekistan B13–C13
Vanuatu E18
Vatican City (see Europe
  map, pages 142–143)
Venezuela D6
Vietnam C15–D15
Yemen D12
Yugoslavia B10–11
Zambia E11
Zimbabwe E11–F11

Wonders of the world

HIGHS AND LOWS
Highest mountains
1 Everest, Nepal/Tibet – 8848 m
2 K2, Kashmir/China – 8611 m
3 Kangchenjunga, Nepal/Sikkim – 8598 m

Longest mountain ranges
1 Andes, S. America – 7242 km
2 Rocky Mountains, North America – 6035 km
3 Himalayas/Karakoram/Hindu Kush, Asia – 3862 km

Lowest lands
1 Dead Sea, Israel, Jordan – 400 m below sea level
2 Turfan depression, China – 154 m below sea level
3 Qattâra Depression, Egypt – 133 m below sea level

▲ Gorges are very deep valleys with almost vertical sides.

Deepest gorge
The Grand Canyon, USA, is the largest land gorge on Earth. It extends over a distance of 446 km, with an average depth of 1.6 km.

WATER WORLD RECORDS
Longest river
The River Nile in Africa stretches from its source in Lake Victoria, Burundi, to the Mediterranean Sea – an incredible 6670 km.

Biggest river
The average flow of water from the mouth of the Amazon River, Brazil, into the South Atlantic Ocean is 175,000 cubic metres per second.

Deepest freshwater lake
At its deepest point, Lake Baykal in Russia is 1637 m.

Highest waterfall
Angel Falls, Venezuela, have a total drop of 979 m. This is more than twice the height of the Petronas Towers, the tallest building in the world.

OCEANS OF THE WORLD
Largest oceans
1 Pacific – 166,240,000 sq km
2 Atlantic – 86,560,000 sq km
3 Indian – 73,430,000 sq km

Deepest oceans
1 Pacific – 10,924 m deep
2 Atlantic – 9219 m deep
3 Indian – 7455 m deep

WEATHER RECORDS
Hottest place in the world
Dallol, Ethiopia, with an annual average temperature of 34.4 °C.

Driest place in the world
Atacama Desert, Chile. The Atacama also holds the world record for the longest drought. When it rained in 1971, it was the first time in 400 years!

Wettest place in the world
Buenaventura, Columbia, has an average annual rainfall of 6743 mm.

Most rainy days in a year
Mount Waialeale, Hawaii: there are often 350 rainy days per year.

Coldest place in the world
Plateau Station in Antarctica has the coldest measured average temperature, of −56.6 °C.

Sunniest place in the world
Eastern Sahara: 97% sunshine – over 4300 hours a year.

Windiest place in the world
Commonwealth Bay, George V Coast, Antarctica, has gales of up to 320 km/h.

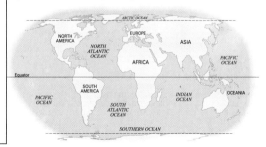

DESERT RECORDS

Largest hot desert
Sahara Desert, 8.4 million sq km

Highest temperature
58 °C, recorded in Libya in 1922

Longest drought
400 years, in the Atacama Desert, Chile

Highest sand dunes
430 m high, in eastern Algeria

AMAZING ANIMALS

Largest animal
The largest animal in the world is a mammal, the blue whale. An adult blue whale can be 30 m in length and weigh over 100 tonnes. Male African elephants are the largest land animals. The largest on record was 3.96 m tall.

Tallest animal
Male giraffes, which live in the savannah and woodland of Africa, can grow to a height of 5.5 m.

Fastest bird
The peregrine falcon can reach speeds of up to 200 km/h as it swoops to catch its prey.

Fastest land animal
For a short distance on level ground a cheetah can run at up to 100 km/h.

▲ A cheetah, the fastest animal on land.

Fastest fish
The sailfish can swim at speeds of up to 109 km/h.

Slowest mammal?
The three-toed sloth from South America moves at an average speed of about 2 m/min. In the trees it speeds up slightly, but only to 4.6 m/min!

Slowest grower
The slowest-growing animal is a type of deep-sea clam. It takes 100 years to grow just 8 mm.

INSECTS AND SPIDERS

Heaviest insect
Male goliath beetles, found in central Africa, can weigh up to 100 g, and measure 11 cm in length.

▲ A violet ground beetle.

Longest insect
A kind of stick insect from Borneo in South-east Asia can have a body length of 33 cm.

Biggest moth
The Hercules moth, found in Australia and New Guinea, can have a wingspan of up to 36 cm.

Fastest insect on land
Some kinds of cockroach can travel at speeds of 5.4 km/h. This is the equivalent of a human runner reaching speeds of 330 km/h.

Biggest spider
The goliath bird-eating spider, found in the rainforests of northern South America, can grow to a size of 28 cm.

Biggest spider's web
Webs of the golden orb-web spider *Nephila* can be up to 3 m in length. They are so strong that they are used as fishing nets.

▼ A tarantula.

PLANTS

Biggest plant
Trees are the biggest plants, and the biggest trees are the giant redwoods of California, USA. 'General Sherman' is the most massive of all: it is 87 m tall and has a girth of 31 m. Another redwood is the tallest living tree – it is 112 m tall.

Oldest plant
The oldest-known living plant is a Bristlecone pine called 'Methuselah' in California, USA. It is 4765 years old.

Biggest and smallest flowers
The biggest single flower is produced by the parasitic plant *Rafflesia*, which grows in South-east Asia. It can measure over 90 cm across. The smallest type of flowering plant is the least duckweed, a tiny water plant scarcely 1mm across.

Wonders of the world

COUNTRIES

Largest
Russia is the biggest country by size: it has an area of 17,075,400 sq km. China is the country with the most people. Its population is 1.21 billion.

Smallest
The smallest country in the world is the Vatican City, within the Italian captial city of Rome. It has a population of only 1000, and an area of 0.44 sq km. The Vatican is the centre of the Roman Catholic Church, headed by the Pope. It has its own police force, and issues its own stamps and coins.

Most crowded
Among larger countries, the most crowded is Bangladesh, with over 800 people per sq km.

TALLEST BUILDINGS

The tallest free-standing tower in the world is the CN Tower in Toronto, at 553 m high. The tallest building that can be lived in is the Petronas Twin Towers in Kuala Lumpur, Malaysia (452 m).

▼ How buildings have grown taller over the ages.

Empire State Building, USA, 1931: 381 m (with mast 449 m)

Eiffel Tower, France, 1889: 300 m

| Great Pyramid, Egypt, about 2580 BC: 147 m | Pharos lighthouse, Egypt, about 280 BC: 135 m | Lincoln Cathedral, UK, AD 1307: 160 m | Petronas Towers, Malaysia, 1996: 452 m | CN Tower, Canada, 1976: 553 m |

TRANSPORT

Fastest land vehicle
In October 1997, at Black Rock Desert, Nevada, USA, the jet-powered car *Thrust SSC* set a world land speed record of 1228 km/h – faster than the speed of sound.

▼ *Thrust SSC.*

Fastest aircraft
The fastest jet aircraft is the US Air Force Lockheed SR-71A 'Blackbird' reconnaissance plane, which can reach speeds of over 3500 km/h.

Fastest train
The French TGV (*Train á Grande Vitesse*) is the fastest train. In 1990 a special TGV reached a speed of 515.3 km/h.

Biggest land vehicle
The 'Marion' crawler is a flat-topped vehicle used to take Space Shuttles to their launch pad. The crawler is 40 m long and weighs over 8000 tonnes when loaded.

Biggest ship
The largest ship is an oil tanker, *Jahre Viking*. It is nearly 500 m long and weighs over half a million tonnes.

Longest railway
The longest train journey you can make without changing trains is the 9297-km trip from Moscow to Vladivostock, Russia, on the Trans-Siberian Railway.

Longest road
The Pan-American highway runs south from Alaska, USA, to Santiago, Chile, then east to Brasilia, Brazil – a total of 24,140 km.

CITIES

World's biggest cities
Different countries measure the population of their cities in different ways, so it is difficult to compare city size accurately. But according to official figures, these are the world's five biggest cities:

1 Tokyo, Japan 26,836,000
2 São Paulo, Brazil 16,417,000
3 New York, USA 16,329,000
4 Mexico City, Mexico 15,643,000
5 Mumbai (Bombay), India 15,093,000

The largest African city is Lagos, Nigeria (10,287,000); the largest Asian city is Tokyo (see above); the largest European city is Paris, France (9,469,000); the largest North American city is New York (see above); the largest South American city is São Paolo (see above).

Time zones

Because the Earth spins, places across the world have day and night at different times. But if everyone used different local times, it would be very confusing. Because of this, the world is divided up into 24 'time zones,' each of about 15° longitude.

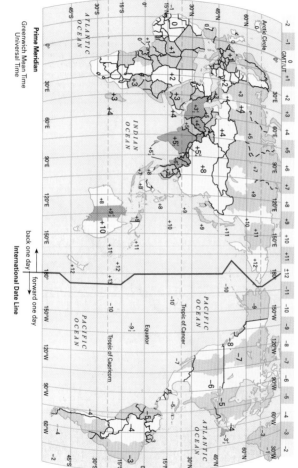

Key

- even number of hours different from GMT
- odd number of hours ahead or behind Greenwich mean Time (GMT) a place is.
- ½-hour difference from adjacent zone
- less than ½-hour difference from next zone

Constellations

The patterns made by groups of the brightest stars are called **constellations**. These star groups all have their own names. Some were named by the Greeks 2000 years ago, and Arab and Chinese astronomers had their own constellations too. These early astronomers probably invented the constellations as a way of referring to particular stars.

There are 88 constellations and they cover the whole sky. Although the stars in a constellation look close together, they are really vast distances apart. The constellations you can see at any one time vary according to the season, the time of night and where you are on Earth. Star charts, like those on this page, will help you find some of the constellations.

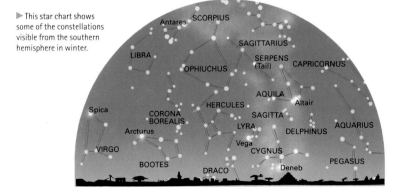

▶ This star chart shows some of the constellations visible from the northern hemisphere in winter.

▶ This star chart shows some of the constellations visible from the southern hemisphere in winter.

Timeline of world history

	Before 10,000 BC	10,000 BC	5000 BC	2500 BC
ASIA	• Hunter-gatherers • A variety of stone tools used – knives, axes, needles, harpoons	• Rice and millet farming begins and spreads • Pottery made in Japan and China	• Horses domesticated on steppes (grassland) • Cities in China • Silk-weaving in China	• Cities in Indus Valley • Cotton grown in Indus Valley • Aryans invade northern India • Beginnings of Hindu religion
AMERICAS AND OCEANIA	• Hunter-gatherers • Cave drawings in Australia from about 40,000 BC	• Hunter-gatherers • Canoes and sledges used	• Maize (corn) farmed in Mexico • Pottery made in South America • Llamas domesticated in Andes • Root crops grown in New Guinea	• Colonization of Pacific Islands by canoe • Temples built in Peru, and cotton cultivated • Metalworking in Peru
AFRICA AND MIDDLE EAST	• First humans • From 100,000 BC people spread through all continents • Cave drawings from about 27,000 BC • Bow invented • Female figurines made	• Cereal farming from 9000 BC • Wheel invented • Dogs, cattle, sheep and goats domesticated • Copper used • City of Jericho built	◄ An early plough • Plough invented • Horses and camels domesticated • Sumer civilization begins • Bronze and pottery made • Writing invented	• Pyramids built in Egypt • Sumer civilization • New Kingdom in Egypt • Beginnings of Jewish religion
EUROPE	• Hunter-gatherers • Cave paintings from 30,000 BC • Bow invented • Female figurines made	• Farming in Balkans and Greece from 7000 BC • Canoes and sledges used • Animals domesticated and herded	• Standing stones and circles • Flint mines • Farming spreads • Ploughs used ◄ Stonehenge, Britain, built around 2800 BC	• Bronze objects made • Minoan civilization in Crete • Mycenaean civilization in Greece ▲ Golden burial mask from Mycenae

422

Timeline of world history

1000 BC	500 BC	AD 1	AD 250	AD 499
• Zhou dynasty in China • Taosim founded in China • Iron objects made in China • Confucius (Kongzi) and Buddha lived	• Mauryan empire in India • Alexander the Great invades India • Great Wall of China built • Qin dynasty unifies China • Great Silk Road opens	• Han dynasty in China • Buddhism reaches China and South-east Asia • Paper invented in China • Emperors in Japan ◀ Terracotta horse from the tomb of Chinese 'First Emperor'	• Gupta empire in India • Horse-collar harness first used in China	
• Settlements in Polynesia • Chavin culture in Peru • Pottery made in Arctic • Olmec civilization in Mexico ◀ A giant stone head made by Olmec sculptors	• Olmec civilization ends • City of Teotihuacán built in Mexico • Early Maya culture in Central America • Hieroglyphic writing develops in Mexico	• Large states in Central America • Huge stone temples built in Peru	• Maya civilization in Central America grows • Nazca civilization in southern Peru	
• Kingdom of Kush in East Africa • Assyrian empire • Kingdom of Israel • First coins, Lydia, Turkey • Persian empire • Assyrians conquer Israel	• Nok culture in Nigeria • Alexander the Great conquers Persian empire • Romans destroy Carthage and conquer Syria, Palestine and Egypt • Birth of Jesus	• Jews expelled from Jerusalem • Beginnings of Christianity • Kingdom of Axum, Ethiopia	▲ Madonna and child from a Byzantine icon • Byzantine empire succeeds Roman empire in east	
• Celts move into Germany and France • Greek city states • Greek alphabet develops • Roman republic founded • Hillforts in western Europe	• Great age of Athens • Alexander the Great conquers Greece • Romans rule all Italy and conquer Spain • Growth of Roman empire • Augustus first Roman emperor	▲ Colosseum, Rome, completed AD 80 • Roman empire at its height • Christianity spreads	• Collapse of Roman empire in west • Spread of Christianity continues • Frankish kingdom founded	

423

Timeline of world history

	AD 500	750	1000	1250
ASIA	• Large Chinese empire under Tang dynasty	• Beginning of Fujiwara period in Japan • Tang dynasty in China • Chinese invent printing and gunpowder	• Genghis Khan creates Mongol empire • Mongols conquer Russia • Khmer kingdom in South-east Asia ▶ A Khmer temple, Angkor, Cambodia	• Yuan (Mongol) and Ming dynasties in China • Conquests of Tamerlane • Russia defeats Mongols • Portuguese reach India • Growth of Vietnam
AMERICAS AND OCEANIA	▲ A Mayan temple • Maya civilization at its height	• Toltec civilization in Mexico	• Vikings sail to North America • Polynesians settle in Hawaii, New Zealand and Easter Island • Growth of Inca empire, Peru	• Aztec and Inca empires at their height • Columbus reaches America
AFRICA AND MIDDLE EAST	▶ Islamic mosque, Persia • Muhammad founds Islam • Sassanid (Persian) empire at its height • Arab conquests in northern Africa	• Abbasid caliphate rules Muslim empire from Baghdad • Empire of Ghana, West Africa • Great Zimbabwe, East Africa	• Christian crusaders invade Middle East • Saladin defeats crusaders • Turks conquer Palestine	• Mongols destroy Abbasid caliphate • Empires of Benin and Mali in West Africa • Black Death ▶ Bronze cast from Benin
EUROPE	• Gregory the Great establishes the power of the pope • Muslims conquer Spain	▶ A Viking longboat • Viking raids and settlement • Empire of Charlemagne • England united • Beginning of Holy Roman Empire	• Break between Roman and Greek (Byzantine) Churches • Normans conquer England and Sicily	• 100 Years War between England and France • Ottoman Turks capture Constantinople • Black Death • Renaissance begins

Timeline of world history

1500	1700	1800	1900 2000
• Babur founds Mughal empire • Beginning of Sikh religion in Punjab • Qing (Manzhou) dynasty in China • Tokugawa shoguns in Japan • Russian expansion reaches Pacific	• Qing dynasty continues • Decline of Mughal empire • British control much of India	• Europeans dominate trade in Asia • Opium Wars in China • Taiping rebellion in China • Indians rebel against British • Japan begins to modernize	• China becomes a republic, then a communist state • Rise and fall of Japanese empire • India and other countries gain independence • World War II • Vietnam War
• Spanish conquer Aztecs and Incas • Fleet led by Magellan sails round world • European colonies in North and South America • Slavery grows	▶ The first US flag, 1776 • British defeat French in Canada • USA gains independence • First European settlers in Australia	• Spanish and Portuguese colonies gain independence • USA expands through Louisiana purchase and Mexican war • American Civil War • Europeans settle in Australia and New Zealand	• USA becomes leading world power • Civil rights movement • Astronauts on Moon • Technological revolution begins ▼ A communications satellite
• Ottoman (Turkish) empire at its height • Atlantic slave trade begins • Dutch settlers in South Africa	• Slave trade grows • Ottoman power declines • Asante kingdom in West Africa ◀ A gold statue of an eagle made by Asante craftspeople	• Slave trade ends • Africa divided into European colonies	• Turkey becomes a republic • African and Arab states gain independence • Israel founded • Apartheid in South Africa
• Reformation (Protestants split from Catholic Church) • Ottomans invade central Europe • Wars of religion • Thirty Years War • France becomes leading European power	• England and Scotland united • Russia dominant in northern Europe • French Revolution • Start of Industrial Revolution	▲ Stephenson's 'Rocket', an early steam locomotive • Napoleonic wars • Industrial Revolution continues • Italy united • Germany united	• World Wars I and II • Russian Revolution • Ireland gains independence • Eastern Europe under Soviet communist control • European Union founded

425

Sports facts

On the following pages we look at different sports, and some of the records that have been set by top sportspeople.

AERIAL SPORTS
Aerial sports are sports that happen in the air, such as gliding, hang-gliding, skydiving, hot-air ballooning and aerobatics.

Around the world in 20 days
In 1999 Brian Jones (UK) and Bertrand Piccard (Switzerland) made the first round-the-world balloon flight. They flew 46,759 km in 19 days, 21 hours and 55 minutes. Their balloon, the *Breitling Orbiter*, used a combination of helium gas and hot air. It was as tall as the Leaning Tower of Pisa and weighed as much as a fighter plane.

Helicopter circumnavigation
In 1996 John Williams and Ron Bower from the USA made the fastest flight around the world in a helicopter. They took 17 days, 6 hours, 14 minutes and 25 seconds.

Glider records
In 1972 Hans-Werner Grosse of West Germany flew 1460.8 km in his glider. The longest hang-glider flight was 495 km, made by Larry Tudor of the USA in 1994.

Oldest fliers
Hildegarde Ferrera made a parachute jump in Hawaii, USA, in 1996, when she was 99. In the same year, at Cust in New Zealand, Florence Laine flew in a hot-air balloon, aged 102.

ANIMAL SPORTS
Sports involving animals include bullfighting, gymkhanas, horse racing, pigeon racing, polo, rodeo, and show-jumping.

An ancient race
The oldest horse-racing contest in the world is thought to be the Palio, a bareback race held in Siena, Italy, which began in the 15th century. The Palio lasts only about a minute, as riders from 10 teams charge three times round the Piazza del Campo (the city square).

Grand National
The Grand National is the UK's best-known steeplechase (horse race over fences). The fastest times for the race are:

1 1990 – Mr Frisk (8 min 47.8 s)
2 1973 – Red Rum (9 min 1.9 s)
3 1995 – Royal Athlete (9 min 4.6 s).

Manifesto raced in the Grand National eight times, winning in 1897 and 1899.

ATHLETIC SPORTS
The term 'athletics' usually includes running, walking, hurdling and 'field' events such as jumping, vaulting and throwing. Other athletic sports are climbing, gymnastics, marathon running and orienteering.

▼ An athletics track showing the starting positions of the running events, all of which finish in the same place.

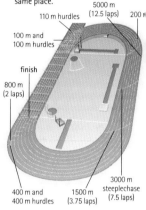

Fastest 100 m
Men's: 9.79 s Maurice Green (USA) 16 June 1999. Women's: 10.49 s, Delorez Florence Griffith Joyner (USA), 16 July 1988.

Fastest 1500 m
Men's: 3 min 26.00 s Hicham El Guerrouj (Morocco), 14 July 1998. Women's: 3 min 50.46 s Qu Yunxia (China), 11 September 1993.

Fastest marathon
Men's: 2 hr 6 min 5 s Ronaldo da Costa (Brazil), 20 September 1998. Women's: 2 hr 20 min 47 s Tegla Louroupe (Kenya) 19 April 1998.

All in a day's work!

On 25 May 1935 Jesse Owens of USA astonished the athletics world when he set four world records in less than an hour! He ran 100 yards (91 m) in 9.4 seconds at 3.15 pm, made an 8.13-m long jump at 3.25 pm, ran 220 yards in 20.3 seconds at 3.45 pm and did the 220-yard low hurdle track in 22.6 seconds at 4 pm.

High jump

Men's: 2.54 m, Javier Sotomayor (Cuba), 27 July 1993. Women's: 2.09 m, Stefka Kostadinova (Bulgaria), 30 August 1987.

Pole vault

Men's: 6.14 m, Sergey Nazarovich Bubka (Ukraine), 1 July 1994. Women's: 4.60 m, Emma George (Australia), 20 March 1998 and Stacey Dragila (USA) 22 August 1999.

Long jump

Men's: 8.95 m, Mike Powell (USA), 30 August 1991. Women's: 7.52 m, Galina Chistyakova (USSR), 11 June 1988.

Javelin

Men's: 98.48 m, Jan Zelezny (Ukraine), 25 May 1996. Women's: 80 m, Petra Falke (Germany), 9 September 1988.

COMBAT SPORTS

Combat sports include boxing, fencing, wrestling, and martial arts such as judo, karate, aikido and kung fu.

Most world wrestling titles

Russian Aleksandr Medved won 10 wrestling titles in three weight categories (1962–1964 and 1966–1972).

Most boxing knockouts

In his entire career Archie Moore from USA finished an astounding 145 bouts with knockouts.

Sumo giants

In the Japanese sport of sumo wrestling, all the contestants are huge, but the tallest and heaviest champion in history is Hawaiian-born Chad Rowan (fighting name Akebono). He was 2.04 m tall and weighed 227 kg when he became grand champion in 1993.

Most judo titles

Yashuhiro Yamashita of Japan won four world and one Olympic judo title.

RACKET SPORTS

Racket sports are all played with a racket and ball or, in the case of badminton, a shuttlecock. Other racket games include squash, table tennis, and tennis.

Most Grand Slam wins

Margaret Court of Australia won 24 Grand Slam tennis tournaments between 1960 and 1973: 11 Australian, five US, five French and three Wimbledon.

Longest Grand Slam match

The 1992 US Open semi-final between Stefan Edberg (Sweden) and Michael Chang (USA) lasted 5 hours and 26 minutes.

Fastest tennis serve

239.8 km/h by Greg Rusedski (GB) on 14 March 1998.

Most successful squash player

Female: Susan Devoy (New Zealand), who won four World Open titles. Male: Geoffrey B. Hunt (Australia), who won four World Open titles.

TABLE SPORTS AND GAMES

These are usually played indoors and include chess, billiards, snooker, and card games.

▲ In snooker, players score points for getting the coloured balls into the pockets.

Most snooker world titles

Joe Davis won the World Professional Snooker Championship 15 times (1927–1940, 1946).

Chess king and queen

The youngest world chess champions in history are Gary Kasparov (Russia) and Maya Grigoryevna Chiburdanidze (Georgia). Gary won the title when he was 22 years and 210 days old. Maya took the women's title when she was 17.

Slowest chess move
2 hours 20 minutes by Francisco Torres Trois (Spain) in 1980.

World's biggest jigsaw puzzle
Completed on 8 July 1992 in Marseille, France, it measured 4783 sq m and was made up of 43,924 separate pieces.

Highest Scrabble score
The highest score recorded for one turn is 392, made by Dr Saladin Karl Khoshnaw (UK) in April 1982.

TARGET SPORTS
Target sports involve aiming a ball or other missile, such as an arrow, at a target or hole. They include archery, bowling, darts and golf.

▲ Archery involves shooting at targets with a bow and arrow. The closer an arrow hits to the centre (the bull's eye), the more points the archer scores.

Koreans on target!
South Korea's female archers are the best in the world. Since 1984 no other country has won an Olympic Gold in women's events. In 1995 Kim Jung-rye scored 1377 points out of a possible 1440.

Youngest golf champion
Thuashni Selvaratnam won the 1989 Sri Lankan Ladies' Amateur Open Golf Championship when she was only 12.

Oldest golf champion
Isa Goldschmid won the 1976 Italian Women's Championship when she was 50 years old.

Most money won at golf
By 1999, Greg Norman of Australia had won $12 million during his career.

TEAM SPORTS
These organized sports usually involve teams of people. There are many team sports, including American football, baseball, basketball, cricket, football, hockey, ice hockey, netball, rounders, rugby and volleyball.

Top career scores, American football
1 George Blanda (2002 points)
2 Nick Lowery (1711 points)
3 Jan Stenerud (1699 points).

Top scores in Test cricket
1 Brian Lara (West Indies): 375 runs, 1993–1994 Test series against England.
2 Gary Sobers (West Indies): 365 runs, 1957–1958 Test series against Pakistan.
3 Len Hutton (England): 364 runs, 1938 Test series against Australia.

Most home runs in a season
Baseball player Mark McGwire of the St Louis Cardinals hit 70 home runs in 1998. In the same season, Sammy Sosa hit 66 home runs. The previous record was 61 home runs, set in 1961 by Roger Maris.

Olympic hockey champions
The Indian hockey team were champions in every Olympic Games from 1928 to 1960.

World Cup champions
Football is the world's favourite team sport and the World Cup is the most famous football tournament. Brazil have won the World Cup the most times (four), and scored a record-breaking 173 goals in 80 World Cup matches.

Top scorers, World Cup rugby
1 Grant Fox (New Zealand) 1987 126 points
2 Gavin Hastings (Scotland) 1995 104 points
3 Thierry Lacroix (France) 1995 103 points.

WATER SPORTS
Water sports include canoeing, diving, fishing, jetskiing, rowing, sailing, surfing, swimming, water skiing, windsurfing and yachting.

Youngest world record–holder
Gertrude Ederle (USA) became the youngest world record-holder in any sport in 1919, when she set a record of 13 min 19 s for the women's 880-yard freestyle swimming in 1919. She was 12 years and 298 days old.

Motorbike or ski?

Jetskiing was invented by an American, Clayton Jacobsen, in the 1960s. He created the jetski – a cross between a motorbike and a giant ski – to combine his love of moto-cross and water skiing. Jetskiing is now a highly competitive sport which is played all over the world.

Highest surfing waves

Waves of 9–11 m are regularly found at Waimea Bay, Hawaii, USA. But a wave of 15.24 m high was ridden by Taylor Knox (USA) in 1998 at Todos Santos, Mexico.

Fastest water-skier

In 1983 Christopher Massey (Australia) reached a top speed of 230.26 km/h on his water skis.

Most water-skiers

In 1986 100 skiers were towed behind one boat at Queensland, Australia.

Americas Cup champions

The USA have won every Americas Cup yacht race except two since the America's Cup started in 1870.

WHEELED SPORTS

These include cycling, drag racing, Grand Prix (races for Formula 1 cars), motor sports, motorcycle racing, rallying and roller skating.

Most Grand Prix wins

1 Alain Prost (France): 51 wins in 1981–1993.

2 Ayrton Senna (Brazil): 41 wins in 1985–1993.

3 Michael Schumacher (Germany): 35 wins up to 1999.

Longest motorcycle ride

Emilio Scotto from Argentina rode his motorcycle over 735,000 km across 214 countries between 1985 and 1995.

Flash Clash!

The world's fastest car race is the Busch Clash Race in Daytona, Florida, USA. In 1987 driver Bill Elliott completed the 80.5 km race on a 4-km-long track with an average speed of 318.331 km/h in a Ford Thunderbird.

Most Tour de France wins

The Tour de France is the biggest cycling event in the world. Four riders have won it five times: Jaques Anquetil (France), Eddy Merckx (Belgium), Bernard Hinault (France) and Miguel Induráin (Spain).

▲ Record-breaking tandem cyclists Laura Geoghegan and Mark Tong rode from London, UK to Sydney, Australia between May 1994 and November 1995 – a total distance of 32,248 km.

WINTER SPORTS

Winter sports are those played on snow or ice. They include bobsleighing, ice hockey, ice skating, skiing, dog-sled racing, snowboarding and tobogganing.

▼ In Alpine skiing competitors race down mountain slopes; Nordic skiing includes cross-country racing and ski-jumping.

Fastest ice-yacht

John Buckstaff (USA) reached a speed of 230 km/h in his ice-yacht on Lake Winnebago, Wisconsin, USA, in 1938.

Champion figure skaters

By 1999 Ulrich Salchow (Sweden) had won 10 men's figure skating titles. Between 1927 and 1936 Sonja Henie (Norway) won 10 women's figure skating titles.

A dog's life?

The Iditarod dog-sled race is held every year between Anchorage and Nome in Alaska – a distance of 1864 km. The race is run to remember an emergency in 1925 when dog-sleds were used to bring medical supplies to Nome. It takes its name from a mining village along the route. The fastest time for the race so far is 9 days, 2 hours, 42 minutes and 19 seconds.

Weights and measures

Metric to imperial units

Length
1 kilometre = 0.6214 mile
1 metre (m) = 1.094 yards
1 metre = 3.647 feet
1 centimetre (cm) = 0.394 inch
1 millimetre = 0.039 inch

Area
1 hectare (ha) = 2.471 acres (1 ha = 10,000 m^2)
1 square metre (m^2) = 1.196 square yards

Volume (liquid)
1 litre (l) = 0.22 gallons
1 litre (l) = 1.76 pints
1 millilitre (ml) = 0.002 pint

Mass
1 tonne = 0.984 ton
 (1 tonne = 1000 kg)
1 kilogram (kg) = 0.1575 stone
1 kilogram = 2.205 pounds
1 gram (g) = 0.0353 ounce

Imperial to metric units

Length
1 mile (1760 yards) = 1.609 kilometres
1 yard (3 feet) = 0.9144 metre
1 foot (12 inches) = 0.3048 metre
1 inch = 2.54 centimetres
1 inch = 25.4 millimetres

Area
1 acre (4840 square yards) = 0.405 hectare
1 square yard = 0.836 square metre

Volume (liquid)
1 gallon* (8 pints) = 4.546 litres
1 pint* = 0.568 litre
1 pint = 568 millilitres

Mass
1 ton (28 stones) = 1.016 tonnes
1 stone (14 pounds) = 6.35 kilograms
1 pound (16 ounces) = 0.4536 kilogram
1 ounce = 28.35 grams

* The imperial pint and gallon are not the same as the pint and gallon measures used in the USA. An American liquid pint is 0.473 litre, and a gallon is 3.784 litres; an American dry pint is 0.550 litre.

Metric prefixes

In the metric system, the basic unit of length is the metre. Mass, time and other quantities also have a basic unit. Units smaller or larger than the basic unit have a prefix, which indicates a multiple or fraction of the unit. Thus, for length:

1 **micro**metre (µm) = 1 millionth of a metre
1 **milli**metre (mm) = 1 thousandth of a metre
1 **centi**metre (cm) = 1 hundredth of a metre
1 **kilo**metre (km) = 1000 metres
1 **mega**metre (Mm) = 1 million metres

Index of people

A

Abraham (about 1800 BC) 213
Aeschylus (d. about 456 BC) 110, 117
Aesop (about 620–560 BC) 261
Akbar, Mughal emperor
  (1542–1605) 197
Alcock, John W. (1892–1919) 15
Aldrin, Edwin 'Buzz' (b. 1930) 353
Alexander the Great
  (356–323 BC) 183, 423
Alfred the Great (849–899) 21
Amundsen, Roald (1872–1928) 24
Anderson, Gillian (b. 1968) 367
Anka, Paul (b. 1941) 394
Aristotle (384–322 BC) 281
Arkwright, Richard (1732–1792) 199
Armstrong, Neil (b. 1930) 353
Arthur, King 74, 216
Atahualpa (about 1502–1533) 195
Augustine of Canterbury, St (d. about
  604) 21, 54
Augustus, Roman emperor (63 BC–AD
  14) 317, 319, 423
Austen, Jane (1775–1817) 410

B

Babur, Mughal emperor (1483–
  1530) 425
Bach, Johann Sebastian
  (1685–1750) 82
Bacon, Francis (1561–1626) 325
Baez, Joan (b. 1941) 294
Baird, John Logie (1888–1946) 366
Bandaranaike, Sirimavo (b. 1916) 179
Becquerel, Henri (1852–1908) 305
Beethoven, Ludwig van
  (1770–1827) 83
Bell, Alexander Graham
  (1847–1922) 90, 365
Benz, Karl (1844–1929) 67, 377
Bergman, Ingrid (1915–1982) 153
Berry, Chuck (b. 1926) 293
Bhutto, Benazir (b. 1953) 179
Bismarck, Otto von (1815–1898) 176
Bizet, Georges (1838–1875) 254
Blackbeard (Edward Teach) (about
  1680–1718) 285
Blake, William (1757–1827) 290
Boccaccio, Giovanni (1313–1375) 410
Bogart, Humphrey (1899–1957) 153
Bolívar, Simón (1783–1830) 350
Bonny, Anne (18th century) 285

Botticelli, Sandro
  (1445–1510) 279–280
Bowie, David (b. 1947) 294
Brahe, Tycho (1546–1601) 325
Brontë, Charlotte (1816–1855) 411
Brown, Arthur Witten (1886–1948) 15
Bruce, Robert (1274–1329) 54
Brunelleschi, Filippo
  (1377–1446) 311
Buddha (about 563–483 BC) 57, 423
Bush, George (b. 1924) 177
Bushnell, David (1742–1824) 362

C

Cabot, John (1450–1498) 145
Caesar, Julius (100–44 BC) 285,
  317, 318, 319
Calvin, John (1509–1564) 309
Cameron, Julia Margaret
  (1815–1879) 282
Canaletto (1697–1768) 280
Carroll, Lewis (1832–1898) 282, 411
Carter, Howard (1874–1939) 25
Castro, Fidel (b. 1927) 65
Catherine the Great, empress of
  Russia (1729–1796) 321
Cayley, George (1773–1857) 15
Cervantes Saavedra, Miguel de
  (1547–1616) 411
Chadwick, James (1891–1974) 35
Chaplin, Charlie (1889–1977) 152
Charlemagne (about 742–814) 169,
  239, 240, 412, 424
Charles I, king of England
  (1600–1649) 54
Ching Shih (d. about 1820) 285
Ching Yih (d. 1807) 285
Christo (b. 1935) and Jeanne-Claude
  (b. 1935) 327
Clinton, Bill (b. 1946) 177
Cnut (Canute), king of England (d.
  1035) 389
Coleridge, Samuel Taylor
  (1772–1834) 290
Collins, Michael (b. 1930) 353
Columbus, Christopher (1452–1506)
  65, 141, 145, 146, 424
Confucius (Kongzi) (about
  551–449 BC) 310, 423
Constantine the Great (about
  274–337) 61, 317
Cook, Frederick (1865–1940) 29

Cook, James (1728–1779) 37, 146
Copernicus, Nicolas
  (1473–1543) 325, 343
Cortés, Hernán (1485–1547) 38
Cornwallis, General (1738–1805) 18
Cromwell, Oliver (1599–1658) 55
Crosby, Bing (1904–1977) 394
Cunningham, Merce (b. 1919) 103
Custer, General (1839–1876) 387

D

Daguerre, Louis (1789–1851) 283
Dahl, Roald (1916–1990) 411
Daimler, Gottlieb (1834–1900) 43, 67
Dalton, John (1766–1844) 35
Dante Alighieri (1265–1321) 410
Darby, Abraham (about
  1678–1717) 199
Darius I, king of Persia (d. 486 BC) 20
Darwin, Charles (1809–1882) 144
David, king of Israel (d.
  921 BC) 214, 260–261
Democritus (about 460–about
  370 BC) 35
Descartes, René (1596–1650) 281
Dias, Bartolomeu (about
  1450–1500) 145, 146
DiCaprio, Leonardo (b. 1974) 153
Dickens, Charles (1812–1870) 411
Disney, Walt (1901–1966) 69
Drebbel, Cornelius (about
  1572–1633) 362
Dürer, Albrecht (1471–1528) 279
Dylan, Bob (b. 1941) 294

E

Edison, Thomas
  (1847–1931) 229, 308
Edward I, king of England
  (1239–1307) 55
Einstein, Albert (1879–1955) 284
Elizabeth I, queen of England
  (1533–1603) 54, 55
Engels, Friedrich (1820–1895) 91
Euripides (5th century BC) 117

F

Faraday, Michael
  (1791–1867) 129, 284
Flaubert, Gustave (1821–1880) 411
Fonteyn, Margot (1919–1991) 102
Ford, Harrison (b. 1942) 386

General index

If an index entry is printed in **bold**, it means that there is an article under that name in the A–Z part of the encyclopedia or in the Data file. When an entry has more than one page reference, the most important one may be printed in bold. References in italic indicate that there is a map, photo or other illustration relating to the entry on that page.

Acknowledgements

Key
t=top; b=bottom; c=centre;
r=right; l=left; b=background;
fore=foreground

Artwork
Allen, Graham: 398b
Allington, Sophie: 46b
Ambrus, Victor: 183c
Arlott, Norman: 149c; 47l
Baker, Julian: 84t; 129b; 130b; 132; 215b; 218b; 222b; 272b; 281t; 295t; 303t; 307b; 324t; 362b; 368b
Barber, John: 166b
Baum, Julian: 123tr; 248br; 341b; 342t; 354b
Beckett, Brian: 41t
Berridge: 119cl
Birkett, Georgie: 374t; 376ct, b
Black, Brad: 233b
Brian Beckett/Gecko Ltd: 60br
Brown, Chris: 417t
Bull, Peter: 336; 395; 405b
Butler, John: 331tl
Connolly, Peter: 179; 182bl; 319b; 389
Cottam, Martin: 427t; 86
Courtney, Michael: 330t;333b
D'Achille, Gino: 422b; 23cl; 424tl; 425bl
Dainton, Paul: 419b; 67b
Gaffney, Michael: 47r
Gecko Ltd: 67t; 73; 97b; 103t; 204c (Brian Beckett); 217t; 282b; 289b (James Sneddon); 299t; 301b; 323b; 365b; 39bl
Gibbons, Tony: 335c
Gulbis, Stephen: 90; 128b; 147b; 403b
Hadler, Terry: 5t; 14; 16
Harding, Robert: 430b (Robert Francis)
Hardy, David: 323t; 361b; 388b; 421
Haslam, John: 229b; 329tr; 344t
Hawken, Nick: 291b; 345b
Hinks, Gary: 3b; 72b; 88b; 105b; 123b; 208t; 249b; 269b; 314; 316; 390b; 392b; 397t
Hiscock, Karen: 158b; 408
Hook, Richard: 38; 121b; 394
Hutchins, Ray: 115b
Jonatronix: 69b
Jones Sewell Associates/James Sneddon: 255–256
Kennard, Frank: 186cr; 51t
Loates, Mick: 154; 155b
Luff, Vanessa: 161b
Madison, Kevin: 167r
Mendez, Simon: 40; 215t; 226br
Michael Woods/James Sneddon: 287b
Milne, Sean: 17b; 124; 148b; 149t; 165b; 184t; 224-225b; 230t; 232tr, br; 251b; 328b; 331tr
Moore, David: 378t
Noon, Steve: 21b
Ovenden, Denys: 108b; 227c
Oxford Designers and Illustrators: 12b; 15t; 34t; 35b; 42cr; 98b; 138b; 139; 207b; 228t; 229tl; 254; 354t; 371t
Oxford Illustrators/James Sneddon: 164t
Oxford University Press: 216b
Parsley, Helen (John Martin and Artists): 1; 76t; 111b; 126b; 184b; 418tl
Polley, Robbie (Virgil Pomfret): 5b; 19t; 28; 58; 59; 70; 116; 117b; 127tr; 264t; 376t, cb; 419t; 422–425; 490
Raw, Stephen: 89b; 219
Richardson, Paul: 46tr; 62b; 71b; 107b; 202c; 232bl; 247; 247; 399b; 400
Robbins, Jim: 359tr; 426l; 427r
Roberts, Steve: 3t; 22fore; 23; 44b; 48t; 95cr, b; 171t; 203; 204tl; 231l; 232tl; 238; 259; 271; 312; 313; 328tr, br; 340; 356; 418cl, bl
Robinson, Andrew: 109; 226tl
Sanders, Michael: 45cr; 50b; 333t; 338b; 364bl
Seymore, Steve: 173c
Sneddon, James: 12t; 22back; 34b; 39br; 53b; 92b; 128t; 137; 156b; 159b; 162c; 174t; 178b; 180; 187r; 205t; 222t; 227back; 229tr; 245; 268t; 275b; 288back; 304; 308t; 309b; 334; 345r; 357tr; 367b; 372b; 393b; 426t
Visscher, Peter: 22fore; 100; 140b; 151b; 157; 212t; 227fore; 286b; 288fore; 375t; 379; 408b; 426b; 427b; 428tr, b; 429tr, cl, c
Ward, Catherine: 152b (Simon Girling and Associates)
Weston, Steve: 107t; 186bl; 192; 193; 49; 49; 51b; 52
Wiley, Terry: 4; 110; 226bl; 485
Woods, Michael: 160b; 171b; 364br
Woods, Michael/James Sneddon: 74
Woods, Rosemary: 261t
Worldwide Fund for Nature: 5t.

Photos
The Publishers would like to thank the following for permission to use photographs.

Aardman Animations Ltd 1993: 69t
Action Plus Photographic: 66b (Richard Francis); 273b (Glyn Kirk); 274b (Glyn Kirk); 274c (Glyn Kirk); 357b (Al Messershmidt); 358b (Mike Hewitt); 358t (Chris Barry); 359tl (Mike Hewitt)
AKG photo: 65cl
ALSTOM: 300b
Ancient Art and Architecture: 119tr (R. Sheridan); 126t; 234b; 326b (R. Sheridan)
Heather Angel: 378b; 379b
Apple Computer Inc.: 106tr
Apple Corporation Ltd: 293b
Bank of England: 325b (©1989 Governor and Company of the Bank of England)
Bibliotheque Royale Albert 1er, Brussels (BR13076.77, f24): 48b
Bridgeman Art Library: 18b; 54b (National Library of Scotland, Edinburgh); 55b (Private Collection); 55t (Woburn Abbey, Bedfordshire); 83t (Private Collection); 101t (Bibliotheque Nationale, Paris); 112b (Lauros-Giraudon); 135t (Private Collection); 144t (Downe House, Kent); 146b (British Library); 170b; 183t (Museo e Gallerie Nazionali Di Capodimonte Naples); 199b (Walker Art Gallery, Liverpool); 235t (Glasgow University Library); 240b (The British Library, London); 240t (Jean Auguste Dominique Ingres); 246tl (Private Collection); 260b (Arthur Rackham Estate/Chris Beetles Ltd); 261b (British Library); 267tr (Walker Art Gallery, Liverpool); 276t (The British Library, London); 278b (Private Collection); 278t (Vatican Museum and Galleries,Vatican City, Italy); 279b (ADAGP Paris and DACS London,1998); 280tl (© Succession Picasso/DACS,1998); 281b (Vatican Museum and Galleries,Vatican City, Italy); 290t (Fitzwilliam Museum, University of Cambridge); 309t (City of Bristol Museum and Art Gallery); 311bl (Palazzo Pitti, Florence); 311br (Biblioteca Ambrosiana, Milan); 318t (Giraudon); 339b (The British Library, London); 343b (Bibliotheque Nationale, Paris); 401t; 409b (Palazzo Ducale, Mantua); 409t (Novosti); 422b (Duomo, Florence)
Michel Brigaud/Electricité de France: 299b
British Airways: 15b
Bronte Society: 411t
Bruce Coleman: 188b (Harold Lange); 189t (Jules Cowan)
Christie's Images: 211b; 298b
Christo and Jeanne-Claude: 327t
Corbis: 223b; 223t (Hank Morgan); 305b; 362t (Ralph White); 402t (Jon Spaul)
Corbis Bettmann/UPI: 162b
Corbis/Getty Images: 176t
Corel: 13tl; 195b; 338t; 368t
Dickens House Museum: 411b
Dominic Photography: 53cr (Zoe Dominic); 102b (Catherine Ashmore)
Dover Books: 279t
E. T. Archive: 80b; 114b; 246b; 405t
Mary Evans: 82t; 146t; 159tl; 216t; 234t; 240; 265b; 310t; 350t; 401b; 410t
Mary Evans/Explorer: 145t (Plisson)
Mary Evans/Sigmund Freud Copyrights: 114b (Max Halberstadt)
Norman Foster and Partners: 26tl
Robert Francis: 335t
Geo Science Features/Dr B. Booth: 140t; 315t, cr, b
Getty Images: 11t (Ian Murphy); 68t (David Hanson); 81b (Oliver Benn); 94b (Bob Thomas); 106bl (Michael Rosenfeld); 135b; 141b (Jerry Alexander); 170t; 175b (Hans Peter Merten); 177b; 181t (Mitch Kezar); 198t; 211t; 220b (David Young-Wolff); 241b; 248t (Oldrich Karasek); 258b (Nabeel Turner); 262b; 272t (James Wells); 274t; 302b; 306t (Paul Chesley); 321t (Natalie Fobes); 330cr (Billy Hustace); 365t; 369t (Steven Weinberg); 373b (Jon Riley); 402b; 407t
Robert Goble & Son Ltd.: 256tl
Ronald Grant Archive: 153b (Twentieth Century Fox)
Sally and Richard Greenhill: 173t
Greenpeace: 95b (Sims)
Hanny/Gamma/FSP: 121b
Robert Harding: 10t (G Renner); 32b (Thomas Laird); 32tl (Nevada Wier); 37t (J. H. C.

Acknowledgements

Wilson); 41t (N. A. Callow); 43t (J. H. C. Wilson); 54t (Adam Woolfitt); 57b (Alain Evrard); 57t (Advertasia); 61b (Teresa Black); 61t (Robert Frerck); 65t (Fred Friberg); 76tr (G Hellier); 78b (Schuster); 79t (Gavin Hellier); 80t (Adam Woolfitt; 88t (Gavin Hellier); 91b (Paolo Koch); 97t (M.Leslie Evans); 158t (T. Waltham); 160t (Rainbird); 169b (Nigel Frances); 169t (David Martyn Hughes); 182t (Tony Gervis); 185b (Adam Woolfitt); 185t (Liba Taylor); 201t (Advertasia); 204b (N. A. Callow); 213b (Richard Nowitz); 213t (Photri); 214b (E. Simanor); 214t (A. S. A. P.); 217b (Michael.J Howell); 218t (Jennifer Fry); 237b (Michael Short); 239b (Peter Scholey); 243b (David Beatty); 249t (Lorraine Wilson); 253t (Tony Gervis); 263b (Julian Pottage); 277b (G Renner); 295b (Thomas Laird); 296b (Roy Rainford); 311t (Philip Craven); 318b (D. Beatty); 321b (G.R Richardson); 324b (C. Rennie); 329b (J. H. C. Wilson); 349t (Nedra Westwater); 352t (Gavin Hellier); 355b (Robert Frerck); 355t; 371b (John Miller); 377b (Schuster); 380b (John Miller); 382b (David Lomax); 382t (C. Bowman); 386b (Simon Harris); 393t (Financial Times)

Michael Holford: 19b; 20t; 21tr; 26b; 27bl; 127t, b; 183b; 199t; 220t; 255t; 264b (Adam Woolfitt); 319t; 327b

Image Bank: 28b (Peter Hendrie); 37b (Peter Hendrie); 42tr (John P. Kelly); 53t (Alan Choijnet); 62t (Margaret Mead); 63t (Andre Gallant); 85t (Eric Meola); 86t (Alvis Upitis); 87b (Carlos Navajas); 98t (Walter Bibikow); 131tr (Steve Allen); 156t (Chris Hackett); 163l (John P. Kelly); 197t (J. Du Bisberran); 209b (Marc Romanelli); 265t (Stuart Dee); 270b (Jeff Hunter); 289t (Marc Romanelli); 292t (Yiu Chun Ma); 298tr (Wendy Chan); 310br (C. Brown); 335t (John P. Kelly); 359b; 384b

Images Colour Library: 115t; 188t

Images of Africa: 11br (Vanessa Burger); 148t (David Keith Jones); 150b (David Keith Jones); 191b (Johann Van Tonder); 252t (David Keith Jones)

Images of India: 27tl; 76b (Roderick Johnson); 133b; 200b (Michael Ravinder)

Japan Information and Cultural Centre: 117t

Katz/Mansell Collection: 117bl

David King Collection: 91t; 201b; 281br; 329br; 406b

Kobal: 152t (United Artists); 153tr (Selznick/MGM); 293t (Paramount)

Link Picture Library: 198b

Charlotte Lippmann: 326tr

London Picture Museum: 375b

MVP, Munich; 374b

Matsumoto/Sygma: 407b

Latha Menon: 147t

NASA: 33t; 122t; 164br; 172b; 187b; 248b; 248t; 283t; 303b; 323cr; 341c; 342b; 343t; 353b; 353t; 360t; 361b; 361tr; 361tr; 363b; 370b; 388t (Space Telescope Science Institute/NASA/SPL)

National Geographic Image Collection: 25tr (Kenneth Garrett); 103b (Volkmar Kurt Wentzel); 105t (George F. Mobley); 159t (Brooks Walker); 194tl (Medford Taylor); 195t (Stephen L. Alvarez); 243t (Lynn Abercrombie); 266b; 296t (Stephanie Maze); 376t (Dean Conger)

National Maritime Museum, London: 276b; 285t; 379tl

National Motor Museum; 377t

Natural History Photographic Agency: 17tr (M.I Walker); 24b (Jonathan Chester); 29b (Rich Kirchner); 40b (John Shaw); 44t (Manfred Danegger); 45b (Stephen Dalton); 46t (E. A. Janes); 60b (John Shaw); 60t (Anthony Bannister; 71t (Stephen Krasemann); 87b (John Shaw); 8br (Nigel J. Dennis); 96t (Kevin Schafer); 104b (Anthony Bannister); 110bl (Daniel Heuclin); 125b (Norbet Wu); 125t (David Woodfall); 133t (Anthony Bannister); 150t (Douglas Dickins); 155t (Norbet Wu); 158cr (John Shaw); 165t (Rod Plank); 190b (Christophe Ratier); 202t (Anthony Bannister); 204t (Stephen Dalton); 212b (B.Jones & M.Shimlock); 231bc (Stephen Dalton); 244b (B.Jones & M.Shimlock); 244t (Hellio & Van Ingen); 283b (Andy Rouse); 286t (Laurie Campbell); 287t (Daniel Heuclin); 288t (John Shaw); 292b (David Woodfall); 330b (Stephen Dalton); 332b (Orion Press); 356b (G.I. Bernard); 398t (Dr Ivan Polunin); 399t (John Shaw); 403t (Stephen Krasemann)

Peter Newark's Pictures: 285b; 387b

Novosti: 322t

Tony O'Keefe: 346t

Oxford Scientific Films: 181b (Martyn Colbeck); 225t (Douglas Faulkner); 269t (Harold Taylor)

Ann & Bury Peerless: 310b; 337t

Planet Earth Pictures: 50t (David Maitland); 230b (Geoff du Feu)

Popperfoto: 65cr; 162t (Sam Mircovich); 177t (Gary Cameron); 302t (Juda Ngwenya, Reuters); 373t; 404b

Zev Radovan: 25b

Redferns: 102t (Pankan Shar); 253b (Chuck Stewart); 275t (Graham Diss); 294t (Marc Marnie); 308b (Suzi Gibbons)

Rex Features: 87t; 118b (C. Brown); 176b; 206t; 221t (Roberto Koch); 322b; 366b; 390t (Arthur Pengelly)

The Royal Photographic Society, Bath: 282t

RSPCA: 149t

Peter Sanders: 257t, b; 258cl; 337b

Science Photo Library: 33b (David Parker); 39t (Omikron); 66t (David Parker); 72t (Vaughan Fleming); 75b (Maximilian Stock Ltd); 75t (Jeremy Burgess); 89t; 92t (David Parker); 93t (Los Alamos National Laboratory); 94t (James King-Holmes); 111t (Hattie Young); 112tl (Mark Clarke); 113b (Geoff Tompkinson); 113t (EM Unit, VLA); 114t (Eddy Gray); 118t (Larry Mulvehill); 122b (NASA); 129t (Alex Bartel/SPL); 130t (Nelson Morris); 131t (Vaughan Fleming); 136b (Peter Menzell); 136t (James King-Holmes); 13br (Dr George Gornacz); 151t (Jim Gipe); 167b (Sinclaire Stammers); 172t (Dr Steve Gull); 174b (Philippe Plailly/Eurelios); 186t (Ken Eward); 194tr

(Pekka Parviaien); 207t; 208b (Douglas Faulkner); 221b (Philippe Plailly); 224t (John Reader); 228b (Will & Deni McIntyre); 236b (John Mead); 236t (Eye of Science); 251t (Dr. Jeremy Burgess); 284t (Patrice Loiez); 291t (NOAA); 296b (National Snow and Ice Data Centre); 301t (Pascal Nieto); 305t; 306b (David Nunuk); 314br; 325t (Dr. Jeremy Burgess); 332t; 341t (NASA); 344b (Richard Folwell); 354b; 35t (Los Alamos National Laboratory); 360t (Martin Bond); 364 (W.Bacon); 364t (Richard Nowitz); 366t; 370t (Alexander Tsiaras); 392t (Martin Dohrn); 396b; 397b (Peter Menzell)

Science Photo Library/CNRI: 51

Sony: 307t

South American Pictures: 136t; 252b; 349b; 350b; 369b

Space Charts Photo Library: 363t

Spice Girls Ltd: 294b (Andrew Southam)

Peter Spilsbury: 269br

Still Pictures: 166t (Daniel Dancer)

Suzuki: 43b

Tate Gallery: 280b (ADAGP Paris and DACS London,1998)

Telegraph Colour Library: 262t (Japack Photo Library)

The Coca-Cola Company: 106bl

The Exploratory Bristol: 223t

The Guardian: 205b (Don McPhee)

The National Museum, Copenhagen: 74t

The Walt Disney Company Limited: 386t

Topham: 56t; 346b; 383b; 387t; 391b (Y. Shimbun)

Topham Picture Source: 161t (G.Marinovich)

Topham/Associated Press: 178t (A. Bradlow)

Trek Bikes: 42b

Twentieth Century Fox: 367t

United Feature Syndicate. Inc., 1993; 69b

United Nations: 383t

Weidenfeld Archives: 56b

Wilberforce House, Hull City Museums: 339t

William Sturgis Bigelow Collection/Museum of Fine Arts, Boston: 260t

Reg Wilson: 529bl

Woodfall Wild Images: 190t (Steve Austin); 191t (Nigel Hicks)

York Archaeological Trust: 389t

ZEFA: 109t